ARISTOTELIAN
INTERPRETATIONS

For Bríd,
with warmest wishes

ARISTOTELIAN
INTERPRETATIONS

FRAN O'ROURKE

Fran O'Rourke

Celebrating Aristotle
21 Oct 2016

IRISH ACADEMIC PRESS

Published in 2016 by
Irish Academic Press
8 Chapel Lane
Sallins
Co. Kildare

© 2016 Fran O'Rourke

British Library Cataloguing in Publication Data
An entry can be found on request

ISBN 978-1-911024-23-1 (Cloth)
ISBN 978-1-911024-24-8 (PDF)
ISBN 978-1-911024-25-5 (Mobi)

Library of Congress Cataloging in Publication Data
An entry can be found on request

Book design by www.sinedesign.net

To the pious memory of
Christopher and Alice O'Rourke
&
Jeremiah and Hannah O'Sullivan
With love and affection to all their descendants
Con un pensiero soave pien d'amore
per l'ultima arrivata, n° 363

ACKNOWLEDGMENTS

I am grateful to the editors and publishers for kind permission to reprint the essays which were originally published as follows:

'Wonder and Universality. Philosophy and Poetry in Aristotle', in *On Aristotle's Poetics and the Art of Rhetoric* (Athens: Society for Aristotelian Studies 'The Lyceum', 2003), pp. 241–63.

'Philosophy and Poetry in Aristotle. Interpreting and Imitating Nature', in *Vita Contemplativa. Essays in Honour of Demetrios N. Koutras* (Athens: National and Kapodistrian University of Athens, 2006), pp. 385–404.

'Human Nature and Destiny in Aristotle', in *Human Destinies. Philosophical Essays in Memory of Gerald Hanratty*, ed. Fran O'Rourke (Notre Dame, IN: Notre Dame University Press, 2012), pp. 19–55.

'Knowledge and Necessity in Aristotle', in *Hasard et nécessité dans la philosophie grecque* (Athens: Académie d'Athènes, 2005), pp. 155–71.

'Aristotle and the Metaphysics of Metaphor', in *Proceedings of the Boston Area Colloquium in Ancient Philosophy*, vol. 21, eds John J. Cleary & Gary M. Gurtler (Leiden: Brill, 2005), pp. 155–77, 186–90.

'Aristotle's Political Anthropology', in *Politics of Practical Reasoning. Integrating Action, Discourse and Argument*, eds Ricca Edmondson & Karlheinz Hülser (Lanham: Lexington, 2012), pp. 17–38.

'Aristotle and the Metaphysics of Evolution', in *The Review of Metaphysics* 58 (2004) pp. 3–59.

'Evolutionary Ethics. A Metaphysical Evaluation' in *What Happened in and to Moral Philosophy in the Twentieth Century? Philosophical Essays in Honor of Alasdair MacIntyre*, ed. Fran O'Rourke (Notre Dame, IN: Notre Dame University Press, 2013), pp. 323–57.

'Aristotle and Evolutionary Altruism', in *ΦΙΛΟΣΟΦΙΑ*, Yearbook of the Research Centre of Greek Philosophy (Athens: Athens Academy, 2011), pp. 136–46.

'James Joyce and Aristotle', in *Voices on Joyce*, eds Anne Fogarty & Fran O'Rourke (Dublin: University College Dublin Press, 2015), pp. 139–57, 311–14.

Research for these essays was made possible by fellowships awarded by University College Dublin, the Fulbright Commission, and the Alexander S. Onassis Foundation. I express my sincere gratitude to these institutions.

I am grateful to the National University of Ireland for a grant toward the cost of publication.

I express my warmest thanks to Philip Harvey, Conor Graham, Sinéad McKenna, Siobhán Prendergast, Peter Costello, Andrew Smith, and Patrick Sammon for their invaluable help with the preparation of this volume.

An electronic version of this book is available free of charge to persons with visual impairment (email orourke@ucd.ie).

Of things constituted by nature some are ungenerated, imperishable, and eternal, while others are subject to generation and decay... Both departments, however, have their special charm... Having already treated of the celestial world, as far as our conjectures could reach, we proceed to treat of animals, without omitting, to the best of our ability, any member of the kingdom, however ignoble. For if some have no graces to charm the sense, yet even these, by disclosing to intellectual perception the artistic spirit that designed them, give immense pleasure to all who can trace links of causation, and are inclined to philosophy. Indeed, it would be strange if mimic representations of them were attractive, because they disclose the mimetic skill of the painter or sculptor, and the original realities themselves were not more interesting, to all at any rate who have eyes to discern the reasons that determined their formation. We therefore must not recoil with childish aversion from the examination of the humbler animals. Every realm of nature is marvellous: and as Heraclitus, when the strangers who came to visit him found him warming himself at the furnace in the kitchen and hesitated to go in, reported to have bidden them not to be afraid to enter, as even in that kitchen divinities were present, so we should venture on the study of every kind of animal without distaste; for each and all will reveal to us something natural and something beautiful. Absence of haphazard and conduciveness of everything to an end are to be found in Nature's works in the highest degree, and the resultant end of her generations and combinations is a form of the beautiful.

Aristotle, *Parts of Animals* 1, 5, 644b22–645a26, trans. William Ogle

CONTENTS

INTRODUCTION

Portrait of the Author as a Young Aristotelian

Despite the gap of two and a half thousand years, the world we inhabit is essentially the same as that experienced by Aristotle. We live in the same universe and, like the philosopher, yearn to discover its secrets. Nature flourishes and unfolds as in his time, performing ageless tasks of wonder. We are fascinated by the same realities; we marvel at the turning of the seasons and the cycle of growth, the world's order and oddities, its beauty and variety. Nature veils and unveils the same ubiquitous mysteries which moved the inquiring spirit of the ancient thinker. What has changed is our attitude. Today we live amid the artefactual surroundings of a postmodern world and are no longer attuned to the simplicity of nature. Immersed in the world of human constructs we are removed from the elemental ground of experience.

I regard it as an extraordinary blessing, therefore, to have lived the first ten years of my life in the country. My father was the schoolmaster in the small townland of Ratheniska, Co. Laois, in the Irish midlands. The teacher's house was located between the school and chapel, which stood at a fork where three roads converged. The countryside gently sloped away for miles, presenting a panoramic vista of serene and varied beauty. My early experience was of an open landscape stretching to a far horizon. A low hill above the chapel and a raised plateau at the county's edge, barely visible in the hazy distance, framed an immense amphitheatre, an arc of earth and sky, which was my childhood universe. It was an enchanting sphere which instilled a sense of vast openness. I did not appreciate this at the time but later understood Seamus Heaney's remark, 'The inner place of your first being is a large solitary gaze out on the world.'[1] Our early being is likewise attuned to surrounding sounds:

the beat of the rain, the song of the stream, the wind in the trees, the prolonged silences of the night. A country childhood affords endless experiences of nature in its fresh sensuality.

The view from our house was expansive. Irregular fields of every size and shape were framed by a network of ditches and hedgerows; clumps of woodland punctuated the landscape. The panorama changed with the seasons: the brown earth and rotting winter stubble turned to delicate green in spring and a brighter tone as the harvest ripened. There is no sight more glorious than the sway of golden corn in the summer breeze. The mood could change hourly as light and shadow played off one another between earth and sky. To the east you could observe a lashing cloudburst, while the sun flashed through rifted clouds in the west. Shadow and sunburst, wind and light, clouds ominous or luminous, the elements fused in dramatic beauty. Rainbows frequently adorned the vaulted expanse; thunderstorms brought fascination and terror. We learned to distinguish between fork and sheet lightning and waited for the rumble, clap, and crack, counting the interval between flash and roar as the storm moved closer; in darkness this was frightening. Seven cattle were once killed by lightning on the hill above the chapel. There had been an old mine there long ago and it was believed the metal underground attracted the lightning.

I was nurtured into the routine of a rural community and learned the rhythms of nature: sowing, harvesting and threshing. The soil and the seasons were constants which sustained and ordered daily life. To feed a growing family my father farmed part-time. He had the use of a nearby farmyard and some adjacent fields. We had two cows and two pigs; also lots of chickens that arrived regularly as day-old chicks in a large cardboard box that emitted a sweet and high-pitched chirping. In the 'six-acre field' my father planted beet, turnips, kale, potatoes, carrots, beans, peas, and other fodder for family and fowl. In the garden behind our home he planted blackcurrants, raspberries, strawberries, onions and lettuce. We had lots of apple and even some pear trees. There was endless weeding of plants, thinning of seedlings, and pulling of vegetables. I spent a summer picking caterpillars off cabbage plants. I could not understand how from these ugly multipedes could burst forth beautiful butterflies.[2] Illustrating Aristotle's theory of act and potency years later, I understood my students' perplexity when asked if such transformation is radical substantial change, or a superficial accidental modification. As a child, to borrow from James Joyce, I 'impossibilized' countless generations of those exquisite creatures. It was more rewarding to watch my father displaying his expert skill at grafting apple trees, splicing vigorous scions onto older stock to produce a varied and richer crop. It was puzzling how you could get a single tree by joining two together.

One Christmas my brother got a handbook on birds and could soon identify every winged creature in sight: the skylark, blue tit, swift, grey partridge, yellowhammer, goldcrest, meadow pipit and house sparrow. My expertise was limited to the easily recognized plover and thrush, but I took enormous pleasure from observing their frequent appearance. Our nearest neighbour, a generous, gentle and patient farmer, indulged my childish curiosity, and let me meddle around his farmyard. He even gave me his best nanny goat, which I hoped to raise as a pet. To my great sadness the goat died soon afterwards, and I was distraught to find that magpies had plucked out her eyes: an early lesson in the inexorable ways of nature. I had more satisfaction when I attempted to milk the gentler of our two cows, enjoying the music of the milk hitting the metallic bottom of the bucket and the deep reverberation as it filled with froth.

Childhood memories are potent. I remember the sweet smell of freshly-cut hay, as well as the pungent, less pleasant scents of a healthy farmyard. Burning hay was fresh and pleasing, burning straw irritated the throat and nose. I liked the smell of the turf fire in the schoolroom but not the clammy touch of ash when it was my job to clean out the fireplace. A fire to dispose of garden rubbish, twigs and leaves – illegal today – gave a rushing sound and smell. Some hedges had a mildly cloying and faintly soporific odour. Outside Notre Dame in Paris a decade ago, walking between low-cut rows of *Buxus sempervirens*, I was in memory swinging again on our neighbour's gate. While not so evocative, memories of touch are also lasting. I can still re-imagine the different sensations of my hand running through ripe stalks of wheat and barley, pleasant to the touch; and ears of oats with their irritating spikes. My left middle finger still has a scar from the crescent blade of a rotary mangold slicer: I wondered if it was sharp to the touch. Curiosity has its price.

There was no running water in the teacher's house, nor in any of the houses at that time; a huge tank on the roof collected rain. Fresh water was taken from a pump across the road; when it occasionally went dry in the summer we went to nearby wells with buckets and cans. Despite the drudgery, I was fascinated by the fact that the ground could deliver something that usually fell out of the sky. One spring well in particular held immense fascination; it was centuries old and gave pure fresh water all year round. You went down some steps before dropping the can or bucket. I enjoyed the metallic clang and the splashing plop as the vessel hit the surface. To keep balance you gripped a stone on the side. Two of the stones were polished soft and shiny from generations of people who drew there the most elementary necessity of life. This was truly amazing: that a stone could become silken smooth from human touch. I have often wondered about the people who came to that well – perhaps daily over millennia. How did they live? What language did they speak? Attempts were made in the locality to find an underground source of water. I was spellbound to see the diviner's hazel tremble and twitch, before triggering determinedly downwards. Sadly, weeks of drilling with a cumbersome mechanical bore that pounded incessantly ten hours a day produced nothing more than a muddy trickle. It was only a decade later that a feasible water supply was piped to the area.

Free-range children, there were no limits to where we could roam or wander. On Sunday afternoons as my brothers, passionate about our national Gaelic games, listened to the commentator's nasal screeching on the battery-powered wireless – for me the acme of boredom – I crossed ditches and walked grassy headlands, exploring, gathering hazel nuts, sloes, rosehips, vetches and berries. The hedgerows were a self-contained ecology of growth, with blackthorn, ivy, honeysuckle, ash, sycamore, elm and elderberry all tangled and enmeshed. They were home to the speckled wood and orange tip butterfly, honeybee and a host of insects. In those days one heard the corncrake, cuckoo and curlew; the countryside buzzed with wildlife. A favourite adventure was to climb the local hill, which was covered in furze, apart from patches of sparse grass where sheep gently grazed. In summer months the hillside was afire with yellow bloom, which gave off a mildly herbaceous scent I later discovered was redolent both of fig trees and coconut. I was intrigued to realize that this spiny, beautiful shrub gloried in three different names: 'furze', 'whin' and 'gorse'.

Growing up in the countryside one acquired a variety of knowledge from which one might extrapolate wider implications. The dock leaf offers a soothing antidote to nettle stings; curiously they are to be found in close proximity to one another. Crops are best rotated for the soil to be renewed: beet or turnips with wheat or barley. We observed as something natural the mating and birthing of animals, and knew when a cow needed to be brought to the bull. We learned which weeds and leaves were poisonous to animals: ragwort was the deadliest. We observed the spawning habits of frogs, and uncovered a badger's sett; I envied a schoolmate who once saw a hedgehog. We carried out our, sometimes cruel, experiments in natural philosophy, most commonly the bisection of earthworms. The puzzle of morphogenesis was not that two complete individuals now wriggled and squirmed, but whether the procedure could be performed on other creatures.

My father allotted to each of us a plot in the garden, where we could plant whatever we chose. I was more interested in flowers than cabbages and lettuce; I was fascinated by the fact that from a sprinkle of dry seeds, which seemed no different from dust, grew marigolds, pansies, wallflowers and forget-me-nots. The springtime miracle of delicate green shoots pushing up through the hardened frozen earth, the stirring of buds and blossoms in summer, desiccated dead heads containing the gift of new seeds, with the promise of a new season – the annual rhythm never ceased to fascinate. A special joy was the crop of mushrooms that sprang up every autumn in meadows covered with morning dew; this was soon followed by a rich harvest of hazelnuts in the ditches that bordered every headland.

While almost everyone now had tractors, one of our neighbours worked his land with horses, ploughing in spring and hauling home the hay in late summer. I found it strange to hear talk of a tractor's 'horsepower'; the only horsepower I knew was that of Denis Drennan's two plough horses, frothing at the mouth, hooves stamping as they strained against the creaking harness and heaved into the tearing earth. With the reins balancing the strength of the stronger against the weaker horse, Denis guided the ploughshare as it sliced the sod into gleaming ridges. At the end of the furrow he turned on the headland and in an elaborate manoeuvre aligned horses and plough in the opposite direction. By evening the field was a glistening spectacle of perfectly parallel lines. Plato's allegory of the charioteer commanding the rival horses takes place for me in a field below the school at Ratheniska.

The community were a robustly god-witted folk who worked hard during the week and devoted the seventh day to the Almighty – at least the early part, since there were duties of play and sport to occupy the remainder of the day. The chapel was full on Sunday mornings. Mass was in Latin; mysterious sounds and paused silences invited the congregation to contemplate the unknown great and adore the great unknown. Everyone knew the Latin hymns and sang at full throttle to the croaking music of an ancient bellows organ, whose inner apparatus creaked like our wooden churn making butter. Some came to church by car, others by pony and trap. Many cycled: there were lines of bicycles outside the chapel and not a lock to be seen. Some worshippers walked; life was slow and there was time.

When I was six we got electricity; our parish was one of the last in the country to benefit from rural electrification. But up till then there was excitement in the evening ritual of dressing the oil lamp. To light the Tilley lamp was a tricky task: one had to be careful not to touch the gauze mantle or it would disintegrate. Schoolwork was often done by the light of a candle. Spending time in the dark increased one's sense of hidden presences; the world had an ominous quality. We also became magically thrilled by celestial phenomena: the *aurora borealis*, or northern lights, darted high in tongues of coloured fire into the evening sky behind the fairy rath (now obliterated in the name of mechanized farming) that gave the townland its name. It was also at that time that we stared unbelieving skywards to descry Sputnik, the first Russian satellite, as it rose behind Dysart and traced its way across the night sky to disappear over Timahoe. Around that time also I saw my first solar eclipse, when the moon passed between the earth and the sun; the entire school went outside to look at the crescent shape, using photographic negatives to protect our eyes from the bright sunshine. In a variety of ways the entire universe entered our senses and took root within the orbit of our childhood imagination. The world came closer too when we were linked to the telephone network.

For weeks crews planted poles along the narrow roads, unfurled and hooked up miles of cable. If you put your ear to a pole you could hear the high warm hum travelling along the wire, a distant diapason in single harmony.

The outside world also entered our awareness in simpler ways, whose importance was not appreciated at the time. For a few years we went through a phase of stamp collecting. Regular assortment packs that arrived by post gave one a sense of the world beyond one's daily reference. My first acquaintance with Greece was to stare unknowingly at the strange letters ΕΛΛΑΣ on stamps adorned with images of gods and mythic heroes; these images conjured up an exotic and ancient land. I do not recall if Aristotle's image featured in my collection. A seasonal reminder of wider horizons was the swarming of swallows in late autumn as they assembled for their flight half way round the globe. This collective phenomenon is one of the rhythmic wonders of the animate world; Aristotle was the first to write systematically about bird migration, as well as to state that one swallow does not make a summer!

My young years in the country awakened in me a loving fascination for all aspects of nature, and this has remained with me. For as long as I can remember, I felt an unexpressed inner glow at the simplest happenings. I constantly marvelled at the mysteries of nature's hidden presence. A country childhood is filled with excitement and experiment unknown in the city. It is not an exaggeration to say there is a spontaneous engagement with the cosmos itself. There is no barrier of artificiality between the natural elements and the hours of the day. Light is not a commodity mechanically switched off and on. Darkness is an intangible presence that preserves physical things in private intimacy. Artificial energy occludes the pace and motion of the earth.

A virtue exemplified in country folk – at least those of the previous generation – was self-reliance. They could not run to the shop to supply every need, but improvised and made do. This was particularly the case with farm implements: equipment was repaired rather than replaced. One of Aristotle's most practical insights into human inventiveness is his descriptive image of the hand as the 'tool of tools', the 'instrument of instruments'. It is the natural organ of the human body which fabricates every artificial implement, to be used as an extension to itself. Perhaps more than any other profession, the farmer must be creative and practical, manufacturing and maintaining the apparatus needed for his work. One of our neighbours was a blacksmith, who mostly mended farm machinery, now that there were fewer horses to be shod. A huge bellows raised a storm of sparks in the forge as iron glowed in red-hot coals. Every time I hear the story of Pythagoras, who supposedly discovered the arithmetic of music on hearing the different pitches of the hammer's clang on the anvil, I think of the forge in Ratheniska.

Another community of resourceful folk were the tinkers who travelled the country roads in horse-drawn caravans. 'Tinker' was not yet a pejorative term, but described an admired trade practised over generations by the knights of the road. Their forebears, we were told, were historical nobility evicted from their lands in less happy times. Every spring a family of three generations arrived in their barrel-shaped caravan, painted bright red and green, drawn by a dappled pony with her foal trotting alongside. Soon a blackened pot sizzled over a fire, as the piebald was let loose to graze the 'long acre', the grassy verge along the roadside. Tinkers were welcome: they sold shiny tin cans, mended pots and basins, fixed bicycles, umbrellas, and anything that needed repair. Their camp was colourful and exciting, with strange sounds and smells suggesting adventure in far corners of the land. They told stories and sang of travels on the road; they were friendly and were made welcome by the locals. My mother was neither surprised nor upset if the hens laid fewer eggs that week or if a chicken went missing, to end her days in the black pot. The tasty smell of wood smoke still evokes a pleasant memory.

Neighbourly cooperation was the welding bond of the community. All kinds of activities were done together, work and play. There was an amateur drama society, a sports club, a branch of the Irish Country-women's Association, and the Pioneers (a temperance association). The parish hall hosted card games on winter evenings and table tennis tournaments on wet weekends. When the hurling team won the county championship we celebrated for three nights with bonfires, biscuits and lemonade; there was music and dancing in the glow of the embers. A major communal effort was at harvest time, when neighbours gathered by turn in each other's haggards for the threshing. It was a great collective task requiring precise and patient coordination. When up and running, the threshing machine rattled and shook as if ready to fly apart in all directions. It was a huge shaking monster, kept in walloping motion by a fan belt from the tractor. All manner of levers and shaking griddles, pulleys, spindle wheels and metal limbs, clattered and clacked as the straw was shaken out, while the grain flowed bounteously into sacks of jute. Equally awesome, but less congenial, was the mammoth lumbering mechanical combine harvester that soon replaced the ingenious threshing machine. Half the size of a small cottage and always painted yellow, it resembled a mechanical dragon as it strode the meadow beast-like and ferociously devoured the golden crop. Operated by a single driver it baled the straw and bagged the grain all at once. *Technik* progressed from year to year with the rhythm of mechanistic time.

Growing up in the country, death was one more event of nature. The graveyard was over our garden wall. A death in the locality brought great excitement as we waited eagerly for neighbours to arrive with picks and shovels to dig the grave. As they reached a depth of about five feet, the shovel sometimes sounded an ominous thud as skulls, femurs, and tibiae of a previous generation were disinterred; these were respectfully covered with a layer of clay. A chilling and macabre dare among the older boys was to climb down into the grave, prostrate oneself on the cold earth, and join hands in pretended prayer. But as the funeral cortege approached all levity vanished and the chapel bell tolled solemnly with a menacing finality that never failed to strike horror in a child's heart.

When I was ten, my family moved to Galway, then still a small port city in the west of Ireland. My father was appointed principal of the primary school in the Claddagh, the traditional fishing village situated between the river Corrib and the shoreline. I was at once fascinated by the sea. Hearing classmates talk of pocket money to be earned picking periwinkles among the rocks at low tide, I took myself off one day after school to engage in this new harvest, not knowing what a periwinkle even looked like; I asked two old-timers sitting on the pier to identify them for me. With some amusement they showed me where to look among the rock pools. One of them prised a barnacle from a rock and slurped it with relish, proclaiming that whatever comes from the sea is healthy and good. My brothers and I sometimes fished off the Claddagh pier but only ever caught pollock, which were bland and tasteless. During a couple of summers in the mid 60s, however, for a few memorable days the beach at Salthill was black with shoals of mackerel that followed the thousands of flashing silver fry that burrowed for microorganisms in the golden sand along the shallow shore. You could snatch a mackerel with a yard of twine and a safety pin. Families feasted on mackerel for days, which was fine if, like me, you were partial to the strong oily texture and taste.

My love of the sea deepened when I spent three months at the age of twelve in the Gaelic-speaking area of Connemara on the edge of the Atlantic, to improve my knowledge of the language. I lived with an elderly couple, whose grown children had emigrated to England and America. They lived a life of near-subsistence, nourished by the riches of the sea and some of the poorest soil in the country. I went fishing with the man of the house in his currach, the traditional light canvas-covered boat. I was always delighted by the catch and surprised by the variety of living forms caught in the net. A man of few words, he once pointed to a catch of speckled mackerel: 'Isn't it a curious thing that the spots on every single one of those are different.' The remark awakened in me an awareness of the endless variety and particularity among individual entities in the natural world. I also helped with the few cows and calves, and picked potatoes in the minuscule rocky fields that were defined by irregular stone walls; some of the boggy fields produced nothing but reeds and were appreciated only by ducks and hens. I had lots of diversion with the dog and donkey. (Aristotle was mistaken in suggesting that Celtic lands are too cold for donkeys to survive!) I went to school through the fields and along the seashore, where I often explored the rock pools and sand dunes. After stormy tides I helped collect seaweed to be used as fertilizer or sent to the factory to make iodine.

I loved the wonderful landscape of the west of Ireland, especially the mutual proximity of mountains and sea. Coming from the flat Irish midlands, I was immediately attracted to the mountains of Connemara. Martin Heidegger once remarked that the philosopher should also be a good mountain climber. This is true not only in a vague metaphorical sense; there is a keen affinity between mountaineering and philosophy, a parallel between the physical action of the one and the spiritual activity of the other. Climbing mountains offers in particular a suitable analogy for metaphysics, which might be defined as philosophy at its widest – the search for an all-embracing vision of the world, from the most radical to the most sublime. The words '*meta*' (beyond) and '*physis*' (nature) convey the quest for a perspective upon reality in its totality, going beneath and beyond the visible world.

As a student I was a regular walker with the university hillwalking club and there is not a hill in the west of Ireland that I have not climbed. I spent many summer days in chthonic contemplation amid the mountains of Connemara. My favourite mountain in the west of Ireland is Mweelrea, the highest in the province of Connacht. Situated at the mouth of Killary Harbour, it is divided by a fjord from Rosroe, Wittgenstein's retreat in Ireland. The most exciting approach is by boat from across the harbour. The ascent from seashore to summit is long and arduous, but beautiful and rewarding. As one climbs, one leaves behind the flatland of daily life and experience, not necessarily to turn one's back, but to attain a new and more complete perspective. One gains an unfamiliar panorama and a novel outlook. The horizon stretches out and extends as one rises, ascending step by step, slowly gaining altitude. You enter a third dimension and attain a bird's-eye glance, a synoptic view of the surrounding spectacle. The elevated vantage-point affords a greater depth of field. The ground plan becomes clear and distinct; you discern the broader features of the landscape, its structure and relief. Contours emerge, the twin patterns of hill and valley become apparent. To quote from a popular song, 'from a distance there is harmony, and it echoes through the land'. The vestiges of geological time, hidden at close range, are revealed in the formation of the landscape, recalling millennia of change and bringing to mind even the earth's genesis. While climbing one becomes, as it were, an eyewitness to an all-embracing sphere of reality and time, of activity past and present: rolling hills traced with miles of stone wall; vast boglands scarred and carved by generations of human habitation and industry; potato ridges in lazy beds, grave reminders of a painful history; deserted cottages and twentyfirst-century wind turbines; forests, lakes and rivers; a tractor in the field, a trawler on the bay.

Hillwalking gives a raw sense of the elements which dominate our existence: land and sky, earth, wind and water. You discern more palpably the patient pace of nature and the annual rhythm of her seasons. One experiences in various ways the concurrence and totality of which we are a part. The moist and fertile scent of humus (whence the word 'human') on a summer's day has a potent redolence, an enveloping, sensual intimacy with Mother Earth as she exudes her generosity. One witnesses the nascent moment in the cycle of water, its emanation and return, a timeless exchange between earth and sky. Water oozes from beneath the surface, rivulets take volume, a trickle becomes a river as it courses inexorably to the ocean. In its eternal return of the same, nature is a great Heraclitean stream. From coastland peaks one perceives too the different densities and depths of water, hues of green and blue which reveal the shape of the submarine land as it retreats below the shore.

I once went with friends of the university speleological club to explore *Poll an Eidhneáin*, the cave in County Clare with the biggest stalactite in the entire northern hemisphere. Decades later walkways were opened to allow visitors stroll with ease to view this massive pendulum accumulated from the calcium in drops of water over thousands of years. We, however, wiggled on our bellies and twisted our contorted bodies around S-bends, slithering and sliding along constricted passages. It was an entirely different ambience to the open mountain air, and bereft of intellectual inspiration. We had no Ariadne's thread to orient our exit from the labyrinth of subterranean straits and I was glad to emerge into daylight. While I appreciate the genius of Plato's image of the cave, I have never warmed to the allegory, possibly because of the claustrophobic oppression that lingers in the memory of that expedition.

Climbing in many ways mirrors the process of abstraction characteristic of philosophy. For Aristotle, 'abstraction' is to 'draw away from' the incidental aspects of what we experience, so as to grasp what is fundamental and essential. In climbing one leaves behind things at ground level, but discovers their wider context, perceiving a thing's individuality in its universal setting. In metaphysics one should never abandon immediate and intimate contact, but simultaneously grasp reality sensibly and comprehend it intellectually.

My late dear friend Norris Clarke suggested that there is a connection between a love of high places and the predilection for metaphysics. He expressed the connection between mountain walking and metaphysics:

'To look out over the countryside from a high place enables one to see how it all fits together, making a single overall pattern. From down below, streams, valleys, hills, etc., all seem to be doing their own thing somewhat separately, without their interconnections being that visible. From higher up, it becomes clear how they all weave together to form a whole. The higher viewpoint yields the unity. This visual physical experience seems to be a kind of symbol, a foretaste, and acting-out on the physical level, of the inner spiritual synoptic vision of how all things in the universe somehow fit together to make an integrated meaningful whole. It is a kind of physical practice for doing metaphysics.'[3] There is good evidence, he suggests, for a 'natural affinity between metaphysicians and high places'. Some philosophers may prefer the ocean or the vast openness of the plains as the symbolic ambience and element for their philosophic theories; the ideal setting for Derridean deconstruction, Clarke teasingly suggested, would likely be the misty half-gloom of the shifting quicksands.

We have no evidence that Aristotle had any special fondness for the mountain peaks of ancient Hellas; on the contrary, his prose is laced with many references to maritime life. He was, however, respectful of Greek mythology and its divine personalities, including the Olympian gods. To climb Mount Olympus is a special experience for the philosopher; I have been fortunate to do so nine times – a pagan novena. As the mythical home of gods and goddesses, Olympus was for centuries the focal point of prehistoric Greek culture and mythology. It shaped the orbit of meaning and destiny for generations of Hellenes. Olympian mythology was crucially both the context and counterpoint for philosophy as it struggled into its own. Physically Mount Olympus is impressive; the rugged peak of Mytikas, hewn of rough vertical tubular crags, is aptly called the throne of Zeus. From the summit one takes in the expanse of contorted rock formations, bare above the timberline, stretching out across the valley to the ocean. On one visit the sea began to churn in a sudden storm. I was enveloped in a fury of cloud, a cauldron of divine discontent; Olympian deities vented their anger, exacting revenge with thunderous rage. Once in a small plane I saw Olympus from above; only the summit was visible through the cloud, presenting an archetypal mythic-religious scene; one imagined the father god upon the throne, thunderbolt in hand. Inspiring too is the vast Plateau of the Muses below the summit; here the daughters of Zeus and Mnemosyne still dance and sing upon a meadow of mountain flora, delicate in colour but robust enough to endure the winter snows. To stay overnight in the cabin of the Hellenic Mountaineering Association and watch the sun rise in the company of these beautiful maidens is an experience to relish. At the vault of the world and the threshold of the skies, it is a panorama that fills one's gaze to overflow.

Mountain climbing can be an arduous exercise requiring effort and exertion. Metaphysics also demands at times mental labour to rise beyond the average, banal appreciation of things. It too has its rewards, moments of illumination, revelation and insight. We transcend the particular to embrace the totality, not abandoning but viewing it within the whole; we discern a cosmos from the welter of apparent chaos. The physical world is an image of the spiritual; the ecology of nature is a cipher for the greater order of the totality, in which are harmonized the physical and the psychic, the natural and supernatural, the human and divine. This is the ambience and element of our everyday reality, but as Shelley well remarked, 'The mist of familiarity obscures us from the wonder of our being.' For me, one of the best ways to refresh this sense of wonder is to walk the hills, to feel the earth under my feet and experience the rhythm of nature which ultimately we cannot dominate or control.

Besides hillwalking I have also regularly sailed in Ireland and Greece. I take delight in discovering throughout the works of Aristotle his many insightful references to maritime activity. He cites the pilot's habitual knowledge as an exemplar of expertise: while the carpenter manufactures the rudder, the captain is the better judge of its suitability and efficacy – as the guest, rather than the cook, is the better judge of the banquet.[4] In the *Politics* he draws an elaborate comparison: 'For as healthy bodies and ships well provided with sailors may undergo many mishaps and survive them, whereas sickly constitutions and rotten ill-mannered ships are ruined by the very least mistake, so do the worst forms of government require the greatest care.'[5] Further parallels are drawn between the building and use of ships, and the construction and ordering of the polis. Each is composed of its respective material – wood or population; and to operate effectively, the statesman can learn from the pilot's treatment of his passengers. Aristotle makes a comparison between the various roles of citizens in the polis and the functions performed by the sailors in a boat: one is an oarsman, another the helmsman, another the look-out, etc. In each case there is shared purpose (e.g. the security of navigation), and a community of excellence; yet 'the most exact definition of their excellence will be special to each'.[6] On the wisdom of appointing magistrates by lot, he remarks that this would be as sensible as drawing lots among the sailors to appoint a helmsman.[7]

In the *Politics* Aristotle states that the polis must be of appropriate size, a fact he illustrates by analogy with a ship: 'To the size of states there is a limit, as there is to other things, plants, animals, implements; for none of these retain their natural power when they are too large or too small, but they either wholly lose their nature, or are spoiled. For example, a ship which is only a span long will not be a ship at all, nor a ship a quarter a mile long; yet there may be a ship of a certain size, either too large or too small, which will still be a ship, but bad for sailing.'[8]

Some of Aristotle's allusions to the sea suggest personal experience. He begins *Movement of Animals* by stating that whatever moves requires resistance from something other than itself: flying and swimming would not be possible unless the air and sea offered resistance. He explains this by the futility of someone trying to move a boat by pushing against the mast while standing on the deck.[9] As an example of optical illusion, he refers to the impression that the land appears to move to those who are sailing past.[10] To illustrate how a small action at the beginning of an activity can have great consequences at the end, he explains that the slightest movement of the rudder will alter the angle of the prow, and cause the boat to change its course.[11] Offering advice on how best to attain the moral mean, Aristotle cites Calypso's advice to Odysseus to 'hold the ship out beyond that surf and spray'; he cites a Greek proverb that the use of oars is the best alternative to sailing when the wind fails.[12] He affirms the paramount importance of navigation,[13] and knows that it may be necessary to throw goods overboard in a storm for the sake of safety.[14] He illustrates the intimacy of the body and soul with the analogy of the sailor and the ship. He contrasts the constancy of virtue with the ebb and flow of the tide: 'The wishes of good men are constant and not at the mercy of opposing currents like a strait of the sea.'[15] I find difficulty, however, in sharing his opinion that men are unaffected by fear if they have never been tested; the example he gives is that in a storm, those who have never experienced danger will remain calm and confident.[16]

We may conclude that Aristotle had accumulated much experience of seafaring from his use of practical data to elucidate difficult concepts; while referring to place as something mysterious and difficult to grasp, he distinguishes between the concepts of space and container by referring to someone seated in a boat that is floating on the sea: place is an immovable container, a container is a movable place.[17] To convey the greater meaning of philosophy, Aristotle employed a sailing analogy: 'The philosopher is the only producer to have both laws that are stable and actions that are correct and beautiful. For he is the only one who lives looking toward nature and toward the divine and, just as if he were some good navigator who hitches the first principles of his life onto things that are eternal and steadfast, he moors his ship and lives life on his own terms.'[18]

Although Aristotle's style is for the most part dry and factual, it is heartening to find occasional touches of humour. He contemplates the quandary exposed in the proverb: 'When choking on water, what do you wash it down with?'[19] The *Constitution of Athens* reports that the tyrant Pisistratus released from all taxes a farmer who complained that all he earned from his labour were aches and pains: 'Pisistratus should get one tenth of these.'[20] There is teasing humour also in the observation that the public only eats sweets at theatre if the acting is bad,[21] and he tells us that it is ridiculous to wish well to a bottle of wine.[22]

It was probably around the age of ten that I first heard of Aristotle. More accurately, I heard of 'Harry Stakle', invoked by my grandmother with admiration whenever she wished to authorize some natural insight of venerable or ancient wisdom. The name of Aristotle has for generations in Ireland been synonymous with wisdom and erudition. The following extract from a German visitor to Ireland in 1842 illustrates how well Aristotle had become established over the centuries in the Irish folk tradition:

I have already mentioned the somewhat antiquated learning, even of the lower classes of the people of Kerry; and I now met with a remarkable instance of it. In the bow of the boat sat a Kerryman, reading an old manuscript, which was written in the Irish language, and in the Celtic character... Some of it, the man told me, he had added himself; some he had inherited from his father and grandfather; and some had, in all probability, been in his family long before then. I asked him what were its contents? 'They are,' answered he, 'the most beautiful old Irish poems, histories of wonderful events, and treatises of antiquity; for instance, the translation of a treatise by Aristotle on some subject of natural history!'... Twice, methought, I heard them speak of Aristotle as a wise and mighty king of Greece, as if they had the same conception of him as of King Solomon.[23]

Aristotle's renown was clearly alive in the mouth of the people. My grandmother's own grandmother was alive in the period described by the German visitor.

It was some time before I made the connection between the character popular in Irish folklore and the Greek philosopher. Later as a student of philosophy it was my reading of Aristotle in particular that helped me to articulate and put shape on my deep-felt sense of nature, those original sensations from my childhood, and my way of experiencing the natural world. Since then Aristotle has provided countless insights, opened up perspectives, deepened my sensibility, widened my horizon. Throughout his works he has the permanent power to surprise; a floating phrase, an incidental comment, a parenthetical elucidation – these repeatedly are to be discovered as they convey a subtle nuance of meaning.

Over the past thirty years I have been fortunate to visit Greece regularly; more recently I have lived for long periods in Athens. Each day I pass the excavated site which it is claimed was the location of Aristotle's Lyceum. I have visited the remains of the ancient city of Eretria on the island of Evvia (ancient Euboea), where in 1891 the American archaeologist Charles Waldstein claimed to have discovered the tomb of

Aristotle. On a sunny autumn afternoon I visited the village of Stagira in northern Greece. I was the only passenger to get off the bus travelling from Thessaloniki to Chalkidiki. As I sat beside the statue of its most famous citizen outside the town, what struck me most forcefully was the manner in which nature imposes herself from all sides upon the senses. The sweltering heat, the scent of tamarisk and pine, the incessant chirping of cicadas, the hooting owl at dusk: reality revealed herself without a mask or veil. The surroundings had little in common with the scents and sounds of my childhood in Ireland; nevertheless it was the same power of universal nature. One of the characteristics that drew me to Aristotle was his common-sense attitude. He could never have been an idealist; nature gives herself directly and immediately. He would agree with Jacques Maritain's remark that there is more excitement in a cherry between the teeth than in all the libraries of idealist philosophy.

I am intrigued by the enigmatic figure of Aristotle that entered the Irish folk tradition. His mysterious character is distilled in one of those medieval triads that are a unique genre of Irish traditional wisdom and folk-poetry. The triplet runs: 'Three things Aristotle did not understand: the coming and going of the tide, the working of the honeybee, and the mind of a woman.' (*Trí rud nár thuig Aristotle: teacht agus imeacht na taoide, obair na mbeach, intinn na mban*). There is some foundation for these apparent conundrums. While there are no tides in the Mediterranean, there are particular currents in the narrow and extended straits between the mainland and the island of Evvia, where Aristotle spent his final years. Aristotle, supposedly, was unable to fathom these erratic 'tides'. An apocryphal story, even mentioned by Galileo in his *Dialogue on the Two Great Systems*, claimed that having observed the currents from some cliffs of Euboea and failing to comprehend them, in a fit of mortal despair Aristotle plunged into the sea below. Assuming consistency between the character of Aristotle the individual and the tenor of his philosophy, which exhibits a humility and equanimity towards life and the world, we may dismiss this story as pure fiction.

In one of his biological treatises Aristotle recognizes his limited understanding of bees. The Irish oral tradition portrays his failed attempt to observe the working of the honeybee; Aristotle placed a glass dome around a swarm, but the bees frustrated his research by covering the inside of the globe with honey. It is hardly necessary to find a textual reference in Aristotle for the universal enigma of the female mind; he does suggest that men have more teeth than women – perhaps neither of his wives, Pythias or Herpyllis, acquired her wisdom teeth, since he himself states that women sometimes acquire them into their eighties! As well as the folk tradition, there are frequent references to Aristotle also in Irish poetry. Like many others, William Butler Yeats contrasted Plato and Aristotle. In the poem 'Among School Children' he wrote: 'Plato thought nature but a spume that plays / Upon a ghostly paradigm of things; / Solider Aristotle played the taws / Upon the bottom of a king of kings.' 'Solid' was the word used also by Goethe to describe Aristotle in a letter to Schiller.

In a variety of ways I encounter in Aristotle's attitude to nature a resonance of my own experience and sentiment; his attitude I find congenial and sympathetic. This is, I believe, because I spent the first decade of my life in a rural environment where I gained a love of the physical and natural world, which primed me for philosophical reflection. Nature comes before nurture, and nature is herself the first great teacher. Our formal education is a guided discovery of the wonders of the world. *Primum vivere.*

INTERPRETING ARISTOTLE

Aristotle was arguably the greatest philosopher who ever lived, but he was also deeply aware of the limits of our knowledge. He may well have inspired Goethe's remark: 'Many things we would know better if we did not wish to know them so precisely.'[24] The world is always more than we can discover, and we always know more than we can ever express. Aristotle realistically recognized the limits of the human condition. While 'man is the best of the animals … he is not the highest thing in the world'.[25] He was, nonetheless, entirely committed to the intelligibility of reality, and the human passion to discern it. Aristotle was no rationalist. Hegel's slogan, 'the rational is the real', he would invert and modify: 'the real is the intelligible'. Jacques Maritain remarked that an error of modern philosophy was to divorce intelligibility from mystery. Are these not opposing qualities? Aristotle made the valuable distinction between what is intelligible in itself, and what is clear and evident to us. The divergence lies in reality's excess of intelligibility which surpasses our capacity to understand. There is an inverted relationship between what we know with clarity and that which is intelligible in itself: 'We advance from what is more obscure by nature, but clearer to us, towards what is more clear and knowable by nature.'[26] In the presence of what is fully intelligible by nature, our mind, he suggests, is like the bat blinded by the light of day. We are dazzled by an excess of light: how curious that Aristotle should speculate, *avant la lettre*, what it is like to be a bat!

The sixteenth-century Italian critic Minturno contended: 'No one can be called a poet who does not excel in the power of arousing wonder.' The same holds for the philosopher and Aristotle recognized wonder as the wellspring of philosophy. His admiring humility towards the world is edifying. The starting point of all investigation and speculation is the recognition 'that it is'.[27] Experience frequently leads the mind to a state of perplexity where, as it were, it gets tied in knots. The first step towards a solution, according to Aristotle, is to acquaint oneself with the problem. It is not possible to unravel a knot that you do not know.[28] He valued the challenge of inquiry, praising those who ignored human interests, seeking instead the 'extraordinary, wonderful, difficult and divine'.[29] He remarks that 'a complacent mind feels no surprise'.[30] Doubtless he would have rejected Dante's estimation that he was 'Master of those who know'; instead he was 'Master of those who seek to know', and he was audacious in that search.

Aristotle was by no means universally praised by poets or philosophers. Dryden lamented his influence:

> The longest tyranny that ever swayed,
> Was that wherein our ancestors betrayed
> Their free-born reason to the Stagyrite,
> And made his torch their universal light.
> So truth, while only one supplied the state,
> Grew scarce, and dear, and yet sophisticate.
> Still it was bought, like emp'ric wares, or charms,
> Hard words sealed up with Aristotle's arms.

The poet reserved his praise for Francis Bacon, champion of the new learning: 'The world to Bacon does not only owe / Its present knowledge, but its future too.' Dryden was voicing the view of those who rejoiced in the experimental philosophy newly championed by Bacon. Jonathan Barnes is scathing in his censure of those who fail to appreciate the fact that our modern notion of scientific method is essentially Aristotelian.[31] As well as Bacon, Barnes targets Dryden's contemporary John Locke, who was apparently under the impression that Aristotle preferred (in Barnes' words) 'flimsy theories and sterile syllogisms to the solid, fertile facts'. Barnes protests: 'The charge is outrageous; and it was brought by men who did not read Aristotle's own works with sufficient attention and who criticized him for the faults of his successors.'[32]

The title of the present collection is chosen to indicate a range of approaches arising from a personal reading. Only one thing is sure: not everyone will agree with my interpretations of Aristotle, or the conclusions to which I commit him. Aristotle's genius is to have investigated so many aspects of the real world, from diverse points of view, that he opened up varied possibilities of method and insight. Much of current Aristotelian scholarship is technical and exegetic; while this is valid we must not forget that Aristotle was concerned with real questions of the living world, and with human experience in all its amplitude. His goal was wisdom; his writings are devoted to questions of genuine value and still have much to offer. Reading the work of ancient philosophers we should aim to make its dry bones live.

Aristotle's phrase 'All realms of nature are marvellous' could serve as a motto for this volume. Each essay is in one way or another motivated by the attitude of marvel that Aristotle recognized as the wellspring of philosophy, which he himself conveys frequently in his writings. In keeping with this underlying tenor of the collection, the opening essay 'Wonder and Universality' has as its theme the philosopher's wondrous outlook upon the universe, an attitude shared with the poet. Philosophy and poetry are both characterized by the universal openness of each upon reality. Although Aristotle does not say so, I suggest that the wondrous perspective of poetry is somehow, like that of philosophy, made possible by its relation towards the totality. The poet has indeed an even greater openness and freedom than the philosopher, since he engages the imagination and deploys parable and allegory in order to articulate insight and emotion. He has licence to affirm things not only as they are, but also as they might be or could be imagined.

The second essay, 'Philosophy and Poetry in Aristotle. Interpreting and Imitating Nature', also deals with the relation between philosophy and poetry in their similarity and difference, as they interpret and imitate nature according to their respective approaches. The philosopher seeks to disclose the principles which lie at the heart of substances in the natural world, as they endure within their identity and unfold in actions; the poet (like other artists) somehow re-enacts the causal activity of nature, assimilating the natural process. There is, I suggest, something of an inverse analogy in the manner in which poetry and philosophy deal respectively with their subject matter. Philosophy reflects upon things in our world of sense experience and aims to grasp their inner nature, interpreting them in light of universal concepts. The poet, on the other hand, illustrates his insight into a universal character-type by recreating the concrete actions appropriate to such a character.

The essay 'Human Nature and Destiny in Aristotle' aims to provide an overview of the philosopher's understanding of human beings, both as they resemble and differ from other animals. Aristotle was convinced that nature had appointed man as the summit of the visible world, hinting at a purpose beyond the visible. Man's physical nature is fitted towards a spiritual fulfilment, a world of *logos*, self-examination and happiness; even his physical comportment suggests a heavenly destiny. In the generation of the human substance, nature, more than elsewhere, shows that she makes nothing in vain, but provides all that is useful and necessary. I emphasize the unity for Aristotle of soul and body as co-constituents of a single substance; I note also his tentative arguments for the immortality of the soul, and recognize the conflict between these two aspects of his teaching. I make explicit Aristotle's remarks on the *selfhood* of human nature, i.e. each one's experience as reflectively individual. This provides valuable insight into the motivation for morality: the virtuous man loves his own existence and consciously forges his own good. But since man's final good seems to lie beyond his natural state, Aristotle urges that we strive to attain immortality as best we can, by seeking to emulate the gods in the intellectual activity by which we most resemble them.

The essay 'Knowledge and Necessity in Aristotle' discusses some aspects of a characteristic which philosophers generally agree pertains to knowledge properly conceived. Aristotle grounds the necessity of knowledge, in the first place, in the action of sensible beings upon our sense faculties; since these by their nature respond to material objects, the knowledge they mediate is immediate and infallible. More generally Aristotle anchors knowledge in the principle of non-contradiction, which is the most certain of principles. The reliability of truth is ultimately grounded in the necessity implicit in the affirmation of existence. The essay also considers the relation of necessity which, in opposition to the modern empiricist view, Aristotle holds, exists objectively between the agent-cause and its effect. The necessity of action is, at a deeper level, grounded in the nature of substance, which determines each thing to be what it is; the primacy of final causality and its role as necessarily orienting the operation of substances is highlighted. The essay concludes with a summary of Aristotle's reasoning to the necessity of the first mover.

In 'Aristotle and the Metaphysics of Metaphor' I suggest that Aristotle has articulated the most satisfactory available explanation for metaphor as a fundamental, ubiquitous, and necessary feature of everyday language. His understanding of metaphor rightly rests upon an appreciation of analogy as the mind's spontaneous recognition of similarities across the widest gamut of difference. Aristotle emphasizes the importance of analogy for biology and metaphysics. Metaphor expresses not properly intrinsic analogy, but an imperfectly analogous resemblance that has its metaphysical foundation in action. Special attention is paid to metaphoric similarities between the physical and mental spheres, indicating both man's citizenship of two worlds, material and spiritual, but also, as *suntheton* or composite, his ability to transcend this duality. The ubiquity of metaphor is a cipher for the unity of reality throughout the multiplicity of beings.

'Aristotle's Political Anthropology' examines a number of questions arising from Aristotle's definition of man as a political animal. Is the term 'political', properly speaking, exclusive to humans? When affirmed of animals, is it to be understood literally or metaphorically? Is the definition biological, rational, or metaphysical? In what sense may the polis be described as natural, if it does not conform to Aristotle's definition of nature (*phusis*)? How may the primacy of the state be reconciled with the fact that the citizen is somehow independent, with autonomous activities and an individual purpose?

Aristotle offers two distinct explanations to establish that man is by nature a political animal and the polis a natural entity. The first is a detailed description and empirical narrative of the genesis of the polis: how it arose, and the evident purpose which it exists to serve. The second is a short, theoretical, compacted explanation of man as a political animal, based on his possession of *logos*. While there is no logical entailment between the two arguments, there is a necessary material connection. The concept 'political' refers properly to man as an animal living in political partnership and community; uniquely endowed with *logos*, he alone shares with his fellow humans the common and universal values upon which society is based. The term 'political' is used in a secondary and metaphorical sense of those gregarious animals that collaborate in a common task. Against a widespread interpretation I argue that Aristotle's definition of man as political animal is not biological, but rational and metaphysical.

The essay 'Aristotle and the Metaphysics of Evolution' was written in reaction to W.K.C. Guthrie's suggestion that Aristotle's doctrine of substantial form (*eidos*) is no longer tenable, since 'it makes Darwinian evolution impossible'. While it is true that in his biological writings Aristotle excludes the evolution of species, I suggest that his metaphysics is theoretically receptive to evolutionary theory. Aristotle provides, moreover, a wider philosophical context for an adequate explanation of evolution. Doctrines that are fundamental for a theoretical consideration of evolution are the concepts of act and potency, form and finality, the nature of causation and the explanation of chance. *Eidos* (form) is for Aristotle the deepest principle of individual substance. Form is inseparable from finality; individuals are properly realized and defined in the completed actuality of their nature: *phusis* is both origin and end. The notion of substantial form, dominant in ancient and medieval philosophy, was rejected by modern thinkers. Darwin also sought to reduce structure to the conditions from which it arose, rather than acknowledge it as structure in itself; hence the suggested incompatibility with Aristotle. It may be argued that the question of form is prior to the debate concerning the origin of species. Aristotle's denial of evolution in his biological writings does not invalidate, a priori, his fundamental insight into form as metaphysical principle. Form is required in order to account for the basic taxonomy of the natural world, and to distinguish the living from non-living. Material causality is insufficient to explain the irreducible complexity of life; biology may not be reduced to mechanics.

Aristotle anticipates certain aspects of evolutionary theory, such as the gradation of species and the dualizing nature of the ape. He rejected pangenesis – the theory that the individual is entirely formed from the start – in favour of epigenesis, according to which individuals grow and develop gradually, actualizing latent potencies. Analogously, his notion of form may be extended prospectively to embrace its dormant potencies. Contemporary scholars recognize in Aristotle's genetics an anticipation of the principle of DNA, the single most important discovery in recent evolutionary biology. With certain adaptations, a theory of evolution may be accommodated to an adapted metaphysics of Aristotle.

The essay 'Evolutionary Ethics: A Metaphysical Evaluation' assesses from an Aristotelian perspective the project of E.O. Wilson, founder of sociobiology, to establish ethics exclusively upon the theory of evolution. The essay deals primarily with the metaphysical presuppositions of the theory. According to Wilson, human behaviour is to be explained in terms of basic universal features of human nature laid down by evolution. Morality is based upon genetics; ethics should be removed from philosophers and biologicized. I argue that because of an excessive reductionism, Wilson fails to recognize the crucial differences between humans and other animals. Restricting the value of morality to the conditions from which it arose, Sociobiology is guilty of the genetic fallacy. An early victim of sociobiological ethics is personal purpose, since all duty is towards the so-called epigenetic rules governing evolution. Wilson dismisses the question of self-existence: the moral question of suicide is a false one, to be overcome by the control centres of the hypothalamic-limbic complex. Such a view, I suggest, not only runs counter to experience, but is the vitiation of morality and ultimately the abandonment of philosophy.

This critique is continued in the following chapter, 'Aristotle and Evolutionary Altruism', in which I examine the theoretical justification provided by Sociobiology for a theory of morality based upon evolutionary ends. Altruism is not an operative concept for Aristotle: benevolence is not included among the virtues. Commentators debate – anachronistically – whether Aristotelian attitudes towards others, presented in the context of friendship, should be viewed as egotism or altruism. Seeking to ground ethics in biological evolution, Sociobiology postulates inherited altruistic tendencies. The sole ultimate purpose of human life is to propagate the species. Against early Darwinism, which emphasized conflict in the struggle for survival, Sociobiology points to the need for cooperation to guarantee continuance of shared genetic material. Sociobiology appeals to 'social' structures in the animal kingdom as indicating, analogously, a biological imperative as the foundation of human morality. E.O. Wilson defines altruism as 'self-destructive behaviour performed for the benefit of others'. This occurs principally in two contexts: kin selection and reciprocal altruism. On an Aristotelian view such extreme selfless demands would be possible only – if at all – for totally virtuous individuals. Aristotle is too much of a pragmatist to accept that humans would universally sacrifice themselves for the species. He agrees with Hume that love is firstly centred upon the self, and that men are 'endowed only with a confined generosity'. While he also maintains that the highest human activity is the perpetuation of the species, he attributes individual goals to the moral agent. If altruism is interpreted as a concern for others for their own sake, Aristotelian friendship is by definition altruistic. Aristotle's views on friendship, and the motivation and sacrifice involved, provide a helpful perspective on evolutionary altruism.

To accept that we have a genetic propensity to behave morally does not yet explain why we are obliged to act morally, or why we might be personally motivated to do so. Aristotle's ethics is immediately appealing because it offers personal reasons and incentives why we should be moral: it is centred upon individual happiness. We are the only animals that can be happy. Other animals have no share in well-being or in purposive living; their purpose is life, that of man is the good life. Morality and happiness are personal; virtue depends upon ourselves. As a result there is no hiatus between 'is' and 'ought': the notion of a 'naturalistic fallacy' is alien. Man's 'is' *is* already an 'ought', his existence embraces obligation. While praising Hieron the victorious charioteer, Pindar urges him: 'Learn and become who you are.'[33] Human life is suffused with values, but they must be conquered and attained. The prize is happiness; the cost of failure is unhappiness in the form of personal non-fulfilment. The distance between 'is' and 'ought' is that between our raw state and the self-project we discern; the dynamism and tension is the freedom experienced as we cover that distance in reflective acts of self-attainment.

The final essay in this collection, 'James Joyce and Aristotle', details the extensive and penetrating influence of Aristotle on one of the greatest figures of modern world literature. During his time at University College Dublin, Joyce was imbued with the spirit of Aristotle. A wayward student, alienated from the ideals of his Jesuit professors, he even confesses to 'Bringing to tavern and to brothel / The mind of witty Aristotle'. The protagonist of the early autobiographical novel, *A Portrait of the Artist as a Young Man*, interrogated about his developing theory of aesthetics, declares: 'For my purpose I can work on at present by the light of one or two ideas of Aristotle and Aquinas.' Joyce read the *Metaphysics* and *De Anima* intensively for two months in Paris; these works provided him with the mental framework of Stephen Dedalus in *Ulysses*. Long afterwards he still regarded Aristotle as the greatest ever philosopher: 'In my opinion the greatest thinker of all times is Aristotle. He defines everything with wonderful clarity and simplicity.' Joyce might find the style of his contemporary, Thomas Speed Mosby, to be somewhat overladen, but would agree with the latter's paean: 'The most versatile intellect that mankind has ever known, the master mind of all antiquity and the great mental phenomenon in the history of human thought, that mighty prodigy of learning known to the world as Aristotle, still gleams adown the ages like a distant sun, a beacon-light of learning that casts its burning rays upon the farthest shores of time.'[34]

One of the merits of Aristotle's approach is its unrestricted openness upon the fulness of reality: 'the soul is in a sense all things'.[35] He refuses resolutely to reduce reality to one or other phenomenon. The mind measures itself against the world, and may not limit experience to its own categories; intelligibility and mystery abide in one another. Being may not be identified with, or reduced to, any of its determinations: such would be to restrict its existential wealth. This attitude is illustrated in the remark that 'no part of an animal is purely material or purely immaterial'.[36]

Aristotle's starting point is the indubitable fact that things are: knowledge is firmly grounded upon reality. His first philosophy (πρώτη φιλοσοφία) coincides with the study of being, and so it should be. Being is the universal and ubiquitous element of the human spirit: the ebb and flow of all we do, the buoyancy and ballast of what we know, the keel on which rests each intellectual advance. It is the anchor of every affirmation, the north which guides our quest – equally each point which encompasses the boundless sphere both of what we know and what yet remains uncharted.

Although his was a philosophy of being, I contend that Aristotle did not himself attain to a concept of existence, in the sense of the radical presence of things in their total separation from sheer nothingness. He provided for Aquinas, however, the nuanced concepts that allowed the latter go deeper than Aristotelian essence to the actuality of existence, understood as the 'act of all acts and perfection of perfections'. In Heideggerian terms Aristotle remained at the ontic level. With his distinction between the act of existing (*actus essendi, esse*) and the essence (*essentia*) of what things are, Aquinas penetrated to the ontological.[37]

Aristotle was for Aquinas *the* philosopher: *philosophus*. He adopted complete and entire the method of Aristotle. Aquinas remarked that it was characteristic of Aristotle never to depart from the obvious.[38] Henri Bergson remarked that if we remove from Aristotle's philosophy everything derived from poetry, religion and social life, as well as from a somewhat rudimentary physics and biology, we are left with a grand framework which, he believes, is the natural metaphysics of the human intellect.[39] When actively engaged in, this natural metaphysics bears much advantage, not just theoretical, but personal and existential. Aristotle remarked that those who choose life in accordance with reason, live more intensely and with greater pleasure.[40] His own work is a valuable guide for those who seek to explore the richness of life.

1

Wonder and Universality
Philosophy and Poetry in Aristotle

Beautiful and very young are Philo-Sophia
And poetry, her ally in the service of the good.
As late as yesterday Nature celebrated their birth,
The news was brought to the mountains by a unicorn and an echo,
This friendship will be glorious, their time has no limit,
Their enemies have delivered themselves to destruction.

Czesław Miłosz[1]

O ne of the most moving documents which we possess from the entire corpus of ancient philosophy is the fragment of a letter written by Aristotle toward the end of his life: 'The more solitary and isolated I am, the more I have come to love myths.'[2] The fragment speaks volumes. Werner Jaeger comments: 'Within the noisy house there sits an old man living entirely to himself, a hermit, to use his own expression, a self withdrawn into itself, a person who in his happy moments loses himself in the profound wonderland of myth.'[3] One recalls Rembrandt's famous painting of Aristotle contemplating the bust of Homer. These words reveal not only how dearly Aristotle treasured the tradition of the ancient mythmakers, but indicate concretely and existentially the profound bond between poetry and philosophy.

The following reflections refer to aspects of similarity and difference between philosophy and poetry. I will focus upon the universal character of each, grounded in the unique relationship of the human psyche (ψυχή, soul) to the totality of being, and its conscious reflection upon universal reality. Aristotle explicitly recognizes the philosophical value of poetry, which he famously contrasts with history. There have been endless interpretations of his assertion: 'Poetry is both more philosophical and more serious than history, since poetry speaks more of universals, history of particulars.'[4] Discussion of the philosophical character of poetry has tended to focus on this distinction and the subject matter of poetry, sometimes simplistically presented as universal natures rather than individual facts. I am not concerned, however, with the meaning of this celebrated passage.[5] Extrapolating from Aristotle, I wish instead to identify some of the wider parameters of poetry. I propose to consider the philosophical character of poetry, not with regard to its specific object, but from the point of view of its universal perspective, a characteristic which, I suggest, is what it most fundamentally shares with philosophy. Poetry exhibits a universality of scope akin to that of philosophy whose object is the totality of being. This universal perspective accounts moreover for their concrete starting point in wonder.

The close kinship of poetry and philosophy has its profound origin in man's radical response to reality, and in his capacity and need, in different ways, to interpret the world. Aristotle begins his treatise on first philosophy with the simple declaration 'All men by nature desire to know',[6] and proceeds to ascribe to poetry and philosophy a common origin in the fundamental human experience of wonder. Both poetry and philosophy are born of marvel and are motivated by a loving fascination and desire for learning. The text of *Metaphysics* 1 is well known: 'From wonder men now begin and at first began to philosophize.'[7] Wondering first at obvious problems, they gradually advanced to the greater realities of nature, the moon and sun, until they finally reflected upon the genesis of the universe itself (περὶ τῆς τοῦ παντὸς γενέσεως). Aristotle continues: 'A man who is puzzled and wonders thinks himself ignorant, whence even the lover of myth (φιλόμυθος) is in a sense a lover of wisdom (φιλόσοφος), for myth is composed of wonders.'[8] The φιλόμυθος relies greatly upon the poet, the 'maker' of myth, who through allegory, symbol and metaphor, shapes a meaning from the welter of human happenings by weaving them into a pattern and narrative of wider cosmic order. Although Aristotle does not state that the poet is engaged in wonderment of the totality (θαυμάζειν τοῦ παντός), the juxtaposition and comparison of philosophy and poetry allow us to make this assimilation. In a particular manner, the poet and philosopher are both captivated by the uniquely human experience of wonder. Elsewhere Aristotle declares: 'Sophia is the knowledge of many wonderful things.'[9]

Two significant aspects of the relationship of man as poet and philosopher to reality are indicated at the start of the *Metaphysics*. Firstly, it is man's nature to wonder. This arises from the desire to escape ignorance, but also from a loving admiration of what is to be known. Secondly, the ultimate horizon of man's inquiry, the final goal of his desire, is the totality of the real. Wonder reaches its ultimate expression in a reflection upon the widest dimensions of human experience. Philosophy seeks to grasp the origin of all things. This is possible through the relationship which constitutes the very nature of the soul itself, expressed concisely in *De Anima*: 'Summarizing what has been said about the soul, let us assert again that the soul is somehow everything that is... the mind becomes all things.'[10]

Wonder is especially revealing of human knowledge and inquiry; it may be described as the reflective admiration of that which we know but do not fully comprehend. While it may not be identified with knowledge (ἐπιστήμη), neither may it be equated with ignorance: there is within it at least some primitive certainty in the face of an object which is affirmed as worthy of admiration and inquiry. It is an incipient knowledge which is aware that what is known surpasses one's understanding. As a unique form of knowledge (γνῶσις) it comprises both a positive and negative element. Nevertheless it is accompanied by joy and hope, rather than resignation to ignorance.[11] In Gabriel Marcel's distinction, it is concerned with mysteries rather than problems.[12] A problem is a question which confronts us; it lies before us. A mystery is a truth which embraces us; it is inexhaustible and remains an abiding source of wonder and fascination.

Aristotle exhibits a fundamental, yet cautious, optimism regarding man's desire for truth and knowledge, based upon a confidence in the generous munificence of nature. Man is marked by a capacity for knowledge; this tendency cannot be in vain since, as he repeatedly declares, 'nature does nothing in vain', but bestows everything that is needed and nothing that is superfluous.[13] Early in the *Rhetoric* he states: 'Men have a sufficient natural instinct for what is true, and usually do arrive at the truth.'[14] Moreover, 'things that are true and things that are just have a natural tendency to prevail over their opposites'.[15]

The paradox of man is that while he is characterized by knowledge, he is aware that his knowledge is limited. Man is defined as a rational animal (ζῷον λόγον ἔχον: an animal having reason) yet knows himself to be ignorant.[16] There is an ambivalence at the heart of wonder. It is not simply the absence of knowledge, but a knowledge which is aware there is something beyond its reach. This finds its explanation in Aristotle's distinction between what is intelligible in itself and what is evident to us.[17] We are caught in a tension between what we know and that which we know exceeds our grasp. What characterizes this attitude, however, is the very *recognition* that it surpasses our understanding; we stand midway between knowledge and ignorance, in a cognition that is conscious of its own limits and accepts that the intelligibility of the real far excels our capacity: 'The cause of the present difficulty is not in the facts but in us. For as the eyes of bats are to the blaze of day, so is reason in our soul to the things which are by nature most evident of all.'[18] It is the constant challenge of poet and philosopher to give expression to the elusive mystery of reality: the philosopher to articulate it conceptually, the poet to announce it imaginatively in metaphor, symbol or image, giving it thus a 'concrete habitation and a name'. Because we are surrounded by mystery, the philosopher and poet ceaselessly ponder and are forever replete with wonder. As the eye of the bat is blinded by the light of the sun, so the human mind is dazzled by the deep and dazzling darkness of reality itself, not a deficiency but an inexhaustible excess of intelligible light.

Awareness of the limits of human knowledge does not cause despair or resignation, but paradoxically a certain joy in the affirmation of what we desire. 'Everything which we desire is pleasing, since desire is a longing for what is pleasant.'[19] Wonder offers in promise the prospect of ever-deepening knowledge. 'Learning and wonder are generally pleasant; for in wonder there is the desire to learn, so that what is wonderful is desirable, and through learning is established what is in accordance with nature.'[20] Even the very desire for knowledge is pleasant: the initial awareness of something to be discovered provokes delight. We love that which makes us wonder. The marvellous is a cause of pleasure (τὸ δὲ θαυμαστὸν ἡδύ) – evidenced by the fact that everyone adds to a story in order to please his listeners.[21] Aristotle suggests the importance of the wondrous as both the motive and subject matter of poetry and drama: arising from a sense of mystery, the purpose of poetry is also to portray the awesome or marvellous (τὸ θαυμαστόν).

It is beyond our present scope to deal exhaustively with the role and nature of the irrational (τὸ ἄλογον) which, according to Aristotle, is the main cause of wonder.[22] Central to that discussion is also the status of the impossible (ἀδύνατον). Aristotle states that in drama and epic poetry, a *likely impossibility* (ἀδύνατα εἰκότα) is preferable to an *improbable possibility* (δυνατὰ ἀπίθανα).[23] One may wonder how it is proper for the poet to portray the impossible, however convincing it might appear. One explanation is to bracket the problem by referring it to popular belief,[24] or to cloak it with the mantle of myth ('things as they are said to be').[25] The latter carries, moreover, the persuasive weight of religious tradition, a frequent source for dramatic plots, with its allied authority of divine intervention in the human order.

Aristotle does not require plays to be representations of philosophical theories; he accepts traditional themes and mythic plots.[26] What he demands, however, is a certain measure of internal credibility. A bad drama is one in which there is neither probability nor necessity in the sequence of episodes.[27] 'Stories should not comprise irrational components (μηδὲν ἄλογον); ideally there should be no irrationality, or failing that, it should lie outside the plot.'[28] Aristotle contrasts the irrational (τὸ ἄλογον) with those necessary or probable elements (τὸ ἀναγκαῖον ἢ τὸ εἰκός), that will explain the reasons for a character's actions or the sequence of events.[29] Hence, 'if a poet posits an irrationality, and a more rational alternative is apparent, this is an absurdity'.[30] There should be nothing irrational in the events portrayed on stage. The unfolding plot should provide its own dénouement. 'The *deus ex machina* should be employed for events outside the drama – preceding events beyond human knowledge, or subsequent events requiring prediction and announcement; for we ascribe to the gods the capacity to see all things.'[31] This privilege is beyond the human condition.

Aristotle declares that the poet describes not what has actually happened, but 'what might happen and which can happen, as either likely or necessary (τὰ δυνατὰ κατὰ τὸ εἰκὸς ἢ τὸ ἀναγκαῖον)'.[32] While the poet errs, for example, if he depicts impossibilities (ἀδύνατα), this is justifiable if he thereby provokes astonishment and thus achieves his goal.[33] Correctness (ὀρθότης) in poetry is not the same as in politics or any other art.[34] Aristotle concedes that impossibility may be accepted for three reasons: for poetic effect, for the sake of an ideal, or because of popular belief (πρὸς τὴν ποίησιν ἢ πρὸς τὸ βέλτιον ἢ πρὸς τὴν δόξαν δεῖ ἀνάγειν).[35] He subtly distinguishes the irrational (τὸ ἄλογον) from the impossible (τὸ ἀδύνατον), explaining the former as 'what people say'. And recognizing the power of reality to cause surprise, he says of irrationalities that 'they are sometimes *not* irrational, since it is probable that improbable things occur'.[36]

Aristotle's suggestion that τὸ ἄλογον, the inexplicable or irrational, is the main element in the wondrous (τὸ θαυμαστόν) might seem to conflict with his definition of man as ζῷον λόγον ἔχον, a rational animal. If philosophy, which has its origin in wonder, is directed to what is in itself intelligible and aims, in Plato's phrase, to 'render reason' for the world (λόγον διδόναι),[37] is it not contradictory to regard the irrational as the primary source of wonder? Aristotle, however, is here dealing with wonder as the response to a spectacle on the stage, or incited by the telling of an epic. Ἄλογον is only paradoxical until its surrounding circumstances or causes have been disclosed; it plays, one may suggest, a crucial role in the early stages of the drama and is resolved in the dénouement. Precisely because man's nature is ζῷον λόγον ἔχον, the best *captatio* is an element which jars and jolts his normal categories of experience and interpretation.[38] Thus Aristotle will permit the poet to introduce the irrational for the sake of surprise and marvel. This can have no place for the philosopher; the wondrous which captivates the philosopher's attention must be of itself open to intelligibility.

Aristotle states that incidents provoke greater amazement when they are unforeseen, yet follow upon one another, than if they happen automatically or by mere chance. 'Such incidents have the very greatest effect on the mind when they occur unexpectedly and at the same time in consequence of one another; there is more of the marvellous in them than if they happened of themselves or by mere chance. Even matters of chance seem most marvellous if there is an appearance of design as it were in them.'[39] As an incident of special significance Aristotle cites the story of Mitys, the murdered King of Argos in whose honour a statue was erected. When his killer came to look at the statue, it happened to fall and kill him. Stressing the importance in tragedy of discovery (ἀναγνώρισις), i.e. the change from ignorance to knowledge,[40] he states: 'The best of all discoveries is that arising from the incidents themselves, when the great surprise comes about through a probable incident (εἰκότων).'[41] It provides an unexpected, but adequate explanation.[42] There is both the pleasure of surprise and the satisfaction of cognitive explanation. The case of Mitys' statue is most compelling, carrying the conviction that there is a greater justice.

According to Jonathan Lear, the relation between wonder and understanding in the *Poetics* is the opposite of that presented in the *Metaphysics*: wonder is provoked by grasping the fact that the events, though unexpected, are intelligibly linked to one another. 'So while in *Metaphysics* wonder provokes us to understand, in the *Poetics* understanding provokes us to experience wonder.'[43] This is a valid but incomplete interpretation. It is characteristic of wonder that with increased insight, there follows *pari passu* an ever-increasing sense of mystery; understanding and wonder feed and fortify one another in an ever-intensifying cycle of contemplation and admiration.

As well as captivating the intellect, wonder also engages the will. What is awesome or marvellous is pleasing; it arouses wonder and incites a desire to learn. Learning is the movement towards the actuality of knowledge, insofar as this is possible.[44] Thus all stages of cognition are marked in varying degrees either by the desire stemming from the need to know, or the pleasure derived from the fulfilment of this need. The love of the marvellous is fulfilled in the discovery of its causes: *felix qui potuit cognoscere causas*. Through discovery (ἀναγνώρισις) the intellect is brought to its proper state, bringing pleasure and happiness in accordance with the natural, fulfilled, state of the human intellect. (In the *Poetics*, ἀναγνώρισις is brought about through the unfolding of the plot itself, so has a parallel effect in the mind of the audience.) Knowledge is an end in itself, hence wisdom causes happiness: man is happy through the simple act (τῷ ἐνεργεῖν) of contemplating.[45] This is his highest activity, in which he is naturally happy and in which he most resembles divine nature.[46]

The distinction between learning and knowledge is best elucidated by Aristotle's distinction between two kinds of activity. Learning is a movement (κίνησις) or incomplete activity (ἀτελές), whereas to know is an actuality (ἐνέργεια) or end which contains its own fulfilment. Κίνησις is the imperfect exercise of becoming actual, ἐνέργεια the pure exercise of actuality without change. In activities proper, as distinct from motions, the goal is the exercise of the faculty itself; it does not lie in an outside product as, for example, in a house. 'The actualization resides in the subject; e.g. seeing in the seer, contemplation (θεωρία) in the one who contemplates, life in the soul.'[47]

Knowledge, accordingly, is marked by happiness, learning by desire. But since man desires knowledge, learning too is pleasant. 'Learning gives the greatest pleasure not only to philosophers but similarly to all other men, although they share this pleasure to a small degree.'[48] Things which appear pleasant are done from desire.[49] Nature determines what is desired, hence activity which leads to our natural state is pleasant. Aristotle even remarks that for the most part it is *necessarily* pleasant to enter into a natural state of being,[50] since 'what is natural is pleasant'.[51] He defines pleasure as the sensation experienced with the awareness of achieving our proper nature. It is the conscious movement (κίνησιν αἰσθητήν) by which the soul as a whole attains natural fulfilment.[52] Central to Aristotle's definition is the perceptible quality of pleasure: one is *aware* of one's experience as pleasant.[53]

Since learning and wonder are pleasant, acts of imitation (μίμησις) such as painting, sculpture and poetry, according to Aristotle, also cause delight, even though the original object may itself be unpleasant: 'For it is not this that causes pleasure, but the inference that the imitation and the object imitated are identical (that 'this is that': ὅτι τοῦτο ἐκεῖνο), so that the result is that we learn something.'[54] According to Aristotle, poetry has its origin in two particular causes, both of which are natural (φυσικαί). Firstly, man has from childhood an innate (σύμφυτον) instinct for imitation and learns his first lessons through imitation. Secondly, he delights in works of imitation; these give joy and pleasure through learning, with the recognition of their likeness to the original.[55]

Aristotle's remarks on man as a mimetic creature, and the connection between knowledge and mimesis, are of fundamental significance for his evaluation of the cognitive value of poetry: 'Man differs from the other animals in that he is the most imitative (μιμητικώτατον).'[56] This description of man is, I suggest, directly related to his fundamental definition of man as an animal with reason (ζῷον λόγον ἔχον). It is because he is rational that man is eminently imitative. In the act of imitation man represents what he already knows. This involves an awareness of one's already existent knowledge and the continual assessment of the imitative process in order to assess its fidelity. This is also the case when one recognizes, rather than creates, a work of imitation; an act of self-knowledge is required. It is not the discovery of something for the first time, but a recognition of the identity of what I observe with what I already know. Mimesis involves a reflexive act; an act of discovery through self-reflection. In recognizing the identity of an imitation with its original, that 'this is that', there is a bending back of knowledge upon itself: not only do I know, but I *know that I know*. Only thus can I relate the imitation to the original, and examine the value and reliability of my knowledge. It should be pointed out that both metaphor and simile (εἰκών) are also acts of imitation, involving a reflexive recognition of identity – metaphor tacitly so – between distinct elements of the semantic synthesis, that 'this is that' (ὡς τοῦτο ἐκεῖνο).[57]

Aristotle, as noted, refers to the particular causes which move poets to create works of literary representation: their instinct for imitation and their delight in works of imitation. However, he goes on to point out that *all men* by nature have a mimetic instinct, and gain enjoyment from representation. These native instincts, the very grounds which Aristotle has proposed as the source of poetry, are thus not confined to poets but are universal. Hence they are not in themselves sufficient to guarantee the existence of poetry.[58] The unique charisma of the poet is the ability to lend an air of elegance and strangeness to what he represents. This he achieves in many ways, portraying persons and things as extraordinary; he enhances his subject through the many modifications of language (πολλὰ πάθη τῆς λέξεως). 'As humans behave [differently] toward strangers and their fellow citizens, so also do they relate toward language; hence we should give to our language an air of strangeness; for men marvel at what is remote and what is marvellous is pleasant.'[59] More than any other element of language, metaphor for Aristotle contributes to excellence of style (ἀρετὴ λέξεως). 'Metaphor above all gives lucidity, pleasure, and strangeness (καὶ τὸ σαφὲς καὶ τὸ ἡδὺ καὶ τὸ ξενικὸν ἔχει μάλιστα ἡ μεταφορά).'[60] A successful metaphor excites a *frisson* of delight with the discovery of a new connection or relation. It opens up a strangeness within an individual through its unexpected association with something far removed. Things which are remote are wonderful and what is wonderful is pleasant.

The power of metaphor sets the poet apart; it is the true sign of genius. It is a gift of nature which cannot be learned from another.[61] Metaphor is the most effective way to 'give to everyday speech an unfamiliar air'; it is a continual reminder of the strangeness of all things, of the marvellous in the quotidian. Metaphor, moreover, brings the surprise and pleasure of fresh knowledge; of all poetic means to provide rapid knowledge (μάθησιν καὶ γνῶσιν... μάθησιν ταχεῖαν) it is the most effective.[62] 'Easy learning is naturally pleasant to all... so that all words which make us learn something are most pleasant.'[63] While the poet's work is fundamentally one of imitation, metaphor is a uniquely creative imitation, bringing into view 'hitherto unnoticed resemblances between things the most apparently dissimilar'.[64] Metaphor, one might suggest, itself involves a special kind of mimesis, effected mentally through a newly-discovered likeness. It is not entirely a new creation since the poet discovers the likeness present already in the world; it is nonetheless a new imitation because the subject is mirrored in a fresh light. In metaphor the poet illustrates how nature, as it were, 'imitates' or mimics herself, repeating her wonders across a variety of modes. The patterns of nature are repeated throughout a multitude of individuals, each analogously exhibiting the marvels of nature. The special gift of the poet is the ability to discover unusual and remote similarities.

The wondrous or marvellous (τὸ θαυμαστόν) is for Aristotle the motivating impetus for all investigation, not only philosophic and artistic or poetic, but also the empirical inquiries of biology and zoology. It suffices to recall the famous passage from *Parts of Animals* which displays a loving fascination with the concrete living individual, and a desire to understand it radically.[65] The passage reveals much about our present topic: the nature of wonder and the attitude of self-conscious admiration toward different objects of knowledge. 'In all things of nature', Aristotle declares, 'there is something marvellous (ἐν πᾶσι γὰρ τοῖς φυσικοῖς ἔνεστί τι θαυμαστόν)'.[66] He contrasts the meagre knowledge which we have of transcendent reality with the detailed knowledge we enjoy of the physical world of nature. 'The scanty conceptions to which we can attain of celestial things give us, from their excellence, more pleasure than all our knowledge of the world in which we live; just as a half glimpse of persons that we love is more delightful than an accurate view of other things, whatever their number and dimensions.'[67] The merit of knowledge does not depend on the accuracy or detail of the knowledge we obtain, but on the value of the object known. The world of wonder is not that of clear and distinct ideas, but the chiaroscuro of mystery. Celestial realities conceal astonishing depths and evoke awe precisely because they surpass our capacity to understand; the little knowledge which we have about them is valued more dearly than the certitude and completeness we have of earthly beings. The latter, however, are also charged with wonder; even lowly substances evoke pleasure by revealing the inner work of nature; such is the sheer pleasure of knowledge characteristic of philosophy.[68]

Aristotle affirms the unity of all things in nature, hence wonder attains its greatest depth when it views its object *sub specie totalitatis*. 'All things, both fishes and birds and plants, are ordered together in some way ... and the system is not such that there is no relation between one thing and another; there is a definite connection.'[69] A being appears most wonderful in the context of this universal connection. Nature is itself a unity, a totality which, although it escapes our comprehension, is intelligible in itself. The search for a knowledge of the totality (περὶ τοῦ παντὸς) is described by Aristotle in the *Metaphysics* as the science which contemplates being as being.[70] Being is itself the totality, and the mystery of each thing is its existence within the ensemble.

Wonder, therefore, is ultimately understood in light of the universality of its object. Poetry exhibits a universality of scope akin to that of philosophy which has as its object the unlimited totality of being. Since being is in itself inexhaustible, it can never be fully fathomed by the human mind; it is an abiding source of wonder and beckons to endless inquiry. Wonder is related to the totality; when man adopts a conscious attitude vis-à-vis the universe, he is confronted by the vertiginous possibility of nothingness.[71] Genuine poetry, together with such profound human experiences as love, proximity to death, marvel in the presence of beauty, all shock us out of the apparent self-sufficiency of everyday life, caught in a web of daily needs and ends.[72] We are obliged to confront the totality itself and to face the fundamental ontological sense of realities over which we have no power. Such boundary experiences invite us to contemplate the gratuitous character of existence. This is, I believe, the meaning that Heidegger finds in the words of Hölderlin: 'Full of merit, yet poetically man dwells on this earth.'[73] The wonderful, we noted, engages not only the intellect, but also the will, which affirms reality as good in itself. Wonder is both an intellectual and affective response to a reality which we wish to understand in its most universal context, and whose ultimate value we wish to explore. Wonder incites desire – not only is knowledge to be desired; its object is equally to be loved.

It is in relation to the universal that Aristotle most significantly discovers the meeting point between poetry and philosophy. By the universal content of poetry, he states, is meant 'the kinds of things which it suits a certain kind of person to say or do'.[74] I suggest, however, that the universality which characterizes both poetry and philosophy might also be taken in another sense, namely, that of the totality of things *tout court*. This is not explicit in Aristotle but may legitimately, I suggest, be concluded by bringing together certain elements and suggestions from diverse writings, and especially by relating the *Poetics* and *Metaphysics*. The ultimate horizon of man's philosophic and poetic pursuit alike, the final goal of his spiritual desire, is the totality of the real, the very fullness of being itself: he seeks to grasp the origin of all things (περὶ τῆς τοῦ παντὸς γενέσεως). One must be careful in the Aristotelian context to avoid speaking of 'infinite being'. Only later did 'infinite' assume a positive sense, indicating the subsistent fullness and perfection of being. For Aristotle, the endless or infinite was imperfect, in the sense of unachieved, and hence 'unpleasant and unknowable (ἀηδὲς γὰρ καὶ ἄγνωστον τὸ ἄπειρον)'.[75]

History relates what has happened; it deals with verifiable events, which it describes and interprets. The historian may indeed wonder about the causes and connections of particular human deeds, which he seeks to explain in a pattern of behaviour and influence. In that aim his work rests. He does not ponder why the very condition of human affairs should at all be such as it is. His wonder is sated with the disclosure of the circumstances of time and place, which exhaust his desire to know. In principle, the poet and philosopher cannot be satisfied by the mere supply of information. The wonder of poetry and philosophy is wider and more radical; in the words of William James, 'to wonder why the universe should be as it is presupposes the notion of its being different'.[76] The possibility of difference opens the intellect and imagination to endless and universal horizons. Most radically it reveals the intransgressible chasm between being and non-being. Philosophic wonder is ultimately expressed in the question which Martin Heidegger, emulating Leibniz, has restored to the centre of philosophical reflection – a question which had already been articulated in the thirteenth century by Siger of Brabant in his commentary on Aristotle: 'Why is there something rather than nothing in reality?'[77]

The philosopher clearly investigates being as being (τὸ ὂν ᾗ ὄν) from a universal point of view. He adopts the widest possible perspective towards reality, in harmony with logic and the laws of thought. How does the poet engage with the totality? Needless to say, he does not investigate τὸ ὂν ᾗ ὄν. He may ponder the mystery of the universe, but does not interrogatively reflect upon the *fons et origo* of existence. He shares with the philosopher, nonetheless, the unlimited theatre of the world in its totality. Aristotle states the poet's unlimited perspective: 'He must always represent one of three things – either things as they were or are; things as they are said and seem to be; or things as they should be.'[78] With this broad definition of mimesis, Aristotle allows full freedom to the poetic psyche (ψυχὴ) and imagination (φαντασία). They range over the entire spectrum of existence, real or imaginary, factual or fictional. The poet has therefore, in a sense, an even more universal scope than the philosopher; he is not restricted to individual events or facts in seeking to express his insights and intuitions. Moreover poetry tells, not necessarily what actually happened, rather what 'might happen', or what might have been.[79] He is not confined to fact, but is free to imagine all manner of possibility. He may embrace what people believe or say, although it is not actually true.[80]

Most significantly, the poet may also resort to allegory to illustrate how things might have happened, although he is aware that it is not a true account. Parables or allegories have the advantage that while it is difficult to find similarities in the past, one can always, according to Aristotle, invent them, if one has the skill of grasping the analogy between fact and fable. This recognition of similarity is a gift which the poet shares with the philosopher: philosophy trains the mind not only in the skill of discovering likenesses, but also of inventing them.[81] The poet's method, of metaphor and allegory, allows him a universality of scope in a manner which itself resembles – is analogous to – the philosopher's application of analogy to discern the similarity of metaphysical principles throughout the universe of beings. Both philosophic analogy and poetic metaphor are an indication of true genius: a gift of nature, a skill that cannot be learned from another.[82] The genius of poetic metaphor is precisely to recognize deep and hidden similarities: 'just as in philosophy also an acute mind will perceive resemblances even in things far apart'.[83]

According to G.F. Else, there is not a word in the *Poetics* 'about the ultimate "secrets of life," about why mankind should suffer or be happy, about Fate, or man's relation to God, or any such metaphysical matters… Thus we are not to ask the poet for ultimate answers'.[84] It is indeed true that in the *Poetics* Aristotle does not engage with the fundamental questions of human existence. That is not his purpose; his aim is to arrive at a correct understanding of 'poetry in general and the capacity of each of its genres'.[85] Aristotle, however, is investigating a form of human discourse which, while distinct from philosophy, is also concerned with ultimate values, although the poet must finally remain silent in their regard: questions of fate and freedom, of moral duty and obedience to divine command.[86] Materially there is much in common between philosophy and poetry; the philosophical inquiry into poetry, however, has a distinct formal perspective, and approaches it, as Aristotle states, 'as is natural, from first principles (ἀρξάμενοι κατὰ φύσιν πρῶτον ἀπὸ τῶν πρώτων)'.[87]

While divergent in method, poetry and philosophy have been seen from the beginning as intimately related in origin and aim. They share a common source in the concrete lived human experience of wonder. Analysis reveals that the ultimate horizon of wonder, and of the human soul itself, is the totality of the real, which the poet and philosopher both seek to fathom in different ways. While the philosopher proceeds discursively, respectful of logic and firmly anchored in fact, the poet 'in nimble thought can jump both sea and land'.[88] Pindar claims that the poet 'knows a shorter path' to knowledge,[89] that he 'moves like a bee from word to word'.[90] The philosophic and poetic paths, of intellect and imagination, run side by side, wandering apart only to return and intertwine. The dialogue between the poet and philosopher arises, as Heidegger declares, 'from a necessity of thinking itself'.[91] Each in its own manner seeks illumination through insight and intuition. Plutarch suggests, therefore, that 'whenever we find any edifying sentiment neatly expressed in the poets we ought to foster and amplify it by means of proofs and testimonies from the philosophers . . . For this is right and useful, and our faith gains an added strength and dignity whenever the doctrines of Pythagoras and of Plato are in agreement with what is spoken on the stage or sung to the lyre.'[92]

2

PHILOSOPHY AND POETRY IN ARISTOTLE
INTERPRETING AND IMITATING NATURE

In morrall doctrine, the chiefe of all knowledges, hee doth not
only farre passe the Historian, but for instructing
is well nigh comparable to the Philosopher,
for moving, leaveth him behind him.

Philip Sidney, 'Defence of Poesie' (1595)[1]

There is perhaps some small significance in the fact that the first
recorded, although unrelated, use of the two words 'philosophy' and
'poetry' occurs in the same work – the history of Herodotus. The word
'philosopher' is applied in a general sense to Solon the Athenian, who
'travelled far in search of wisdom (φιλοσοφέων)'.[2] Herodotus states of
Homer and Hesiod that they 'made' (ποιήσαντες) for the Greeks the birth
of gods, giving to them their names, honours and arts, and expressing
their outward forms; the poet is thus regarded primarily as a maker or
creator.[3] The early poets expressed in story a primitive view of the world
and of man's destiny. Homer moulded an ideal combining nobleness in
action with the tragedy of death, the power of the gods with the
inevitability of fate. This view of the world was for centuries the
inspiration of Greek thought and education. The words of Aristotle may
be applied to Homer: 'what is ancient seems akin to what is natural (τὸ
ἀρχαῖον ἐγγύς τι φαίνεται τοῦ φύσει)'.[4] To better appreciate Aristotle's

contribution to an understanding of the relationship between poetry and philosophy, I will briefly outline the development of this relation in early Greek culture.

The ancient poetic vision of the cosmos was a prelude to the critical and reflective inquiry of philosophy. The twentieth-century Austrian writer Hermann Broch remarked: 'Homer stood at the cradle of the Greek world; creator of language, painter of myths, a poet and philosopher, and held in his hand the germ of the future.'[5] It was not by chance that philosophy arose in a milieu formed by the epic vision. The ancients themselves, according to Strabo, considered poetry 'a kind of elementary philosophy which introduced one early to life and taught through the enjoyment of character, feeling and action'.[6] According to Plutarch, poetry opens and awakens the minds of the youthful to the teachings of philosophy.[7] Porphyry regarded Homer as a great philosopher and wrote a multi-volume work entitled *Homeric Questions*.[8]

Philosophy thus emerged within a culture shaped by the mythic vision of the Greeks, and its origin and development are revealing of its distinctive nature. One cannot overestimate, for example, the importance of cosmogonic myths, in which personified powers provide imaginary answers to real questions. The philosopher, however, must distinguish between real explanation and the allegorical account, which was intended to show that a rationale was at work within the universe: not necessarily the one described, but one that was analogous.[9]

The 'ancient quarrel between philosophy and poetry', of which Plato speaks,[10] began in the sixth century, when the authority of Homer and Hesiod as the teachers of the nation was questioned by the early philosophers. The homeric view of the cosmos was not altogether satisfactory and at times inconsistent. The gods, for example, although declared all-powerful, were at times subject to fate. Xenophanes, himself a poet and philosopher, criticized Homer for giving to the gods the frailties of men. For this anomaly Pythagoras portrays Homer as suffering in Hades. Heraclitus also despises the authority of the poets, contrasting the much learning (πολυμαθίη) of Hesiod with the true knowledge of the philosopher.[11] Hesiod, the 'revered teacher of many', for example, taught that 'Day was the daughter of Night',[12] which to Heraclitus' philosophy of opposites made little sense, since for him day and night must be one.[13] Heraclitus criticized Homer's prayer for the healing of strife which, he claimed, is the principle of all things. Homer ought to be 'expelled from the games and given a beating'.[14]

Soon, however, other philosophers, including Anaxagoras and Theagenes, accepted that the poets had in their myths 'concealed profound wisdom in enigmatic and symbolic fashion',[15] and that on the level of allegory a deeper meaning could be discovered in their works. The words 'symbol' and 'allegory' convey the twofold level of poetic expression. 'Symbol' (σύμβολον, from συμβάλλω, 'to throw together') is defined by Liddell and Scott as 'a sign or token by which one infers a thing'.[16] To 'allegorize' (ἀλληγορέω = ἄλλος + ἀγορεύω), is 'to speak so as to imply something other than what has been said'. Allegory (ἀλληγορία) is the 'description of one thing under the image of another'.[17] This way of poetic expression had been recognized already by Homer and Hesiod, who claimed to express, not always the truth of things (τὰ ἔτυμα), but its likeness (ἐτύμοισιν ὁμοῖα).[18] The words of Alan of Lille (1128–1202) in *De Planctu Naturae* (*The Complaint of Nature*) hold for ancient Greek poetry: 'Poetry's lyre sings with vibrant falsehood on the outward literal shell of a poem, but interiorly it communicates a hidden and profound meaning to those who listen. The man who reads with penetration, having cast away the outward shell of falsehood, finds the savoury kernel of truth wrapped within.' These words of Dame Nature distinguish the dual potencies of poetry to both adorn the outward apparel and reveal the inner substance of things.[19] Plutarch employs another metaphor: myth is the rainbow which reflects the sun of truth.[20]

The protagonist in the ancient dialogue between poetry and philosophy, to which he refers, was Plato himself; he was the first to consider the origin and nature of poetry in depth philosophically. His theory of poetry was essentially determined by his philosophy of being and theory of knowledge. Truth is the privilege of philosophy and could be attained only by reflection. The work of artists and poets is not to explore truth but 'to seek the nature of what is beautiful and elegant'.[21] Poetry attains not true reality but a mere imitation; it is primarily an influence rather than a reliable source of instruction. Plato attacks the importance of Homer in Greek education: philosophy alone can seek the true meaning of the world and guide man's action. If the poet appears wise it is because, inspired by the gods, he utters many great things, knowing nothing of what he says.[22]

The poet speaks, according to Plato, 'not from art, but as inspired and possessed'.[23] This was indeed the traditional belief; Homer begins his work with an appeal 'for inspiration to utter the truth of things'.[24] Hesiod tells how the Muses breathed into him a divine voice while he was tending his flock on Mount Helicon, inspiring him to sing 'of the things that shall be and have been long ago'.[25] 'The Muses', he declares, 'have taught me to sing in marvellous song'.[26] The Greek word for 'inspired', ἔνθεος, means to be filled with the god; the state of the poet was ἐνθουσιάζων – whence the word 'enthusiasm'. To be inspired the poet must, according to Plato, abandon his own self, so that the gods may enter his mind and speak through him. 'For a poet is an airy thing, winged and holy, and he is not able to make poetry until he becomes inspired and goes out of his mind and his intellect is no longer in him.'[27] This 'being-beside-oneself' is a kind of mania but, according to Plato, the greatest of blessings come through this madness, which is in essence an openness to the gods. In the *Phaedrus* Plato distinguishes between various kinds of mania: 'prophetic', 'cathartic', and a 'third kind of possession or mania which comes from the Muses. This takes hold of a gentle and pure soul, arousing and inspiring it to songs and other poetry.'[28] Whoever arrives at the gates of poetry without a divine mania, thinking he will be a good poet by art alone, will be unsuccessful.

Socrates declares in the *Lysis* that poets 'are to us as fathers and guides in wisdom'.[29] In the *Meno* he states that poetry is a gift from the gods, and that the poet speaks of things divine (τὰ θεῖα).[30] In the *Republic*, however, Plato refuses to listen to the poet's wisdom and scorns his words as a pale imitation of truth. All art, including poetry, is an imitation (μίμησις) of the sense world – itself a copy of the world of Forms, the only true reality (ὂν ὄντως).[31] The poet, therefore, imitates what is itself but a shadow of reality. Homer, whom Plato addresses as 'dear Homer' and describes as 'the best poet and most divine',[32] is thus 'at a third remove from truth and virtue, a creator of appearances'.[33] Poetry is as unreal as the images in a mirror: it knows nothing of reality, only semblance.[34] According to Plato, therefore, poetry should not be regarded seriously as attaining to the truth and whoever listens to her should be on guard against her seductions.[35] As well as being untrue, poetry is also harmful to the spirit; by arousing the emotions, it seduces the mind. Whereas we regard as best the poet who arouses our sympathy, in our own lives we strive to be calm. Therefore unless feelings and passion rather than reason are to rule the state, poets must be banished. Hymns to the gods and eulogies which honour noble men are the only poetry allowed in Plato's republic.[36]

Despite the fact that Plato scorned the poets, his contribution to the understanding of poetry is significant. Aristotle soon restored to poetry its unique value and healed the rift with philosophy. The difficulty with Plato's evaluation of poetry is that of his entire philosophy: the separation of truth from sense experience and its location in transcendent universal Forms. Aristotle restored the unity of knowledge and rooted man's search for universal truth in sensible reality. What really exists, according to Aristotle, are active, autonomous, individuals; in the first place, sensible substances or φύσεις: plants, animals and humans. It is through our experience of these that universal ideas are acquired. Sense objects are the proper domain of human knowledge, and provide in turn the models and material for the poet and artist. Aristotle recognized the profound affinity between poet and philosopher; each is in his own way engaged in man's search for the universal meaning, truth and purpose of the world. He articulated more adequately the symbiotic relation of poetry and philosophy implicit in early Greek culture. There has been much speculation regarding the exact meaning of his famous statement, 'Poetry is both more philosophical and more serious than history, since poetry speaks more of universals, history of particulars.'[37] In the following reflections I wish to consider yet another aspect of comparison, namely the value which the universal has for poetry in its activity of imitating nature.

There is, I suggest, a certain inverse analogy in the manner in which poetry and philosophy deal respectively with their subject matter. Philosophy reflects upon the world of sense experience, composed of substances and understood primarily as natures (φύσεις). This it does by means of universal concepts. The philosopher inductively acquires such concepts in his discovery of the world and employs them deductively in its interpretation.[38] In each case rational activity relates general concepts to the world. The poet, on the other hand, 'makes' or creates a plot, representing the actions of an individual of the kind investigated by the philosopher. The philosopher seeks insights which will elucidate the agent; the poet proceeds with a pre-formed characterization, which implicitly contains the logic of the unfolding action. The philosopher aims to disclose the inner form (εἶδος) of an individual substance (οὐσία); the poet, with the aid of imagination, imposes an εἶδος pre-formed within the soul upon materials drawn from experience.[39] In this the poet emulates nature; at another level he also resembles the philosopher: presenting plots in plays and narrative, he draws attention to the marvels and mysteries of human life, in an attitude akin to philosophic θεωρία or contemplation.

Their distinct, but complementary, speculation is well stated by S.H. Butcher: 'Philosophy seeks to discover the universal through the particular; its end is to know and to possess the truth, and in that end it reposes. The aim of poetry is to represent the universal through the particular, to give a concrete and living embodiment of a universal truth.'[40] The poet presents to his audience, that they may ponder and wonder, an action of the kind the philosopher encounters in the real world. He may not *ab initio* foresee the complete dénouement, but he has advance knowledge of the plot and *dramatis personae*, which the philosopher must gain after the fact. Through its method of representation poetry analogously resembles philosophy, not through plain imitation or direct replication, but in a certain inverse parallel. The idiom of each, moreover, is suited to its task: whereas philosophy is rational, poetry is figurative, wielding a wealth of lexical tropes and dramatic strategies.

Aristotle includes poetry in the genus of mimetic arts (τέχναι). In what way does poetry imitate nature? On a variety of occasions Aristotle draws an analogy between the creative work of the poet and the immanent activity of φύσις. Defining tragedy as the representation (μίμησις) of an action which is complete, whole and with a certain magnitude, he refers to the beauty of a living being, which also consists of parts with a certain magnitude and which are arranged in an orderly manner.[41] The parallel holds both for the epic poet and the dramatist: 'As for the art of imitation in narrative verse, it is clear that the plots ought

49

(as in tragedy) to be constructed dramatically; that is, they should be concerned with a unified action, whole and complete, possessing a beginning, middle parts and an end, so that (like a living organism) the unified whole can effect its characteristic pleasure.'[42] The analogy is reversed in the *Metaphysics*: 'The phenomena show that nature is not a series of episodes, like a bad tragedy.'[43]

The highest achievement of artistic creation – and this is the sense of the statement 'ἡ τέχνη μιμεῖται τὴν φύσιν'[44] – is that it somehow reenacts the causal activity of nature itself. Directing his creative attention to the works and actions of φύσις, the poet in a twofold manner imitates nature: he replicates, in some transformed fashion, a work of nature, and in doing so vicariously assimilates his own creative activity to the action of nature itself. It is not simply the end product of artistic creation which provokes admiration and pleasure, rather the illustration through artistic activity of the immanent unfolding of nature. The famous passage from the *Nicomachean Ethics* is enlightening: 'All art deals with bringing something into existence; and to pursue an art means to study how to bring into existence a thing which may either exist or not, and the efficient cause of which lies in the maker and not in the thing made; for art does not deal with things that come to existence of necessity or according to nature, since these have their (efficient) cause in themselves.'[45] The work of art, as Liberato Santoro notes, 'lacks the substantial perfection of physis, the self-unfolding process from itself to itself'.[46]

Imitating nature, the artist functions as a surrogate principle of determination, replicating the self-unfolding activity of φύσις. The creative activity of the artist, operating extrinsically, reenacts by way of imitation the intrinsic self-unfolding activity of nature. The point is not that the product of art is simply a mirror image of a natural substance; rather the human creative process itself imitates the growth process of nature. It is by comparison a feeble and crude imitation, but is nevertheless a genuine resemblance. The analogy from art to nature is deficient and fails to express the full power of nature since, as Aristotle recognizes, 'the final cause and the beautiful are more fully present in the works of nature than in the works of art'.[47] Nature, moreover, is ever-present and all-powerful. Intimately active in all her works, she resembles the artist who models in clay rather than the carpenter, since she shapes her product not at arm's length through an intermediate tool, but by palpably touching it herself in direct action.[48] One might extend Aristotle's analogy, suggesting that the action of the poet is likewise more intensely and intimately effective in his creation, and therefore better resembles the work of nature.

Poetry as an imitation of nature may be further examined in light of the contrast between poetry and history. The question of φύσις vis-à-vis the universal is central and fundamental to the distinction between poet and historian, a distinction more profound than that of rhyme and prose. Aristotle explains: 'The distinction is this: the one says what has happened, the other the kind of thing that would happen. For this reason poetry is more philosophical and more serious than history. Poetry tends to express universals, and history particulars.'[49] To say that poetry is more universal is not to say that it is a contemplation of universal essences or φύσεις. There is, nevertheless, an inevitable connection: the universal is that which pertains to, and may be predicated of, several individuals.[50] For Aristotle, φύσις is the principle of living individuals. The distinction of poet and philosopher inevitably raises the question of the truth value of poetry with respect to the reality of universal essence.

There is a temptation in the light of some remarks by Aristotle to view the poet as idealizing the work of nature.[51] As the portrait painter who enhances his subject, the poet also transforms his characters into figures of worth.[52] The model should excel the actual.[53] 'Art in some cases completes what nature cannot bring to a finish, and in others imitates nature.'[54] Moreover, as Aristotle comments in the *Politics*, 'The beautiful are said to differ from those who are not beautiful, and works of art from realities, because in them the scattered elements are combined, although if taken separately, the eye of one person or some other feature in another person would be fairer than in the picture.'[55] To the charge that the poet's imitation is not true, one may respond that perhaps it should be; Sophocles claimed that he portrayed people as they ought to be, Euripides as they are.[56] Dramatists resemble painters in that some depict men better than they are, others as worse. Tragedy represents men as better than they are, comedy as worse. Homer, for example, portrays people to be better than they are.[57]

Typical of the view that poetry idealizes nature is the classic interpretation of S.H. Butcher. His position may be summed up: 'Art in imitating the universal imitates the ideal; and we can now describe *a work of art as an idealised representation of human life—of character, emotion, action—under forms manifest to sense*.'[58] Butcher equates the universal of poetry with an ideal and perfected form (εἶδος), grasped by an abstract concept but never attained by nature.[59] In line with his aim to present the *Poetics* in the context of Aristotle's broader philosophy, Butcher might have cited textual evidence for the unity of nature (φύσις) and form (εἶδος), thus strengthening his case for the imitation of nature as a portrayal of εἶδος. Seeking the substance (οὐσία) of things in *Metaphysics* 7, Aristotle identifies it primarily with εἶδος. And in the *Physics* he identifies φύσις or nature as the distinctive 'shape and form' (ἡ μορφὴ καὶ τὸ εἶδος) of things which have within themselves their own source (ἀρχὴ) of movement and change.[60] Nature (φύσις), he elaborates, determines each living thing in its shape and form as the kind of thing which it is by definition (ἡ μορφὴ καὶ τὸ εἶδος τὸ κατὰ τὸν λόγον).[61] Φύσις and εἶδος are virtually identical; imitating nature as a model, the artist thus imitates the εἶδος. Butcher's appeal, however, to the principle that nature always works for the better is misplaced.[62] Since Aristotle's φύσις is the counterpoise of Plato's ideal Form, but which nevertheless struggles to do its best in every circumstance, he cannot here be speaking of an idealized nature. The poet is not concerned with an ideal εἶδος; poetry deals with concrete actions, which are in a continual process of genesis and movement towards a real – not an idealized, unattainable – final cause. It is a contradiction to suggest that nature strives towards a final goal which it can never attain. Nature attains her final cause in the maturity of each living substance.

Aristotle's explanation of the 'universal' content of poetry is not so sublime as Butcher suggests, but much more human. It refers, he states, to 'the *kind* of speech or action which belongs by probability or necessity (κατὰ τὸ εἰκὸς ἢ τὸ ἀναγκαῖον) to a certain *kind* of character'.[63] From this it is clear that while Aristotle maintains that poetry is concerned with universal actions, he does not have in mind the philosopher's contemplation of abstract universals. The poet, therefore, does not portray the universal essence or nature of man, the one-beyond-the-many, the 'general concept which the intellect spontaneously abstracts from the details of sense'.[64] Human nature itself allows for a great many 'types': the courageous, cowardly, brave, wise, ambitious etc. Needless to say, as an act of verbal representation poetry relies – as every discourse[65] – upon universal concepts and meanings. The subject matter of poetry, however, cannot be the human essence of the abstract universal. Human types are merely different ways in which common human nature comes to concrete embodiment, manifesting the variegated richness of nature in general. Such types are indeed grasped by means of universal concepts, but refer not to universal man in general, but to specific modes of character or personality. The human εἶδος allows for many types; without such diversity there is no drama. The poet depicts living, acting individuals (μιμούμενοι πράττοντας).[66] Each individual acts autonomously, but illustrates a general type. Concepts have universal validity, but refer to concrete persons. The figures on stage must therefore exhibit human characteristics 'in a representative and not an idiosyncratic way'.[67]

Actions are particulars;[68] however a complete action – *a fortiori* that of drama – is not the work of a single agent, but of many individuals acting around a comprehensive plot. And it is precisely the organic interrelations of the latter which together contrive to exemplify the general principles involved in epic and dramatic poetry, in the first place the universal rule of necessity and probability.[69] Malcolm Heath argues convincingly that the universality of a plot 'is realized proximately in the necessity or probability of each character's words and deeds, but ultimately in the necessity or probability of the product of their interaction, that is, in the necessity or probable consequences of the events which constitute the action as a whole'.[70]

For Aristotle, the ideal of philosophical knowledge is the grasp of universal concepts and their mutual implication. Poetry is clearly not such a contemplation of universals, charged in addition with emotion and embellished by rhyme; it is a representation of human events and their interaction. It does not engage in abstract speculation, but portrays universal aspects of human life in concrete situations. The poet does not describe universal essences or ideas, but particular human actions; not arbitrary, disjointed incidents, but actions consistent with certain characters. Poetry employs universal ideas in a way history does not. Historiography too relies, as every intellectual activity, upon general terms and universal concepts; its application however is different. While history seeks patterns of influence and inevitability, placing human action in the widest relevant context of antecedent events, its speculation is confined to what has actually happened. It is therefore less universal and philosophical.[71] Poetry, on the other hand, sets human action within the broadest possible parameters, factual or fictional: human action as it has happened, may be imagined to happen, or should happen. There are no limits to its hermeneutic. The modalities of possibility, probability and necessity are more significant of universal knowledge than the contingencies of actual historical events. More than relate them, poetry interprets, investigates, balances and ponders their significance and implication; in this it is more resemblant of philosophy.

It would be tempting to conclude that Aristotle did not have a very high opinion of history. One can indeed understand the suspicion of Martha Nussbaum[72] and Jonathan Lear,[73] that he was unfamiliar with Thucydides. This, however, is highly unlikely; Aristotle was well versed in all available literature. His purpose, however, was not to divest history of philosophic value; he merely states that it is not so serious as poetry. His comparison of history with poetry is itself recognition of its relative philosophic merit. A superficial knowledge of Thucydides suffices to indicate how closely the investigative mentality of the Greek historian resembles that of the philosopher. He is not content to record isolated events; he traces patterns and sequences, seeks explanations, identifies causes and draws general conclusions.

There is indeed acute philosophic awareness in Thucydides' own self-evaluation. Ironically he believed that the poets were unreliable, with little regard for truth. He questions Homer's reliability – suspecting that he exaggerated the size of the expedition to Troy for the sake of embellishment.[74] He is convinced of the truthfulness and value of his own account, and considers himself superior to the poets. Thucydides recognizes the difficulties involved in the search for truth (ζήτησις τῆς ἀληθείας),[75] and warns against the exaggerated fancies of the poets (ἐπὶ τὸ μεῖζον κοσμοῦντες).[76] The absence of myth (τὸ μυθῶδες) from his narrative may make it less pleasing, perhaps, than the tales of the chroniclers who aim to please the ear, but whose reliability cannot be tested. His own work, he declares, is an accurate account 'both of the events which have happened and of those which will some day, in all human probability, happen again in the same or in a similar way'. It has been composed, not for passing gain, but as a 'possession for all time (κτῆμά ἐς αἰεί).'[77]

The historian catalogues various events and seeks inductively to order them in a coherent pattern of categories and causes. He aims to clarify events in their broader perspective. At its most profound he aspires to lasting insights into human behaviour, even perhaps the predictability of human actions. In his creative work, the poet assumes such predictability, based upon a generalization of human character and destiny, and proceeds to illustrate it deductively through particular actions and situations. Like the historian, the philosopher too begins with a posteriori experience and proceeds inductively until he acquires the general notions required to analyze reality in its broadest dimensions. His investigation however goes deeper than that of the historian. Philosophy investigates the ultimate natures of things, seeking the grounds for action in the substances of the world. As we have seen, poetry represents the actions of individual human beings; it thus imitates nature and reveals something of human φύσις. It is, by the same token, concerned with universals, since φύσεις, the forms or essences of natural substances, are the fundamental principles of explanation for the realities and qualities expressed by universal ideas. Imitating φύσις, the poet deals in a unique manner with the universal, not as the philosopher does, but analogously in his own idiom.

Aristotle states that while experience is of particulars, and actions and events are individual, 'art is knowledge of universals'.[78] Poetry, however, does not deal explicitly with universal ideas, but with what happens probably or by necessity with concrete living natures (φύσεις). These admit of exceptions and differences, but follow regular patterns of behaviour. Aristotle's rule of dramatic action, that poetry is concerned with what belongs 'by probability or necessity (κατὰ τὸ ἐικὸς ἢ τὸ ἀναγκαῖον)' to a certain kind of character,[79] approximates to the law of nature, according to which things of their nature happen 'for the most part (ὡς ἐπὶ τὸ πολύ)'.[80] This close parallel allows us to clearly ground the impetus of poetry in φύσις. Poetry therefore, is not only, as we have seen, an imitation of nature by extrinsically re-enacting the immanent self-unfolding of φύσις; it also 'holds up a mirror' to the work of nature in what it describes. Needless to say it is not an exact imitation; its reflection of life is refracted in multiple ways, but the relation to the original is always present. The poet has therefore the authority to say: this is what happens for the most part (ὡς ἐπὶ τὸ πολύ), when such characters interact in certain circumstances. Poetry satisfies the demands of verisimilitude when a plot unfolds 'by probability or necessity (κατὰ τὸ ἐικὸς ἤ τὸ ἀναγκαῖον)'. A bad drama is one in which there is neither probability or necessity (οὔτ' εἰκὸς οὔτ' ἀνάγκη) in the sequence of episodes.[81]

In dealing with what may possibly happen, the poet goes beyond the particular event in the life of an individual in order to grasp the vast range of possibilities within the compass of a human character. This is reminiscent of Leibniz' remark that an adequate knowledge of Caesar's nature would allow one understand 'why he decided to cross the Rubicon rather than halt there, why he won rather than lost the battle of Pharsalus, and that it was reasonable, and therefore certain, that that would happen'.[82] An individual's acts are somehow inscribed within his nature. Aristotle's poet beholds in the depths of human nature the domain of probable action, and plots a narrative to illustrate the character; the character he points out, however, is secondary to the action.[83]

The celebrated passage from *Parts of Animals* places in suitable perspective the status of artistic imitation, and its value vis-à-vis the philosophic investigation of nature.[84] It throws light, moreover, on the ultimate meaning of the principle 'Art imitates nature.'[85] The pleasure gained from works of imitation, Aristotle declares, is secondary to the delight derived from the discovery of the intrinsic work of nature itself, giving as it does 'amazing pleasure in their study to all who can trace links of causation, and are inclined to philosophy'. Aristotle gives an ultimate evaluation of all imitation: 'It would be strange if mimic representations[86] of [animals] were attractive, because they disclose the mimetic skill of the painter or sculptor, and the original realities themselves were not more interesting, to all at any rate who have eyes to discern the causes. We therefore must not recoil with childish aversion from the examination of the humbler animals ... for each and all will reveal to us something natural and something beautiful. Absence of haphazard and conduciveness of everything to an end are to be found in nature's works in the highest degree, and the end for which those works are put together and produced is a form of the beautiful.' Art is an imitation of nature, not a substitution. It should not distract from nature but provoke greater admiration. While imitation in itself, as we saw, is a source of wonder through discovery of agreement between object and original, its primary goal is to increase one's marvel at the original. Poetic mimesis will thus enhance the philosopher's contemplation of nature.

3

HUMAN NATURE AND DESTINY
IN ARISTOTLE

Aristotle's inquiry into human nature is manifold and far-reaching.[1] Each aspect of his philosophy discloses an understanding of man as unique – distinguished by his very diversity. Aristotle's man merits the Odyssean epithet πολύτροπος: of many turns, versatile and resourceful. Superficially his creative and adaptive character is confirmed by the titles of Aristotle's various treatises. A cursory review indicates that man is a living, breathing animal endowed with soul; he investigates the world and deliberates how he himself should live, pondering his actions as dramatically represented by the tragic poets. Aristotelian man sleeps, dreams, and is anxious about old age; living in a political state and fascinated by the animal world, he looks to the heavens in hope of discerning his destiny.

Unsurprisingly man is the model and exemplar for Aristotle's investigations into the world of living things. Man is at once that which he knows best, and the best of what he knows. Aristotle introduces the *History of Animals* with an appropriate analogy: 'First we should consider the parts of the human body. Every nation reckons currency with reference to the standard most familiar to itself; and we must do the same in other fields: man is, of necessity, the animal most familiar to us.'[2] In *Parts of Animals* he declares: 'The shape of his external parts is better known than that of other animals.'[3] Through his observations as biologist

Aristotle claims to indicate a variety of physical characteristics marking man off from other species. Man is the only creature whose hair goes grey, who laughs and can be tickled.[4] He is the only animal with different eye colours – or at least with the greatest variety – and the only one, moreover, with eyelashes on both lids.[5] While uniquely he can learn to make equal use of both hands, he is also the only animal that cannot move its ears.[6]

These quirky characteristics are of course mere *obiter dicta* and in no way intended as a serious catalogue. Most philosophically significant is Aristotle's observation that man is the only animal that stands upright, looks ahead, and projects his voice straight in front.[7] There is for Aristotle a higher purpose in this anatomical difference: 'For nature, as we declare, does nothing without purpose; and man alone of the animals possesses speech.'[8] What distinguishes man most properly from other animals is the possession of *logos*. This is the source of all that is distinctive of human nature and behaviour. It provides, moreover, the internal goal or *telos* for the elements which together make up his constitution.

In one of those universalizing accounts which reveal his deep sense of metaphysical order and synthesis, Aristotle offers the following panorama concerning diverse life forms:

> Since it is the nature of plants to permanently remain in one location, they do not have a great variety of heterogeneous parts. For where there are few functions, few organs are required for their performance... In those animals, however, that have not only life but also sensation, there is a greater multiplicity of parts; there is more diversity in some than in others, the greatest variety being found in those animals whose nature it is to share not only in life (τοῦ ζῆν), but in the good life (τοῦ εὖ ζῆν). Such is mankind, for of the animals known to us, man alone partakes of the divine, or at least more than all the rest.[9]

Man's special place in the cosmos provides the ultimate reason why certain aspects of his makeup are indispensable to his nature and function. Aristotle discerns cosmic purpose in the unique design of human anatomy. Instead of forelegs and forefeet, man has hands and arms, which allow him turn his upper body toward the higher regions of the universe.[10] There is even transcendent purpose in the distribution of the human body: 'Man is the only animal that stands upright, and this is because his nature and essence are divine. Now the business of that which is most divine is to think and to be intelligent; and this would not be easy if there were a great deal of the body at the top weighing it down, for weight hampers the motion of the intellect and of the common sense (κοινὴ αἴσθησις).'[11] Anatomy thus favours man's special place in the universe. Nature never makes anything without a purpose;[12] moreover, out of given conditions, she always effects that which is the better.[13] Nature provides the necessary means to fulfil the various functions performed by each living substance.

The theory of 'intelligent design' is applied with particular detail by Aristotle to man's head and face, since these are clearly associated with his ability to interpret the world and communicate his thoughts. His comment upon the face is noteworthy: 'In man the portion of the body between the head and the neck is called the face (πρόσωπον), thus called, it would appear, from the function it performs. Man, the only animal that stands upright, is also the only one that looks straight ahead (πρόσωθεν ὄπωπε) and who directs his voice straight before him (πρόσω).'[14] Aristotle's explanation accords with the standard explanation of 'person' – the actor's mask that is worn to portray a character and that helps to project the voice on stage. The structure of the head also serves a purposive goal, in keeping with the different operations of sight and hearing. 'Nature has located the sense-organs in a very satisfactory manner. The ears are half-way round the circumference of the head, because they are to hear sounds from all directions alike and not only from straight before them. The eyes face front: this is because sight is along one straight line, and we must be able to see along the line in which we are moving, which is directly forward.'[15]

Nature's handiwork may be observed likewise in the structure of the mouth and tongue, which are coordinated to make speech possible. Whereas in other animals, the lips serve as protection for the teeth, in man 'they are more especially intended to serve a higher office, contributing in common with other parts to man's faculty of speech. For just as nature has made man's tongue unlike that of other animals … for the perception of savours and for speech, so also has she acted with regard to the lips, and made them serve both for speech and for the protection of the teeth.'[16] He provides a detailed description:

> For vocal speech consists of combinations of the letters, and most of these it would be impossible to pronounce, were the lips not moist, nor the tongue such as it is. For some letters are formed by closures of the lips and the others by applications of the tongue… It was necessary that the two parts should from the start be severally adapted to fulfil the office mentioned above, and be of appropriate character. Therefore are they made of flesh, and flesh is softer in man than in any other animal, the reason for this being that of all animals man has the most delicate sense of touch.[17]

The articulation of meaning through the manipulation of sound requires that the organs of speech be free and easily adaptable. If man were tongue-tied – literally, like other animals, – he could not produce the endless sounds required to express thoughts symbolically through the physical medium of sound. 'It is in man that the tongue attains its greatest degree of freedom, of softness, and of breadth.'[18] The human tongue is designed to articulate various sounds and produce speech; it has a looseness and freedom lacking in the tongues of other animals. 'It has, also, to articulate the various sounds and to produce speech, and for this a tongue which is soft and broad is admirably suited, because it can roll back and dart forward in all directions; and herein too its freedom and looseness assist it.'[19] The voice, moreover, manifests the deeper presence of human soul: 'Voice is the sound produced by that which has a soul; for none of the soulless creatures has a voice; they can only be said metaphorically to speak.'[20]

Aristotle contends that man's erect stature is in keeping with his divine nature. Instead of legs in front, nature has given him hands and arms. Anaxagoras had earlier claimed it was the possession of hands that made man the most intelligent of animals. Aristotle argues it was the other way around; it is more plausible that man is endowed with hands because he is the most intelligent. 'Hands are an instrument; and Nature, like a sensible human being, always assigns an organ to the animal that can use it.'[21] It is worth citing his view at length:

> We may conclude, then, that, if this is the better way, and if Nature always does the best she can in the circumstances, it is not true to say that man is the most intelligent animal because he possesses hands, but he has hands because he is the most intelligent animal. We should expect the most intelligent to be able to employ the greatest number of instruments to good purpose; now the hand would appear to be not one single instrument but many; it is, as it were, an instrument for instruments. Thus it is to that animal which has the capacity to acquire the greatest number of arts that Nature has given the most useful of instruments, namely the hand.[22]

It must be recognized that there is a circularity in Aristotle's explanation of the stewardship of nature. He declares that nature always provides the apparatus appropriate for the operations performed by any particular kind of animal or plant. Should he not affirm, more importantly, that it is nature itself which is the very origin of such living individuals in the first place?

Aristotle rejects the view that man is the least well constructed of animals, because he is barefoot, unclothed, and without a weapon to defend himself. He points out that all other animals have just one means of defence, which they cannot exchange for another. 'They are forced to always sleep and perform every action, as it were, with their shoes on.'[23] Man, on the other hand, is not restricted to a single mode of defence, but has a great many at his disposal from which he can choose the most appropriate. The secret of his armoury is his hand, whose marvellous versatility is extolled by Aristotle: 'For the hand is talon, claw and horn; it is spear and sword, and any other weapon or tool whatever: it can be all of these, because it can grasp and hold them all.'[24] Aristotle outlines in detail the marvellous manner in which nature has designed the shape (εἶδος) of the hand so that it can fulfil all of these tasks: its diversity and adaptability, its joints, parts, mutual order and arrangement, the varying length of fingers and their relative position vis-à-vis one another.

There is an obvious parallel between this passage and *De Anima* 3, 8, where Aristotle compares intellect (νοῦς), paramount among the powers of soul, with the hand as the principal organ of the body. The hand is the tool of tools, as νοῦς is the form of forms. The hand literally *manu-factures* all physical tools – just as νοῦς cognitively receives into its own intellective form the essential forms of all natures. Given the parallel between body and soul, yet the priority of soul, the primacy of the hand in the physical world derives from its role in the service of intellect.

In the *Politics* Aristotle declares outright that man is the summit and goal of all nature. There is an evident hierarchy between all living substances within the cosmos. Plants exist for the benefit of animals, and animals for the good of man: 'Now if nature makes nothing incomplete, and nothing in vain, the inference must be that she has made all animals for the sake of man.'[25] The universe presents for Aristotle a scale of value and perfection, with man at the summit of the observable world. Within human nature there is also an order and hierarchy: the soul is superior and therefore the natural ruling principle; the hierarchy of the natural world is reflected within the individual. Reason and intelligence are the goal toward which our nature strives (ὁ δὲ λόγος ἡμῖν καὶ ὁ νοῦς τῆς φύσεως τέλος).[26] Both the birth and education of humans are ordered toward this end. While recognizing that man's nature manifests a number of dualities, Aristotle stresses that these comport a series of subsidiary and subservient functions, all of which point to the supremacy of reason.

> As soul and body are two, so we observe that the soul also has two parts, the irrational part and the part possessing reason (τὸ λόγον ἔχον), and their corresponding states, desire (ὄρεξις) and intelligence (νοῦς). And as the body is prior in its development to the soul, so the irrational part of the soul is prior to the rational. And this also is obvious, because passion and will, and also appetite, exist in children even as soon as they are born, but it is the nature of reasoning and intelligence to arise in them as they grow older. Therefore in the first place it is necessary for the

> training of the body to precede that of the mind, and secondly for the training of the appetite to precede that of the intelligence; but the training of the appetite must be for the sake of the intellect, and that of the body for the sake of the soul.[27]

Man's natural superiority above animals, and his moral and social nature are grounded, as noted, in the possession of intellect and language. While some animals have a 'voice' with which to indicate pain and pleasure, speech enables man to articulate the meaning of the world. Animals sense pleasure and pain, but man alone grasps their nature and cause; he distinguishes between what is beneficial and harmful, and he alone knows right from wrong. The possession of *logos* explains why he is more political than even the most gregarious of animals. Aristotle again invokes his guiding maxim that nature does nothing in vain.[28] 'For it is the special property of man in distinction from the other animals that he alone has perception of good and bad and right and wrong and the other moral qualities, and it is partnership in these things that makes a household and a city-state.'[29] The endowment of *logos*, with its fruits of reason, deliberation, speech and logic, however, has its associated dangers: 'For man, when perfected, is the best of the animals (ὥσπερ γὰρ καὶ τελεωθὲν βέλτιστον τῶν ζῴων ὁ ἄνθρωπός ἐστιν), but, when separated from law and justice, he is the worst of all; since armed injustice is the more dangerous, and he is equipped at birth with arms, meant to be used by intelligence and virtue, which he may use for the worst ends. That is why, if he has not virtue, he is the most unholy and the most savage of animals, and the most full of lust and gluttony.'[30]

Viewed also with regard to emotional and moral dispositions, man is the most advanced creature. Aristotle engages in his characteristic search for similarity with an investigation into the 'character' of animals.[31] He even detects constant patterns of behavioural difference between male and female across the animal world. He catalogues all animal species according to gender with respect to such dispositions as compassion, shame, deceit, memory, courage and cunning.[32] 'There are traces of these characters in virtually all animals, but they are all the more evident in those that are more possessed of character and especially in man. For man's nature is the most complete (ἔχει τὴν φύσιν ἀποτετελεσμένην), so that these dispositions too are more evident in humans.'[33] Both the continuity of nature and the excellence of mankind are again observed.

According to Aristotle, all living things necessarily possess a principle distinguishing them from nonliving beings: 'That which has soul is distinguished from what does not, by living.'[34] Soul (ψυχή) is the actualizing form (εἶδος) or animating element which causes a substance to live, investing it with relative autonomy. He notes that his predecessors defined the soul by three properties: movement, perception, and incorporeality – each of which, he remarks, refers to a basic principle.[35] 'What primarily distinguishes something which has a soul from that which does not, is movement and sensation.'[36] Ψυχή is for plants the principle of nutrition; animals are endowed, in addition, with sensation,[37] and humans with intellection. Of all investigations, that into the soul is one of the most difficult, but also the most important – recall Heraclitus' remark that we could never fathom the depths of the soul, so deep is its *logos*.[38] Aristotle repeatedly notes the difficulties associated with the study of soul and mind.[39] The soul is the most elusive of targets and cannot be fastened upon by reason. The difficulties arise from its excellence. Aristotle begins his treatise *On the Soul* with the declaration: 'We regard all knowledge as beautiful and valuable, but one kind more so than another, either in virtue of its accuracy, or because it relates to higher and more wonderful things. On both these counts it is reasonable to put an inquiry into the soul among subjects of the foremost rank. Moreover this investigation seems likely to make a substantial contribution to the whole body of truth, and particularly to the study of nature; for the soul is in a sense the principle (ἀρχή) of animal life.'[40]

According to Aristotle, the distinctive characteristic of soul is that it is itself its own cause of movement;[41] in turn it is the source of movement in the body.[42] It is fundamental for Aristotle that the soul unifies all vital activities of the human individual: vegetal, sensitive, and intellective. 'It is the soul by which we primarily live, perceive, and think; so that soul is the *logos* or form, and not the matter.'[43] Although it has distinct capacities and operations, the soul itself is one – the body certainly cannot be the source of unity for the individual: 'On the contrary the soul seems rather to combine the body into a whole; for when the soul departs the body disintegrates and decays.'[44] Aristotle provides the radical explanation for the unity of the body in his definition of soul as the 'first actuality of a natural body which potentially possesses life'.[45] The soul gives to the body its unity, existence, and life. While unity and existence are used in many senses, their primary sense is that of actuality.[46] He explains: 'In living beings life is their existence, and of these the soul is the cause and first principle.'[47]

Aristotle was obliged to coin a new term to formulate his definition: 'Soul is the first actuality (ἐντελέχεια, i.e. completeness, perfection) of a natural body with organs.'[48] The soul is the primary perfection which completes the body, determining it as the kind of essence it is. The soul is said to be the 'cause and first principle of the living body' and 'the essence of a particular body'.[49] The unity of the individual substance is guaranteed by the actualizing force with which the soul organizes the body into a unitary whole; it is grounded in the relation of act to potency. The activity of the soul pervades all of its aspects; even the unity of the organs which feed the blood supply is attributed to soul. They begin from a single source, yet extend throughout the body: 'the reason why these vessels coincide in one principle and begin from a single cause, is that the sensory soul is in all animals actually one'.[50]

According to Aristotle, it is a universal law of nature that in every whole that is composed of parts, there is a commanding principle and a submissive element.[51] This is verified most clearly in living things, where soul is the ruling principle. 'In the first place an animal consists of soul and body, the former naturally ruling, the latter being ruled.'[52] If the individual is corrupted, the soul will be dominated by the body, but nature ordains that the soul should rule the body, and intelligence the appetites. Similarly men are the natural rulers of non-rational animals since these submit not to *logos* but to their passions.[53]

Aristotle emphasizes the unity of actions performed by the soul-body composite. Thinking, remembering, loving and hating, for example, belong not to the mind, but to the individual.[54] It is more accurate to say, not that the soul pities, learns or thinks, but that the individual man does these things by means of the soul.[55] Aristotle recognizes the intimate bond between soul and body, as illustrated by the psychosomatic character of such affective states as anger, gentleness, fear, pity, courage, joy, love, and hatred. Referring to the 'affections' of the soul (πάθη), he remarks:

> If we consider the majority of them, there seems to be no case in which the soul can act or be acted upon without involving the body; e.g. anger, courage, appetite, and sensation generally... It seems that all the affections of soul involve a body – passion, gentleness, fear, pity, courage, joy, loving, and hating; in all these there is a concurrent affection of the body. In support of this we may point to the fact that, while sometimes on the occasion of violent and striking occurrences there is no excitement or fear felt, on others faint and feeble stimulations produce these emotions, viz. when the body is already in a state of tension resembling its condition when we are angry. Here is a still clearer case: in the absence of any external cause of terror we find ourselves experiencing the feelings of a man in terror. From all this it is obvious that the affections of soul are ideas expressed in matter (λόγοι ἔνυλοι).[56]

The relation between soul and body is one of the most challenging topics of *De Anima*. Though Aristotle has declared that there obtains between soul and body a relationship of act to potency, the nature of soul remains as obscure as ever. In *De Anima* Aristotle states that while the soul cannot exist without the body, neither is it in any sense a body.[57] It is the form of the body, but is not itself corporeal. One of the most testing remarks in *Parts of Animals* is the statement that no part of an animal is either purely material or purely immaterial.[58] By emphasizing the simplicity of the individual substance, and the unity of body and soul, Aristotle raises the greatest obstacle to the independence of the soul and its survival after death: 'One need no more ask whether body and the soul are one than whether the wax and the impression it receives are one, or in general whether the matter of each thing is the same as that of which it is the matter.'[59] We are confronted with two fundamental and related problems in Aristotle's psychology: the relation between body and soul, and the ultimate nature of soul. Aristotle's basic premise is that the soul is the form of the body. The question is whether its entire being and activity are exhausted by that function and role, or whether it has independence beyond its actualization of the body. Is it a 'real particular' ('τόδε τι', *hoc aliquid*) in itself as well as the form (εἶδος) of the body? Can it exist independently as an incorporeal reality?

Aristotle is concerned from the start of *De Anima*, not only with the nature of the soul, but also with its ultimate destiny: Is it indissolubly bound to the body, or is it immortal? This would be an expected corollary of its 'divine' nature which – possibly for cultural reasons – he seems to accept. From the frequency of his assertions it appears that Aristotle hopes, if possible, to establish the immortality of the soul – or at least of the intellect. Early in *De Anima* he outlines the context for his discussion of the soul's ultimate status and its possible survival. Having emphasized the unity of body and soul, and having clearly stated the problems of the soul acting in separation, he states: 'Thinking seems the most probable exception; but if this too proves to be a form of imagination or to be impossible without imagination, it too requires a body as a condition of its existence. If there is any way of acting or being acted upon proper to soul, soul will be capable of separate existence; if there is none, its separate existence is impossible.'[60]

In the first book of *De Anima* Aristotle tentatively proposes the immortality of the intellect: 'Νοῦς seems to be an independent substance implanted in us, which cannot be destroyed.'[61] He remarks that if the intellect, like the sense organs, were subject to decay, this would inevitably occur with the debility of old age; this, as we know, does not happen. Sensation on the other hand usually declines with the ageing of the body's sense organs: Aristotle suggests that if an old man were to receive a young man's eyes he would regain a young man's sight.[62] The mind is unaffected since it has no special organ; it is affected only indirectly, because its activity belongs to the individual, whose body is clearly affected by the ageing process. The individual ceases to think when the substance is corrupted, and the compound of body and soul dissolved. 'Thinking, loving and hating are not affections of the mind, but of the individual man who possesses the mind.'[63] It is the individual who thinks, just as it is the individual who perceives, loves, and hates;

the individual is a unity of body and soul. The dependence of intellect upon the body, however, is not the same as that of sensation. Aristotle makes an important distinction: memory and love terminate with the death of the individual, but thought and reflection (τὸ νοεῖν καὶ τὸ θεωρεῖν) are beyond destruction.[64] The mind, he suggests, is perhaps more divine and therefore unaffected (ὁ δὲ νοῦς ἴσως θειότερόν τι καὶ ἀπαθές ἐστιν).[65]

In *De Anima* 2 Aristotle restates his belief in the immortality of the mind, while recognizing the intrinsic obscurity of the inquiry: 'In the case of the mind and the thinking faculty nothing is yet clear; it seems to be a distinct kind of soul, and it alone admits of being separated, as the immortal from the perishable.'[66] While once again the mind's immortality is tentatively proposed (ἔοικε), it is clear (φανερόν) that while other parts of the soul may be conceived in isolation from the body they cannot exist separately. He stresses the essential difference between senses and intellect. 'There is', he asserts, 'a difference between the faculties of sensation and thought, just as perceiving is different from thinking.'[67] Animal and plant souls may indeed be conceived by thought as separate, but can have no independent existence. And while strict hylomorphism theoretically requires that the human soul should perish with the individual's death, νοῦς may be an exception since it is not material (i.e. composed of parts) and cannot suffer disintegration.[68]

Aristotle's hylomorphism has been praised by some as best safeguarding the unity of the human individual;[69] for others it is intrinsically linked to an outmoded physics and hence no longer sustainable. The current orthodoxy regards Aristotle's views on the immateriality of νοῦς as an awkward inconsistency. H.M. Robinson remarks: 'More often than not nowadays the favoured opinion is that Aristotle is essentially or in spirit some sort of materialist. I say that the favoured opinion is that he is a materialist *essentially* or *in spirit* because few dare to say that he actually *is* a materialist, because few dare to deny that his doctrine of *nous* is immaterialist.'[70] While expressing reservations concerning Robinson's exposé, Christopher Shields agrees that 'the majority of commentators have disregarded Aristotle's conception of an immaterial *nous*'.[71] The immateriality of νοῦς, however, is pivotal to many aspects of Aristotle's theory of man and may not be readily dismissed.

Before dealing with νοῦς we should point out that, according to Aristotle, sensation is also an immaterial activity, since it is 'receptive of the form of sensible objects without the matter' (ἄνευ τῆς ὕλης).[72] Thus while physically absent the objects of knowledge can be present immaterially through sense images.[73] Aristotle distinguishes between the *organ* of sensation, which has spatial magnitude (μέγεθος), and the (immaterial) *power* of sensation, which resides within the organ but is without magnitude.[74] Aristotle notes the obvious parallels between intelligence and sensation.[75] The fundamental difference is that sensation depends intrinsically upon a physical organ while intellect does not. The senses know individual things here and now, confined in time and space; νοῦς knows universal realities. These exist in some manner, he suggests, within the soul itself. A person may contemplate his thoughts at will but cannot arbitrarily choose to sense a particular object; the object must itself be present, since sensation knows what is individual and external (τὰ αἰσθητὰ τῶν καθ' ἕκαστα καὶ τῶν ἔξωθεν).[76]

Borrowing from Anaxagoras, Aristotle states that, since the soul knows all things, it must be 'unmixed' (ἀμιγῆ).[77] For Anaxagoras, the universal mind must be untainted in order to control the universe; for Aristotle, the human soul must be unadulterated in order to know. There is good reason, he says, to affirm that it is not mixed with the body, but is noncorporeal or immaterial.[78] If it were corporeal, it would inevitably have a determinate quality (such as hot or cold), which would make cognition of its contrary impossible. It would also require a physical organ, similar to those of the senses.[79] Were it material, it could not receive the intelligible natures of all things; it must therefore be immaterial, simple and impassible, without a determinate nature of its own.[80] The soul, Aristotle states, has been well described as the 'place of forms' (τόπος εἰδῶν);[81] this applies, he explains, not to the soul as a whole, but to its thinking element; and the forms are contained not actually but potentially. He also defines it as the 'form of forms' (εἶδος εἰδῶν),[82] since it assimilates the forms of all things.

The immateriality of the intellect is established in the first place by its universality; the clearest proof is its unlimited openness to every possible object. The sense faculties function, each infallibly in a particular domain, because they have a clearly limited range, determined by the receptivity of the sense organ. Sensation is directed towards a particular material object here and now, located narrowly in time and space. The intellect is open to the totality because it has no such organ. Its universality is a consequence of its immaterial capacity. Its target is universal reality – the unrestricted totality of beings in general (τα πάντα), as well as the universal concepts of those essences which are instantiated in countless substances (τὰ καθόλου). There is nothing in being whose essence cannot be the object of intellect; universality is the mark of immateriality. While the senses grasp particular individuals, the intellect knows universal essences according to their immaterial intelligibility.[83]

The nonmaterial character of intellect, and especially its independence from a physical organ, is further evidenced by its impassibility, that is, its imperviousness to damage by its object. The sense organ can be destroyed by violent stimulation: the ear by deafening sounds, the eye by intense light.[84] The intellect does not suffer damage from intense thought; on the contrary, Aristotle remarks that if it has struggled with difficult matters it reflects more easily upon simpler matters. This allows him conclude that 'the faculty of sense is not apart from the body, whereas the mind is separable'.[85]

Of its nature immaterial, and independent of a physical organ, the intellect has neither magnitude nor parts: these would be a hindrance to the process of thinking. Examining Plato's theory of the world-soul, Aristotle denies that it could be a magnitude;[86] his reflections are equally valid for the human intellect. 'The mind is one and continuous like the process of thinking; thinking consists of thoughts, but these are continuous in the same sense as numbers and not as magnitudes. So also the mind is not continuous in this sense, but it is either indivisible, or at any rate is not continuous as a magnitude. For, if it is a magnitude, how will it think with any one of its parts?'[87] The mind must be single and complete, as are its thoughts, which are simple and indivisible. Mind grasps thoughts once and entire, not successively piece by piece, one part after another. If the mind were a material magnitude, it would have to know its object through its divisible parts. As Aquinas points out, 'The intellect's object is intelligibles, and intelligibles compose a unity.'[88]

In *De Anima* 3, Aristotle considers the specific character of νοῦς, the thinking part of the soul; he specifically asks whether it is separable –

either actually or only in thought. To explain the process whereby the forms of all things cognitively enter into the soul, he distinguishes between two functions of mind: a passive element, which 'becomes' everything, and an active element, which 'makes' everything.[89] The latter is a positive state or 'habit', resembling that of light, which illuminates the potential meanings latent in sense images, and transforms them into actually intelligible concepts to be received by the passive intellect. In this role, Aristotle states, the mind is separable, impassible, and unmixed, since its essence is activity.[90] He then makes one of the most contested and controversial pronouncements to be found anywhere in his work: 'Only when separated (χωρισθείς) does it achieve its proper nature, and this alone is immortal and eternal.'[91] Aristotle's reasoning is that since it is entirely active this element of the mind cannot itself be acted upon (ἀπαθές)[92] and will thus be unaffected by the processes causing death; by contrast, the passive intellect is perishable (ὁ δὲ παθητικὸς νοῦς φθαρτός).[93] To act upon is always superior to being acted upon; the active intellect is fully constituted in itself as cause and agent.[94] Eternally active, it cannot be affected in any way and is entirely independent of the senses. It alone fulfils the condition laid down by Aristotle for immortality.

To establish the soul's immortality, Aristotle must prove that it is independent of matter, entirely free from the processes of the body. Any dependence whatsoever will negate the possibility of immortality. Thus if in order to *act* the intellect needs the cooperation of the senses, it will be unable to *exist* in separation from the body. Aristotle states repeatedly that the soul cannot think without images (ἄνευ φαντάσματος);[95] these are received through the senses and must be illuminated by the agent intellect. Thus Aristotle has no alternative but to declare that the passive intellect is mortal. The active intellect alone can exist separately from the body.

Much debate and controversy would have been spared if Aristotle had explained more carefully what he meant by 'separate'. Aquinas for one has no doubts about its meaning and expresses surprise at the controversy it provoked: 'Indeed it is astonishing how easily some have let themselves be deceived by his calling the intellect "separate"; for the text itself makes it perfectly clear what he means, – namely that, unlike the senses, the intellect has no bodily organ. For the nobility of the human soul transcends the scope and limits of bodily matter. Hence it enjoys a certain activity in which bodily matter has no share; the potentiality to which activity is without a bodily organ; and in this sense only is it a "separate" intellect.[96]

One of the most disputed questions is the nature of immortality and eternity referred to by Aristotle. The meaning of this passage turns upon the meaning of 'separate' (χωρισθείς). In an interesting interpretation, Gérard Verbeke rejects the customary reading of the passage as referring to the intellect in the state of separation which ensues after death, when the soul is removed from the accidental modifications which characterized its union with the individual.[97] According to such an interpretation, death would restore the active intellect to its pure essence. Verbeke suggests, however, that the passive aorist of the verb here has, not a temporal meaning (i.e. '*having been* separated'), but a causal meaning (i.e. '*because* it is separated'). Aristotle is thus contrasting the agent intellect, not with its own previous condition of union, but with a different power (the passive intellect). Because the active intellect is separate, it is exclusively that which it is, namely cause and agent (αἴτιον καὶ ποιητικόν).[98] The passive intellect, by contrast, depends upon the senses for its intelligible content; instead of being fully itself, it becomes all things (πάντα γίνεσθαι),[99] in that identity with its object which, for Aristotle, is the essence of knowledge.

In his discussion of the successive emergence of the distinctive souls, together with their graded powers, in *Generation of Animals*, Aristotle raises what he calls 'the question of greatest difficulty' (ἀπορία πλείστη): 'When and how and whence is a share in reason (νοῦς) acquired by those animals that participate in this principle?'[100] His suggestion in that context is that it is not generated by the parents, but can only come from outside (θύραθεν): 'It remains, then, for the reason alone so to enter and alone to be divine, for no bodily activity has any connexion with the activity of reason.'[101] According to Hicks, the latter phrase correctly explains the meaning of the word χωριστός in *De Anima* 3, 5: the intellect is not only separable, but actually separate, that is, 'not involved in physical life'.[102] This passage refers to the undifferentiated intellect, as does Aristotle's statement at *Metaphysics* 12, 3, 1070a26, that there is nothing to impede the survival of νοῦς.

Aristotle's view on the immortality of the soul is far from definitive. His hesitation and lack of clarity allowed some to conclude that he denied the soul's immortality. Martin Luther pronounced harshly: 'Why, this wretched man, in his best book, *On the Soul*, teaches that the soul dies with the body, although many have tried with vain words to save his reputation.'[103] The position of *De Anima*, that only the thinking function of the soul is immortal, involves a twofold inconsistency. First, it poses an obstacle for the unity of the individual, which is essential to his hylomorphic theory. Man's substantial unity was a fundamental point of disagreement with Plato; for the latter the body was an impediment, whereas for Aristotle the soul needs the body to actualize its proper nature. Aristotle emphasizes in particular the unity of knowledge as the collaboration of mind and body. Knowledge is a continuity from sense and intellect, a progression from the sensible grasp of the individual physical object, to an immaterial, intellectual insight into its universal character. While distinct, body and soul are inseparably united in the cognitive process: inseparable but not identical. Rejecting Plato's view that the soul is separate, Aristotle himself argued: 'It is quite clear that neither the soul nor any parts of it, if it has parts, can be separated from the body.'[104] He himself, however, introduces such a distinction into the soul and proposes that νοῦς may be separable; to further compound the problem, he suggests that νοῦς properly constitutes the essence of the individual.

The first objection against the immortality of the active intellect is that it jeopardizes the unity of the complete individual. A second objection is that it threatens the unity of the soul. Early in *De Anima* Aristotle emphasized that by the soul we live, perceive and think; he is committed to the unity of all powers, vegetative, sensitive and intellective, in a single soul. The human soul is origin of both the physical and immaterial operations of the individual. Aristotle's requirement for survival is that at least one of the soul's activities be independent of the body: one noncorporeal activity suffices to prove its essentially immaterial nature. If this requirement is fulfilled (by the agent intellect, as he argues), logically the entire soul should be immortal, not only a single isolated function. As we saw, Aristotle has a strong sense of the unity of the acting, living individual; this has been illustrated in a particular way by the close bond between the affective states of the soul and the condition of the body.[105]

Before considering the ultimate destiny of man in the light of a wider examination of his nature, I wish first to briefly consider the status of self-knowledge as treated by Aristotle. One of the most disputed questions of his psychology is how we know that we know. In his discussion of perception, Aristotle asks how we come to perceive that we see and hear (αἰσθανόμεθα ὅτι ὁρῶμεν καὶ ἀκούομεν).[106] He takes it as an evidence that the perceiver is aware of himself; in sensation we are aware not only of the object, but also of the very activity of sensation and of our own existence.[107] Were he troubled by Cartesian doubt, he could without hesitation assert: 'I perceive, therefore I exist.' In *De Anima*, he suggests that the self-awareness accompanying perception is the work of the sense faculty itself.[108] This, however, cannot be a satisfactory explanation in light of his distinction between sense and intellect. Intrinsically dependent upon a physical organ, sensation cannot be reflexive; consisting of parts outside parts (*partes extra partes*), the senses cannot bend back upon themselves in an act of self-knowledge. The activity of perception cannot be itself the object of sensation. He remarks in *De Somno* that it is not by sight that we become aware that we see.[109] The solution may be found, I suggest, in the assertion that the soul is 'in a sense' all that is.[110] Aristotle states that when the soul has become each of its objects (ὅταν δ᾽ οὕτως ἕκαστα γένηται), then the mind is capable of thinking itself (αὐτὸς δὲ αὐτὸν τότε δύναται νοεῖν).[111] Thus a significant consequence of the soul's universality is its self-reflection. Because of its universal scope, the intellect may introspectively and concomitantly know every cognitive act of the individual, whether sensible or intellectual.

The intellect knows itself, Aristotle suggests, as it does any other immaterial object: 'And it is itself an object of thought, just as its objects are. For, in the case of those things which have no matter, that which thinks and that which is thought are the same; for contemplative knowledge and that which is known in that way are the same.'[112] Aristotle applies to cognition his own metaphysics of causation: the action of the agent is identical with the passivity of the subject[113] – thus there is identity between the act of intellect and the reality of the intelligible as

75

actually known. In knowing its intelligible object, the intellect knows itself; such knowledge, however, is always indirect.[114] Although there is no direct knowledge of the self, this does not mean there is no substantial reality at the core of each human individual; the problem has to do rather with the very nature of knowledge and its origin in the senses. Considered in isolation, the mind as such has no complete nature in actuality; it must be activated through the objects of perception. In itself it resembles a tablet upon which nothing has been actually written. Until it thinks, the mind is itself nothing in actuality (ἐντελεχείᾳ οὐδέν).[115]

Awareness of oneself and of one's activities is therefore concomitant with a knowledge of objects.[116] All knowledge begins with the senses; 'The mind in itself can have no nature (φύσιν μηδεμίαν) except its capacity to receive. That part of the soul, then, which we call mind ... has no actual existence until it thinks.'[117] Self-consciousness for Aristotle is always an attendant awareness of the self as acting. As Joseph Owens notes, 'In that concomitant cognition, however, there is immediate and unshakable awareness of a single agent, namely oneself. This immediate awareness is not of a sense, or of a mind, or of a soul. It is of the man or woman as cognitive agent. It is of the *anthropos*, or, as we would say today, of the person who thinks and acts by means of those faculties or parts.'[118] In an insightful passage of *De Anima*, already referred to, Aristotle points out that it is more accurate to say, not that the soul pities, learns or thinks, but that the individual man does these things by means of the soul.[119] 'Thinking, loving and hating are not qualities of the mind, but rather of the individual man who possesses the mind.'[120] In his treatise *On Sense and Sensible Objects*, he notes that vision occurs not in the eye but in the observer.[121]

Aristotle's most important inquiry into man's nature and destiny may be found in the *Nicomachean Ethics*, where he treats explicitly the question of man's end and purpose. He begins this work with the general observation that all things seek the good. This description has indeed the value of a definition: 'The good is that which all things seek.'[122] The ultimate human good has a special name, 'happiness' (εὐδαιμονία).[123] Man's supreme good and the nature of happiness may be ascertained, he suggests, if we determine the function of man. Just as the goodness and efficacy of a flute player, sculptor, or any craftsman with a function is considered to reside in the fulfilment of that function, so also with man – if indeed he has a function. Aristotle asks rhetorically: 'Are we to suppose that, while the carpenter and the shoemaker have definite functions and activities man as such has none, but was designed by nature without any purpose to fulfil? Must we not rather assume that, just as the eye, the hand, the foot and each of the various members of the body manifestly has a certain function of its own, so a human being also has a certain function over and above all the functions of his particular members?'[124]

Man's function cannot be simply the activity of either growth and nutrition, which he shares with plants, or of sensation which is shared with animals. Since man's distinguishing mark is reason, his proper function must be action and activities of the soul in accordance with reason (ψυχῆς ἐνέργεια καὶ πράξεις μετὰ λόγου).[125] The function of the good man is to perform these actions well and nobly. Aristotle sums up therefore: 'If a function is well performed when it is accomplished in accordance with its own proper excellence (i.e. virtue), it follows that the good of man is the active exercise of his soul's faculties in accordance with excellence or virtue (τὸ ἀνθρώπινον ἀγαθὸν ψυχῆς ἐνέργεια γίνεται κατ' ἀρετήν).'[126] Human happiness, the highest good of all individual men, consists in activity of the soul; this life of active virtue is, moreover, essentially pleasant (ὁ βίος αὐτῶν καθ' αὑτὸν ἡδύς).[127] It is at once the best, noblest, and the most pleasant of all things.[128]

Aristotle's definition of a friend as 'another self' is deservedly well known; intuitively it offers immediate evidence in its own right.[129] Less explicit is the deeper metaphysical basis for his definition and the insight it provides for Aristotle's understanding of selfhood. His exemplar is the 'good man' (ὁ σπουδαῖος), whose virtue is the moral measure of all things. The virtuous man is well-centred and self-rooted in all respects. Aristotle makes repeated use of the reflexive personal pronoun (ἑαυτὸν/ἑαυτοῦ/ἑαυτῷ): the σπουδαῖος 'is of one mind with himself (ὁμογνωμονεῖ ἑαυτῷ), and desires the same things with all his soul (κατὰ πᾶσαν τὴν ψυχήν).'[130] The good man wishes for himself his own good (ἑαυτῷ τἀγαθά), striving actively to attain it for his own benefit. 'He does it for the sake of the intellectual element in him, which is thought to be the man himself.'[131] The good man, moreover, desires his own life, seeking especially to preserve his rational part (μάλιστα τοῦτο ᾧ φρονεῖ). There follows a powerfully personalist statement, which conveys a clear sense both of the fundamental character of existence, and the inalienable and intimate nature of the thinking and acting individual: 'For existence is good for the virtuous man (ἀγαθὸν γὰρ τῷ σπουδαίῳ τὸ εἶναι); and everyone wishes his own good: no one would choose to possess every good in the world on condition of becoming somebody else ... but only while remaining himself, whatever he may be; and it would appear that the thinking part is the real self, or is so more than anything else.'[132] In a similar vein Aristotle refers again to the intellect, which 'though small in bulk, in power and value far surpasses all the rest. It may even be held that this is the true self of each, inasmuch as it is the dominant and better part; and therefore it would be a strange thing if a man should choose to live not his own life but the life of some other than himself.'[133] Paradoxically the deep bond of friendship is experienced only when individuals retain their distinct and inalienable identity. Aristotle points out that parents love their children as themselves (ὡς ἑαυτούς) – they are 'other selves' – because they are separate (ἕτεροι αὐτοὶ τῷ κεχωρίσθαι).[134]

Aristotle offers the following metaphysical description of the individual's interior life: 'The good man desires his own company; for he enjoys being by himself, since he has agreeable memories of the past, and good hopes for the future, which are pleasant too; also his mind is stored with subjects for contemplation. And he is keenly conscious of his own joys and sorrows; for the same things give him pleasure or pain at all times, and not different things at different times, since he is not apt to change his mind.'[135] It is in light of this self-understanding that the philosopher offers his definition of a friend as 'another self'. Friendship is best fulfilled between individuals of such character: 'Good men's wishes are steadfast, and do not ebb and flow like the tide, and they wish for just and expedient ends, which they strive to attain in common.'[136]

The sense of self-being, and the ineradicable link between existence and action, are likewise conveyed in a passage where Aristotle explains why the artist loves his work, the poet his poems, parents their children, and benefactors the fruits of their generosity: 'The reason of this is that all things desire and love existence; but we exist in activity, since we exist by living and doing; and in a sense one who has made something exists actively, and so he loves his handiwork because he loves existence.'[137] Action is an affirmation and enactment of some new modality of being. Through πρᾶξις and ποίησις new potencies are actualized and actualities perfected.

Aristotle states as a fundamental principle of nature: 'What a thing is potentially, its work reveals in actuality' (τοῦτο δὲ φυσικόν· ὃ γάρ ἐστι δυνάμει, τοῦτο ἐνεργείᾳ τὸ ἔργον μηνύει).[138] We are close to the insight of medieval metaphysics that *agere sequitur esse*: insofar as something is actual it acts through a necessity which, rather than restrictive, is natural and self-fulfilling. Prime matter is inert although it provides the receptivity necessary for new modes of being to take shape. Beyond the incomplete action of motion (κίνησις), which involves potency, there is the perfect action of self-complete activity whose exercise is its own fulfilment.[139] Expressed by the term *energeia* (ἐνέργεια), this is the primary goal of human desire: 'While the actuality of the present (τοῦ παρόντος ἡ ἐνέργεια), the hope of the future, and the memory of the past are all pleasant, actuality is the most pleasant of the three, and the most loved.'[140] Only ἐνέργεια is self-contained and complete in itself and, as we will see, the highest human actuality is the activity of θεωρία.

Aristotle repeatedly asserts that intellect is the real self. In *Nicomachean Ethics* 9 he argues this in detail, in the course of a discussion of the moral merits of self-love. He distinguishes between egotistical self-love, dominated by passion and irrational desires, and the noble self-love of the individual who in all things strives for moral excellence. 'Such a man might be held to be a lover of self in an exceptional degree. At all events he takes for himself the things that are noblest and most truly good.'[141] These are attained by self-control – effectively domination by the intellect. Drawing an analogy with a political sovereign, who in a sense may be said to *be* the state, and suggesting that any composite may be identified with its dominant part, Aristotle concludes that the intellect *is* man, adding: 'It is our reasoned acts that are felt to be in the fullest sense our own acts and voluntary acts.'[142]

Aristotle provides a deeper metaphysical dimension for his definition of happiness, viewing it as an actuality to be attained as final fulfilment. It is an unenunciated principle for Aristotle that action is the natural consequence of being. Each thing will actualize itself precisely in the measure that it is actual: if it is perfect, its actuality is already complete and will not cease; if it is imperfect, it will be actualized through the imperfect actuality of change as it moves from potency to ever more perfect actuality. Life is a form of activity (ἡ δὲ ζωὴ ἐνέργεια τίς ἐστι),[143] and happiness is activity in accordance with virtue (ἡ εὐδαιμονία κατ' ἀρετὴν ἐνέργεια.).[144] Such activity must be self-sufficient (αὐτάρκης); lacking nothing, it is an end in itself (τέλος γὰρ αὕτη).[145] We exist in our activities, and it is in the optimal exercise of these activities that happiness is to be found.

Human nature is defined by Aristotle as the capacity for sensation and thought.[146] He elucidates this definition in light of the primacy of actuality: 'A capacity is referred to its activity, and in this its full reality consists. It appears therefore that life in the full sense is sensation or thought (ἔοικε δὴ τὸ ζῆν εἶναι κυρίως τὸ αἰσθάνεσθαι ἢ νοεῖν).'[147] He even asserts that 'being is [defined as] perceiving or thinking' (τὸ γὰρ εἶναι ἦν αἰσθάνεσθαι ἢ νοεῖν).[148] It is in keeping with this intensive notion of being, which identifies human existence with the highest activities of sensation and thinking, that he asserts that being is desirable. It is personal being that is desired – vital and intellective – not just the brute fact of being there; for living things, existence is their life itself (τὸ δὲ ζῆν τοῖς ζῷσι τὸ εἶναί ἐστιν).[149] Since happiness consists in activity, it is not something that we possess but something we must continually actualize. It consists of living and acting (ἐν τῷ ζῆν καὶ ἐνεργεῖν)[150] in accordance with the excellences proper to the highest capacities of the soul; such activity, Aristotle has emphasized, is pleasant in itself.[151] And since, for living things, to exist is to live, existence is naturally desirable; to be happy is to actualize human existence in the best possible manner.

We do not have simply a vague desire for the fact of being. Our happiness derives from the awareness of our own life as good; each man's existence is desirable for himself: τὸ αὐτὸν εἶναι αἱρετόν ἐστιν ἑκάστῳ.[152] 'It is the consciousness of oneself as good that makes existence desirable, and such consciousness is pleasant in itself.'[153] Self-awareness is a certainty; it is the concomitant self-awareness of ourselves in our activity of knowing the world, and as agents within the world: 'If one who sees is conscious that he sees, one who hears that he hears, one who walks that he walks, and similarly for all the other human activities there is a faculty that is conscious of their exercise, so that whenever we perceive, we are conscious that we perceive, and whenever we think, we are conscious that we think, and to be conscious that we are perceiving or thinking is to be conscious that we exist.'[154]

Because he identifies existence with perception and thought, to exist is to be self-aware as perceiving and thinking. This passage is a remarkable expression of selfhood and of the experience of personal existence, not usually associated with Aristotle. He concludes that 'to be conscious that one is alive is a pleasant thing in itself (τὸ δ' αἰσθάνεσθαι ὅτι ζῆ τῶν ἡδέων καθ' αὐτό)'.[155] For good men, existence is good and pleasant (τὸ εἶναι ἀγαθόν καὶ ἡδύ),[156] because they are aware that their activities, which constitute their existence, are directed toward their final goal and happiness. Their entire existence is an actualization of their prospective happiness. The context of these reflections, the foundation of friendship, provides a suitable analogue for the affirmation of personal happiness: the joy at the existence of one's friend, another self, is reflective confirmation of the value of our own being. One ought to share one's friend's consciousness of his existence and to rejoice in a friend's existence as in one's own.[157]

The happy life is one in accordance with virtue (εὐδαίμων βίος ὁ κατ' ἀρετήν);[158] it consists in noble and serious activity – not pastime and amusement. The nobler the activity, the better and more productive of happiness. The activity of highest virtue is that of our best part, namely, the intellect (or whatever else naturally governs us), which has knowledge of what is noble and divine, being either itself divine or the most divine part of us. It is the activity of this part, in accordance with its proper virtue, that constitutes perfect happiness. According to Aristotle it is the activity of contemplation.[159] He summarizes: 'Contemplation is at once the highest form of activity (since the intellect is the highest thing in us, and the objects with which the intellect deals are the highest things that can be known), and also it is the most continuous, for we can reflect more continuously than we can carry on any form of action.'[160] Contemplation is the only activity that is loved for its own sake, since it produces nothing other than the very act of contemplating; it is its own fulfilment. As an activity it is self-sufficient: whereas the just man needs others in order to act justly, the wise man is able to contemplate by himself. It is moreover the most pleasant of the virtuous activities; it is the activity of leisure par excellence.[161] 'If the attributes of this activity are self-sufficiency, leisuredness, such freedom from fatigue as is possible for man, and all the other attributes of blessedness: it follows that it is the activity of the intellect that constitutes complete human happiness.'[162]

Having reasoned carefully to the conclusion that human happiness consists in the virtuous exercise of activity in accordance with reason, Aristotle curiously remarks that it is effectively beyond human attainment and may be achieved only through a higher agency:

> Such a life as this will be higher than the human level: not in virtue of his humanity will a man achieve it, but in virtue of something within him that is divine; and by as much as this something is superior to his composite nature, by so much is its activity superior to the exercise of the other forms of virtue. If then the intellect is something divine in comparison with man, so is the life of the intellect divine in comparison with human life.[163]

There is no doubt for Aristotle but that man should aim for divine and immortal life. He criticizes those, such as Pindar, who counselled men to confine their thoughts to mortal affairs and not to covet kinship with the gods. (The poet scornfully discouraged the most glorious athlete of his day: 'Die, Diagoras, you will not be able to reach Olympus.')[164] Aristotle countered: 'We ought so far as possible to achieve immortality (ἀθανατίζειν), and do all that man may to live in accordance with the highest thing in him; for though this be small in bulk, in power and value (δυνάμει καὶ τιμιότητι) it far surpasses all the rest.'[165] If intellect is the true self, this means that man should seek his happiness in the perfect activity of contemplation. Echoing his earlier teaching that it is absurd to want to live as another, he states: 'It may even be held this is the true self of each, inasmuch as it is the dominant and better part; and therefore it would be a strange thing if a man should choose to live not his own life but a life of some other than himself.'[166] He repeats his essential teaching: 'That which is best and most pleasant for each creature is that which is proper to the nature of each; accordingly the life of the intellect is the best and the pleasantest life for man, inasmuch as the intellect more than anything else is man; therefore this life will be the happiest.' [167]

Whereas intellectual virtues pertain to activities of the intellect, moral virtues relate to the bodily nature of man and the passions and therefore lead only to a second-rate happiness. The distinction is grounded in the metaphysical constitution of man: moral virtues, which are purely human, belong to the composite (τοῦ συνθέτου) of body and soul, whereas the happiness of the intellect is separate (ἡ εὐδαιμονία . . . τοῦ νοῦ κεχωρισμένη). [168] We are confronted again with the paradox that man's ultimate happiness is located beyond his natural condition, in some disembodied state.

To illustrate that 'perfect happiness is some form of contemplative activity (ἡ δὲ τελεία εὐδαιμονία ὅτι θεωρητική τίς ἐστιν ἐνέργεια),'[169] Aristotle compares man to both the gods and animals. The gods, who are understood to be happy and blessed, are thought of as alive and active (ζῆν καὶ ἐνεργεῖν). If one removes from the gods the limited activities of 'doing' (πράττειν) and 'making' (ποιεῖν), only contemplation (θεωρία) remains.[170] 'It follows that the activity of God, which is transcendent in blessedness, is the activity of contemplation; and therefore among human activities that which is most akin to the divine activity of contemplation will be the greatest source of happiness.'[171] The kinship of human nature with divinity becomes obvious in *Metaphysics* 12, where Aristotle defines the prime mover as self-thinking thought (νόησις νοήσεως).[172] Mind is the 'most divine' (θειότατον) of phenomena.[173] Because he is the only animal that can contemplate – albeit intermittently – man is the only animal that can be happy; at least he can approximate in a deficient manner to the happiness of the gods. By contrast:

> The lower animals cannot partake of happiness, because they are completely devoid of the contemplative activity. The whole of the life of the gods is blessed, and that of man is so in so far as it contains some likeness to the divine activity; but none of the other animals possess happiness, because they are entirely incapable of contemplation. Happiness therefore is co-extensive in its range with

contemplation: the more a class of beings possesses the faculty of contemplation, the more it enjoys happiness, not as an accidental concomitant of contemplation but as inherent in it, since contemplation is valuable in itself. It follows that happiness is some form of contemplation.[174]

It appears that for Aristotle, in the final analysis, man is what he is because he contains an element of divinity. Though it threatens the unity of his metaphysics as applied to the human individual, the destiny of Aristotle's man lies beyond his natural state, and is in some sense beyond his control.

It seems likely that the man who pursues intellectual activity, and who cultivates his intellect and keeps that in the best condition, is also the man most beloved of the gods. For if, as is generally believed, the gods exercise some superintendence over human affairs, then it will be reasonable to suppose that they take pleasure in that part of man which is best and most akin to themselves, namely the intellect, and that they recompense with their favours those men who esteem and honour this most, because these care for the things dear to themselves, and act rightly and nobly. Now it is clear that all these attributes belong most of all to the wise man. He therefore is most beloved by the gods; and if so, he is naturally most happy.[175]

In *Generation of Animals*, Aristotle presents another grand panorama on the existence and purpose of living things. He pronounces the most basic evaluation possible: being is better than not being, living than not living.[176] Whereas divine and eternal being exists of necessity, contingent beings might equally not exist; thus they must strive to preserve their being and to perpetuate life. 'For any living thing that has reached its normal development... the most natural act is the production of another like itself, an animal producing an animal, a plant a plant, in order that, as far as its nature allows it, it may partake in the eternal and divine (τοῦ ἀεὶ καὶ τοῦ θείου).'[177] All animals have a natural impulse to participate in the divine and eternal, and since they cannot do so by continuity of individual existence, they do so in the only manner possible, namely through the perpetuation of their kind.[178] This is for Aristotle the radical reason for male and female: unable to live eternally as individuals, living beings strive to maintain their kind through the process of generation. Since the being of things resides in the particular, nature cannot be eternal in the numerical identity of the individual, but only through the specific form.

Is man likewise governed by this universal law of nonpersonal life? Is human individuality nothing but a transient link in the advance toward an indeterminate cosmic telos? Is man simply a transitory unit in the endless chain of a collective species, the carrier of a selfish gene? While it seems Aristotle hoped to discern in man a cipher of transcendence, an element rising above the stream of biological continuity, he did not fully succeed within the terms of his own philosophy. He provided, nonetheless, a context within which later philosophers would continue to discuss the question of human nature and destiny.

4

Knowledge and Necessity in Aristotle

'To think at its best is to find oneself carried down the current of necessity.'

Brand Blanshard[1]

Brand Blanshard's remark aptly conveys the impetus of thought in its commitment to truth. Truth occurs when the intellect is obliged to affirm its own acknowledged and self-reflected agreement with reality. It recognizes that such agreement cannot be otherwise, but is compelling in its own right. Intuitively and instinctively philosophers generally assume that there is an inextricable link between truth and necessity. Knowledge simply could not function – would have no value – if truth were a matter of arbitrary and changing circumstance. Knowledge must involve, either on the part of the knower or the reality known, a stability which guarantees reliability in our dealings with the world. The crux of the matter is the scope, status and grounding of such stability; on these questions philosophers diverge.

In the ancient world, the question of permanence in knowledge was keenly experienced by Socrates. Aristotle perceptively remarked: 'Disregarding the physical universe and confining his study to moral questions, Socrates sought in this sphere for the universal and was the first to concentrate upon definition.'[2] Socrates had identified the famous problem of universals – a question which has lost none of its urgency for philosophy: to what do our general ideas or concepts refer? Although nothing within our experience exactly corresponds to them, our interpretation of the world depends primarily on these universal concepts; if they have no validity, they are worse than useless – they are misleading. A philosopher's position on universals will determine his entire system. It is not merely a theoretical 'issue'; the problem assumes everyday importance with regard to the very foundation of morality and human rights. In a modern day evocation of Socrates' moral injunction, Albert Camus declares in *The Rebel*: 'If men cannot refer to a common value, recognized by all as existing in each one, then man is incomprehensible to man.'[3]

In response to the problem of stable, scientific knowledge Plato proposed his theory of Forms. His entire metaphysics could in fact be described as an attempt to provide a satisfactory foundation for Socrates' belief in the existence of stable and universally valid moral values. Plato's theory, ingenious though it was, failed because it did not explain what it set out to do; moreover, by introducing a second world of reality it duplicated the problem. Aristotle, like Plato, also sought the foundations for scientific knowledge, which would have universal validity. He adopted a more empirical approach, guided at every stage by the evidence of ordinary experience rather than the *a priori* requirements of a rationalist theory.

Suzanne Mansion notes the coordinates for Aristotle's approach to science: 'Science is a *universal* and *necessary* knowledge, it attains the *essence* of things and explains them through their *cause*. These are the four most obvious characteristics of ἐπιστήμη for Aristotle.'[4] In this essay I propose to consider some broad aspects of the relationship between knowledge and necessity as viewed by Aristotle. The question bears both upon the necessity associated with the process of knowledge, and the necessity inherent in the reality known. The former gives way to the latter; ultimately for Aristotle, the necessity of knowledge is determined by a knowledge of necessity.

In *Metaphysics* 5, his summary lexicon of philosophical terms, Aristotle provides a comprehensive survey of the various meanings of the term 'necessity'.[5] It will be worthwhile to review these before considering their relevance to the nature and object of knowledge:

(1)   Aristotle first refers to the necessity pertaining to a *concomitant cause* (συναίτιον): that which is necessary for the existence of another, e.g. breathing and food for the survival of living things.

(2)   A related, but distinct, necessity is that of a *condition* that is required for the benefit of another, or in order to remove an obstacle which impedes its proper functioning. This is referred to elsewhere as 'hypothetical necessity' (ἐξ ὑποθέσεως).[6]

(3)   Thirdly, Aristotle cites the necessity of *violence* (βία), which removes all choice and deliberation, with the result that an individual cannot function in any other way. In the words of Sophocles, quoted by Aristotle: 'Force makes me of necessity act thus.'[7] Compulsion is contrary to nature; it thwarts the natural 'necessity' of living substances.

(4)   Necessity most basically denotes *that which cannot be otherwise* than it is – this is its primary meaning, implicit in all other modes of necessity.

(5)   He notes finally the necessity proper to *demonstration*. If a conclusion is based on 'first premises' which need no proof, and is demonstrated unconditionally (without qualification, but simply and absolutely), such a conclusion cannot be otherwise.[8]

Aristotle makes the crucial distinction between things the necessity of which is caused by another, and necessary things which have no cause beyond themselves. This is the distinction between simple or absolute necessity (ἁπλῶς) and conditional or hypothetical necessity (ἐξ ὑποθέσεως). Absolute necessity characterizes those realities which are of their very nature immutable; they contain within themselves the ground of their own necessity. Hypothetical necessity is the condition of realities which cannot be other than as they are, by virtue of their dependence on another.[9]

NECESSITY AND SENSATION

Since all knowledge begins with the senses, its necessity too must be rooted in sensation. The renowned Aristotelian scholar Joseph Owens has remarked: 'The sensed object does not leave one free to regard it as nothing. Necessity is in this way seen in the object. It accordingly exercises its compelling force in sensation, even though there it is not given any separate status.'[10] A fundamental necessity pertains to the realities which we encounter; we cannot deny their brute facticity. Once something is, it is irrefutable and cannot be denied. While necessity is not expressly thematized as such by Aristotle, it is central to his doctrine of the proper sensibles. In *De Anima* Aristotle makes the important distinction between the proper and the common objects of perception; colour is the proper sensible of the eye, sound the proper sensible of the ear. Size, shape, speed and distance, on the other hand, are among what he calls the 'common perceptibles', which may be grasped by more than one sense faculty; the perceiver is liable to err if he carelessly judges an object on the evidence of only one of the senses. There is a necessity, however, attaching to our knowledge of the proper sensibles; this derives from the very nature of our faculties of sensation, which must grasp their proper objects correctly.

According to Aristotle, each of the senses is infallible within its particular, very restricted, domain; in the simple apprehension of their respective objects they cannot err. This follows by definition from the nature and function of the sense faculty itself: the eye is the organ equipped exclusively to grasp colour; the ear is the faculty which necessarily and inevitably grasps sound. To suggest that a particular sense faculty, operating according to its nature, is deceived in its grasp of its proper object is a contradiction; it is to deny that it is a faculty of knowledge. A faculty is defined by the object for which it is equipped. Faculty and object are correlative; Aristotle is justified in making infallibility a defining property of each faculty as such. Given the existence and nature of a sense organ, its sensations are necessarily true: 'if indeed we lack any sense, we must (ἀνάγκη) lack the corresponding sense organ also.'[11] Aristotle thus declares: 'The sensation of particular things is always true.'[12] This follows of necessity from the existence and purpose of the diverse sense organs, and their unique dedication to a well circumscribed domain of sensible reality. The infallibility of sense knowledge is a necessary consequence of the nature of the sense faculties. It would be contradictory to suggest that the eye, whose function it is precisely to know colour as its proper and unique object, were subsequently in error with respect to its specified domain. James Joyce, a keen reader of Aristotle in his youth, captures the kernel of Aristotle's theory of sensation in the twin phrases: 'ineluctable modality of the visible' and 'ineluctable modality of the audible.'[13] These phrases summarize with accurate clarity Aristotle's fundamental teaching regarding the infallibility of sense knowledge.

NECESSITY OF NON-CONTRADICTION

If, to borrow Descartes' phrase, Aristotle found the *fundamentum inconcussum veritatis*, the unshaken ground of truth, not in the prior certainty of the self, but in the ineluctability of sensation, he likewise sought to identify and validate those principles of reasoning which would guide and guarantee all elaboration of experience. Importantly he points out that it is not possible to prove everything: 'A demonstration of everything is impossible; for the process would go on to infinity, so that even in this manner there would be no demonstration.'[14] Nor is it necessary to prove everything, since some truths are immediately evident of themselves. Reasoning rests upon principles that are directly grasped in the light of their own evidence. Aristotle twice refers to the 'most certain of all principles' (πασῶν βεβαιοτάτη ἀρχή), about which it is impossible to think falsely.[15] Seeking an absolute, necessary, non-hypothetical, principle which would guarantee all others, he codified the famous law of non-contradiction: 'The same attribute cannot at the same time both belong and not belong to the same thing and in the same respect.'[16] In the order of discovery, the principle of non-contradiction is primary. What, therefore, is the origin of the notions it employs? Avicenna sums up Aristotle's position when he suggests that the primitive notions of 'being', 'thing', and 'necessity' are simultaneously impressed upon the soul with the initial knowledge of an object.[17]

Referring to the principle of non-contradiction, Aristotle uses the word 'necessary' four times (ἀναγκαῖον) within a short passage: 'Such a principle *must* be most known ... and be also non-hypothetical. For a principle which one *must* have if he is to understand anything is not an hypothesis; and that which one *must* know if he is to know anything *must* be in his possession for every occasion.'[18] The law of non-contradiction articulates an absolute, necessary, non-hypothetical truth about all things. It is, Aristotle argued, self-validating: whoever denies it, reduces himself to the status of the plant. Non-contradiction is the fundamental law pervading all reality and governing all thought: insofar as something is, it cannot not-be; insofar as we affirm, we cannot simultaneously deny. It is rigorous, compelling and comprehensive, admitting of no exceptions. Necessity enters into the warp and woof of knowledge in all its modes and phases: discovery and investigation, interpretation, explanation and demonstration.

Necessity and Truth

Aristotle states that the primary meaning of being is 'being as truth' (τὸ δὲ κυριώτατα ὂν ἀληθές).[19] His words from *De Interpretatione* may be applied to every true assertion: 'What is, necessarily is, when it is; and what is not, necessarily is not, when it is not.'[20] Every judgment is implicitly a judgment of either existence or non-existence, and hence shares in the rigorous necessity of the principle of non-contradiction. Aristotle remarks: 'Perhaps, indeed, the necessary and not necessary are first principles of everything's either being or not being, and one should look at the others as following from these.'[21] *De Interpretatione* treats of the modalities of possibility, contingency, and necessity pertaining to propositions. Without dwelling upon the variety of these modes, we may consider in a general way the necessity which attaches to the character of existence as enunciated in the copula.

Necessity marks every true affirmation. The kind of necessity varies: it can be absolute or simple; or it may be hypothetical, i.e. contingent or conditional. Every true affirmation is necessarily subject to the laws of logic. Since the truth function is located in the copula 'is', a certain absolute character attaches to every true affirmation; it shares in the unrestricted and undeniable existential value which marks all reality. It exhibits the simple necessity of being. Truth is the affirmation of reality as it is: in so far as something is, it necessarily is; in so far as a judgment is true, it is necessarily true. Truth has an absolute and necessary quality deriving from the unconditional character of existence itself. Once being is, it cannot not-be; insofar as an assertion is true, it is true for all time. Parmenides had already grasped the stark necessity which attaches to being: 'Justice has never released Being in its fetters and set it free ...

powerful necessity holds it in the bonds of a limit (κρατερὴ γὰρ Ἀνάγκη πείρατος ἐν δεσμοῖσιν ἔχει).'[22]

We can make assertions regarding possible future events; these are contingent, i.e. not necessary. Statements about future contingencies cannot, therefore, be true in the same sense as past contingent events; Aristotle is greatly exercised by these in his discussion of the sea battle that may or may not take place. In so far as they are contingent, future events belong to the domain of possibility and are free from necessity. Contingent events of the past, however – by the very fact that they have occurred – are removed from the realm of possibility and inscribed in the world of fact which cannot be undone. Aristotle declares: 'What has happened cannot be made not to have happened'; he quotes the poet Agathon: 'Of this alone even God is deprived, the power of making things that are past never to have been.' [23] Once a potency has been actualized, it cannot be 'de-actualized'; when something is done, it cannot be undone. The necessity attaching to the truths of past events derives from the principle of non-contradiction, the distinction between act and potency, and the primacy of actuality.

NECESSITY AND CAUSATION

Necessity is a hallmark of Aristotelian causality. A cause is productive of some element or aspect indispensable for the effect. Each substance depends necessarily upon its constitutive causes. Science, as Aristotle repeatedly asserts, is knowledge through causality.[24] Modern philosophy has largely dispensed with formal and final causality, and the principle of efficient causality has indeed not fared too well. Aristotle has given the classic formulation of this principle: 'That which moves is *necessarily* moved by another (ἅπαν τὸ κινούμενον ὑπό τινος ἀνάγκη κινεῖσθαι).'[25] All change is the transition from potency to act; since the potential is powerless to actualize itself, it depends necessarily for its actualization on another being which is actual.

For Aristotle causative action offers the evidence of a necessary connection, grasped by the intellect when it interprets the phenomena given to the senses. It is a relationship of action, passivity, production and dependence, experienced by the senses and elucidated by intellect in the light of metaphysical principles. Doubt has been cast in modern philosophy, most famously by Hume and Kant, upon the ability of mind to grasp necessary relations. For Hume, the mind is intrinsically incapable of knowing any necessity whatsoever: causality is a subjective habitual knowledge, with no more than a psychological, associative, power acquired through repetition. He saw correctly that causality could not be conceived as an analytic relation of cause and effect. It is rather, in Aristotelian terms, a synthetic relationship given, not as Kant believed, as an *a priori* category, but in an *a posteriori* judgment which affirms the empirical evidence of sense experience in which the action of cause is joined synthetically and necessarily with the production of the effect. Aristotle and Kant view knowledge and necessity quite differently. For the latter, the necessity of the law of causality derives from its status as synthetic *a priori* knowledge. The principle 'Whatever begins to be has a cause' operates within the sphere of mental forms and categories; its necessity derives from the structure of the knowing subject, which imposes order on sense data. For Aristotle, its necessity is grounded in the order of things themselves, a necessary relationship of production and dependence, experienced by the senses and grasped conceptually by the mind.

Empiricism limits the principle of causality to the domain of observable sense data. For both Hume and Kant, whatever lies beyond the range of sense experience is unknowable; the phenomena of sense experience are themselves intelligible only in terms of empirically observable causes. Carried to its ultimate conclusion, empiricism leads to scientific determinism, which is to confuse efficiency with necessity. It is by no means obvious in advance that there cannot be events or realities knowable by the mind but beyond the range of the senses. A free decision, for example, is caused and is therefore intelligible; however, it is not amenable to explanation in positivist scientific terms. Causality is not determinism; every effect necessarily depends upon its cause, yet not every action is necessitated.

Aristotle's view of causation has wider scope than that of Hume and Kant, and is more in tune with everyday experience. Quine's quip is well known: 'The Humean predicament is the human predicament': we are supposedly incapable of grasping necessary connections.[26] This clearly belies experience: normal persons have no difficulty grasping necessary connections and predicting inevitabilities in everyday life. Gravity is an inescapable property of physical bodies; poison acts inexorably according to its nature. Daily experience proceeds in the awareness of necessity: people take the stairs rather than exit through an upstairs window; we put medicines beyond the reach of children. Reading Quine, one wonders what has become of the original meaning of ἐμπειρία ('experience'), from which the term 'empiricism' takes its origin. What of the adage *primum vivere deinde philosophari*?

KNOWLEDGE AND THE NECESSITY OF NATURE

For Aristotle, as already noted, the scientific knowledge of things must be necessary in character, universal in scope, and furnish explanation through causes. He states in the *Nicomachean Ethics*: 'Scientific knowledge is a mode of conception dealing with universals and things that are of necessity.'[27] Ἐπιστήμη (*episteme*) is the knowledge of essence (εἶδος); the proper object of the intellect is the immanent form or nature present in the individual (τὰ μὲν οὖν εἴδη τὸ νοητικὸν νοεῖ).[28] Whereas the senses grasp the individual subject to changing conditions, the mind knows the indispensable necessary nature of the individual in its stable universal character. The key to knowledge, according to Aristotle, is the power of abstraction. Through an act of abstractive insight, the intellect grasps the universal in the particular, the permanent in the changing, the necessary in the contingent. This it does through universal concepts, which the scientist inductively acquires in his discovery of the world and deductively employs in its interpretation.[29]

Aristotle formulated the classic essentialist theory, according to which substances have of their nature certain necessary and indispensable properties. The question arises: which characteristics are necessary, and which are incidental? Essentialism has enjoyed a revival in recent decades. It has been labeled 'The New Essentialism' by the Australian author Brian Ellis.[30] Ellis states clearly the importance of necessity for essentialist theories: 'Metaphysical necessities are propositions that are true in virtue of the essences of things. Of course, if one does not believe that there are any natural kinds, or if one does not accept that things have essential natures, then one will not believe that there are any metaphysical necessities. But for an essentialist the concept of metaphysical necessity is fundamental.'[31] Ellis is careful to point out the differences between the new and old essentialism:

> The new essentialism retains the Aristotelian idea that there are natural kinds of substances (roughly, kinds of things of a material nature), but rejects Aristotelian essentialism about animal and plant species. According to the new essentialism, the true natural kinds of substances exist only at a much deeper level than that of living species. They include the basic kinds of physical and chemical substances, such as the various species of atoms, molecules and subatomic particles, but not the biological kinds. The biological species concepts are really *cluster concepts*, a modern essentialist will say. They have some similarities with natural kinds concepts, but the biological species are not natural kinds.[32]

In response, it may be suggested that the difficulty is partly one of knowledge: as one rises in the hierarchy of nature it is not so easy to circumscribe and rigorously define the operational horizon of living individuals, as is the case with elementary particles. Our knowledge of essential natures must be analogical, in accordance with their differences. At lower levels nature is relatively determinate; ascending the order of the living world, there is less predictability. As William Wallace remarks: 'Nature's necessity is far from absolute.'[33] Due to ever-changing contingent conditions and circumstances living things do not always act in the same definite manner.

Some of the difficulties associated with Aristotle's essentialism are obvious from his statement in the *Nicomachean Ethics* regarding scientific knowledge: 'We all conceive that a thing which we know scientifically cannot vary; when a thing that can vary is beyond the range of our observation, we do not know whether it exists or not. An object of scientific knowledge, therefore, exists of necessity. It is therefore eternal, for everything existing of absolute necessity is eternal; and what is eternal does not come into existence or perish.'[34] It is axiomatic for

Aristotle that living things are eternal as a species, but not individually. We have the paradox that the class or kind is eternal, yet what exists is the individual. Can there be scientific knowledge of changing individuals?

It is not a necessary truth that all men are rational, if by that is meant that every person is at all times engaged in rational activity. It is true that most humans have the power of rationality, even when it is not actualized, e.g. when they are asleep. A specific problem arises regarding humans who are retarded or incapacitated: incapable of rational behaviour, are they devoid of humanity? As Wallace points out, in relation to another difficulty, 'It is here that final causality, instead of being ruled out of the science of nature, offers a distinctive way through its difficulties.'[35] Ellis declares, however: 'Aristotle's concept of final cause – that is, that for the sake of which a thing exists – has no role in the new essentialism.'[36] This is to overburden Aristotle's notion of final cause; at most he believes that each living thing ultimately exists in order to perpetuate the species. More concretely, the final cause is the perfection which the individual itself attains; this it does in the majority of cases. But, as William Wallace explains: 'The necessity of nature is not absolute: rather it is a conditional or suppositional necessity, a *necessitas ex suppositione*.'[37] Attainment of an individual's final immanent purpose is dependent upon the natural conditions being present for its development; this occurs, not by necessity, but for the most part (ὡς ἐπὶ τὸ πολύ).[38] What is necessarily the case is that, given the adequate and proper circumstances, the acorn will become an oak. It is necessity bound – if it matures – to become an oak and nothing else (it cannot become a birch); there is, however, no iron-clad universal necessity regulating all circumstances which would compel the actualization of its natural potency.

The necessity of nature for Aristotle is therefore hypothetical, and functions with a view to the final cause of the individual. In his explanation of the generation of individuals he states: 'There are then two causes, namely, necessity and the final end. For many things are produced, simply as the result of necessity.'[39] The necessity he refers to is a conditional necessity, governed by the integral construction of the individual: 'The whole body, as each of its parts, has a purpose for the sake of which it is; the body must therefore, of necessity, be such and such, and made of such and such materials, if that purpose is to be realized.'[40] Necessity, for Aristotle, is that of the necessary self-construction, survival, and evolution of the individual towards the goal immanent within its form. It is a necessity emanating from its *eidos* or formal cause which tends dynamically towards its own finality. It is a natural necessity governing the development of a living substance from potency to completion. It is not a physical coercion since, as he points out, every growth has a τέλος and, unless hindered, proceeds naturally towards its achievement.

NECESSITY OF THE FIRST MOVER

Aristotle's affirmation of a first mover is nothing less than an elaboration of the ultimate ground for the principle of causality: for any single instance of movement or change to be ultimately explained, it is necessary to affirm the existence of an unmoved mover or uncaused cause. His proof for the prime mover depends, firstly, on the relation of cause and effect, based upon the distinction of act and potency and, secondly, on the inadequacy of an endless causal regress to provide complete explanation of an effect. Necessity imbues both the content and method of the proof at every phase. The distinction of act and potency is necessary to explain any occurrence of change. The effect exists potentially, but cannot realize its own actuality; it is necessarily dependent upon an actualizing cause. By identifying the immediate cause of any effect we provide an explanation for the observable phenomenon. Our attention has moved to another layer within a network of interacting realities, thus raising a new problem: is that cause (which explains the initial problem) self-explanatory in itself, or has it equally the status of an effect?

The inefficacy of an endlessly regressing explanation, discussed at length in *Physics* 7 and 8, may be illustrated as follows. Something which moves (A), is moved by another (B). B will only give a fully satisfactory explanation of A if it contains within itself its own explanation, and is thus self-explanatory. Since the initial fact we are trying to explain is the movement of A, B will provide an adequate explanation, not only if it is the source of A's movement, but if it is itself unmoved or uncaused. If it is itself dependent upon something else, then the explanation is pushed back along the line, as it were, and simply delayed: we have to wait until we discover the cause of B. When we identify it (C), we will ask, in turn, if C is moved and caused, or if it is self-sufficient. If it is self-sufficient, then the movement of B and A are satisfactorily explained, while C is self-explanatory; reason then rests in its search for explanation. If C is dependent, i.e. if it has itself the status of an effect and is likewise dependent, reason is still in the same state of inquiry as when initially confronted by the movement of A; the mind is still seeking reasons. An endless chain of explanations, each of which is itself in need of explanation, can in principle never provide an adequate explanation: 'the series cannot go on without limit, but there must be a prime cause of the motion'.[41]

The affirmation of a prime mover is the logical finale to Aristotle's search for explanation through causes; the conclusion is attained by a necessity inscribed in the dynamism of thought itself in its search for understanding. The final signpost on the path of investigation reads Ἀνάγκη στῆναι: it is necessary to halt. As Aquinas remarks in a commentary on another text of Aristotle, no action is completed if it depends upon an endless series of incomplete actions.[42] The search for causes can never be fulfilled unless there is a cause which is itself uncaused. In *Metaphysics* 5 Aristotle explains the ground for the unique necessity of the prime mover: it is utterly simple, and hence not open to any change whatsoever. It has no parts; free from generation and corruption it cannot be other than as it is. The prime mover is thus characterized by absolute or simple necessity in virtue of itself alone; through it, other things in turn are necessary.[43]

By way of conclusion we may refer to what Aristotle refers to as the 'coercive' power of truth. He notes that his predecessors 'as if compelled by truth (ὥσπερ ὑπ' αὐτῆς τῆς ἀληθείας ἀναγκασθέντες)' recognized a conclusion even when the reasons were not fully obvious.[44] Parmenides was obliged to follow the phenomena (ἀναγκαζόμενος δ' ἀκολουθεῖν τοῖς φαινομένοις),[45] Empedocles was 'forced by the truth' (ἀγόμενος ὑπ' αὐτῆς τῆς ἀληθείας) to say that substance and nature are reason.[46] In the *Physics* he notes that his predecessors accepted the elements as the principles of the contraries – a position adopted without rational motive – as if the truth itself coerced them.[47] In the *Metaphysics* he notes that the earliest philosophers, having discovered certain principles, recognize that these do not provide an adequate explanation and 'were again compelled by truth itself to investigate the next first principle'.[48]

It is also notable that Aquinas on six occasions makes use of Aristotle's phrase, translated by William of Moerbeke as '*quasi ab ipsa veritate coacti*'.[49] He remarks that Plato and the other ancient philosophers, 'as if forced by the truth itself', tended towards positions later enuntiated by Aristotle. The Presocratics misinterpreted the first principle,[50] and Plato the status of the ideas.[51] Compelled by the evident nature of things (*ipsa rei evidens natura*)[52] they somehow dreamt the truth, as though compelled by truth itself.[53]

5

ARISTOTLE AND THE METAPHYSICS
OF METAPHOR

Asked what his first decree would be, were he to become emperor, Confucius allegedly replied that he would fix the meaning of words. It is easy to appreciate the good intentions of the eastern sage; Aristotle may have had something similar in mind when he stated that a word which does not have a single meaning has *no* meaning.[1] This expresses a central truth about the nature of language, thought and reality: not however the full truth, since language does not lend itself to such Procrustean fixity; Aristotle recognized this better than most. Only a tyrannical philosopher king could legislate as suggested by the anecdote concerning Confucius. Perhaps the clearest challenge to such a decree is analogy; this occurs most commonly as metaphor, which is surely one of the most marvellous feats of language. Bereft of metaphor, everyday language would remain flat and univocal, each word atomically attached to a single object. Indispensable to our way of understanding and articulating the world, metaphor is richly revealing of the relationship between knowledge and reality. It deeply penetrates our way of perceiving and expressing the world. John Middleton Murry did not exaggerate when he remarked: 'To attempt a fundamental examination of metaphor would be nothing less than an investigation of the genesis of thought itself.'[2]

'Metaphor' means literally 'transfer' or 'transport'. The word is used as such by Herodotus, who relates that the Athenian tyrant Pisistratus 'removed all the dead that were buried within sight of the temple and carried them to another part of Delos'.[3] He also uses the word to describe the use of levers for the lifting of stone in the construction of pyramids.[4] These are both strongly physical and visual uses of the term. The first, as it were, 'metaphorical' use of the word – as a noun – is found in the orator Isocrates, who describes the wealth of stylistic means enjoyed by poets, compared to the dearth of literary devices available to prose writers: 'The poets are granted many methods of adorning their language, for besides the use of normal words they can also employ foreign words, neologisms, and metaphors while prose writers are allowed none of these last three, but must severely restrict themselves to such terms alone as citizens use and such arguments as are precisely relevant to the subject matter'.[5] Metaphor was primarily understood by Isocrates, therefore, as a means of poetic adornment.

While he was himself a master of metaphor, Plato does not name it as such.[6] He uses 'μεταφέρειν', meaning to 'transfer' an object from one place to another. Interestingly he employs the expression 'μεταφέρειν ὀνόματα', meaning to 'translate' from one language into another. Aristotle was the first to offer a systematic study of the essential nature and structure of metaphor. Umberto Eco has convincingly suggested that 'of the thousands and thousands of pages written about metaphor, few add anything of substance to the first two or three fundamental concepts stated by Aristotle'.[7] This is a bold claim in light of the voluminous literature that has appeared, especially in recent decades. Another author refers to 'the Stagirite's astonishingly modern description of metaphorical processes'.[8] While Aristotle could not have anticipated the variety of theories now current, many interpretations will find support in his stated views; his perspective, however, may not be reduced to any one in particular. In the following reflections I wish to consider some of the presuppositions of Aristotle's theory of metaphor, and relate them to other aspects of his philosophy, especially his metaphysics, epistemology and psychology. My focus is metaphor as a token for the analogous unity pervading the diversity of the world, and as an index of man's psychosomatic unity. The key to Aristotle's approach is his understanding of metaphor as analogy; much discussion of metaphor as a linguistic or literary device has unfortunately neglected this. Analogy is of the essence of metaphor; it relies on the diversity and unity both of human knowledge and human nature, and on the diversity and interconnection of beings within the cosmos.

Aristotle famously defines metaphor in the *Poetics*[9] as the transfer to one thing of a term belonging properly to another, i.e. an alien or strange name (ὀνόματος ἀλλοτρίου ἐπιφορά). This may occur, he explains, in one of four ways: from genus to species, from species to genus, from species to species or, finally and most significantly, according to analogy or proportion (κατὰ τὸ ἀνάλογον),[10] expressing thereby a similarity of relations. Metaphor through proportional analogy, he explains in the *Rhetoric*, is valued most of all.[11] While metaphor traditionally refers only to the fourth type – proportional metaphor – the first three also illustrate different levels of unity and diversity. These forms of so-called metaphor function, however, on the basis of a manifest similarity which is transferred univocally rather than by analogy.

Aristotle's definition of metaphor proves, if proof were needed, that there is nothing more elusive or difficult to define. The word 'metaphor' is already metaphorical; the best Aristotle can do is to coin a variant (ἐπιφορά), simply by changing the prefix. Metaphor is the 'imposition' upon the object of a name belonging to another. Ἐπιφέρειν conveys the notion of adding to, or placing something *upon* something else – for Thucydides ἐπιφορά meant an additional payment.[12] Is there a tautology here? Is Aristotle's definition circular? Perhaps, but not viciously so. It reveals rather a hermeneutic circle in which we find ourselves firmly centred and which allows us extend the horizon of our world. We are on sure ground, since we spontaneously affirm the existence of diverse beings, recognize simultaneously their similarities, and deny their identity. Since we are also able to distinguish between the proper (κύριον) and transferred meaning of our conceptual terms, Aristotle's definition merely articulates what we already experience.

For a definition of proportion we may consult the *Nicomachean Ethics*, where it is defined as 'an equality of ratios, implying at least four terms'.[13] In the *Poetics* Aristotle prescribes the following formula: 'Proportional metaphor is possible whenever there are four terms so related that the second is to the first, as the fourth to the third; for one may then put the fourth in place of the second, and the second in place of the fourth.'[14] He illustrates this by the imagined parallel between the shield of Ares and the cup of Dionysus. Ares is the god of war, for whom the shield is essential equipment; Dionysus is the god of wine, whose indispensable implement is the drinking bowl. Thus, as the shield is to Ares, so is the drinking bowl to Dionysus. The cup is, as it were, 'Dionysus' shield', and the shield 'Ares' cup'.[15] Another correspondence is between the duration of the day and the span of a lifetime. 'Old age is to life as evening is to day.' Thus old age is called the 'evening of life' or 'sunset of life'.[16]

What is transferred in metaphor? A likeness of relationship between two or more unrelated pairs of individuals. Metaphor is essentially the recognition of likeness in unlike things. The merit of metaphor is to recognize deep and hidden similarities: 'just as in philosophy also an acute mind will perceive resemblances even in things far apart'.[17] The key to proportional metaphor is the perception – perhaps imaginatively – of a novel resemblance between two pairs of coordinates not normally conjoined. Aristotle goes so far as to declare that the gift for metaphor – the perception of unlikely likeness – is a true sign of genius: it is the one thing, he states, which cannot be taught by another.[18] (It is interesting that in the *Nicomachean Ethics* he states that the moral vision whereby one discerns what is truly good is also a gift of nature – 'the greatest and most noble' – which likewise cannot be acquired or learnt from another.)[19] Having enumerated all the means and literary devices which the poet has at his disposal, Aristotle declares in the *Poetics*: 'It is a great thing, indeed, to make a proper use of these poetical forms, as also of compounds and strange words. But the greatest thing by far is to be a master of metaphor (πολὺ δὲ μέγιστον τὸ μεταφορικὸν εἶναι). It is the one thing that cannot be learnt from others; and it is also a sign of genius, since a good metaphor implies an intuitive perception of the similarity in dissimilars (τὸ γὰρ εὖ μεταφέρειν τὸ τὸ ὅμοιον θεωρεῖν ἐστι).'[20]

With delightful irony George Eliot chides the philosopher: 'O Aristotle! if you had had the advantage of being "the freshest modern" instead of the greatest ancient, would you not have mingled your praise of metaphorical speech, as a sign of high intelligence, with a lamentation that intelligence so rarely shows itself in speech without metaphor, – that we can so seldom declare what a thing is, except by saying it is something else?'[21] It is indeed true that intelligence 'rarely shows itself in speech without metaphor'. Aristotle remarks in the *Rhetoric* that alongside ordinary, regular, words (τὸ δὲ κύριον καὶ τὸ οἰκεῖον), *everybody* uses metaphor in normal conversation (πάντες γὰρ μεταφοραῖς διαλέγονται).[22] This is evidence of a natural and universal inclination towards metaphor. The spontaneous and unreflective use of metaphor has been seen as indicating something elemental in human knowledge. According to Giambattista Vico, in order to understand how 'primitive man' interprets the world, we need simply examine his metaphors. Benedetto Croce sums up Vico's view: 'Poetry ... is the primary activity of the human mind. Man, before he has arrived at the stage of forming universals, forms imaginary ideas. Before he reflects with a clear mind, he apprehends with faculties confused and disturbed: before he can articulate, he sings: before speaking in prose, he speaks in verse: before using technical terms, he uses metaphors, and the metaphorical use of words is as natural to him as that which we call "natural".'[23] While this is certainly exaggerated, it is doubtless true that everyday language is suffused with metaphor. There is no contradiction in Aristotle's statements that while everybody uses metaphor, the mastery of metaphor is a sign of true genius. Cicero later distinguished between the creation or invention of metaphor, and its use; even children and fools use metaphor! Metaphor manifests itself at diverse levels of intelligence.

I wish to distinguish between those metaphors with limited cultural value and those which are universal in scope and which, I suggest, indicate something essential in human nature. To illustrate I will refer to a common scene in the modern Greek capital. Standing on any busy street in Athens, you would not have to wait long to see a truck drive by with the word 'metaphors' (μεταφορές) printed on the side. This is, of course, not a dial-up delivery service for poets with writer's block but more prosaically a removals company vehicle; as already noted, the word 'metaphor' means literally 'transport'. There is an entire stoa or covered archway in the centre of the city occupied by companies specializing in 'metaphors'. It is interesting that while some advertise εθνικές μεταφορές, i.e. 'national metaphors', others offer 'international metaphors' (διεθνείς μεταφορές); yet more promote γενικές μεταφορές, general metaphors. (The Greeks even have a government minister for metaphors! The Athens telephone directory has ten pages advertising topical metaphors, frozen metaphors, air and sea metaphors; you can even chose between esoteric and exoteric metaphors.) The basic division which I wish to note is that between 'ethnic' and 'international' or 'general' metaphors.

Speaking of ethnic or national metaphors, we can agree with Vico that we can learn much about the mentality and tradition of a people from the metaphors embedded in its language. Consider the countless maritime metaphors in English, inconceivable in the language of a landlocked nation. The frequency of nautical and maritime terms reflects the importance of the sea in English history; I have counted no less that sixty expressions originating in sailor's language which are part and parcel of English. Other languages have copious terms drawn perhaps from military or agricultural life. Thus there are what we may loosely call cultural metaphors, particular to a people or nation. However we may also note, above and beyond the diversity of individual languages, a host of metaphoric meanings which transcend regional boundaries. These indicate, not particular cultural, geographic or historical characteristics, but essential aspects of human nature and man's fundamental relationship with the world. They are truly international or universal metaphors.

Predominant among such universal metaphors which may be observed across cultural divisions are those intended to explain mental activity by means of terms drawn from the physical world. I will give just two examples, taken from the vocabulary used to describe knowledge. Firstly perception: English and all the Romance languages adopt the Latin word *perceptio*, deriving from *capere*, to 'take', 'seize' or 'lay hold of'; the Greek word ἀντίληψις likewise derives from λαμβάνω, also 'to take'. Similarly the language of conceptual comprehension: the Latin *concipere*, its synonym *comprehendere*, the Greek καταλαμβάνειν and German *begreifen*, likewise understand intellectual knowledge as a 'seizing' or 'grasping'. The psychic activity of knowing is conveyed with terms drawn from the physical activity of taking hold of, seizing and gripping.

The transfer of physical terms to intellectual activities makes perfect sense in light of Aristotle's insistence that all concepts are founded upon sense experience. Because of his composite nature man needs metaphor to bind the physical and the psychic, the external and internal, the sensible and intellectual. Aristotle remarks: 'The beauty of the body is seen, whereas the beauty of the soul is not seen.'[24] In keeping with the Aristotelian concept of man, it is entirely natural for us to elaborate abstract concepts from our knowledge of concrete objects – natural, because necessary. Man needs to figure his speech, so that it can turn from the domain where it initially belongs and for which it is properly fitted, towards the realms which surpass the physical.

Aristotle continually created linguistic analogies by enlisting everyday concepts in the service of philosophy. Porphyry begins his commentary on the *Categories* with the question why Aristotle chose as a title for his work a term which in ordinary language refers to the speech of the prosecution against the accused in the law courts. He explains that while ordinary language communicates everyday things, philosophers are interpreters of things that are unknown to most people and need new words to communicate the things they have discovered. 'Hence either they have invented new and unfamiliar expressions or they have used established ones in extended senses in order to indicate the things they have discovered... So even though κατηγορία is applied in ordinary usage to the speech of the prosecution which presents evidence against a defendant, he adopted the word, and chose to call those utterances in which significant expressions are applied to things "predications" (κατηγορίαι).'[25] Simplicius likewise recognizes the clear fittingness for Aristotle of the transition by analogy from sensible to intelligible things (ἡ κατὰ ἀναλογίαν αὕτη μετάβασις ἀπὸ τῶν αἰσθητῶν ἐπὶ τὰ νοητά).[26]

Just as intellectual knowledge is rooted in the senses, so too are those various terms we use to describe cognition itself. We have no terms other than physical with which to denote non-physical, immaterial or psychic activities. The reason we transfer to mental acts the names of physical activity is because of the analogous similarity perceived between the two. Consider what we do with ideas and what they do to us. We can trace an idea, pursue it, get our head around it, embrace it, take it to heart and dwell on it; we may put it on the table or into someone's head. Ideas dawn upon us, cross our mind and enlighten us; they trickle down and perhaps inundate us.[27] Among the natural processes which provide rich metaphoric motifs for mental or spiritual realities and activities are those of physical force, light, nutrition, growth, reproduction and birth. The world of the psyche mirrors the realm of nature; in the words of Emerson, 'The whole of nature is a metaphor of the human mind.'[28]

The language of mind is largely metaphorical and refers to phenomena and processes of the body. An adequate explanation of metaphoric signification must account for the unity which necessarily underlies the duality of the domains from which this wide array of expression is drawn. Aristotle's doctrine of the distinction of body and soul, yet their complementarity and unity, provides precisely such a foundation. The unitive power of metaphor, expressing a mental function by analogy with its physical parallel, can only be explained by recognizing a unitary subject of cognition, whose mode of knowledge equally involves physical and mental operations. Metaphor effects between disparate domains a unity which mirrors the relation of body and mind. Aristotle refers repeatedly to man's composite nature; man is a 'σύνθετος'.[29] Similarly metaphor is a 'σύνθετον'.

As already stated, metaphor is the transfer of a name from one object to another on the basis of analogical similarity, i.e. of likeness through 'equality of ratios' (ἡ γὰρ ἀναλογία ἰσότης ἐστὶ λόγων, καὶ ἐν τέτταρσιν ἐλαχίστοις).[30] Analogy is a similarity of relationship, a correspondence of proportion – or, as both Alasdair MacIntyre and Martin Heidegger term it, a 'relation of relations'.[31] Before considering the kind of analogy which constitutes metaphor, it will be helpful to review the broader meaning of analogy for Aristotle, and the use made of it throughout his system. Aristotle uses it extensively in his overall synthesis of knowledge, particularly his metaphysics and biology. The aspect of analogy which I wish to emphasize is its power of universal reference and comprehensiveness; it is this which ultimately allows metaphors of proportion to be predicated across the most widely diverse contexts. Analogy refers not to any or every aspect of unity, but to the resemblance of relations within and among a diversity of beings; it is the agreement of correspondent relations which are diversely realized in different domains; it thus provides the widest possible framework for universal unity among diverse substances.

In *Topics* 1, 7 Aristotle distinguishes between three senses of *sameness* (τὸ ταὐτόν): numerical, specific and generic.[32] Ten chapters on – without naming it as analogy – he speaks of the *likeness* (ὁμοιότητα) which belongs to *different genera*: 'As one thing is to another, so a third is to something else. For example, as knowledge is to the knowable, so is sensation to the sensible thing (ὡς ἐπιστήμη πρὸς ἐπιστητόν, οὕτως αἴσθησις πρὸς αἰσθητόν). And as one thing is in another, so a third is in something else. For example, as sight is in the eye, so the mind is in the soul (ὡς ὄψις ἐν ὀφθαλμῷ, νοῦς ἐν ψυχῇ), and as a calm is in the sea, so is stillness in the air.'[33]

The unity of analogy is clearly not the unity of the individual, species or genus,[34] but of a likeness transcending all three. It is wider than genus: 'things that are one by analogy are not all one in genus'.[35] In accordance with the root meaning of ἀνα-λογία, it is the similarity of an intrinsic proportion which is repeated and realized across an endless number of disparate relationships. G.E.R. Lloyd explains: 'In such four-term proportional analogies, what is claimed is that the relationship within each pair is the same, a sameness distinct from sameness in number, sameness in species and sameness in genus, and labelled, precisely, sameness by analogy.'[36] Analogy offers the widest possible ground for unity, overarching that of genus, which in turn embraces the more limited unity of species and individual. Analogy links different categories because it transcends them.

In *Metaphysics* 5 Aristotle defines both sameness and likeness as forms of unity: 'Some things are one numerically, some in species, some in genus, some by analogy. Those things are numerically one of which the matter is one: those things are specifically one of which the definition is one; those things are generically one which belong to the same category; those things are analogically one that have the same relationship as two other things have to one another.'[37] The unity of analogy transcends the unity of the individual, species and genus; it runs through all three because it surpasses them.

In his zoological investigations Aristotle uses analogy to introduce order among disparate species on the basis of similarity of function or operation; put simply: birds have wings, fish have fins.[38] 'There are some animals whose parts are neither identical in form nor differing in the way of excess or defect; but they are the same only in the way of analogy (ἀλλὰ κατ᾽ ἀναλογίαν), as, for instance, nail to hoof, hand to claw, and scale to feather; for what the feather is in a bird, the scale is in a fish.'[39] Each member of these distinct pairs performs a similar function within their respective natures. Analogy, according to Aristotle, also facilitates the work of taxonomy: for example, 'pounce' (the internal shell of the cuttle-fish), spine and bone are all analogues of animal bone, and may thus be classified together.[40]

Aristotle intentionally exploits analogy as a method of scientific order. To treat all common attributes separately would involve endless and needless reiteration, whereas to study the operation of a function in one animal will cast light upon a corresponding function in another. Aristotle therefore proposes to investigate all animals, insofar as possible, according to their similarities, principally that of function.[41] It is, he states, 'a reputable opinion (ἔνδοξον) that among similars what is true of one is true also of the rest'.[42]

Most far-reaching is Aristotle's use of analogy in metaphysics. Going beyond species and genus he seeks those features and principles common to all beings precisely as beings. Some first principles are common to particular sciences; they are common, however, 'only in an analogical sense', since each is valid only insofar as it falls within the genus of the particular science.[43] He declares however: 'There is analogy between all the categories of being (ἐν ἑκάστῃ γὰρ τοῦ ὄντος κατηγορίᾳ ἐστὶ τὸ ἀνάλογον).'[44] In *Metaphysics* 12 he states: 'In one sense, the causes and principles of distinct things are distinct, but in another sense, if one is to speak universally and analogically, they are the same for all.'[45] The principles of corruptible bodies are form, privation and matter. They are fulfilled differently in each case, but relate similarly to one another precisely as principles in every unique instance. There are four distinct causes, but each acts in a mode proper to itself: cause is analogical. Matter causes the effect by supporting or sustaining form; form determines the matter. The efficient cause produces the effect, while the final cause attracts the efficient cause.

Analogy operates most clearly in Aristotle's elucidation of the distinction between act and potency. The distinction is disclosed inductively, and grasped analogically by way of example. It is the difference between that which builds and that which is capable of building, that which sees and that which has its eyes shut but has the power to see, the finished product compared to the raw material.[46] The relation of act and potency is verified analogically in the duality of prime matter and substantial form,[47] and in the distinction of substance and accident.

The analogous principles of act and potency; matter, form and privation; the reciprocal and dynamic relationship of causes, all conspire to shape Aristotle's vision of a unified cosmos. Nature is inherently coherent; it is not, as he expresses it, a 'series of episodes, like a badly constructed tragedy'.[48] The perception of the world as an interrelated wickerwork of substances and causes gives foundation to the conviction that the cosmos is essentially and integrally united. 'All things are ordered together somehow, but not all alike, – both fishes and fowls and plants; and the world is not such that one thing has nothing to do with another, but they are connected. For all are ordered together to one end.'[49]

Aristotle would doubtless agree with Thomas de Vio, Cardinal Cajetan, who wrote in his highly influential work *De Nominum Analogia* (1498): 'An understanding of this doctrine is so necessary that without it no one can study metaphysics, and ignorance of it gives rise to many errors in other sciences... Metaphysical speculation without knowledge of [proportional] analogy must be said to be unskilled.'[50] Analogy is intrinsic to our human mode of cognition, discovery and creativity; it is a mental crossing of the barriers from one science, art, or region of experience, into another. Analogy is the key – a veritable *passe-partout* – which unlocks the structure of thought in its dual attitude to the unity and multiplicity of the world, as it engages in the twin approaches of analysis and synthesis. Aristotle clearly grasped the importance of his own insight that the causes of all things are the same analogically; Marie-Dominique Philippe suggests that Aristotle's use of analogy 'best characterizes his philosophical approach'.[51]

Proportionality, moreover, is important for Aristotle in all areas of reality and human activity. Justice is defined as proportion. The demands of justice must take into account the circumstances of the individual situation; instead of being imposed in unbending fashion as an iron rule, it must adapt itself with equity to the situation. Aristotle aptly conveys this with the image of the leaden rule used by the builders of Mytilene to harmonize the uneven edges of the building stones.[52] Political life demands equitable harmony; in *Rhetoric* 1 he draws a parallel between the balance required between leniency and severity in a democracy, and the mean between aquiline and snub in a handsome nose.[53] There should be a certain proportion and fittingness between one's position in life and the possession of goods.[54] In friendship among unequals, love should be proportional, i.e. analogously balanced by different levels of dedication and response.[55]

It is this fundamental ontological, analogical, relatedness among beings which provides the profound basis for metaphor. We need however to distinguish between metaphor and analogy in its proper sense; this is also to clarify the distinction implied by Aristotle's definition of metaphor between the proper meaning of a word (τὸ δὲ κύριον καὶ τὸ οἰκεῖον), and its metaphorical or non-proper meaning. Aristotle's definition of metaphor as the transfer of a name from its proper to an alien context is echoed in the medieval characterization of metaphor as 'improper' analogy. This is found in Aquinas, and canonized in Cajetan's influential work *On the Analogy of Names*.

In order to distinguish between simple analogy and metaphor (what we might call intrinsic and incidental analogy, rather than proper and improper analogy), let us examine the various ways in which beings resemble one another analogically. Firstly, for Aristotle the metaphysical principles of being are perfectly realized in every individual; they are properly and intrinsically affirmed in the case of every particular entity in all its uniqueness. Metaphysical principles are affirmed proportionately of every entity by proper analogy, whereas metaphor is the proportional, but imperfect, transfer of a perfection or activity from its primary to a secondary subject. Secondly, similar functions, operations and actions are also predicated properly and analogically, of substances belonging to different genera, because of a real similarity in the corresponding roles which they perform in accordance with their own nature: the bird flies, the fish swims – both move. In metaphor, however, and here is the point, what is affirmed is not a proper analogy, but an *imperfectly analogous resemblance*: the quality, perfection or action belongs perfectly and intrinsically only to one substance, and is transferred to another because of some perceived but imperfect likeness. In the assertion 'Achilles is a lion', the poet is not attributing to the hero either the nature of a lion, nor its beastly rapacious activity as such, but rather a certain secondary likeness. Metaphor is the proportional, but imperfect, transfer of a perfection or activity from its primary to a secondary subject. In metaphor, a name which belongs intrinsically to one being is transferred to another, not by virtue of what it is properly in itself, but through a relation of proportional similarity in some secondary or accidental respect. This similarity is frequently glimpsed only through the creative imagination.

At this point I wish to propose that it is action which constitutes the metaphysical foundation of metaphoric resemblance. Aristotle hints at this, but does not make it explicit. In *Rhetoric* 3 he repeatedly notes that one of the primary virtues of analogous metaphor is to 'place things before the eyes (πρὸ ὀμμάτων)', i.e. to bring them to life. Things are set before the eyes, he explains, by words which 'represent them in a state of activity (ἐνεργοῦντα)'. A metaphor may be nominally complete, but will lack vitality unless it conveys the notion of activity (ἐνέργεια). By happy coincidence the word ἐνέργεια is close to ἐνάργεια, meaning clarity, vividness, brilliance. Through metaphor Homer frequently speaks of lifeless things as living (τὰ ἄψυχα ἔμψυχα); his poetry is thus distinguished through the effect of activity (τῷ ἐνέργειαν ποιεῖν).[56] Aristotle cites a number of Homeric metaphors 'in all of which there is appearance of actuality (ἐνέργεια), since the objects are represented as animate', such as 'the shameless stone' or 'the eager spearpoint'. He explains: 'Homer has attached these attributes by the employment of proportional metaphor (κατ' ἀναλογίαν μεταφορᾶς); for as the stone is to Sisyphus, so is the shameless one to the one who is shamelessly treated.'[57]

The expression to 'place things before the eyes' is itself metaphorical for the sensible character of metaphor. There are here two significant aspects worthy of note. Sensation is itself an activity, as Aristotle makes clear in *De Anima* 3, 2; hence an image or metaphor is all the more potent when it conveys an action (ἐνέργεια). Secondly, in line with Aristotle's metaphysics of the categories, action is the most appropriate similitude to be expressed through metaphor. The substances of different genera cannot resemble one another in essence or nature. The only resemblance which may be affirmed between them is either the perfectly analogous similarity of their metaphysical principles or the imperfectly analogous resemblance of action. The similarity which metaphor conveys is not that of substance, but activity. Beings of different genera resemble one another not in what they *are* (essence or nature) but in what they *do* – each in accordance with its own nature and identity.

For Aristotle, as already noted, metaphors should place an idea πρὸ ὀμμάτων: before the eyes. The vast majority of everyday metaphors originate from sensible images, although most have lost their imagic character; they have become dead metaphors, no more than clichés. Happily we continue to create new metaphors, and there is delight in both inventing and recognizing these. Allow me to mention a few metaphoric images which surprised me recently, and which confirmed the validity of Aristotle's remark that the vitality of metaphor is to place something before the eyes. I was struck by Hugh Kenner's assertion that 'Language is a Trojan horse by which the universe gets into the mind',[58] and by Plutarch's suggestion that myth is the rainbow which reflects the sun of truth.[59] Hearing a woman describe her reaction to the murder of her father, overcome with the black lava of grief and hate, I recalled vivid images of carbonized bodies among the ruins of Pompeii. I was fascinated with Seamus Heaney's description of the intellectual condition of Boston in the seventeenth century: 'Nothing stirred. The future was a verb in hibernation.'[60] Since the tragic catastrophe of the Indian Ocean earthquake in December 2004 it has become a cliché to speak of a 'tsunami of information'. Aristotle's point is well illustrated: the power of metaphoric expression comes from its sensible, imagic character. 'The faculty of imagination', he states, 'is identical with that of sensation.'[61] Image is defined in the *Rhetoric* as feeble sensation.[62]

Aristotle declares that 'metaphorical expressions are always obscure';[63] this does not jeopardize its value but denotes its double character as *clair-obscur*, projecting and diffusing its light, prism-like, although itself opaque. Cecil Day Lewis remarked: 'There are such things as unverifiable truths, and it is the unverifiable element in poetry which carries the conviction of truth.'[64] (It is a strange characteristic of mystery that, while obscure in itself, it has frequently a remarkable capacity to illuminate other things.) The distinction between the metaphorical and the proper (κύριον) use of words allows Aristotle to praise metaphor in poetry but scorn its use in philosophy. While obscurity (τὸ ἀσαφές) has a place in poetry, and metaphor lends an air of wondrous strangeness (τὸ ξενικόν), philosophy seeks clarity (τὸ σαφές). Analogy is one of its most valuable tools; from a scientific point of view metaphor by contrast is deviant, defective and wanting in definition.

Aristotle's sharpest criticism of Platonic participation in the *Metaphysics* was to dismiss it as a poetic word or empty metaphor.[65] In the *Meteorology* he illustrates the opposing values which metaphor has for philosophy and poetry: 'It is absurd to suppose that anything has been explained by calling the sea "the sweat of the earth", as Empedocles does. Metaphors are poetical and so that expression of his may satisfy the requirements of a poem, but as to knowledge of nature it is unsatisfactory.'[66] Empedocles' metaphor provides a graphic image, but nothing of scientific value. Metaphor is for science a semantic hybrid; it flourishes and blooms, but is itself infertile.

Dealing in the *Topics* with the tactics of argument, Aristotle provides another reason for caution. By using metaphor the opponent may escape through sleight of argument.[67] Definition requires strict unity and coherence; metaphor lives in the *double entendre*, a duality of denotation which may give rise to ambiguity. One may refute such an opponent, however, if one can turn his metaphoric meaning against him, on the ironic assumption that he has used words in their proper sense.[68] In rational discourse, however, one should seek clarity of definition and eschew equivocation: 'If we are to avoid arguing in metaphors, clearly we must also avoid defining in metaphors and defining metaphorical terms; otherwise we are bound to argue in metaphors.'[69] One cannot reason syllogistically by metaphor; equivocation ensues, as does incongruity if we confuse metaphor and literal description: 'Socrates has a sharp mind and a snub nose!'

Aristotle's approach to metaphor is comprehensive and multifaceted. While various theories have emphasized one or other aspect of metaphor, Aristotle's approach cannot be reduced to any in particular. Of the elements which he associates with metaphor we may note primarily, however, ornamentation, emotion, and cognition. Aristotle recognizes the importance of metaphor as adorning language; it is essential to what he calls ἀρετή λέξεως, the virtue of the word: 'The materials of metaphor must be beautiful to the ear, to the understanding, to the eye or some other physical sense.'[70] Metaphor no doubt embellishes but cannot be reduced to ornament; these are explicitly distinguished by Aristotle.[71]

With regard to emotion, the states which Aristotle explicitly notes are wonder and the pleasure of knowledge. Metaphor is equally effective, it could be argued, with regard to such affective states as fear, horror or disgust. These too can simultaneously evoke the marvel of knowledge. Vital to metaphor is the contrast between the familiar and the strange, which is the hallmark of wonder. Metaphor is one of the most effective ways to 'give everyday speech an unfamiliar air'.[72] 'Things which are remote are wonderful and what is wonderful is pleasant.'[73] Metaphor is a continual reminder of the strangeness of things all around, the marvellous in the quotidian. 'Easy learning is naturally pleasant to all, and words mean something, so that all words which make us learn something are most pleasant. Now we do not know the meaning of strange words, and proper terms we know already. It is metaphor, therefore, that above all produces this effect.'[74]

Most discussion of metaphor considers it as an event occurring at the semantic level of the object. The effect on the speaking or listening subject, however, should not be overlooked. As well as the transfer of a name from its proper setting to a strange or inhabitual context, metaphor transports the speaker, listener or reader, beyond the confines of his present experience to a new horizon. With its power of estrangement metaphor arrests our habitual relationship with the world. The miracle of metaphor is its power to evoke marvel and astonishment. According to Aristotle metaphor introduces the element of strangeness (ξενικὸν); he has in mind the strangeness of expression, but beyond language it also serves to make things strange. Malebranche's invitation comes to mind: 'I will not bring you into a strange land, but show perhaps that you are a stranger in your own country.'[75] An effective metaphor can bring about a dramatic displacement in the Brechtian sense of *Verfremdung*. There ensues the surprise of recognition, the joy of discovery.

This brings us to the cognitive function of metaphor – already implicit throughout the preceding discussion. Metaphor discerns similitude, discovers novel connections, establishes new resemblances, thus offers new insight; it deepens our understanding of what we know. It provides a cipher for the unknown; Aristotle remarks that even though there is sometimes no word for some of its terms, analogy loses none of its expressive power.[76] Metaphor too can give names to nameless things.[77] Most witty sayings, according to Aristotle, are derived from metaphor and beguile the listener in advance: expecting something else, his surprise is all the greater. His mind seems to say, according to Aristotle, 'How true, but I missed it.'[78] Such discovery provides the pleasure of easy and rapid learning (μανθάνειν ῥᾳδίως . . . μάθησιν ταχεῖαν).[79] Successful metaphors, as in the case of Homer, succeed in creating new learning and knowledge (ἐποίησε μάθησιν καὶ γνῶσιν).[80] Here Aristotle sees the difference between metaphor and simile. Simile does not captivate the listener's attention so powerfully as metaphor. It does not declare outright 'this is that' (ὡς τοῦτο ἐκεῖνο), and thus jolt the mind to examine the strange connection between the objects.[81] The more cryptic quality of metaphor draws the listener to a closer examination of the similarity which he must discover for himself.

As Aristotle notes, the difference between metaphor and simile is minimal.[82] Similes, if they are good, can also have the effect of brilliance. However, the unstated nature of the similarity in metaphor forces the listener or reader to invent it for himself; it has thus an added element of surprise and discovery.[83] The impact of metaphor is to say that 'this' *is* 'that'; the mind is aroused by a Socratic sting that shocks the mind to new recognition. Simile, moreover, is less pleasant because it is longer; metaphor is elegant and clever (ἀστεῖον) because it delivers rapid instruction.

In its cognitive function, we can discern in Aristotle an aspect of metaphor which has rightly been emphasized in recent decades, namely its interactive character, heralded by I.A. Richards and championed by Max Black.[84] Richards referred to the tension between the two contexts that are juxtaposed in metaphor; these he denotes with the terms 'tenor' and 'vehicle'.[85] Black used the terms 'focus' and 'frame' in place of 'tenor' and 'vehicle'. (Ernan McMullin has proposed 'target' and 'illuminator').[86] Metaphor involves the conjugation of ideas or images from distinct domains of experience. In Dr Johnson's celebrated phrase, metaphor gives us 'two ideas for one'.[87] (James Joyce in *Ulysses* offers what is itself an impressive metaphor to describe analogy: 'Though they didn't see eye to eye in everything, a certain analogy there somehow was, as if both their minds were travelling, so to speak, in the one train of thought.')[88] But as well as juxtaposition, there must be an element of opposition or antithesis. Aristotle notes that metaphors should be drawn between kindred objects, but emphasizes that the kinship should not be too obvious: otherwise there is no need for metaphor. The virtue of metaphor is precisely to discover likeness in unlikeness.[89] What is either too obvious or obscure conveys nothing new and is without interest, whereas a successful metaphor provides new learning and insight.[90]

In metaphor the speaker assumes a certain conscious ambivalence. Metaphor asserts one thing, individual and unique, to be what it is not. The speaker is aware of this seeming contradiction, but is saved from absurdity by a concomitant awareness that it is not *really* asserted as such. There is a doublethink, a parallelism or duplicity of intention. When Homer refers to Achilles as a lion, he is not really asserting that he is a member of the species *Panthera leo*, but that in a certain aspect his actions resemble those of a lion. With poetic licence metaphor implicitly exercises an existential bracketing (ἐποχή) with respect to the copula; it declares both that 'it is' and 'it is not', perhaps more precisely: 'it is this, but not really'; it affirms a substance, but intends an accident. It asserts identity, but includes otherness. It is a transgression of genus (μετάβασις εἰς ἄλλο γένος),[91] a category mistake such as Aristotle expressly prohibits when he states one cannot prove a geometrical proposition by arithmetic.[92] The genius of metaphor, however, is not to transgress but to transcend boundaries, categories and genera, by lighting upon latent similarities.

Aristotle's distinction between the normal and the strange use of a word is echoed by the interactive theory, which emphasizes the *tension* between the two usages as a basic constituent of metaphor. To state that one thing is another offends the most basic principle of all discourse, the principle of non-contradiction. Of course Achilles is not a lion: should we not mean what we say? The tension of this doublethink forces the mind beyond itself. There is a fruitful tension at the heart of metaphor, which impels the mind to new discovery. Analogy is the intuitive leap

117

by which mind connects the known with unknown experience. It is the spark that ignites the mind to light up similarities below the surface; it is a lamp borrowed from one domain to illumine the recesses of another. It brings objects from distinct arenas into a reflective relationship, that one may clarify the other. The mind shuttles between one and the other term, and back again, in a quick movement of thought which at once affirms identity and difference, thus extending our knowledge of the given.

What are the metaphysical requirements of metaphor? What does the activity of metaphor reveal to us about man, in terms of Aristotle's philosophy? Metaphor brings out in a unique manner the metaphysical nature of human knowledge. By metaphysical I simply mean the ability of human cognition to pass beyond the sense experience of an individual object to grasp it in its universal aspect, to view an individual – however insignificant – *sub specie totalitatis*. It brings an increase of metaphysical awareness, a heightened pitch of abstractive and intuitive activity: intuitive, because it grasps a concrete feature of the object, abstractive because it sets it in relation with a reality from a distinct, perhaps distant domain. Metaphor is the embodiment in miniature of man's metaphysical knowledge, and illustrates in a unique manner his ability to surpass the physical confines of immediate experience. He may thus view any object of experience, sensible or intellectual, within a wider context according to whatever similarity he perceives. He can associate one individual with any other, even a thing unknown. His arena of reflection is ultimately the unlimited horizon of being in its totality. Summarizing his treatise on psychology, Aristotle states that 'the soul is in a sense all things'.[93] This is the openness requisite for the spontaneous play of metaphor; the subtle tendrils of mind and imagination recognize no obstacle in their glimpse of similarity in the most unlikely places.

In agreement with Aristotle's view of things, metaphor indicates a duality in human nature between body and psyche, sense and intellect; but the ability also to surpass this division. It reveals a more profound unity in human nature. Just as the diversity of sense perceptions is unified by the power of the common sense,[94] so also the acts of cognition which operate in tandem to produce metaphor demand a single subject who is aware of identity in difference. The dual optic must be brought into single focus. Only a common element can bind what is diverse. Moreover, the fact that in countless metaphors the physical and psychic mirror one another indicates the underlying unity of reality itself.

Man's citizenship of two worlds, material and mental, is already inscribed in the very nature of language: a material medium which carries a metaphysical meaning. Language encapsulates the human capacity and impulse for self-transcendence. Using sensible symbols man surpasses the confines of the material world. Frege has put it well: 'Signs have the same importance for thought as the discovery of using the wind to sail against the wind has for seafaring.'[95] Words are somehow a summation of man's sensible and intellectual unity. Language is laden both with the inner tension of sense and intellect and the further struggle to express, beyond cognition, a reality which in principle it can never fully disclose. In metaphor the human impulse for transcendence achieves one of its deepest, most metaphysical, moments. More than any other mental act, analogy, including metaphor, reveals the ability to rise beyond a single individual and establish its relationship with other beings.

The poet Cecil Day Lewis has expressed much of what I wish to convey – which I believe to be in harmony with the fundamentals of Aristotle:

> Relationship being in the very nature of metaphor, if we believe that the universe is a body wherein all men and all things are 'members one of another', we must allow metaphor to give a 'partial intuition of the whole world'. Every poetic image, by clearly revealing a tiny portion of this body, suggests its infinite extension... Poetry's truth comes from the perception of a unity underlying and relating all phenomena... Poetry's task is the perpetual discovery, through its imaging, metaphor-making faculty, of new relationships within this pattern, and the rediscovery and renovation of old ones... The poetic image is the human mind claiming kinship with everything that lives or has lived, and making good its claim.[96]

In keeping with its importance in the *Poetics* and *Rhetoric*, metaphor exhibits a pervasive power for creative insight; it lives in the tension between unity and diversity both in human nature and in the universe. It is moreover a token both for the simplicity of human nature which acts through a diversity of levels, and for the unity of reality throughout the multiplicity of beings. All of these elements are present though not explicit in Aristotle. They are, I suggest, the implicit background to his theory of metaphor. In the absence of genuine metaphysical analogy, which binds entities through a proper likeness and similitude, there would be no real foundation for transferred or metaphoric resemblance. One Shakespearean critic has expressed as follows the profound implications of metaphor: 'I believe that analogy – likeness between dissimilar things, which is the fact underlying the possibility and reality of metaphor – holds within itself the very secret of the universe.'[97] This is close to the passages from the *Metaphysics* cited earlier to illustrate Aristotle's vision of a unified cosmos.

Metaphor is vital to daily language; it attains its fullest expression in poetic creation. Analogy, on the other hand, finds its fullest application in metaphysics. The poet suggests in metaphor what the philosopher asserts through analogy. Metaphor depends upon imagery; analogy operates by means of concepts. Each engages and activates in its own way the universal character of human intentionality: the unique relationship which human φύσις has towards the totality of being. Man's nature is sensible and intellectual; his knowledge is a unity of both, beginning with and relying upon the senses. His ability to surpass the physical is attested to primarily by the intellectual power of abstraction, which is the pulse and drive of philosophy; and heightened by the associative power of imagination, reaching its highest intensity in the act of creative metaphor.

Metaphor always retains an element of paradox, whether viewed as ambiguity or surplus of meaning; it uniquely blends the luminous with the obscure. It cannot enter as such into syllogistic reasoning; it is not a tool of philosophy, but a profound phenomenon which summons philosophic reflection. The process of metaphor is highly revealing of human experience and expression; it discloses a relational similarity between diverse contexts: a resemblance the significance of which is not merely rhetorical or ornamental, but essentially metaphysical. The ultimate philosophical value of metaphor, therefore, from an Aristotelian perspective, is not its argumentative role but, I suggest, its power to disclose the relational solidarity of diverse substances; this in turn calls for philosophic explanation. Aristotle does not himself offer a comprehensive explanation in these terms, but provides the concepts and principles which are required.

According to Henri Bergson, if we remove from Aristotle's philosophy everything derived from poetry, religion and social life, as well as from a somewhat rudimentary physics and biology, we are left with the grand framework of a metaphysics which, he believes, is the natural metaphysics of the human intellect.[98] It seems to me that metaphor, which so profoundly characterizes our intellectual cognition, as it cooperates with sense and imagination, is best explained by such a natural metaphysics.

6

Aristotle's Political Anthropology

Aristotle concludes the *Nicomachean Ethics* by announcing his treatise on politics (περὶ πολιτείας). Only thus, he explains, will his 'philosophy of human affairs' (ἡ περὶ τὰ ἀνθρώπινα φιλοσοφία) be complete.[1] The transition from the *Ethics* to the *Politics* is natural and essential, since human beings attain happiness and fulfilment only within the political community. The *Politics* opens with the assertion that the city or political community (ἡ καλουμένη πόλις καὶ ἡ κοινωνία ἡ πολιτική) aims at the supreme human good.[2] While all partnerships aim at some good, political partnership is paramount. Aristotle confirms this priority by describing the human being as a political animal. In the present essay[3] I consider a number of interrelated questions arising from this description.[4] Is the term 'political' proper to humans, and predicated only metaphorically of animals? Or does Aristotle's definition refer to an elementary zoological characteristic common to members of all gregarious species that collaborate in a common task? In what sense may the polis be described as natural if it does not conform to Aristotle's definition of what it is to be a nature (φύσις)? How may the primacy of the polis be reconciled with the fact that the citizen is somehow independent, with autonomous activities and a separate purpose?

ORIGIN OF THE POLIS[5]

At the start of the *Politics* Aristotle sets out to establish that humans are by nature political animals, and the polis accordingly a natural entity. He offers what are apparently two distinct explanations. The first is a detailed description and empirical narrative of the genesis of the polis: how it arose, and the evident purpose which it exists to serve. The second is a compacted theoretical explanation of humans as political animals, based on the possession of *logos*. Later I shall consider the relationship between these two arguments. For the moment let us note that in the first he seems at pains to emphasize that the polis exists by nature (κατὰ φύσιν, φύσει); the second argument is itself a reflection on human nature.[6]

Aristotle suggests that the best way to investigate things is to see how they have grown (φυόμενα) from the beginning.[7] He explains that the first natural human association is the family or household: 'a union of those who cannot exist without each other'.[8] This is the union of male and female, which exists for the continuance of the human race, motivated by the desire – common to all living things – to leave behind another of the same kind. It also incorporates the relationship of master and slave, grounded in their shared need for security; the one who envisages the means of defence is a natural ruler, the one who provides these is a natural subject. Aristotle defines the family as 'the association established by nature for the supply of men's everyday wants'.[9]

Aristotle goes on to explain that families in turn combine to form a village, an association which aims at something more than the supply of daily needs.[10] Finally, when several villages coalesce into a self-sufficient community, they constitute a polis. Aristotle notes: 'A polis only begins to exist when it has attained a population sufficient for a good life in the political community'.[11] There is a graded hierarchy in the goals respectively of family, village, and polis, responding incrementally to the citizen's needs, from daily necessities to the fulfilment of the good life. Aristotle emphasizes that all three associations – family, village, polis – come about in accordance with nature (κατὰ φύσιν). The polis is natural because it derives from the family and village, which grow out of the citizen's essential and immediate dependence on human cooperation.

In his ethical works Aristotle adds valuable remarks on the social or political role of the family. In the *Nicomachean Ethics* he remarks that the love of husband and wife exists by nature (κατὰ φύσιν), 'for human beings naturally tend to form couples more than to form cities, to the extent that the household is prior to the city, and more necessary'.[12] He also points out that 'human beings cohabit not only for the sake of begetting children but also to provide the needs of life (τῶν εἰς τὸν βίον)'.[13] More important from our point of view is his emphasis in the *Eudemian Ethics* on the foundational character of the family: 'In the household are first found the origins and springs of friendship, of political organization and of justice.'[14]

While the family exists for the sake of everyday needs, and the village for non-essential goods, Aristotle makes a significant distinction between the *genesis* and continued *existence* of the polis: it *came into being* for the sake of life (γινομένη μὲν τοῦ ζῆν ἕνεκεν), but *exists* for the sake of the good life (οὖσα δὲ τοῦ εὖ ζῆν).[15] The polis was instituted to provide for the daily necessities of living – for the sake of survival – , but once in existence offers its citizens an enhanced mode of life. It provides added benefits not envisaged in advance. These correspond, presumably, to the pre-eminent, outstandingly human capacities of individual citizens. The city came into being so that men might be *able* to live, but continues to exist so that they may live *well*. As Christopher Rowe remarks, Aristotle 'does not want to claim that all, or indeed perhaps *any*, actual cities in fact "exist for the sake of the good life". We have to live and survive, but what we live *for* is the realisation of our potential as human beings, which is impossible outside a political community.'[16] Aristotle repeatedly affirms that 'the polis was formed not for the sake of life only but rather for the good life (εἰ δὲ μήτε τοῦ ζῆν μόνον ἕνεκεν ἀλλὰ μᾶλλον τοῦ εὖ ζῆν)'.[17]

In his first argument that the polis exists by nature, Aristotle has so far referred to the collective combination of families and villages, both of which result from nature.[18] To emphasize the point he changes perspective from the material, compositional, origin of the polis to its purpose as the goal, end or *telos* of the family and village (τέλος γὰρ αὕτη ἐκείνων). The most important principle in any reality is its end and purpose; finality defines and determines the nature of each substance: 'That which each thing is when its growth is completed we speak of as being the nature (φύσις) of each thing, for instance of a man, a horse, a household.'[19] The polis has a clear and indispensable goal, the self-sufficiency of its citizens. Aristotle is thus able to carry his genetic explanation to its ultimate conclusion and identify the purpose for which the polis exists. 'The object for which a thing exists, its end, is a chief good; and self-sufficiency (αὐτάρκεια) is an end, and a chief good. From these things therefore it is clear that the polis is a natural growth, and that man is by nature a political animal.'[20] One of the strengths of Aristotle's method is his reliance upon observation, and the most obvious reason for the polis is the human dependence upon cooperation. No individual is self-sufficient, but attains adequacy in collaboration with others. Aristotle reinforces the point by noting that whoever is either incapable of, or has no need of, partnership, must be either an animal or a god.[21] He illustrates the fate of the individual deprived of city life by referring to the 'clanless, lawless, heartless' man reviled by Homer.[22] Sophocles conveys the same plight in Philoctetes' lament that without a polis (ἄπολις) he is a living corpse.[23] Self-sufficiency is a requisite for happiness, but the self-sufficiency of the citizen ultimately depends upon the self-sufficiency of the polis, 'for it is felt that the final good must be a thing self-sufficient in itself. The term self-sufficient, however, we employ with reference not to oneself alone, living a life of isolation, but also to one's parents and children and wife, and one's friends and fellow citizens in general, since man is by nature a social being.'[24] Aristotle first establishes through observation the *fact* that humans are political beings. In his second argument he proceeds to examine the *reason* for their political nature. The answer appears obvious: 'Why man is a political animal in a greater measure than any bee or gregarious animal is clear. For nature, as we declare, does nothing without purpose; and man alone of the animals possesses speech (λόγον δὲ μόνον ἄνθρωπος ἔχει τῶν ζῴων).'[25] While other animals have voice (φωνή), which allows them communicate pain and pleasure, they are restricted to the domain of the senses. Human beings experience deeper levels of value within reality: 'Speech is designed to indicate the beneficial and the harmful, and thus also what is right and wrong; for it is special to man as distinct from the other animals that he alone has any sense of good and bad, of right and wrong and other moral qualities: it is association in these things that makes a family and a polis.'[26] This short passage has raised two fundamental questions. What is the exact meaning and scope of the term 'political'? What is the context of Aristotle's definition: is it biological, rational, or metaphysical?[27]

'POLITICAL ANIMAL': LITERAL OR METAPHORICAL?

There are two interpretations of the meaning and scope of 'political' as understood by Aristotle in his definition. According to one, the concept refers properly and primarily to humans as animals that live in political partnership and community – the only ones capable of doing so since, uniquely endowed with *logos*, they alone share with their fellow humans the common and universal values upon which society is based. According to this interpretation, the term 'political' is used for those gregarious animals that collaborate in a common task (bees, ants, and so on) in a secondary, derived, and metaphorical sense. Such creatures are not properly 'political' but, resembling humans in the performance of a common project, merit the transferred application of the term on the basis of this similarity. This interpretation appeals to the etymological roots of the word, and Aristotle's penchant for analogy and metaphor.

According to the second interpretation, the use of the term 'political' in respect of animals is not metaphorical, but proper and intrinsic; its meaning is not confined to human society, but refers equally to every animal group engaged in communal activity. This interpretation appears confirmed by Aristotle's definition of political animals at the start of *History of Animals* as 'those which have some one common task (κοινὸν ἔργον)';[28] Aristotle lists humans, bees, wasps, ants and cranes.[29] The word has an extensive – rather than extended – meaning which covers many and diverse degrees of sociality. Thus when Aristotle says that humans are 'more' political than bees or other gregarious animals (*Pol.* 1, 2, 1253a9), he is referring to a superior grade along a continuum.

In *History of Animals* 7 Aristotle distinguishes two ways in which qualities may be common to animals and humans. Some are common 'more or less', others by analogy (τὰ μὲν γὰρ τῷ μᾶλλον καὶ ἧττον . . . τὰ δὲ τῷ ἀνάλογον διαφέρει). Examples of characteristics that can be found in varying degrees are tameness/wildness, gentleness/roughness, courage/cowardice, fear and boldness. While admitting of gradation, such qualities (we may add uncontroversially) are understood intrinsically and properly and thus univocally. By contrast art, wisdom, and comprehension are proper to man, while 'certain animals possess another natural capability of a similar sort'.[30] Had Aristotle placed 'political' in one or other of these two categories, the present discussion would never have arisen; but tantalizingly he did not. I will argue that the qualification 'political' in its intrinsic sense is unique to humanity, but that it is recognized analogically, according to varying degrees, in select animal groups.

Whatever about Aristotle's supposed metaphorical use of the word πολίτης, there was undeniably in ancient Greek an extension beyond the original meaning of the word. As Fred D. Miller, Jr. points out, 'The word "*polis*" originally referred to a high stronghold or citadel to which the Greeks of the dark ages repaired when their villages were under attack.'[31] Πολίτης, *polites*, originally meant the watchman on the citadel, and was later generalized as 'citizen'. Significantly the word contrasts with ἰδιώτης (*idiotes*), which referred to the private city-dweller who took no part in the affairs of his community.

The case for a literal interpretation of 'political', when affirmed of animals, would be strengthened if the intention of Aristotle's definition were shown to be biological, rather than rational or metaphysical. Because Aristotle invokes the principle 'Nature does nothing in vain' ('the basic proposition of his zoology'), Wolfgang Kullmann takes Aristotle to mean that man is political by nature, 'insofar as he is a biological being'.[32] He suggests that 'the reference to bees and herd animals makes clear [that] man is indeed understood as a biological species'.[33] He explains:

> The political is a characteristic which necessarily results from the special biological nature of man. In this connection, Aristotle proceeds as if it is self-evident that this concept is not coextensive with the concept of man, but has a wider scope. It is only when compared with certain other animals that men are political to an especially high degree... It also follows from the description of man as *zoön* that 'political' above all describes a biological condition of a group of animals.[34]

This, Kullmann argues, is also the meaning of Aristotle's assertion that 'man is a political animal in a greater measure (μᾶλλον) than any bee or gregarious animal'.[35] A different interpretation is defended by Richard Bodéüs, who argues that Aristotle does not intend with this remark 'that the human species possesses a political character more marked than every other species of the same genus, but that the human species, rather than any species of bee or gregarious animal, possesses this character'.[36] Before stating my reasons for also adopting this reading, I will examine in closer detail the case for a broader, literal and biological, reading.

If I understand Kullmann correctly,[37] he maintains that for Aristotle the concept 'political', while initially deriving from humans' political character understood as a *biological* function, is recognized as applicable – properly and with equal validity – to all gregarious animals sharing a common task.[38] From the fact that Aristotle invokes the 'statement from his writings on natural science' that Nature does nothing in vain, Kullmann deduces that Aristotle is proposing here a biological description of humanity. This conclusion, I suggest, is not entirely obvious. While it is true that Aristotle employs the principle with great frequency in his biological writings, his commitment to its validity is not confined to these. Perhaps it was necessary to affirm it more frequently as a programmatic maxim with regard to the lower level of physical minutiae, than in the domain of human experience where purposiveness is more apparent. Aristotle's confidence in the beneficence of nature extends throughout the living world, human and subhuman, confirming his overall teleological concept of the universe and humanity.[39] The principle is cited twice in *De Anima* 3, which culminates in a discussion of the human soul.[40] Aristotle notes that since the goal of politics is human excellence and happiness, the student of politics should study the activities of the soul.[41] The soul, ψυχή, is a synonym for the φύσις or nature of living things – the principle of all their activities, from digestion to contemplation. In the *Nicomachean Ethics* Aristotle asks rhetorically if we could suppose that, while the carpenter and the shoemaker have definite functions – as also the eye, hand and foot – human beings themselves have none.[42]

Aristotle's conviction that nature does nothing in vain extends to the highest desires of human nature. From the fact that we always act for the sake of a goal, he concludes there must be a final end which satisfies our tendencies: otherwise the process would go on infinitely, so that the desire would be vacuous and futile.[43] When he declares that all people by nature (φύσει) desire to know, this does not mean that metaphysical reflection has its roots in human biology. A person's φύσις or nature is his or her ψυχή, soul, which, as well as defining their biology, opens them through the intellectual capacity of νοῦς or reasoning upon the totality of the real (ψυχὴ πώς πάντα),[44] which they are drawn through wonder to explore. Aristotle is convinced that humans' desire for truth and knowledge is not in vain; in the *Rhetoric* he states that 'men have a sufficient natural instinct (πεφύκασιν) for what is true, and usually do arrive at the truth'.[45] Humans have likewise a natural propensity for what is good and noble; it would seem that it is upon the shared experience of these that political partnership is ultimately established. Wolfgang Kullmann suggests that the 'strong biological elements' of Aristotle's thought are not confined to the *Politics*; he points to Aristotle's repeated appeal to natural human impulses across a wide area of human activity in philosophy, morality and creativity in the *Metaphysics*, *Ethics* and *Poetics*.[46] I propose that rather than characterize these activities as biological, it is Aristotle's spirit to understand their nature (φύσις) as embracing not only humans' biological aspect, but also their metaphysical nature, since these are inseparable.

Kullmann[47] refers to a distinction between *phusis* (φύσις) understood in the general sense of *universitas rerum*, and as referring to the nature of a particular thing. Thus when Aristotle declares 'Nature does nothing in vain', the expressions φύσει and κατὰ φύσιν do not refer to individual natural things in the world, but to the overall economy of nature. However, for Aristotle the realist, nature has no existence apart from particular things that grow. His commitment is not to a universal Platonic law in light of which the world is interpreted; it is a profound insight, based upon his empirical observations as biologist, but also on his observation of human affairs and aspirations.

A biological interpretation of humans' political nature might suggest that it is their biological instinct to congregate, as a bird builds its nest and the spider weaves its web. While there is doubtless a biological foundation to humans' social character, the *ground* for their political engagement is, within an Aristotelian framework, primarily rational with a metaphysical foundation. Language, as it were the tangible epiphen-

omenon of reason, an expression of rationality and vehicle of conceptualization, is the requisite medium of community, allowing us to
articulate our thoughts and values, first for ourselves and secondly to
fellow humans.

At the logical level it is correct to read Aristotle as offering through
his definition a class description, setting humans apart from other
animals; in this sense the definition is biological. His purpose, however,
is to give the profound reason why humans are by nature political. It is
true that humans constitute a distinct biological species, something
which cannot be said, for example, of the gods. That does not mean that
their essence is entirely biological. Humans are essentially biological, yet
their essence or φύσις is not exclusively biological, but eminently rational
and intellectual. Admittely one might take the definition as referring to
human beings in an exemplary or normative sense: they are 'natural to
a higher degree than other animals'.[48] For Aristotle human beings are the
most natural of animals; they most perfectly embody what it is to be an
animal.

I suggest that the essential meaning of 'political' is the distinctively
human meaning; it is then applied by derivation and metaphorically –
analogously and in a weaker sense – to ants and bees and other such
beings.[49] We cannot say that bees live in *poleis*; we may observe parallel
similarities between their collective life and mode of organization, and
the manner in which humans dwell in cities, and thus validly apply the
term 'political' to non-intelligent creatures. Aristotle's definition indicates
that it is part of man's nature to live in cities. The etymological
connection between *politikon* and *polis* is clear. According to John M.
Cooper, Aristotle 'means that human nature demands that, in general
and as a normal thing, human beings live in cities of some sort: cities
(*poleis*) themselves or citizens (*politai*) are explicitly mentioned . . . the
etymological connection between *politikon* and *polis* is plainly in the
forefront of Aristotle's mind'.[50] As R.G. Mulgan notes, since the word
πολιτικά, as used by Aristotle in *History of Animals*, cannot mean
'belonging to the πόλις', most translators of this work resort to the word
'social' – which simply implies a common group activity without
specifying anything further either about the activity or the group. 'But
this obscures the fact that Aristotle is taking a word with a clear, literal

sense, "belonging to the πόλις", and giving it a wider, metaphorical extension, meaning roughly speaking, "belonging to a πόλις-like association".[51]

According to David Depew, the worst mistake one can make about 'political animal' is to think that this phrase picks out the defining essence of humankind, and to hold that in consequence Aristotle must be speaking metaphorically when he says that animals other than humans are political.[52] Depew is correct in his criticism of Heidegger, Arendt,[53] and others for locating the 'defining essence of humankind' in man's political nature. Although the phrase ζῷον λόγον ἔχον, a living being that has reason, was coined by later commentators, it approximates more satisfactorily to what one would expect an Aristotelian definition to be. Depew's criticism will not apply if we seek to derive humans' political nature, at least in part, from their rational nature.

The phrase 'political animal' does not express the 'defining essence of humankind'. We may, however, legitimately conclude that their political nature inevitably ensues from humans' nature as material, biological, dependent animals, endowed not only with rationality, but with the intellectual power that provides them with an openness to their fellow humans, and the recognition of a common task. Conscious of this shared condition, and the obligation to make their way in the world, they recognize that their situation is one of shared solidarity, not solitary isolation. Human beings are by essence political animals since participation in life of the city is indispensable for the realization of their well-being and happiness, the optimal attainment of human excellence and maximal exercise of virtue. While the term 'political animal' does not define the essence of human nature, it indicates a uniquely human property (*Wesenseigenschaft*),[54] as also – though clearly more significant than – laughter. In that sense the terms 'human' and 'political animal' are interchangeable.[55]

Aristotle recognizes that in their natural state, compared with most animals, humans are physically weak, though his point is that manual dexterity and intelligence more than compensate.[56] They are least well equipped for survival as regards food, shelter, and defence. They have the longest period of total dependence after birth, hence the prolonged need of family for survival. Of all animals they are the most dependent upon others of their species; this need is greatest for their mental development – the most obvious example being language – and this dependence is lifelong. Aristotle stresses the importance of language for humans' social nature and the formation of the polis. While *logos* refers primarily to the rational character of humans, it is the ground of language. To reason, deliberate, and articulate our thoughts we need language, which we can only learn in a community. Offering the deepest explanation for the existence of the polis and of the family, Aristotle does not refer to the practical needs of survival, but to shared participation or communication (κοινωνία) in such universals as good and bad, right and wrong. According to Aristotle, humans are political beings because they are by nature social, and this social nature is grounded through rationality upon a community of metaphysical values. We may speculate as to the order of priority between humans' rationality and their social character. It seems to me that humans' communicative and communal dispositions are essentially simultaneous. Aristotle appears to allot primacy to humans' rational character when he remarks that 'just as statesmanship does not create human beings but having received them from nature makes use of them'.[57]

In the *Nicomachean Ethics*, Aristotle provides a valuable insight into the personal motivation for society, in which he emphasizes the rational and metaphysical dimension:

> It is the consciousness of oneself as good that makes existence desirable, and such consciousness is pleasant in itself. Therefore a man ought also to share his friend's consciousness of his existence, and this is attained by their living together and by conversing and communicating their thoughts to each other (ἐν τῷ συζῆν καὶ κοινωνεῖν λόγων καὶ διανοίας); for this is the meaning of living together as applied to human beings, it does not mean merely feeding in the same place, as it does when applied to cattle.[58]

In the *Politics* also he notes the importance of friendship for political partnership. All societies are the work of friendship, for it is friendship to choose to live together.[59] In the *Nicomachean Ethics* he goes so far as to declare:

Friendship appears to be the bond of the polis; and lawgivers seem to set more store by it than they do by justice, for to promote concord, which seems akin to friendship, is their chief aim, while faction, which is enmity, is what they are most anxious to banish. And if men are friends, there is no need of justice between them; whereas merely to be just is not enough – a feeling of friendship also is necessary. Indeed the highest form of justice seems to have an element of friendly feeling in it.[60]

Dependence is therefore not the only reason for political partnership. Aristotle notes that even if a person were equipped with all the goods he desired, he would not wish to live alone: 'Surely it is absurd, to make the blessed man a solitary; for no one would choose to possess all good things on condition of being alone, since man is a political creature and one whose nature is to live with others.'[61]

In *Politics* 4 we find an interesting variation on Aristotle's statement that man is by nature a political animal (φύσει μέν ἐστιν ἄνθρωπος ζῷον πολιτικόν). He presents the paradoxical thesis that humans seek society not only when the necessities of life have been provided, but also when they cannot be provided. In the first condition, the aim of society (συζῆν) is the good life (τοῦ ζῆν καλῶς); in the second, political partnership (πολιτικὴν κοινωνίαν) is sought for the sake of mere life itself (τὸ ζῆν αὐτὸ μόνον). Bare life – living at subsistence level – must contain some element of value, provided it is not excessively burdened by hardship. He seems to imply that there is a sweetness and satisfaction simply in the fact of being alive, and that one of the delights is the fellowship of being that all people share together. The text is best cited in full:

Man is by nature a political animal; and so even when men have no need of assistance from each other they none the less desire to live together. At the same time they are also brought together by common interest, so far as each achieves a share of the good life. The good life then is the chief aim of society, both collectively for all its members and individually; but they also come together and maintain the political partnership for the sake of life merely, for doubtless there is some element of value contained even in the mere state of being alive, provided that there is not too great an excess on the side of the hardships of life, and it is clear that the mass of mankind cling to life at the cost of enduring much suffering, which shows that life contains some measure of well-being and of sweetness in its essential nature.[62]

The point of this passage seems to be that political life is essentially sought without regard for the necessities of life. Not only do humans seek society when replete with the requirements of life; when deprived of the minimum necessities we also benefit from society, even when no physical gain is to be had.

Jean-Louis Labarrière suggests that there is no intrinsic link between the two reasons given at *Politics* 1, 2 for man's social nature.[63] According to Aristotle's first argument, man is destined to live in the city through a natural law governing the union of male and female; it is not a matter of agreement or convention. He subsequently argues that man is *more* political than other social animals,[64] since he not only has voice (φωνή) but also λόγος, intellect or reason, which permits him to apprehend good and bad, justice and injustice. However, it is precisely partnership in goodness and justice, as highlighted by the second argument, that makes possible the household and polis described in the first argument; animals do not form families or cities. There is no logical entailment between the first and second arguments. There is more importantly a material connection: humans enter into family partnerships for the same reason they enter political society – for the sake of the good life; both presuppose a community of goodness and justice (ἀγαθοῦ καὶ δικαίου κοινωνία).[65] There is an intrinsic and fundamental link between man's naturally social nature and the fact that he is endowed with *logos*.

For Aristotle the polis results inevitably from the kind of beings that we are; it is not the coincidental or arbitrary result of human compact or agreement, but has its origin in the essential and universal nature of human beings as such. It arises spontaneously wherever humans are found. We may thus reject the interpretation that the Greek citizen historically *became* a political animal during the apogee of the Greek polis.[66] At the other extreme we may reject the view that to be human in ancient Greek society was automatically to be a politically active citizen.[67] Humans' sociality defines their place within the natural cosmic hierarchy, midway between beast and divinity. Brutes are unable to enter society: they lack the requisite openness to share common projects, ideals and values. The gods, on the other hand, entirely sufficient in themselves, have no need of association.[68] Human beings' situation between the two is precarious: 'perfected, man is the best of animals; separated from law and justice he is the worst'.[69]

Applying the categories of Aristotle's metaphysics, we are obliged to seek the origin and explanation for the polis in its constituents, in other words in individual citizens. Neither the family, village, nor city contains within itself the principle of individuality or identity that defines φύσις. The polis is natural in a derived sense, having grown gradually – organically 'as it were' – from lesser associations, which it embraces and organizes into a structural unity. The polis is an outgrowth of the nature of individual citizens, as they establish ever wider spheres of relationship for their survival and fulfilment. The polis is a product of nature, having developed from the first forms of human association. It has grown accumulatively out of the family, clan and village; empirically it is the most advanced form of community, and humans are plainly dependent on it. The metaphysical ground of the polis is the need and capacity of its citizens: the conjunction of their reciprocal dependence and support.

We should not seek to diminish the strong biological elements in Aristotle's political anthropology, which as Kullmann points out, are not confined to the *Politics*.[70] If human beings were disembodied souls, they would not be political. Aquinas notoriously theorized that each angel might be considered a complete and distinct species, without need of others of its kind: it has no need for society (although as pure spirit it can communicate perfectly). Given that humans are in nature biological *and* rational/intellectual, their political nature is together detemined by both essential aspects – in various combinations and at diverse levels. Kullmann writes: 'The political polis is for Aristotle neither a purely rational construction in a Hegelian sense, nor merely a community of bees. It has something of both.'[71] While I entirely agree with this assertion, it seems to me that Kullmann introduces too sharp a separation between alternative biological and rational interpretations of humans' political nature as understood by Aristotle. I do not share the view of those who maintain that ζῷον as used by Aristotle in the political context has no biological connotation, because of their reluctance to rank human beings among the animals. (This view takes support from Aristotle's reference to God as the 'best eternal living being', ζῷον ἀΐδιον ἄριστον).[72] I merely question Kullmann's opposing assertion that the context for Aristotle's definition in the *Politics* is first and foremost biological.[73]

Polis as Natural

Aristotle repeatedly affirms that the polis exists 'by nature'.[74] It is 'one of those things that exist by nature', 'one of the things that are constituted according to nature'.[75] He likens the polis to an animal or living being (ζῷον).[76] Understandably there is considerable debate regarding the meaning of these assertions, since the polis is obviously not an individual natural substance. *Physis* (φύσις) is the paradigm for *ousia* (οὐσία) – a living entity with an intrinsic principle of identity, growth and activity, and is also the exemplar of *eidos* (εἶδος), which profoundly determines the individual in its entirety as it unfolds from within. The polis is not φύσις in that sense, since it does not have a single principle of autonomous growth, but is composed of a multitude of individual substances.

In referring to the goal and purpose of the polis we cited Aristotle's declaration: 'That which each thing is when its growth is completed we speak of as being the nature (φύσις) of each thing, for instance of a man, a horse, a household.'[77] This statement is problematic, since the assumption could be that the polis, like the household, has its own φύσις or nature. But this is impossible, since neither may be counted among those things that 'have within themselves a principle of movement and rest'.[78] While the polis has its origin in nature and provides for its citizens' natural development, it does not possess an immanent organic formal principle that governs its constituent material elements, directing them dynamically toward their *telos*. The polis certainly has a defining *eidos* or form, which may perhaps be understood after the manner of a work of art; it is more natural however than an artefact, since it emerges spontaneously as the result of intrinsic natural tendencies within its members. It would seem that Aristotle is speaking loosely when in *Politics* 1 he refers to the polis as φύσις. That the polis may not be viewed *simpliciter* as a natural entity is obvious from his analogy with the craft of the weaver or the shipwright who need a suitable working material: 'So also the statesman and the lawgiver ought to be furnished with their proper material in a suitable condition.'[79]

One of the merits of Aristotle's naturalist explanation for the polis is that he is using a richer concept, for example, than Hobbes who regarded the state as contravening man's natural condition.[80] Aristotle was familiar with the view that the law is nothing more than a covenant (συνθήκη), in Lycophron's view a surety (ἐγγυητής) of men's just claims on one another, but that it is not intended to make the citizens good and just. For Aristotle, good government must be concerned with political virtue and vice (περὶ δ' ἀρετῆς καὶ κακίας πολιτικῆς).[81] He recognizes the practical difficulties involved, which sometimes lead to the belief that justice and goodness are conventions without real existence in the nature of things.[82] Aristotle distinguishes: 'Political justice (πολιτικὸν δικαίον) is of two kinds, one natural, the other conventional. A rule of justice is natural that has the same validity everywhere, and does not depend on our accepting it or not.'[83] He sees a parallel between the immutable laws of natural justice that have the same force everywhere, and those of the physical world: fire burns in the same manner in Greece as in Persia.[84] He is aware that rules of justice (natural and conventional) vary according to circumstances, but affirms that some of these are nonetheless laws of nature.[85]

CITIZEN AND SOCIETY

One of the charges made on occasion against Aristotle is that of totalitarianism. This is understandable in light of his assertion: 'We ought not to think that any of the citizens belongs to himself, but that all belong to the polis, for each is a part of the polis, and it is natural for the superintendence of the several parts to have regard to the superintendence of the whole.'[86] A variation is found in his statement: 'The whole must necessarily be prior to the part.'[87] Having asserted the importance of the family as providing the basic necessities of life, he states that 'the polis is prior in nature to the household and to each of us individually.'[88] His analogy with a living organism illustrates not only the primacy of the polis in relation to its citizens, but also its natural character. Citizens are likened to the organs of the polis, fulfilling a subordinate role, which cannot function or survive apart from the body. When the body ceases to exist, one speaks ambiguously of its hands or feet, as of those of a sculpture. 'All things are defined by their function and capacity, so that when they are no longer such as to perform their function they must not be said to be the same things, but to bear their names in an equivocal sense.' Aristotle concludes: 'It is clear therefore that the polis is also prior by nature to the individual; for if each individual when separate is not self-sufficient, he must be related to the whole polis as other parts are to their whole.'[89]

We have seen why the polis may not be described as an individual natural substance; however, on the basis of similarity in certain respects between the natural organism and the polis we speak figuratively of the 'body politic'. The weakness of Aristotle's position is inherent in the metaphor. Insofar as the polis lacks a single animating principle (ψυχή or φύσις), as far as the most essential – life itself – is concerned, it resembles the statue or the deceased body.[90] The parallel between the body politic and living organism may not be taken as implying that the members of the community resemble those of the physiological body whose purpose is entirely absorbed in subservience. Nor is there a hierarchic command structure between higher and lower members, since the polis is a community of equals and freemen.[91] The analogy of the polis as a living body is limited, and in the final analysis breaks down at the limit. As Fred Miller, Jr points out: 'Certain terms such as "nature", "prior", and "political" may be used in an imprecise manner.'[92] At most one may accept the analogy in respect of secondary activities that are exclusively social.

Aristotle has, needless to say, a nuanced view of the relation between the polis and its citizens; W.L. Newman emphasizes that he is less totalitarian than Plato.[93] The polis is a multiplicity of citizens (πλῆθός πολιτῶν),[94] not an undistinguished mass or artificial aggregate. It is a unity and a whole. It is a unity of individuals, each more unified than either family or polis.[95] It is a whole composed of individuals, each an intrinsic and integral whole; the citizen is a ὅλον or integral unit, the polis a σύνολον or ensemble. The city is an accidental whole: not a chance multitude of people, rather one that aims at self-sufficiency of life.[96] Although a unity and a whole, the polis is not simple or single, but differentiated from within and composed of dissimilars. 'Not only does a city consist of a multitude of human beings, it consists of human beings differing in kind. A collection of persons all alike does not constitute a polis.'[97] Since they share a common goal he can say without contradiction that the city is a community of similar people whose purpose is the best life possible.[98] The polis is a partnership (ἐστι κοινωνία τις ἡ πόλις), with a continuity of community in spite of a continually changing membership. Aristotle reverses Heraclitus' image: the river remains the same though streams flow in and streams flow out. The principle of identity of the polis is its constitution.[99]

Aristotle's emphasis upon the status of citizens at the start of Book 3 seems to contradict the primacy of the polis which had been stressed in Book 1. Peter Simpson remarks: 'It is tempting to claim that there are signs here of confusion and contradiction in Aristotle's text.' While some commentators have suggested this, I believe that Simpson resolves the problem satisfactorily by pointing out that instead of confusion it is rather a difference of emphasis: 'For the city, one may say, is prior [to the individual] as the whole to the parts that it perfects, but the citizens are prior [to the city] as the parts to the whole that they define. Individuals as individuals thus exist for the city (since it perfects them) but the city subsists in the individuals as citizens (since it *is* them).'[100]

The city is a diversity ordered together as one; its unity is that of purpose, the good life of its members. It needs a unity of control, according to a minimum and maximum limitation of space suitable for efficient self-sufficiency; it differs from a nation, which is a society amorphously related by race and spatially dispersed. The aims of the polis go beyond defence and prosperity, so it is more than a trade alliance: 'All those who are concerned with good government take civic virtue and vice into their purview. Thus it is also clear that a polis truly so called, and not merely in name, must pay attention to virtue; for otherwise the community becomes merely an alliance, differing only in locality from the other alliances, those of alliances that live apart.'[101] A city exists not for security or commerce, which though necessary are not sufficient. The polis is a 'partnership of families and clans in living well' for the perfect and independent life (τοῦ εὖ ζῆν κοινωνία ... ζωῆς τελείας χάριν καὶ αὐτάρκους).[102] This constitutes the happy and noble life (τὸ ζῆν εὐδαιμόνως καὶ καλῶς); political society exists for noble actions and not merely for life in common.[103]

Aristotle warns against excessive unification of the polis: 'It is certain that both the household and the polis must somehow be a unit, but not entirely.'[104] Individual citizens retain their independence and autonomy: 'The city is a partnership of free men.'[105] Its unity is one of purpose: 'The polis is a plurality, which should be united and made into a community by education.'[106] The poet Simonides proclaims: 'The polis teaches the man' (πόλις ἄνδρα διδάσκει),[107] and it is in the context of education that Aristotle argues that no citizen belongs to himself alone, but that all belong to the polis: 'Inasmuch as the end for the whole polis is one, it is manifest that education also must necessarily be one and the same for all and that the superintendence of this must be public, and not on private lines.'[108] The education of citizens is best achieved collectively; the good of each coincides with the good for all, but is only possible if citizens submit to a common regime. The polis exists for the sake of the individual citizen. It does not possess an end in itself, apart from its members; its only importance is that citizens depend upon it for their development, and ultimately their happiness. They retain their identity and differences. The unity of the family and the polis resembles a musical harmony which will be destroyed if reduced to unison, or a poetic rhythm that is lost if reduced to a single beat.[109]

The question of the primacy of the polis occurs at the start of the *Nicomachean Ethics*,[110] where Aristotle argues that Politics is primary among the sciences. The reason given is extrinsic: he asks which science deals with man's ultimate end or supreme good (ἀνθρώπινον ἀγαθόν) – that for the sake of which he desires everything else. Politics, he argues, is the master science (ἀρχιτεκτονική) for two reasons: firstly it regulates the study of all other sciences in the polis, prescribing those which must be studied, by whom, and to what level; secondly Politics exploits all lesser arts or powers (δυνάμεων); even the most noble (ἐντιμοτάτας) are subordinate to it, military strategy, economics and rhetoric. His reasoning is that since Politics employs all the other sciences and practical arts, legislating what citizens should and should not do, it embraces the goals of the other sciences and has as its end man's comprehensive good. He affirms: 'The good of man must be the end of the science of Politics. For even though the good is the same for the individual and for the polis, nevertheless, the good of the polis is manifestly a greater and more perfect good, both to attain and to preserve. To secure the good only of one person is better than nothing; but to secure the good of a nation or a polis is a nobler and more divine achievement (κάλλιον δὲ καὶ θειότερον).' Politics is concerned, he remarks, with the noble and the just (τὰ δὲ καλὰ καὶ τὰ δίκαια).[111]

There should be no conflict between the citizen and the polis. On the contrary, Aristotle suggests that personal happiness cannot exist without politics.[112] The happiness of the polis coincides with the happiness of each individual citizen.[113] The good constitution pursues alike the interest of the polis and the common welfare of citizens.[114] We may assume Aristotle is stating his own view when he remarks: 'If anybody accepts the individual as happy on account of his virtue, he will also say that the polis which is better morally is the happier.'[115] Again: 'It is evident that that form of government is best in which every man, whoever he is, can act best and live happily.'[116] In the perfect polis, the virtue of the good man and that of the good citizen are necessarily the same.[117] The collective virtue of the polis derives from the virtue of its citizens: 'For even if it be possible for the citizens to be virtuous collectively without being so individually, the latter is preferable, since for each individual to be virtuous entails as a consequence the collective virtue of all.'[118] In harming himself or committing suicide, he remarks, the citizen commits an injustice to the polis.[119]

This argument for the primacy of politics seems contradicted when shortly afterwards Aristotle distinguishes three possible modes of life: pleasure, politics, and contemplation.[120] In the final book of the

Nicomachean Ethics he confirms that the highest human happiness consists primarily in θεωρία, contemplation; the intellect is our highest capacity, and deals with the highest realities.[121] We may ask how we should span the divide between man as active and contemplative. We find a hint in a cryptic remark in the *History of Animals* where, having distinguished between gregarious and solitary animals (τὰ μὲν γὰρ αὐτῶν ἀγελαῖα τὰ δὲ μοναδικά), he notes that man partakes of both characters (ὁ δ' ἄνθρωπος ἐπαμφοτερίζει). Man is the only animal that 'dualizes' between solitary and social existence.[122] He exercises certain activities that can only be done individually; in contemplation he exercises his truest self, and most closely resembles divine reality.[123] Θεωρία (contemplation) is not a group activity, although Aristotle suggests that in the company of others we can engage in it for longer periods: 'A solitary man has a hard life, for it is not easy to keep up continuous activity by oneself; it is easier to do so with the aid of and in relation to other people. The good man's activity therefore, which is pleasant in itself, will be more continuous if practised with friends.'[124] The polis is prior in that it provides the means necessary for the citizen to exercise precisely this kind of independent activity and attain full perfection as an individual. The priority of the polis is that of a necessary condition, without which he could neither survive nor prosper.

The polis relates to the kinds of beings we are in a dual sense. It is the highest historical instantiation of human beings' dependence on relationships in family, clan and village for their survival and fulfilment; they depend on it entirely if they are to achieve their highest development. The essential point of its continuance lies in this conjunction of citizens' needs with their abilities: their dependence on each other and their capacities to afford each other support. The sense in which the polis is primary to the citizen takes a nuanced view of individuals. It depends on them and their participation, but they need the city in a sense so profound that they could not be themselves without it. Our social and political nature is grounded in our dependence on each other: *logos*, the capacity to reason and communicate, can only be fulfilled within a community. The deepest aspect of our dependence on family and polis is thus our shared participative communication in standards of good and bad, right and wrong. Politics and political reasoning are in this sense supreme: not only do they make use of all others, their aim is human beings' comprehensive good in the form of life fundamental to them.

7

ARISTOTLE AND THE METAPHYSICS OF EVOLUTION

'Aristotle was nature's scribe, his pen dipped in mind.'
Ancient saying[1]

'Linnaeus and Cuvier have been my two gods, though in very different ways, but they were mere schoolboys to old Aristotle.'
Charles Darwin[2]

'I recall that in 1951 Harold Cherniss told me that Aristotle's biology was the key to his metaphysics; unfortunately I did not have the wit to interpret this Delphic utterance.'
J.L. Ackrill[3]

Does Aristotle's philosophy rule out evolution? The short answer is 'Yes, but ...!'; the long answer: 'No, ... however!' Summarizing his excellent account of the reasoning which led Aristotle in Book 7 of the *Metaphysics* to identify substance (*ousia*) in the first place with specific form (*eidos*), W.K.C. Guthrie, in the final volume of his monumental history of Greek philosophy, concluded: 'Doubtless this is not a satisfactory explanation of reality. For one thing it makes Darwinian evolution impossible.'[4] The matter, needless to say, is not quite so simple. Two questions immediately arise: Does the doctrine of substantial form necessarily exclude evolution? If so, is this of itself sufficient reason for us to reject form? With these questions in mind, I propose to consider some broader aspects of the relation between Aristotle's metaphysics and his biology, in order to speculate how he might respond to the modern theory of evolution.

Aristotle's metaphysics was continually nourished by his experience as a biologist; the data of Aristotle the biologist were in turn frequently illuminated by his insights as metaphysician. In our own time, biology and metaphysics are obliged to enter into dialogue regarding the theory of evolution, through questions which are central to both disciplines. Evolution is viewed by some, proponents and opponents alike, as a claim for total explanation, not only of how the living cosmos came to be, but also as an exhaustive account of its ultimate origins and final purpose – or absence thereof. Such a claim is tantamount to a metaphysics of total reality. It is provoking to speculate how Aristotle would judge such a theory. While Aristotle indeed explicitly rejects evolution, I will argue that his philosophy is in many ways eminently receptive to the theory. His metaphysics, furthermore, will elucidate many of the philosophical questions encountered by any evolutionary theory. Aspects of his metaphysics which I maintain are fundamental for a theoretical consideration of evolution are his concepts of act and potency, form and finality, the nature of causation and the explanation of chance.

It is appropriate to relate themes of biology and ontology in the work of Aristotle. It is impossible to read the famous passage from *Parts of Animals* and remain unmoved by the philosophic eros which it expresses: these are not just the words of a biologist, but of one inspired by a loving fascination with the concrete living individual, filled with the desire to understand it radically.[5] The passage is close to the hermeneutic of philosophy given in *Metaphysics* 1, which begins with the simple declaration: 'All men by nature seek to know.' Aristotle engaged firstly in exhaustive and widespread empirical observation and proceeded through reflective analysis toward a synthetic grasp of causes, in which the desire for knowledge is ultimately fulfilled. This impulse for unified comprehension is exemplified in his biology as much as his metaphysics.[6] It will be of interest to recall briefly Aristotle's significance as a biologist.

ARISTOTLE AS BIOLOGIST

Opinions vary regarding the value of the biological works of Aristotle. A longstanding problem, now thankfully a thing of the past, was that of ignorance.[7] Another was ridicule; Aristotle's biological treatises abound in risible *curiosa*, which suggest that they are not to be taken quite seriously: men have more teeth than women[8] (perhaps neither of his wives, Pythias or Herpyllis, acquired their wisdom teeth, since he himself states that women sometimes acquire them into their eighties!); the bison defends itself by projecting its excrement – in extraordinary quantities – to a distance of eight yards and it is so pungent that it sears the hair of pursuant hounds[9] (reported in conversation with a drunken Latin-speaking hunter,[10] losing perhaps some of its accuracy in translation); the Celtic lands are too cold for donkeys to survive;[11] only humans have a heartbeat, since unique among animals man alone lives in hope and expectation of the future.[12] These and others, however, Ingemar Düring suggests, should not cause us to dismiss Aristotle's serious contribution as a scientist, unparalleled for centuries.[13] As Jonathan Barnes remarks, the *History of Animals* 'is not flawless, but it is a masterpiece… a work of genius and a monument of indefatigable industry'.[14] Aristotle is regarded by many today as the founder of biology as a science.[15] Some of his empirical work, moreover, has stood the test of time; recent fieldwork carried out by Jason Tipton on the island of Mytilene confirms that Aristotle's detailed observations of the natural history characteristics – including diet, sexual dimorphism, spawning details and habitat – of the kobios (*Gobius cobitis*) and phycis (*Parblennius sanguinolentus*) were largely accurate.[16]

The German scholar Wolfgang Kullmann, in a masterly and comprehensive work on Aristotle and modern science,[17] notes a widely held cliché that the theory of gravity finally rendered Aristotelian science redundant. According to this view, progress in the natural sciences is linear; earlier discoveries continuously become obsolete. The truth however, Kullmann suggests, is that despite an increase in detailed scientific knowledge, 'the total perspective and foundation is not in every case always better'. Scientific progress is viewed more adequately as a spiral curve which advances with the accumulation of more detailed knowledge, but which oscillates like the radius of a circle with respect to basic positions. Kullmann argues that Aristotle's works have repeatedly given new impulses to modern science and that many of Aristotle's positions have in recent times acquired an actuality which they lacked for centuries.[18] As an example of spiral-like progress in scientific knowledge, Kullmann cites biology, especially embryology and genetics; in these areas of research, theories have alternated from ancient to modern times quite independently of scientific detail.[19] According to this model, many of Aristotle's fundamental insights retain their validity. No less an authority than Max Delbrück, preeminent among the pioneers of molecular genetics, has declared: 'Anyone who is familiar with today's physics and biology, and who reads Aristotle's writings in these two fields, must be struck by the aptness of many of his biological concepts . . . his biology abounds in aggressive speculative analysis of vast observations on morphology, anatomy, systematics, and, most importantly, on embryology and development.'[20]

Of particular relevance to the discussion on evolution is Aristotle's approach to the genetic development of living individuals. Democritus first formulated the theory of 'pangenesis', according to which semen is drawn from all the organs of the body, and the embryo contains all its parts already fully preformed in miniature. Aristotle rejected this, maintaining that there is a true formation of new structures as the embryo grows: organs emerge gradually and successively.[21] The individual develops progressively from a simple to a more complex form. Aristotle's distinction of act and potency here provides the profound metaphysical insight, guiding and enabling the biological explanation: the parts of the animal are formed successively, with the gradual actualization of what is initially present in potency, under the agency of what is actual.[22]

While the term 'epigenesis'[23] is much later, the concept was first elaborated by Aristotle: embryonic development is a chain of new constructions, each perfecting the preceding, with the final differentiation of the living individual emerging at the end. Epigenesis was championed, among others, by William Harvey (1578–1657), founder of modern biological and medical science, who famously discovered the circulation of blood. The pendulum subsequently oscillated once more towards pangenesis, gaining tentative adherence among others from Charles Darwin, according to whose 'Provisional Hypothesis of Pangenesis', the complete body contributes to heredity: atoms from the entire body of both mother and father are united in their offspring.[24] The spiral turned again in the twentieth century towards an Aristotelian view of embryonic development with the definitive, experimental, proof of epigenesis – the successive emergence of organs.[25] Wolfgang Kullmann remarks: 'Despite the infinite distance in detailed knowledge between Aristotle and modern biology, common to both is the conviction that hereditary disposition is present in the entire body (in blood or the genes of every cell), but is transmitted in coded form and with delayed action to the developing embryo.'[26] Kullmann thus concludes: 'Aristotle's genetics, considered as an abstract model,[27] has an extraordinary similarity with the modern theories in molecular biology of DNA and the genetic code. While Aristotle's position is not superior to modern science, compared to which it is greatly deficient in detail, it is *more balanced* than the picture of embryology and genetics in the first half of the 20th century.'[28] Max Delbrück declares: 'If that committee in Stockholm, which has the unenviable task each year of pointing out the most creative scientists, had the liberty of giving awards posthumously, I think they should consider Aristotle for the discovery of the principle implied in DNA.'[29]

ARISTOTLE'S METAPHYSICS OF NATURE

W.K.C. Guthrie remarks: 'Aristotle's philosophy was rooted in nature, especially living nature, and the characteristic of natural beings which called above all for explanation, and offered the greatest challenge to the philosopher, was that they moved about, changed, were born and died.'[30] In his analysis of beings, Aristotle sought to discern the metaphysical principles involved in the world of the many, changing, active beings encountered in sense experience. A being which is open to change reveals an inherent diversity; a diversity not of beings, but of principles or *archai* (ἀρχαί). It was by observing the difference and distance between what beings *are* and what they *can be* that Aristotle was led to distinguish between actual being and potential being. This distinction is disclosed inductively, and grasped analogically by way of example. It is the difference between that which builds and that which is capable of building, that which sees and that which has its eyes shut but has the power to see; the finished product compared to the raw material. These contrasting pairs make clear to Aristotle the distinction between act and potency. First discovered by distinguishing between dormant states and active motions, it is verified – again analogically – at more primordial levels: (1) the duality of principles required to make sense of substantial change, namely prime matter and substantial form; (2) the distinction of substance and accident, which accounts for accidental change, for example when the individual is perfected by its actions. At these levels the distinction has profound metaphysical import.

Our grasp of this distinction and of the deep presence of potency as a principle of reality is for Aristotle, it would appear, intuitive rather than discursive. On the nature of such intuitive knowledge Coleridge quotes Plotinus, that 'we ought not to pursue it with a view of detecting its secret source, but to watch in quiet till it suddenly shines upon us'.[31] (Coleridge gives as good an account of potency as I have encountered: 'They and they only can acquire the philosophic imagination, the sacred power of self-intuition, who within themselves can interpret and understand the symbol that the wings of the air-sylph are forming within the skin of the caterpillar; these only who feel in their own spirits the same instinct which impels the chrysalis of the horned fly to leave room in its involucrum for antennae yet to come. They know and feel that the *potential* works *in* them, even as the *actual* works on them!').[32]

Aristotle explains that the notion of actuality properly belongs first to motion or movement (κίνησις, *kinesis*), and is then extended.[33] The deeper meaning of actuality is expressed in the words '*energeia*' (ἐνέργεια), to be at work, that is, to be active; and '*entelecheia*' (ἐντελέχεια), to have completed one's action and so in some respect be perfect. Ἐντελέχεια is thus the completed reality of substance or '*ousia*' (οὐσία). (John Herman Randall, Jr has put it in lapidary form: 'Things with powers exercise those powers – they proceed from "can work" to "working" to "work done", from δύναμις [*dunamis*, potency] to ἐνέργεια to ἐντελέχεια').[34] Aristotle makes an important distinction between two kinds of activity, which throws light on the nature of actuality and, as we shall later see, on the role of form. Some actions are a means to an end. They do not contain within themselves their own goal, and are thus incomplete activities (*ateleis*, ἀτελεῖς) – for example, slimming, learning, walking and building. One does not go on a diet for its own sake, but in order to feel better; one does not learn simply for the sake of learning, but in order to know. On the other hand, to see, to think or to contemplate, can be ends in themselves; they are also their own fulfilment. More obviously, to live well or to be happy. The first, Aristotle calls motions (κινήσεις), the second actualizations (ἐνέργειαι). Κίνησις is the imperfect exercise of becoming actual; ἐνέργεια the pure exercise of actuality without change.[35]

Movement is incomplete activity.[36] In activities proper, as distinct from motions, the goal is the exercise of the faculty itself; it does not lie in an outside product as, for example, in a house. 'The actualization resides in the subject; for example, seeing in the seer, contemplation (θεωρία, *theoria*) in the one who contemplates, life in the soul.' Aristotle forcefully declares: 'It is therefore evident that substance and form are actuality.'[37] This is because substance, through form, is the ground of all its operations and activities as origin, agent and end. Substance has a certain completeness in itself; it is the centre and foundation of its activities, which proceed from it and perfect it in return.[38]

As a *flatus vocis*, 'form' is an exceptionally flat-sounding term with which to denote what is for Aristotle the defining element of a real life substance. It carries for the ordinary ear the meaning of external or superficial, suggesting 'outline', 'condition', 'contour', 'shape' or 'appearance'. The popular perception is of an outer shell rather than the inner core; it is shallow in contrast with the philosophical significance of Aristotelian form. *Eidos* is not a profile or lineament which simply may be perceived as *Gestalt*, but the intrinsic, determining, principle which actualizes a corresponding potential prime matter and thus radically constitutes the composite as a single individual. For Aristotle, the thing's εἶδος is the origin of its identity in *what it is*, distinct from all others in its mode of being. It is what makes each thing at its very foundation that which it is, determining what he calls its '*to ti ēn einai*' (τὸ τί ἦν εἶναι), that is, the basic characterization of what in principle and *ab initio* was its role and destiny in the scheme of things – its intrinsic essence. For Aristotle, *eidos* was the *ousia* of the individual, its 'beingness', in virtue of which it is an existent individual, endowed with concrete determination.

The most significant instance of form for Aristotle is the soul, which he defines as 'the first actuality of a natural body endowed with organs'.[39] The body will act, and actualize itself through its various organs, but in order to do so, these must first be determined and coordinated as the organs of this particular body. Before it can do anything whatsoever, the body must itself be actualized as such. The soul fashions the body with all its components into an individual and is therefore its basic, most rudimentary, determination. It is the soul which first moulds the body into a unitary, self-subsistent, living being. The body's activities are a second actualization, but without the first actualization by soul there is no thinking or perception, movement or rest, reproduction or nutrition, growth and decay. 'It is the soul by which we primarily live, perceive, and think; so that soul is the *logos* or form, and not the matter.'[40] Ψυχή (*psyche*) distinguishes living from nonliving: a cadaver is not a body but only the remains, an aggregate of disparate chemicals. 'A corpse has the same shape and fashion as a living body; and yet it is not a man.'[41] (Mark Antony will not address Caesar as a man, but as a 'bleeding piece of earth... the ruins of the noblest man that ever lived in the tide of times'.[42])

'Nature' (φύσις) is another name for the form of growing bodies. Φύσις, as defined by Aristotle at *Physics* 2, is the 'principle of that which has within itself its own source of motion and change'.[43] However, it is not only the principle of change, but also of rest (τοῦ κινεῖσθαι καὶ ἠρεμεῖν). It is the intrinsic principle of each living thing in its self-possession as well as its self-perfecting activity:[44] an artifact has no intrinsic identity, does not have within itself the principle of its own making.[45] Nature is, he concludes, the distinctive 'shape and form' (ἡ μορφὴ καὶ τὸ εἶδος) of things which have within themselves their own source (ἀρχή) of movement and change.[46] It determines each living thing as the kind of thing which it is by definition (ἡ μορφὴ καὶ τὸ εἶδος τὸ κατὰ τὸν λόγον).[47] As Joseph Owens observes, Aristotle exploits two basic significations of nature in the Greek tradition, 'the stable constitution of a thing and the thing's growth and development. Against this historical background of both change and permanence, Aristotle seems to take the best of both worlds. He finds the basic philosophical meaning of "nature" to be the *unchangeable* components of *changeable* things.'[48]

Since *phusis* (φύσις) derives from φύειν ('to grow'), the cognate concept of *genesis* (γένεσις) opens up another dimension of εἶδος and φύσις. 'Nature as γένεσις is the path to nature... That which is born starts as something and advances or grows toward something. Toward what, then, does it grow? Not toward that from which it came, but toward that to which it advances. It is form (μορφή), therefore, which is nature (φύσις).'[49] It is form as ἐντελέχεια which is the τέλος of γένεσις, that is, of the coming-to-be of φύσις. In its state of completion, φύσις is synonymous with ἐντελέχεια, the fulfilment of εἶδος. These various terms reveal distinct nuances of the same reality, substantial form in its various stages of potency and actualization, development and completion. 'Whatever each thing is when its coming-to-be (γένεσις) is completed, is what we call its φύσις, whether we are speaking of a man, a horse, or a family. Besides, the final cause and end of a thing is the best, and to be self-sufficient is the end and the best.'[50] A reflection on the generation and growth of living substances brings to light the intimate and dynamic relation between formal cause – the substantial form enduring through the process of γένεσις – and the final cause, substantial form as ἐντελέχεια complete and fully achieved.

The primacy of the final cause is also confirmed through a comparison with the moving or efficient cause:

> Furthermore, we see that there are more causes than one concerned in the formation of natural things (γένεσις φυσική): there is the cause *for the sake of which* the thing is formed, and the cause to which *the beginning of the motion* is due. Therefore another point for us to decide is which of these two causes stands first and which comes second. Clearly the first is that which we call the final cause – that for the sake of which the thing is formed – since that is the *logos* of the thing – its rational ground, and the *logos* is always the beginning for products of nature as well as for those of art.[51]

The final cause ultimately provides us with the clearest explanation, since it indicates the goal of substance and, for that very reason, its most adequate definition.

In seeking the *fundamentum inconcussum* of metaphysics, Aristotle remarks that it is neither possible nor necessary to prove everything.[52] It is equally futile and superfluous in the life sciences to demonstrate the existence of nature: 'It is ridiculous to try to prove that *phusis* (φύσις) exists.'[53] It is a manifest fact, unnecessary and impossible to prove. It would be to prove the apparent from the obscure, showing ignorance of what is self-evident and what is not, as if one were to use words without a grasp of what they mean; it would be as ludicrous, he suggests, as a man born blind arguing about colours. Aristotle declares: 'It is evident that many things with nature exist (φανερὸν γὰρ ὅτι τοιαῦτα τῶν ὄντων ἐστὶ πολλά).' Nature, moreover, is ever-present and all-powerful. Intimately active in all her works, she resembles the artist who models in clay rather than the carpenter, since she shapes her product not at arm's length through an intermediate tool, but by palpably touching it herself in direct action.[54] This analogy, as Aristotle recognizes, itself fails to express the full power of nature, since 'the final cause and the beautiful are more fully present in the works of nature than in the works of art'.[55]

Nature is at once both origin and end; the essence of natural things is that they develop and construct themselves from within. This construction is not arbitrary or random, but self-guiding and self-limiting; it is directed towards a concrete goal or τέλος. 'Now, the nature of a thing is its end and its purpose, since in any case of continuous change which comes to an end, this concluding point is also the purpose of the change.'[56] Nature, in its original sense of φύσις, denotes the growth and development of a living being from its beginnings to the fullness of maturity. A living body acts according to its natural form; of itself form 'actualizes' (ἐνεργεῖ).[57] It exists to exercise its powers, first within itself as it tends towards self-completion, but overflows also into outward action, culminating in the activity of propagation. Within the larger perspective animals reproduce because they seek the eternity of the unmoved mover; unable to achieve it as individuals, they seek to attain it in the species. Since the being of things (οὐσία τῶν ὄντων) resides in the particular, nature cannot be eternal in the numerical identity of the individual, but only through the specific form.[58]

Aristotle declares: 'There is purpose (τὸ ἕνεκά του) in things that come about and exist by nature... It is absurd to presume that there is no purpose because one does not observe the agent deliberating. Art does not deliberate either. If the art of shipbuilding were in the timber, it too would act like nature. If purpose is inherent in art, it is also in nature... It is clear then that nature is a cause, that is, a final cause.'[59] Teleology is equally obvious for Aristotle both within the internal behaviour and the outward activity of the living organism: here too there is manifest order. From his observations of animals, Aristotle concluded that the structure of the body is so constructed by nature as to best fulfil a definite function; so too, more minutely, are its parts. The bird's wings are shaped so that it can fly; the fins of the fish are so designed since its nature is to swim in water. 'Nature', Aristotle declares, 'makes nothing without a purpose but always with a view to the best possible for each individual, preserving the particular substance and essence of each (διασώζουσαν ἑκάστου τὴν ἰδίαν οὐσίαν καὶ τὸ τί ἦν αὐτῷ εἶναι).'[60]

To appreciate Aristotle's fundamental attitude to nature, one should keep this principle to the fore. 'We must begin our inquiry by assuming the principles which we are frequently accustomed to employ in natural investigation, namely, by accepting as true what occurs in accordance with these principles in all works of nature. One of these principles is that nature does nothing in vain, but always does the best possible for the substance of each kind of animal (τῇ οὐσίᾳ περὶ ἕκαστον γένος ζῴου τὸ ἄριστον); therefore if one way is better than another, this is also the way of nature.'[61] He does not explicitly call this guiding motif a 'principle' in the way, for example, the principle of noncontradiction is the most certain of all principles (πασῶν βεβαιοτάτη ἀρχή);[62] it is however, an assumption adopted at the beginning which guides his investigation. It cannot command the apodictic power of analysis, but is revealed through the natural patterns of the world; translators of Aristotle invariably render it as 'principle'. It is the starting point of natural inquiry and has the effective status of a first principle.[63]

Aristotle compares nature to a good housekeeper (οἰκονόμος ἀγαθός)[64] which provides everything that is necessary but nothing wasteful or superfluous. The finality of nature is, however, immanent to the cosmos itself; there is no economist, lawgiver or demiurge. Τέλος is confined to the individual itself and ultimately the species; the eternity of the species indeed precludes any such global finality or teleology.

154

Aristotle's concept of orderedness and finality – a basic tenet and evidence – it has been suggested is best expressed by the recent term 'teleonomy'; here he is close to modern biology, which circumscribes the import of orderedness. The term 'teleonomy' was introduced in 1958 by the American biologist C.S. Pittendrigh, to refer to the finality of nature without any suggestion of outside conscious design. Pittendrigh was haunted by J.B.S. Haldane's quip that 'Teleology is like a mistress to the biologist: he cannot live without her, but he's unwilling to be seen with her in public.'[65]

William A. Wallace helpfully distinguishes between three senses of 'end'. There is, firstly, end as *terminus* or goal, that is, the point at which a process, when completed, stops; secondly, the good or *perfection* attained through the process; finally end as the *intention* or aim purposively pursued by a cognitive agent. It is clear that finality in the first two meanings is central to Aristotle's biology. Confusion arises when the notion of τέλος is laden with intention and conscious purposiveness, thus raising problems which lie outside the scope of biological observation.[66] The more limited term 'teleonomy', therefore, more adequately describes Aristotle's grasp of finality and is helpful since it allows biology to proceed to the limits of its inquiry with a clearly circumscribed model of investigation, free from metaphysical or theological concern. The question of the origin and ultimate purpose of finality within nature is thus bracketed from the examination of living things. Kullmann suggests that Aristotelian 'teleology' is not in reality teleological, but eminently teleonomic, since the finality which is observed is not intended.[67] Τέλος in Aristotle's biology does not mean 'plan' or 'purpose'.[68] Purposive action requires deliberation and choice – Aristotle's concern in the *Ethics*. Natural processes, however, are not the result of deliberation. The ends of nature are the forms intrinsic to natural bodies. Form is a principle of actuality, determining a corresponding matter organically disposed in a body. It determines also the sphere of action and interaction proper to an individual substance.

Aristotle's concept of form occupied a central place in the worldview of the medieval period and beyond. That it attained widespread currency is evident from the lines of Edmund Spenser: 'For of the soule the bodie forme doth take / For soule is forme and doth the bodie make.'[69] However, to quote from the opening lines of Newton's preface to the *Principia*, 'the moderns, *rejecting substantial forms and occult qualities*, have endeavored to subject the phenomena of nature to the laws of mathematics'.[70] Substantial form could not be measured by mathematics or verified through experiment and was thus rejected by the new physics. Francis Bacon struck a heavy blow: 'Matter rather than forms should be the object of our attention, its configurations and changes of configuration, and simple action, and law of action or motion; for forms are figments of human mind, unless you will call those laws of action forms'.[71] He inaugurates the modern attitude to final causality: 'Investigation into final causes is fruitless and, like the virgin consecrated to God, produces nothing'.[72] Potency likewise, since it cannot be grasped in a clear and distinct idea, is also jettisoned. Descartes reduced the natural world to outer extension; only geometric form remained. Causality is viewed as an external, efficient, relation; Aristotle's comprehensive understanding of αἰτία is abandoned.

Reduced in this manner to the dimensions of external extension, the natural world is, I suggest, deprived of its inner dynamism and natural tendency. Some of Aristotle's richest insights are lost: intrinsic form and the potency of being. Unless we affirm, however, the presence in natural beings of some element akin to immanent form, it is difficult to understand why they act in the determinate and intelligible ways continually disclosed by science at ever more microcosmic depths. Bereft of form and potency, bodies are deprived of the dynamic structure which orients them by natural tendency.[73] As the life sciences reveal more and more marvellous instances of determination and directional behaviour throughout the world of nature, these provide fresh illustrations of Aristotle's deepest metaphysical intuitions.

EVOLUTION: FORM AND FINALITY?

One of the dominant narratives of our time is the theory of evolution. It is one of the most far-reaching interpretations of the world, and uniquely of man, and equally invites urgent dialogue with every tradition which claims to have relevance today; it imposes the challenge of self-reflection and renewal. Evolution thrives in a chiaroscuro between the brilliance of creative theory and the darkness of evidence shrouded in the past;

perhaps the subtlety of Aristotle's thought will illuminate some aspects of the question in its philosophical relevance. My leitmotif in the following pages is the status of form, as raised by the remarks of W.K.C. Guthrie reported at the outset.

If we are to believe Marjorie Grene, Charles Darwin followed Descartes in exorcising the spectre of form; his view is diametrically opposed to that of Aristotle. She writes: 'Here I believe we really meet the ruling passion of Darwinism: in the determination not to look at structure. Structure must be explained *away*; it must be reduced to the conditions out of which it arose rather than acknowledged *as* structure in itself.'[74] This would explain Guthrie's rejection of Aristotle in opting for Darwin. However, against Guthrie's summary dismissal I wish to suggest some reasons why, on the contrary, one should consider substantial form necessary to make sense of the world in all its multifarious variety, as experienced both prescientifically and as interpreted by the life sciences. My principal aim is one of methodic procedure: the question of form is prior to the debate regarding evolution. Aristotle's denial of evolution in his biological writings does not, *a priori*, render unsatisfactory his fundamental insight into form as a metaphysical principle of beings. I will argue, to the contrary, that evolutionary theory must not only affirm the reality of a principle akin to form but must embrace, moreover, other elements of Aristotle's metaphysics.

It is axiomatic for Aristotle's biology that the world is eternal and composed of kinds which are more or less constant in themselves.[75] However, no less a specialist than David Balme writes: 'Reproduction is part of self-preservation, and its continuance is part of the continuance of the universe. The *fixity* of species is a different matter, not entailed by the continuance of species . . . There is nothing in Aristotle's theory to prevent an "evolution of species", i.e. a continuous modification of the kinds being transmitted.'[76] In favour of evolution, Balme cites the possibility of new species arising from fertile hybrids, and the fact that on the *scala naturae*, it is not always possible to distinguish between certain types of plants and animals. As against this, James G. Lennox objects: 'If to continue a species is to continue replicating its form, it does entail fixity.'[77] This is the interpretation most consistent with Aristotle's view that the goal of living things is to preserve the good of the kind.

The apparent conflict between Balme and Lennox may be resolved by distinguishing between a consideration of the biological data as such, and the presuppositions involved in their metaphysical interpretation. Balme records what might be regarded as adumbrations of evolution; Lennox sets out the ultimate demands of species. Precisely because occasional deviations from the formal control of generation are chance events, Aristotle could not accept them as fixed within the population – that is, as part of its nature. If faced with the evidence for chance variation as *part of nature*, however, Aristotle would no doubt be lead to change his metaphysical interpretation. It may be argued *a fortiori*, in reply to Balme, that it is metaphysical presuppositions which must change, not merely low level biological conclusions. Since, as Lennox notes, 'metaphysical principles interacted in subtle ways with [Aristotle's] biological explanation of reproduction',[78] the recognition of evolution demands, more importantly, a change of metaphysical perspective. That is precisely the pivotal problem of the present essay.

Commenting on Lennox's view that the continuity of species demands fixity, Alasdair MacIntyre has remarked: 'What Lennox does not take into account perhaps is the ὡς ἐπὶ τὸ πολύ character of the relevant generalization. To continue a species it is necessary that characteristically and for the most part the individuals who are members of that species continue replicating its form. But there may come to be individuals in which *per accidens* modifications take place, so that their descendants in time come *not* to replicate that form. From an Aristotelian point of view then the history of Darwinian evolution viewed prospectively is a series of accidental changes.'[79] This fully accords with the interpretation of Lennox which I have proposed: evolution cannot be accommodated without a change of metaphysical perspective. What is ultimately at stake is the metaphysical status of the deviations from the pattern ὡς ἐπὶ τὸ πολύ, what happens 'for the most part'.[80] MacIntyre offers a very plausible suggestion how evolution could be viewed in Aristotelian terms. When members of a species migrate to a new environment, succeeding generations may be modified gradually to such an extent that they cannot mate with the descendants of their ancestors remaining in the original habitat; the original form has been replaced. This is the classic Darwinian case of nature selecting those random genetic mutations which are best suited for survival in the new environment. It could be asked, however, whether a series of 'accidental changes' can amount to a change in the specific nature of the offspring. Are we obliged to speak in evolution of an alteration analogous to substantial change? Or must we locate ultimate metaphysical identity – axiomatic for Aristotle – at some other level which bears the potency for novel determinations?

Given constant circumstances, for Aristotle, each member of a species, having grown to maturity, propagates its like. Other factors, through chance or luck, sometimes thwart the normal progression of events. Nature, however, as a good housekeeper, is not accustomed to discard anything if it can serve some purpose. She always does the best in every circumstance;[81] what is more appropriate than to modify such deviations and determine new life forms? The point to be stressed, however, is that the question of fixity within species is secondary to the reality itself of εἶδος as a principle of fundamental explanation. If Aristotle's metaphysical analysis of growth and change is correct, the principles of form and the affirmation of potency will hold *a fortiori* for the evolutionary process. The validity of the theory of evolution is best decided in the light of empirical evidence – of fossil data and molecular analysis; Aristotle's metaphysics, however, will both accommodate the empirical data and oblige us to ask fundamental questions about the nature of the reality which evolves.

At the most obvious level, form fulfils the basic function of taxonomy – the need to order the variety of beings and account for their differences. There must be some entitative presence – an element or principle – intrinsic to the parrot which is the source of its distinction from the oak tree.[82] It somehow shares this 'something' with other parrots and transmits it to its offspring. Form accounts for the basic similarity that exists within classes of like individuals. At a more radical level, there must be an element within it which distinguishes it as living from dead; the well-known Monty Python sketch on the demise of a pet parrot – a parrot 'bereft of life', a parrot which 'is no more', an 'ex-parrot' – reveals with delightful humour the profound contrast, such that, from a linguistic point of view: 'All statements to the effect that this parrot is still a going concern are from now on inoperative.' In simple ontological terms: 'He has ceased to be.'

The determinative importance of form in living things is summed up by James G. Lennox: 'Aristotle held that any case of a biological generation presupposed the presence of the form of what came to be ... it is clear that this was a metaphysically fundamental principle for him. Matter could never organize itself into a functional organism of high complexity – that kind of organization could only be provided by a pre-existent instance of the kind reproduced.'[83] Lennox expresses the prevailing interpretation: living beings, according to Aristotle, cannot irreducibly be explained by matter, or by a necessity deriving from their originating conditions. The question becomes sharper with respect to the inner teleology of living things. Allan Gotthelf[84] is perhaps the leading exponent of the 'strong irreducibility' thesis at the core of Aristotle's biological thought, summed up as follows: 'Living organisms and their parts do not come to be by material necessity alone.' He states: 'In my view, the absence of a full material-level account requires the presence of an irreducible potential for form, and this irreducible potential provides a primitive directiveness upon an end which is the ontological basis for Aristotle's natural teleology.'[85] While other interpretations argue for more limited, or 'weak irreducibility', there is a general consensus that, according to Aristotle, form cannot be reduced to matter.[86] It lies beyond our present scope to discuss whether, and in what sense, Darwin embraced teleology;[87] it is certain, however, that he did not share Aristotle's belief in final causality as the dynamic potency of the formative cause, proceeding by natural propensity towards its own completion.

Aristotle's irreducibility thesis has more than historic interest. It is widely held that in spite of the successes of reductionistic molecular biology there remain biological problems which are inexplicable by mechanistic causation; another principle is required – a formal cause. Terence L. Nichols enumerates some examples:

> One of these is morphogenesis – the development of form in organisms. Another is the regeneration of organs which have been damaged or removed. If for example the lens is removed from the eye of a newt, the eye grows a new lens. A third is the ability of many organisms to regenerate

themselves from parts: if a flatworm is cut into pieces, each piece will develop into a complete flatworm. Morphogenesis and regeneration are completely beyond the capacity of any machine. Machines cannot be grown from simple units like eggs or single cells, nor can they regenerate parts of themselves, or regenerate the whole machine if they are broken into pieces. Thus morphogenesis and regeneration point to a difference between natural organisms and artifacts.[88]

These facts suggest that the status of natural forms is still of immediate concern for our understanding of living beings. The debate suggests, moreover, that the question of the existence of an intrinsic principle of the organism is prior to the problem how recent or remote its ancestry. The question of evolution, that is, how form came about historically, is secondary to its role as intrinsic, determining, cause of the concrete living beings which we experience here and now.

On the other hand, to emphasize the importance of form as an inner constituent of the individual does not necessarily commit one to the fixity of species. What is stated is that as long as a natural substance of a determinate kind persists, its distinguishing and determining element is form. It may cease to exist; if, however, it mutates to such a degree as to be transformed, it is equally the presence of a new form which accounts for the change – the very word 'transform' conveys as much. But there must remain at least some element which makes the transformation possible; the old must be potential to the new. In all of this, some principle akin to form – however one choses to describe it – exerts both a formative and transformative role.

Many questions regarding the nature and status of finality are raised by Darwinian evolution. The philosophical problem concerns not evolution as such, but rather *how it happened*, and how it was *possible* for it to happen. Did the profusion of life forms come about by chance, or does evolution harbour an inner teleology? Living beings clearly manifest an inherent organization: the reciprocal interdependence of heterogeneous parts and their mutual cooperation in the service of a whole which is greater. The intrinsic organicity – the confluence of instruments – cannot be explained in the same way as the mechanical interaction of the homogeneous parts of an artefact. It cannot be communicated by the impact of an extrinsic motor cause. Is it conceivable that accidental forces can explain the origin, emergence and nature of an individual, all of whose activities are directed by an innate tendency towards a final intrinsic goal: the preservation of itself and its self-fruition in generation? Is it possible to conceive that man, marked by intelligence – a capacity defined precisely in terms opposed to blind chance – has emerged through a series of haphazard mutations? In his discussion of the successive emergence of the distinctive souls, together with their graded powers, in *Generation of Animals*, Aristotle raises what he calls 'the question of greatest difficulty' (ἀπορία πλείστη) which is equally urgent for the evolutionary biologist of today: 'When and how and whence is a share in reason (νοῦς) acquired by those animals that participate in this principle?'[89]

Much has been made of the role of chance in evolution. This term, perhaps more than any other, needs to be clarified; Aristotle's analysis is illuminating. He distinguishes between two kinds of incidental or 'chance' events: that which happens spontaneously, 'of itself' (τὸ αὐτόματον),[90] when an agent acting without deliberation produces an unintended effect; secondly, when an unforeseen effect derives from a deliberate action, it is due to 'fortune' or 'luck' (τύχη).[91] Aristotle realistically recognizes the occurrence of results which are unintended and unforeseen, both by nature and deliberation; but these always result from the activity of an agent. So-called 'chance' events may be unintended, unforeseen or unpredicted; they are, however, caused and may be explained. The results of spontaneity and chance *might* have been the goal of mind or of nature, but in the circumstances have emerged coincidentally. Nothing, however, occurs simply through incidental causation: 'Since there can be nothing incidental unless there is something primary for it to be incidental to, it follows that there can be no incidental causation except as incident to direct causation. Chance and fortune (τὸ αὐτόματον καὶ ἡ τύχη), therefore, imply the antecedent activity of mind and nature as causes.'[92] Chance presupposes an order of natural teleology, and is posterior to that order.[93] Chance is thus coincidence: the accidental concurrence of a sequence normally due to natural teleology. Aristotle may thus declare: 'Both luck and chance, then, are causes that come into play incidentally and produce effects that possibly, but not necessarily or generally, follow from the purposeful action to which in this case they are incident, though the action might have been taken directly and primarily for their sake.'[94] As Wolfgang Wieland states: 'Chance is possible because different independent teleological connections can coincide.'[95]

A number of Aristotle's principles are thus at work in a metaphysical network which accounts for chance effects in living beings: the existence of active autonomous substances; the profound presence of potency and its dependence upon actuality for realization; the providence of nature, which does the best in every circumstance. Natural substances are adaptable; they harbour deep possibilities and are affected by their environment. Since ours is an uncertain world of adventure, freedom and chance, the environment may cultivate or thwart, but nature will adapt. Nature continually asserts herself and is continually inventive. As animals and plants reproduce, there is indeed a natural process towards the selection and survival of the fittest: breeders and gardeners alike are familiar with mutations. Those which are best suited to their environment are most likely to survive.

Thus rather than speak of chance as though to relinquish the need for explanation – surely the antithesis of science, as if to say things could happen without reason – one should speak, with Aristotle, of accidental causes. The appeal to chance does not absolve one from explanation, but obliges rather that one seek to identify the surrounding circumstances – coincidental causes – which somehow favourably influence the unfolding of molecular processes and alter their normal invariance. What are these causes and how do they work? The appearance of new organs or new species would seem to be entirely inexplicable unless one admits the quiescent presence, within the genetic code, of 'virtualities' or potencies which 'e-volve', that is, unfold when favourable circumstances permit. Even if one excludes the finality of goal, there is an immanent, emergent, directionality which points each agent in the direction proper to its resources. The goal may be unpredicted but, given its determinant resources, may perhaps be extrapolated. The form which is to undergo the transformation must harbour within itself a determinate openness to develop the new mode and acquire the new determination: it must

163

have potency, and this potency must be real; it is not a vacuum to be filled. *Natura non facit saltum*. Nature is a continuity; not, as Aristotle puts it, a 'series of episodes, like a bad drama'.[96]

Stephen Jay Gould recognizes that randomness 'is an unfortunate term because we do not mean random in the mathematical sense of equally likely in all directions. We simply mean that variation occurs with no preferred orientation in adaptive directions.'[97] Ernst Mayr further explains: 'It does not in the least mean that any variation can occur anywhere, any time. On the contrary, mutations, in a given species, are highly "constrained". . . When it is said that mutation or variation is random, the statement simply means that there is no correlation between the production of new genotypes and the adaptational needs of an organism in the given environment. Owing to numerous constraints, the statement does not mean that every conceivable variation is possible.'[98]

From the Aristotelian perspective it must be stressed, however, that even if the development of an organ comes about through random mutation, with the nonsurvival of countless unsuccessful stages, whichever one becomes established must be in some sense pre-ordered in the nature of things. Darwin declared: 'If it could be demonstrated that any complex organ existed, which could not possibly have been formed by numerous, successive, slight modifications, my theory would absolutely break down.'[99] In *The Blind Watchmaker*, Richard Dawkins states: 'Not a single case is known to me of a complex organ that could not have been formed by numerous successive slight modifications . . . If it is . . . I shall cease to believe in Darwinism.'[100] There is nothing illogical about the gradual evolution of a complex system or organ; from the Aristotelian point of view, however, what is unacceptable is that such development occur through exclusively material and efficient or mechanistic forces; the gradual evolution, for example, of the eye entirely makes sense in the perspective of formal and final causality – it has been constructed uniquely in order to see. It is fully consistent with the prior, virtual, presence of a real and determinate potency, which comes to actuality under external factors. The case for final causality – the unfolding towards a goal not yet attained, latent but targeted – is strengthened by the hypothesis of gradual evolution.

Here it is crucial to point out a fundamental difference between the so-called 'teleonomies' of Aristotle and Neo-Darwinism. Rejecting all suggestion of a teleology proper to evolution, Ernst Mayr declares: 'If *teleological* means anything, it means *goal-directed*. Yet, natural selection is strictly an *a posteriori process* which rewards current success but *never sets up future goals*. Natural selection rewards past events, that is the production of successful recombinations of genes, but it does not plan for the future.'[101] Among Neo-Darwinians, Francisco Ayala makes a stronger case than usual for teleology within natural selection; he agrees however on the essential point: 'The end-state is causally – and in general temporally also – posterior.'[102] There seems to be a confusion here of the different senses of telos: 'terminal', 'perfective' and 'intentional'. For Aristotle, final causality, both terminal and perfective, is not exerted by a future goal or preexisting end-state; rather the potency proper to form, latent within the individual, simply takes its natural course and comes to fruition under the influence of efficient agents in its environment. Aristotle stresses the dynamic unity of formal and final cause. In order to grasp this, it is first necessary to affirm the unquestionable reality of potency; otherwise it makes no sense. To suggest that 'end-states' of themselves initiate the action whereby they are brought to completion involves the contradiction that something preexists itself and causes its own existence.

In the absence of purpose and finality, chance and necessity are the factors which shape the course of evolution: as well as random variation, Darwinians also appeal to the inescapable demands of natural selection imposed by environment. Aristotle likewise appeals to necessity to explain the generation of new individuals – the operative factors are for him necessity and final causality.[103] Necessity, for Aristotle, however, is a conditional necessity, governed by the integral construction of the individual: 'The whole body, as each of its parts, has a purpose for the sake of which it is; the body must therefore, of necessity, be such and such, and made of such and such materials, if that purpose is to be realized.'[104] Necessity therefore, for Aristotle, is that of the necessary self-construction, survival, and evolution of the individual towards the goal immanent within its form. It is a necessity emanating from φύσις, that is, its formal cause rather than its matter, since 'nature is much more a first principle than is matter' (ἀρχὴ γὰρ ἡ φύσις μᾶλλον τῆς ὕλης)'.[105] It is a natural necessity governing the development of a living substance from potency to completion. It is not a physical coercion since, as he points out, every growth has a τέλος and, unless hindered, proceeds naturally towards its achievement.[106]

ARISTOTLE AND EVOLUTION

Guthrie suggests that 'Aristotle remained too much of a Platonist' to countenance anything like a theory of evolution.[107] The matter, I venture, is not quite so simple. Aristotle's Platonism is his belief in form, but his concept of form is literally worlds apart from that of his master. In the words of W.B. Yeats, 'Plato thought nature but a spume that plays upon a ghostly paradigm of things;'[108] it was, to borrow from F.H. Bradley, 'some spectral woof of impalpable abstractions, or unearthly ballet of bloodless categories'.[109] For Aristotle, on the contrary, nature is a form immersed in blood and bones, flesh and marrow; not transcendent but incarnate. It is a 'this something', a τόδε τι, which replicates its incarnate likeness through the sexual union catalogued in such variety by Aristotle. By repeatedly emphasizing that 'man generates man', he draws attention to the existential mode of substantial form and its concrete reality. This simple fact refutes, better than any elaborate theory, Plato's theory of otherworld Ideas: 'Evidently there is no necessity for the existence of the Ideas. For man is begotten by man, each individual by an individual.'[110] Form is generated by one living substance and bestowed upon a new individual within the species. Guthrie writes: 'The specific form, the essence of the individual, is a changeless, *non-material* entity which exists, but exists only in the manifestations of nature, i.e. in conjunction with matter, not in a transcendental world.'[111] This is, I venture, somewhat too Platonic a view to attribute to Aristotle; if one views form as an immanent, incarnate, principle, rather than 'a non-material entity', the problem is removed. For Aristotle, at least as regards non-intellectual animals, the soul is nothing separate from the organism; the species subsists in its members.

Guthrie, as many others, attributes to Aristotle a false 'essentialism'; this understanding has been the most stubborn obstacle to a rapprochment with Darwin. As one of the leading Neo-Darwinians,

Ernst Mayr, notes, essentialism has 'dominated Western thinking for more than two thousand years after Plato'. According to this view, Mayr explains, 'the changing variety of things in nature is a reflection of a limited number of constant and sharply delimited underlying *eide*, or essences. Variation is merely the manifestation of imperfect reflections of the constant essences... For an essentialist there can be no evolution, there can only be a sudden origin of a new essence by a major mutation or saltation.'[112] Indeed Mayr himself for many years attributed such a view to Aristotle, but changed his opinion under the influence of a number of scholars, notably David Balme, who in 1980 published an article entitled 'Aristotle's Biology was not Essentialist'.[113] According to Balme, Aristotle's teleology deals with the question 'What benefits an [individual] animal of this kind?', and not with the question 'What benefits *all* animals of this kind?' 'Species' is treated by Aristotle as 'merely a universal obtained by generalisation'.[114] Balme sums up the distorted position: 'The extraordinary later misinterpretations of Aristotle, the magical entelechies and real specific forms, must be largely due to these imported concepts – Species, Essentia, Substantia – which presided like three witches over his rebirth in the Middle Ages, but should be banished to haunt the neoplatonism from which they came.'[115] Essentialism is the reification of essence into changeless categories of mental concepts; it is a confusion of the logical with the natural. Clearly it is not Aristotle's understanding of nature.[116]

I propose that in the light of his basic metaphysical principles, with minimal modification to his philosophy of nature, Aristotle might readily accommodate an evolution of species. He already anticipates some features of evolutionary thought. One of the most exciting doctrines of evolution is its thesis of common ancestry, that all living beings are genetically related. From the metaphysical point of view, evolution offers a beautiful, panoramic, synopsis of life, a narrative for the unity of the variegated living world – this is confirmed by molecular biology where the fossil evidence is lacking. Aristotle, for other reasons, also believes that the cosmos is essentially and integrally united: 'All things are ordered together somehow, but not all alike – both fishes and fowl and plants; and the world is not such that one thing has nothing to do with another, but they are all connected. For all are ordered together to one end.'[117]

Aristotle recognized moreover the ascending grades of living things, the *scala naturae*: reality as a graded crescendo from the lifeless through the animate and animal, ascending to the human. According to Joseph Needham, 'the Aristotelian doctrine of the "ladder of souls" – vegetative, sensitive, rational – is a foreshadowing, in fact, of the evolution-concept which ensues as soon as the ladder is realised to exist within time.'[118] Given the graded relation between various species, Aristotle's form-concepts are to some extent elastic: 'Nature proceeds from the inanimate to the animals by such small steps that, because of the continuity, we fail to see to which side the boundary and the middle between them belongs.'[119] Again: 'Nature passes in a continuous gradation from lifeless things to animals, and on the way there are living things which are not actually animals, with the result that one class is so close to the next that the difference seems infinitesimal.'[120] In *Generation of Animals* he comments: 'There is a good deal of overlapping between the various classes (συμβαίνει δὲ πολλὴ ἐπάλλαξις τοῖς γένεσιν).'[121] The point at which a form in its evolutionary unfolding requires a new taxonomy is hence a matter of discretion – though not entirely arbitrary, since there are grounds for whichever order is selected. Thus whether Aristotle chooses to class the sponge as a plant or as an animal, he has valid reasons for both.[122] Without exaggerating its importance, Aristotle recognizes man's link to the primates: the ape, the monkey and the baboon, he states, 'dualize in their nature with man and the quadrupeds (ἐπαμφοτερίζει τὴν φύσιν).'[123] 'The ape is, in form (διὰ τὴν μορφὴν), intermediate between man and quadruped, and belongs to neither, or to both.'[124]

With his declaration, 'Man is begotten by man *and by the sun as well*,'[125] Aristotle affirms the influence of the cosmos in the generation of new living beings; along with heredity, external factors also play a role in determining the progeny. The offspring is a new individualized incarnate form, not a cloned replica. Unlike Aristotle, we now appreciate that throughout geological time the environment is itself subject to change. The environment conceivably enters into the determination of the living individual to an intimate degree. In parallel with geological change or upheaval, major adaptations may occur over time; living forms undergo transformation, unfold latent virtualities and acquire new determinations. Such long term changes under external influences can be more than transient; they may intimately alter the genetic identity of the molecular blueprint, such that the new determination is in turn transmitted to succeeding generations. Should the environment influence the process of heredity to such a degree that it immeasurably alters the form which is transmitted or, to use a phrase of Aristotle, 'should the abnormal increase be one of quality as well as of quantity, it may even take the form of another animal'.[126]

Most significantly, Aristotle interprets Empedocles' theory of the survival of the fittest in light of his own theory of cause and chance: 'In cases where all of the organs were combined as if they had been arranged on purpose, such things survived, having been suitably formed by the operation of chance (ἀπὸ τοῦ αὐτομάτου).'[127] Crucially, however, because of his insistence upon form, he rejects Empedocles' explanation of the generation of animals in terms of the circumstances of their development.[128] Guthrie[129] regards the following remark of Aristotle as antievolutionary: 'The ordered and definite works of nature do not possess their character because they developed in a certain way. Rather they develop in a certain way because they *are* that kind of thing, for development depends on the essence and occurs for its sake. Essence does not depend on development.'[130] This text is indeed anti-Darwinian, since Aristotle here affirms the priority of the formal cause over the process of becoming. For Aristotle, as outlined, γένεσις is governed by the dynamic bond between the individual in its initial potency and the goal towards which it tends. Growth and development are consequent upon essence. Guthrie is correct: evolution exclusively in terms of material and external factors would be unacceptable to Aristotle. Form must play a central role in the unfolding development of living beings. Rather than explain essence by appeal to prior material and efficient causes, Aristotle explains development of the individual through the kind of individual it is, its nature or form. His reply to Empedocles is clear: 'Empedocles was wrong when he said that many of the characteristics which animals have are due to some accident in the process of their formation . . . he was unaware that the seed which gives rise to the animal must to begin with have the appropriate specific character; and that the producing agent was preexistent: it was chronologically earlier as well as logically earlier: in other words, men are begotten by men, and therefore the process of the child's formation is what it is because its parent was a man.'[131] Empedocles did not know that the εἶδος of an animal is predetermined through its λόγος.[132]

Guthrie rejects Aristotle's metaphysics of form and substance, because he believes it to be incompatible with evolution, which he understands exclusively in terms of prior conditions and influences, without regard to formal or final causes.[133] Aristotle does allow a certain role to the efficient and material causes in determining some incidental aspects of an organism: the 'conditions' (παθήματα) in respect of which the parts of animals differ. Thus while the existence and the formation of the eye is for the sake of a definite purpose, because it is in accordance with the λόγος of the individual, the fact that it has a certain colour, however, does not serve a particular purpose; it is incidental to its essence and must of necessity (ἐξ ἀνάγκης) be traced back to its matter and moving cause.[134] In a detailed discussion in *De Anima*, Aristotle distinguishes the difference between explanations in terms of material and final causes.[135] In a distinction, which recalls Socrates' contrasting accounts of his presence in prison, he considers two possible explanations of anger. The διαλεκτικός will respond that it is a craving for retaliation, giving thus an account of its form and essence (εἶδος καὶ τὸν λόγον . . . τοῦ πράγματος). The φύσικος will reply that it is a surging of the blood and heat around the heart, an explanation in terms of ὕλη. The real philosopher of nature will include both in his definition. There is no doubt, however, which is the more significant for Aristotle.

Aristotle, Evolution and Modern Biology

Given the fact of evolution, it is incumbent to ask: Can it be explained by the principles of Aristotle? Is there place for form, or does 'evolution of form' equate to its denial?[136] The notion of 'evolving essence' seems intuitively to contradict the very definition of essence itself. It is necessary to recall the primacy of the natural before the logical; Aristotle was a keen student of nature, and was guided by the actions and operations exhibited by living things. How would he interpret the data of modern biology? I propose the following interpretation in Aristotelian terms, retaining the central, but extended role of form. A living individual is a unitary, single, substance; it is not, however, simple but is itself composed of multiple ingredient components, determined by their own formal structure: atoms, molecules, cells, minerals, and so forth, each of which retains its own identity even though subordinate, perhaps suspended, in the overall service of the organism. Aristotle himself notes that while the elements do not actually persist in a compound, 'neither are they destroyed or altered… for their power is preserved (σώζεται γὰρ ἡ δύναμις αὐτων).'[137] Commenting on this text Aquinas notes that 'The *forms* of the elements are present in compounds not actually but virtually.'[138] The individual is thus determined not only by its own substantial form, but embraces within itself a multiplicity of subsidiary forms, which retain the power of their specific nature. William A. Wallace's use of the term 'natural form', as distinct from 'substantial form', is appropriate to denote these subordinate forms.[139] The individual organism may be viewed as a single substance, governed by a unifying substantial form, but comprising a diversity of parts and elementary constituents which are determined in turn by their own natural forms; the organism is itself composed of a plurality of unities. Substantial form is the coalescent principle of a vast diversity within the individual; it is a unity of unities. Darwin himself aptly remarks: 'An organic being is a microcosm – a little universe, formed of a host of self-propagating organisms, inconceivably minute and numerous as the stars in heaven.'[140]

From the point of view of heredity, and therefore of evolution, most important among the constituent elements within the makeup of the parent are the gene cells. While in one sense dependent upon the entire body for their existence and sustenance, they have an autonomous identity of their own. They carry *in nuce* the elements which, combined from both parents, form the new and unique offspring; Aristotle, needless to say, was ignorant of gene cells. In the *Generation of Animals*, he outlines in detail the roles of semen and menses, which he believed to be the active and passive factors in generation. According to Aristotle, the active element within semen is the living heat of pneuma, endowed with the actuality to enact the movements required for the generation of new offspring. The bodily aspect of semen as such (το σῶμα) plays no part; the active cause (ἡ ποιοῦσα) is the power and movement it contains (ἐν αὐτῷ δύναμις καὶ κίνησις).[141] As Montgomery Furth explains, 'Aristotle's hypothesis is that there is in the semen, not the form itself, nor any portion destined to become the form, but the power of constructing new individuals *of* that form. The nature of this power is informational (thus it is frequently referred to as a logos, a formula) . . . the semen is several times referred to as having in it the "logos *of* these movements", for which various analogies can be found elsewhere in the natural world, but whose operation here is nevertheless *sui generis*.'[142] The semen therefore is as it were, in Gotthelf's phrase, an 'internal transmitter'.[143] As an intermediary or instrumental cause in the process of reproduction, semen is possessed of its own power and nature, separate and distinct from those of the father, the external agent.

Like all instrumental agents, semen acts in virtue of its own powers and natures, distinct from those of the principal cause. From genetics we know that the gene cells of the parent, that is, those which determine and transmit the DNA of the offspring, can possess major differences to those of the parent. Hereditary information is carried by the sequence of nucleotides whose groupings as genes form the DNA molecule.[144] Gene cells are subject to mutation: by radiation, for example, from the external environment; or endosomatically through the action of chemicals within the body itself. All that is required for mutation to take place in the gene cell is the change of a single nucleotide; this suffices to provide the code for a new protein. If the new genetic structure in time becomes predominant within the gene pool, the way is open for evolution of the species itself. In light of Guthrie's dismissal of Aristotelian form as incompatible with Darwinian evolution, it is ironically indicative both of the pace of scientific discovery, as well as a more refined historical appreciation, that many biologists today regard the discovery of DNA – the strongest vindication of evolution – as a more accurate elaboration of Aristotelian form.

Although Aristotle never espoused it, his metaphysics is, I suggest, with certain modifications, compatible with evolution, understood as the development of virtualities latent within specific form. This would entail extending the meaning of potency beyond individual members of the species, viewed in isolation, to the prospective potency of the entire species, that is, beyond the phenotype to the genotype and genepool itself. Such evolution would be governed for Aristotle by a 'teleonomy' rooted in the bond between formal and final causes, and influenced by the external circumstances of generation. This, admittedly, would involve a refocus of explanation. It would require, analogously, a shift away from a 'pangenetic' view of form, in which species as a whole are already globally preformed, to an 'epigenetic' unfolding of new forms, present within the deep potency of the genotype. Despite Guthrie's suggestion of a Platonic prejudice, there is nothing fundamentally uncongenial in Aristotle's metaphysical thought to prevent us from incorporating an evolution of species in the light of modern discoveries. This would not be a violation of his thought, but rather a response to his deepest metaphysical intuitions and attitude to nature, as well as his scientific spirit, that is, the desire to submit to the empirical evidence and shape one's vision accordingly.

The single greatest stumbling block in attempting to incorporate evolution into Aristotle's world is the fixity of species – for the Philosopher a preordained goal of cosmic, even transcendent significance. The primary aim of all living things is to replicate their type faithfully through reproduction, thus guaranteeing the perpetuity of the species. This results from the primitive impulse in all things to persist in being. Aristotle declares: 'Being is better than not-being, and living than non-living.'[145] This, he affirms, is the radical reason for male and female: unable to live eternally as individuals, living beings strive to maintain their class (γένος) and species (εἶδος) through the process of generation. To deviate from specific form would be entirely contrary to this purpose, and confer no advantage. In the context of modern biology, however, one might recognize that the drive for perpetuity operates not only within the species, composed of discrete and autonomous individuals (men, horses, parrots and so forth), but throughout all subsidiary life-forms. (Dawkins merely substitutes the selfish gene for Aristotle's singleminded species – the opposite extreme.) Aristotle's observations focused on living things as whole and complete substances; εἶδος determines the individual and orders it within its class, which in turn it aims to perpetuate. I have suggested that in modern biology natural form is seen to operate not only at the over-arching and all-commanding level of complete substance, but also throughout the diverse range of lesser structures and determinations which cohere in substance. Heredity is not dependent upon the agency of the individual, but is determined by the genetic cells.

Genes have their *eidos*, but are open to mutation. By recognizing *eidos* as operative at this level we can integrate Aristotle's metaphysics and the theory of evolution; interpreted in this manner, Aristotelian form thus contributes to the mutational mechanism of evolution. Here we can meet the objection against the concept of 'evolving essence': it is in the nature of genes to adapt and mutate, while still performing their stable function of transmitting the code of life. In the universal context of whole and complete substances, it is a discovery of modern genetics that all living beings are fundamentally related. Aristotle's fixity of species is no longer tenable; in the light of the evidence, however, the principles of his metaphysics acquire new verification and relevance.

The notion of Aristotelian form thus continues to perform an indispensable role within contemporary biology, a timeless revenant defying all attempts to have it banished.[146] The abiding and actual relevance of Aristotelian εἶδος is clearly expressed by Ernst Mayr, who suggests that we substitute modern terms such as 'genetic program':

> One of the reasons why Aristotle has been so consistently misunderstood is that he uses the term *eidos* for his form-giving principle, and everybody took it for granted that he had something in mind similar to Plato's concept of *eidos*. Yet the context of Aristotle's discussions makes it abundantly clear that *his eidos* is something totally different from Plato's *eidos* (I myself did not understand this until recently). Aristotle saw with extraordinary clarity that it made no more sense to describe living organisms in terms of mere matter than to describe a house as a pile of bricks and mortar. Just as the blueprint used by the builder determines the form of a house, so does the *eidos* (in its Aristotelian definition) give the form to the developing organism, and this *eidos* reflects the terminal *telos* of the full-grown individual.[147]

It is not possible, however, to simply equate *eidos* with DNA, as perhaps implied by Mayr. DNA is present in every cell of the body, yet each organ develops differently; this would be impossible if they were following the same program. There is a higher level of organization which governs the genetic program and translates the blueprint into the construction process of the organism. The gene, furthermore, is a dependent part within the overall makeup of the parent, yet has a certain autonomy and individual identity. No single part controls the whole, and while the individual unites all its parts and constituent elements within itself, it does not entirely dominate them – heredity is independent of the parent. Multiple forms of organization, with overlapping but distinct roles, must therefore be affirmed; there is a diversity of εἴδη within the individual. Aristotle's attention was on the single, all-enveloping, form which determines complete substance. This is admirably conveyed in *Parts of Animals*, in the continuation of the famous passage, referred to earlier, which expresses his basic scientific motivation and attitude:

> When any one of the parts or structures, be it which it may, is under discussion, it must not be supposed that it is its material composition to which attention is being directed or which is the object of the discussion, but rather the total form. Similarily, the true object of architecture is not bricks, mortar or timber, but the house; and so the principal object of natural philosophy is not the material elements, but their composition, and the totality of the substance, independently of which they have no existence.[148]

Substantial form is not the only one, but it is the most important. Aristotle's εἶδος retains its explanatory role. Many evolutionary authors have a comparable principle in mind when they reject extreme reductionism, arguing instead for a holistic, integrative biology.[149] They place the organism, rather than the gene, at the centre of life, and aim at 'Making Biology Whole Again'.[150] Stephen Jay Gould (a self-professed 'dyed-in-the-wool Darwinist') rejects Dawkins's 'ultimate (and logically false) reductionism to the selfish gene', emphasizing that natural selection is 'a hierarchical process working simultaneously at several levels of Darwinian individuality (from genes to organisms to demes to species to clades)'.[151] There are distinct degrees of irreducible organization and complexity, none of which can be reduced to its lower elements. Using a very simple illustration, Steven Rose (from a proclaimed materialist perspective), explains how the physiology of a frog's leap 'requires a set of irreducible organizing relations' which are absent from either the biochemistry or chemistry involved; it is a case, he states, of the whole being more than its parts.[152] He declares: 'Each level of organization of the universe has its own meanings, which disappear at lower levels.'[153] Noting, moreover, that 'Every molecule, every organelle, every cell, is in a constant state of flux, of formation, transformation and renewal', he concludes, in words echoing the metaphysics of Aristotle: 'Dynamic stability of form persists, although every constituent of that form has been replaced.'[154]

Taking his cue from Karl Popper,[155] who argued for what he called 'active Darwinism' – the living organism 'helping to determine its own fate by itself challenging and modifying its environment to meet its own needs'[156] – Rose emphasizes that living things are not merely products of their environment, but firstly wholes which themselves influence in turn their own environment. Stuart Kaufmann likewise claims that besides random mutation and natural selection, self-organization plays an important part in the evolutionary process.[157] That there are different *levels* of biological identity and function accords with our earlier suggestion, in Aristotelian terms, that as well as the all-enveloping, singular and unitary form of the individual, there are lower or subsidiary levels of formal determination and organization. The term 'holon', adapted by Arthur Koestler from the Greek ὅλον,[158] is particularly suited to convey the role of such lesser, relatively independent sub-wholes, complete in themselves yet open to further determination as elements within a higher totality; it is an apt substitution for subsidiary 'form'.[159] The ontological unity of the universe is thus, as Rose puts it, 'a nested hierarchy of holons'.[160]

In light of the intrinsic connection for Aristotle between formal and final causality, it will be of further interest to refer to a daring suggestion that evolution is not entirely bereft of inherent directionality. This has arisen from laboratory experiments by the microbiologist Barry G. Hall of the University of Connecticut, published in 1982 in an article entitled 'Evolution on a Petri Dish'.[161] Hall deleted from the bacteria *E. coli* the structural gene which enables it to metabolize lactose (milk sugar), and then challenged these bacteria to grow on a culture of lactose.[162] Initially they were unable to grow, since they could not produce the enzyme needed to digest the sugar. After 9 days, however, strains of bacteria emerged which, contrary to expectation, metabolized the lactose. It appears that the bacteria reconstructed the code from the missing gene by manipulating another dormant or 'cryptic' gene, thereby bringing about a mutation in an existing enzyme so that it could perform the function of the one deleted. Crucially another, prior, mutation was also needed, namely in the gene which *regulated* the dormant gene. According to Hall, the random chance that both mutations would occur together in the same bacterium was 1 in 10^{18}, which in normal conditions, he calculated, would require 100,000 years; it had ocurred in 9 days. Hall declared: 'We can only conclude that under some conditions spontaneous mutations are not independent events – heresy, I am aware.'[163]

The results of this accelerated and artificial sequence of enforced 'evolution' offer the strongest evidence that, contrary to Neo-Darwinian orthodoxy, these mutations were far from random, that is, unrelated to the individual, but were clearly directed to the organism's benefit. Although Hall's conclusion has been challenged, his critics were obliged to accept the much higher frequency of favorable mutations under controlled conditions.[164] If vindicated, the recognition of such 'directed mutations' would lend empirical weight to Aristotle's conviction of internal finality within the organism itself in the ineradicable bond between formal and final causes.

Having attempted to defend the indispensable role of form, there remains the pertinent question: What *is* form? How is it to be defined? Need we affirm, for example, in every human a *homunculus*, as some early users of the microscope imagined they saw in spermatozoa? Are we committed to some mysterious principle such as Bergson's *élan vital*, or the immaterial entelechy of Hans Driesch's vitalism? Εἶδος, for Aristotle, is indeed ἐντελέχεια, that is, completeness or perfection; form is determined actuality. What does this tell us? What is the reality of form which actualizes and determines one individual living being to be a human being, another a parrot? Where does it reside? I suggest that while this is a pressing and legitimate question, it is not one which needs to be fully resolved in order to justify the validity of what is asserted. In other words, we may affirm the reality of form although we do not fully grasp its nature. It is sufficient to point to its effects and operations, that is, the actions of the individual substance which proceed from it. Substances are known through their actions, since these reveal how something actualizes itself according to a determinate mode of being.

Form is the real and actualizing principle which determines the essences of things. A helpful scientific parallel is the synonymous term 'structure'. Quantum mechanics affirms the existence of elementary particles and assigns to them very definite characteristics which can be identified and measured; they are distinguished from one another by their different roles and behaviour.[165] Each particle has its particular specificity: electric charge, mass, spin, location within a range of time and place and so forth. As we proceed to higher modes of being or essence, it becomes increasingly more difficult to delimit structure. Uniqueness is more easily recognized, but less easily measured. Individuality is clearer the more perfect the substance, but yields less readily to investigation. Substances become more inscrutable with the increase of selfhood or inner complexity.

The example of the comparatively stable knowledge which the physical sciences have of elementary particles, allied with the continuity and differences which obtain among distinct modes of being, allows us analogously to conclude that higher modes of life equally have an intrinsic structure and specificity, proper to their kind, which is the ground of the actions and operations which they exercise. Substances of different kinds act in different ways; thus diverse actions reveal diverse modes of substance, although they do not disclose them entirely or exhaustively. Aristotle distinguishes between living organisms on the basis of their proper powers: plants exhibit the fundamental powers of nutrition, growth and reproduction; in addition, animals enjoy motion and sensation; humans have intellection and will. Nevertheless, with respect to the immediate object of knowledge, the principle inevitably holds true: *individuum est ineffabile*. Our knowledge is indeed limited and deficient, yet adequate for us in the concrete to distinguish amongst different kinds of essence by virtue of their characteristic operations.[166]

Does this commit us to the 'essentialism' condemned by W.V. Quine?[167] In his own words, 'This is the doctrine that some attributes of a thing (quite independently of the language in which the thing is referred to, if at all) may be essential to the thing, and others accidental.' Most likely, but it is a charge one may carry lightly. Are not some accidents indeed more important to an individual's essence than others? Is it not more important to humans that they are rational than to have feet? It is moreover a necessary stratagem in mapping the world through human knowledge. Εἶδος is the object of Aristotelian νοῦς,[168] but it can only work through abstractive insight and distinction: by isolating some features of the object as referentially more significant than innumerable others. This was but another of Aristotle's insights which may not be easily discarded.[169]

In an exhaustive and well-grounded study, the German scholar Johannes Hübner compellingly argues that soul is to be understood as *activity*.[170] He takes this suggestion from Aristotle's illustration in *De Anima* 2, 1, of the two senses of ἐντελέχεια by the analogous distinction between ἐπιστήμη and θεωρεῖν, knowledge as possession or disposition, and knowledge as the very act of knowing itself. Going beyond the standard interpretation of soul as prerequisite of action, he suggests that the very essence of soul is activity. Representative of the 'traditional interpretation' is D.W. Hamlyn: 'The soul is actuality only as *hexis*, i.e. in a dispositional way, since something may still be alive when asleep and not *doing* something.'[171] Of the authors cited in the present study, we can cite James Lennox, who understands Aristotelian soul to be 'a unified set of goal-oriented capacities – nutritive, reproductive, locomotive, and cognitive'.[172] A disposition, however, is by definition itself a potency and therefore dependent on a more primitive actuality. In the example employed by Hamlyn, it is not enough to say that while something is asleep, it is not '*doing* anything'; quite to the contrary, it is very active indeed: it is alive. To be alive is its manner of being. In a significant phrase (not invoked by Hübner), Aristotle declares that 'to be alive' is itself the very being of living things: τὸ δὲ ζῆν τοῖς ζῶσι τὸ εἶναί ἐστιν, αἰτία δὲ καὶ ἀρχὴ τούτου ἡ ψυχή.[173] This is underpinned moreover by Aristotle's statement in *Metaphysics* 12, that God's act of thinking is his very life and actuality, that is, his being: ἡ γὰρ νοῦ ἐνέργεια ζωή, ἐκεῖνος

179

δὲ ἡ ἐνέργεια.[174] Risking what may seem an apparent tautlogy, actuality is the primary reality of anything. This happens for each being in the measure of its form – in the case of living things, according to their soul.

It is easier in this context to understand why Aristotle, having distinguished in the *Metaphysics* between motions (κινήσεις) which are incomplete (ἀτελεῖς), and activities (ἐνέργειαι) which contain within themselves their own completion and fulfilment (ἐντελέχειαι), declares: 'It is therefore evident that substance and form are actuality (ἐνέργεια).'[175] The sheer activity of an act of contemplation (θεωρεῖν) does not seek fulfilment beyond itself in the further discovery of truth, thereby actualizing residual potential, but rests in the enjoyment of an insight already attained; likewise the actuality of substantial form is already complete in itself, as the fundamental and completed actualization of matter which it constitutes as an individual. (This is not to deny the potency which characterizes all beings other than the First Mover; each being is open to new actualizations, but not at the basic level of form. While I continually realize latent potencies, I cannot become a human being to a higher degree; as Aristotle notes in the *Categories*, there are no grades of substantiality.) We may also grasp the definition of form as activity in light of the discoveries of particle physics. The structures of subatomic particles are not inert, but consist of energy; the basic building blocks of the material world undergo endless recombinations, but retain clear levels of identity, recognized by their dynamic inner activity.

Careful not to confuse act with movement in suggesting that form is activity, it is equally important to grasp the analogical nature of actuality. The act of the soul in actualizing the body is not the same kind as the act of contemplation exercised by the soul, but of a prior order. The concept of actuality is itself fundamental and cannot be further analyzed into any notion more elementary. It coincides with our basic grasp of being; for Aristotle, actuality is the primary sense of reality.[176] Form is primary actuality – activity – , not in the existential order, but in the order of essence or modality; it signifies the *modus agendi* according to which each thing exists. For reasons which lie beyond our present scope, modes of being, that is, essences, are themselves potential with respect to the primary, actualizing, power or presence of existence; form is thus, consequent upon existence, the secondary activity of beings, causing each thing, not radically *to be* (that is, in the primary sense of *exist*), but to be *what* it is: determining its essence or τὸ τί ἦν εἶναι.[177]

We must recognize here the inevitable limits of our knowledge; since we have no direct, illuminative, knowledge of forms or souls, the best we can do is describe them in terms of the most revealing and perfect attributes which they exhibit, elucidated through the fundamental concepts at our disposal. Such knowledge is of its nature deficient. It is not possible (in Leibniz's phrase – misattributed to Bacon, whose motive he thereby sought to praise)[178] to put nature 'on the rack' and with screws to wrest her secrets. As Goethe saw, 'Nature falls silent under torture.'[179] It is not within our power, in words of the Bard, to 'pluck out the heart of mystery'; yet, as Aristotle recognized, the occasional and scanty insights we attain of profound realities are more worthy than the detailed knowledge afforded by the senses.

Aristotle's biology provided a richness of experience and insight which greatly nourished his metaphysics; his metaphysics provides, in turn, a deeper dimension and perspective within which to understand and evaluate the undercurrents which inwardly sustain living things in their operations. Aristotle's metaphysics offers perennial insights which are of fundamental value to human experience and which are necessary if the life sciences are themselves to be adequately articulated – even if such insights themselves lie beyond the scope of science. As a scientist of abiding relevance and perennial philosopher par excellence, his wisdom is a valuable guide in assessing whatever theories may emerge regarding man and the cosmos. Leibniz declared that Aristotle's utterances regarding the basic concepts of natural philosophy were 'for the most part entirely true'.[180] Henri Bergson states that if we remove from Aristotle's philosophy everything derived from poetry, religion and social life, as well as from a somewhat rudimentary physics and biology, we are left with the grand framework of a metaphysics which, he believes, is the natural metaphysics of the human intellect.[181] These views echo the opinion of Aquinas, according to whom the characteristic of Aristotle is never to depart from the obvious.[182]

The preceding reflections have been concerned in the first place with εἶδος as an undeniable principle of being, verified analogously at diverse levels of reality; and secondarily with the theory of evolution, insofar as it explains the emergence of multitudinous life-forms. My belief in the validity of Aristotle's insight was strengthened by an experience far removed from philosophic speculation regarding the metaphysical origins of biodiversity. I visited the Lebanon shortly after the civil war. After years of relentless destruction Beirut was an overpowering shock to the senses and an assault on one's comprehension: bombed-out buildings, their façades shrapnel-scarred, stood desolate amongst charred surroundings, pitiably ironic monuments to the failure of human purpose. It was at the time the biggest building site in the world and also – given the many-layered civilizations (Phoenician, Greek, Roman, Byzantine, Medieval) being unearthed – the greatest archaeological site. The most striking story I heard concerned the excavation of a Roman site. The archaeologist was distressed when the contents of a jar were accidentally spilt. When it rained, corn began to sprout – after 2000 years! This suitably Aristotelian chance event provided, to my mind, a striking illustration of what Aristotle meant by φύσις or nature, the 'something extra' (ἕτερόν τι),[183] – however one chooses to name it: εἶδος, vital principle, *élan vital* – which abides deeply within all living things and which distinguishes them from the inanimate. Another picture stays in my mind – a mature tree growing from the balcony of a wrecked and tangled building, germinated years earlier from a seed blown by the wind or carried by a bird. Life defiantly asserts itself after a gap of two millennia in the fire and flare of man's folly and destruction. Despite the tragic consequences of human deliberation perhaps we can after all share in Aristotle's optimism that Nature is not in herself a malign tragedy and does nothing in vain.

8

EVOLUTIONARY ETHICS
A METAPHYSICAL EVALUATION

'The *Origin of Species* introduced a mode of thinking that in the end was bound to transform the logic of knowledge, and hence the treatment of morals, politics and religion.'

John Dewey[1]

'Darwin's theory has no more to do with philosophy than any other hypothesis in natural science.'

Ludwig Wittgenstein[2]

'One's only owned by naturel rejection. Charley, you're my darwing. So sing they sequent the assent of man.'

James Joyce[3]

Evolution is the prevailing paradigm for today's understanding of human nature. It is championed by some not only as a biological explanation for the origin and unity of living beings, but as a response to all questions of human life and the universe itself, as well as its purpose – or absence thereof. It is rejected by others, who fear that acceptance of the biological theory of evolution entails a naturalistic vision of the world, and of man as a product of nature no different from other animals. Both see in evolutionary theory the equivalent of a metaphysical claim to total explanation. Ethics unsurprisingly has been brought into engagement with evolution, in both dialogue and dispute. Systematic attempts have been made by some theorists to ground morality entirely upon evolutionary principles. Evolution, it is claimed, is the key to all moral questions; ethical norms are laws of evolution: biology is our destiny, morality 'a legacy of evolution'.[4] Others fear that evolutionary interpretations of human nature must inevitably lead to the obliteration of uniquely human morality. In this essay I propose to outline one twentieth-century approach to evolutionary ethics and examine some assumptions of evolutionary theory that have a bearing upon the ethical evaluation of man. Although I will not explicitly develop the context in detail, my evaluative comments are largely from an Aristotelian viewpoint. The wider perspective is that of the question of being, which features neither in Aristotle nor in evolutionary theory, but which must finally be confronted to respond ultimately to the ethical question. My wider theme is thus the metaphysical background to the intersection of ethics and evolution.[5]

EVOLUTIONARY ETHICS OF SOCIOBIOLOGY

Among Darwin's disciples who have in recent decades sought to ground ethics upon the biological theory of evolution, the most prominent has been Edward O. Wilson, a renowned Harvard entomologist; other well-known representatives are Michael Ruse and Richard Dawkins.[6] In 1975 Wilson published his monumental work *Sociobiology: The New Synthesis*, which defined sociobiology as 'the systematic study of the biological basis of all social behavior'.[7] His aim was to lay bare the biological underpinnings of animal behavior and to apply these to man. This was a revolutionary renewal, following upon the Modern Synthesis which a generation earlier had fortified Darwinism with the insights of molecular genetics. The new discipline of sociobiology sought to integrate the social and human sciences into evolutionary theory. Novelist Tom Wolfe proclaimed: 'There is a new Darwin. His name is Edward O. Wilson.'[8] Having catalogued in great detail the 'social' features of animal behaviour, in the final chapter Wilson applied his conclusions to *homo sapiens*: all human behaviour, including morality and religion, is based upon genetics. Sociobiology was founded on the conviction that behaviour may be explained in terms of basic universal features of human nature laid down by evolution. The implications for moral philosophy are stark, the claim is ambitious: 'Scientists and humanists should consider together the possibility that the time has come for ethics to be removed temporarily from the hands of philosophers and biologicized.'[9]

By presenting a selection of passages from the authors under consideration I will first outline the claims of evolutionary ethics. One of the attractions of their writing, frequently lacking in mainstream philosophers, is its clarity; Wilson twice won the Pulitzer Prize for General Nonfiction.[10] In the opening paragraphs of *On Human Nature*, written as a popular introduction to sociobiology, he summarizes the essentials of his evolutionary naturalism: 'If humankind evolved by Darwinian natural selection, genetic chance and environmental necessity, not God, made the species… The human mind is a device for survival and reproduction, and reason is just one of its various techniques… The intellect was not constructed to understand atoms or even to understand itself but to promote the survival of human genes.'[11] Michael Ruse expresses the consequence for ethics: 'The position of the modern evolutionist is that humans have an awareness of morality – a sense of right and wrong and a feeling of obligation to be thus governed – because such an awareness is of biological worth. Morality is a biological adaptation no less than are hands and feet and teeth… Morality is just an aid to survival and reproduction, and has no being beyond or without this.'[12] In *Sociobiology* Wilson contends that ethical knowledge and motivation have a physiological source: 'The hypothalamic-limbic complex of a highly social species, such as man, "knows," or more precisely it has been programmed to perform as if it knows, that its underlying genes will be proliferated maximally only if it orchestrates behavioral responses that bring into play an efficient mixture of personal survival, reproduction, and altruism.'[13] Science, according to Wilson, has supreme authority in matters of human destiny:

> I consider the scientific ethos superior to religion: its repeated triumphs in explaining and controlling the physical world; its self-correcting nature open to all competent to devise and conduct the tests; its readiness to examine all subjects sacred and profane; and now the possibility of explaining traditional religion by the mechanistic models of evolutionary biology. The last achievement will be crucial. If religion, including the dogmatic secular ideologies, can be systematically analyzed and explained as a product of the brain's evolution, its power as an external source of morality will be gone forever.[14]

All human activities, including the most lofty, function in the service of genetic evolution: 'If the brain evolved by natural selection, even the capacities to select particular esthetic judgments and religious beliefs must have arisen by the same mechanistic process. They are either direct adaptations to past environments in which the ancestral human populations evolved or at most constructions thrown up secondarily by deeper, less visible activities that were once adaptive in this stricter, biological sense.'[15]

Physiologically the most important organ, 'the brain is a machine of ten billion nerve cells and the mind can somehow be explained as the summed activity of a finite number of chemical and electrical reactions.'[16] But, states Wilson: 'More to the point, the hypothalamus and limbic systems are engineered to perpetuate DNA.'[17] All physiological and cerebral reality and activity are conceived exclusively in the service of purposeless evolution. Ruse states: 'Vanity and ignorance alone support the claim that human reason has a privileged status. Because we are the product of a long, directionless, evolutionary process, we are forced to accept that there is something essentially contingent about our most profound claims.'[18] Evolution is everything; there is no purpose beyond the evolutionary process: 'No species, ours included, possesses a purpose beyond the imperatives created by its genetic history. Species may have vast potential for material and mental progress but they lack any immanent purpose of guidance from agents beyond their immediate environment or even an evolutionary goal toward which their molecular architecture automatically steers them.'[19] Briefly for Wilson: 'The species lacks any goal external to its own biological nature.'[20] Richard Dawkins spells it out: 'We are survival machines – robot vehicles blindly programmed to preserve the selfish molecules known as genes... We, and all other animals, are machines created by our genes.'[21] Dawkins claims that the world is void of all purpose whatsoever, and draws the following conclusion: 'In a universe of electrons and selfish genes, blind physical forces and genetic replication, some people are going to get hurt, other people are going to get lucky, and you won't find any rhyme or reason in it, nor any justice. The universe that we observe has precisely the properties we should expect if there is, at bottom, no design, no purpose, no evil and no good, nothing but pitiless indifference.'[22]

Ultimately and solely important for sociobiology is the perpetuation of genes. They are the units of natural selection and have evolved to manipulate the individuals – 'gigantic, lumbering robots'[23] – in which they dwell; the gene, and not the individual, is paramount. If we are nothing more than an aggregate of cells and molecules, what of personal identity and free will? Why be moral? What it is to be moral? The response of Wilson, Ruse, and Dawkins is consistent: the origin, purpose, and content of morality are likewise a function of the genetic imperative: morality is a mechanism inherited from biology to ensure the survival of genetic material into the future. Genes alone are of enduring value and purpose; the individual and the group are too large to be units of natural selection. Dawkins states: 'The genes are the immortals ... genetic entities that come close to deserving the title. We, the individual survival machines in the world, can expect to live a few more decades. But the genes in the world have an expectation of life that must be measured not in decades but in thousands and millions of years... Genes are denizens of geological time: genes are forever.'[24] Morality is necessary for the continued success of evolution. Ruse and Wilson assert: 'As evolutionists, we see that no justification of the traditional kind is possible. Morality, or more strictly our belief in morality, is merely an adaptation put in place to further our reproductive ends. Hence the basis of ethics does not lie in God's will or any other part of the framework of the Universe. In an important sense, ethics as we understand it is an illusion fobbed off on us by our genes to get us to cooperate. It is without external grounding. Ethics is produced by evolution but not justified by it, because, like Macbeth's dagger, it serves a powerful purpose without existing in substance.'[25] According to Michael Ruse: 'The time has come to take seriously the fact that we humans are modified monkeys, not the favored Creation of a Benevolent God on the Sixth Day. In particular, we must recognize our biological past in trying to understand our interactions with others. We must think again especially about our so-called "ethical principles." The question is not whether biology – specifically, our evolution – is connected with ethics, but how.'[26]

According to Wilson and Ruse, morality exerts its biological imperative through what are termed 'epigenetic rules', laws that have grown accumulatively over evolutionary time. These rules have 'proven their adaptive worth in the struggle for existence';[27] they constitute the 'hereditary regularities of mental development'.[28] The principles governing logical deduction, scientific induction, mathematics, science, religion, and ethics are 'rooted in our biology' and are justified by their adaptive value to our proto-human ancestors.[29] The methods of investigation, analysis, inference, judging, and reaching conclusions evolved epigenetically and were inherited by us; they were obeyed by our ancestors because of their selective advantage and survival benefit. Ruse illustrates this, for example, with hypothetical alternative reactions by our ancestors to the threat of tigers: those who reasoned correctly survived, thus validating the reasoning patterns they had obeyed, which were in turn transmitted to their descendants.[30]

Morality is adaptively useful; it is a function of genetic survival, governed by rules of biology. Genes dominate morality and keep cultural evolution under control. Wilson sums up the relationship between nature, nurture, culture, and morality:

> Can the cultural evolution of higher ethical values gain a direction and momentum of its own and completely replace genetic evolution? I think not. The genes hold culture on a leash. The leash is very long, but inevitably values will be constrained in accordance with their effects on the human gene pool. The brain is a product of evolution. Human

behavior – like the deepest capacities for emotional response which drive and guide it – is the circuitous technique by which human genetic material has been and will be kept intact. Morality has no other demonstrable ultimate function.[31]

I will argue that sociobiology is marked by various deficiencies, methodological and doctrinal. Before I assess the theory from different theoretical points of view, it is worth noting the dearth of references to the historical tradition. In *Sociobiology*, Wilson limits his discussion to the 'oddly disjunct conceptualizations' of intuitionism ('the belief that the mind has a direct awareness of true right and wrong'), and behaviourism ('moral commitment is entirely learned, with operant conditioning being the dominant mechanism'). Both approaches, he charges, neglect the 'genetic evolution of ethics', despite the fact that proponents are obliged to consult and interpret the 'emotive centers of their own hypothalamic-limbic system'. In *Consilience* Wilson considers the alternatives of transcendentalism and empiricism. Dawkins confidently dismisses the entire tradition: 'There is such a thing as being just plain wrong, and that is what, before 1859, all answers to those questions were.'[32] Since the luminaries of the philosophical tradition knew nothing of evolution or the selfish gene, their ethical theories may be dismissed as worthless: philosophers speak in paradigms lost. [33]

ARISTOTLE AND SOCIOBIOLOGY

Surprising is the absence in the literature of sociobiology of all reference to Aristotle, founder of biology and author of the first ethical treatises, regarded by Darwin as his greatest master. On the biological level, Aristotle can readily accommodate many aspects of sociobiology. While he did not teach a theory of evolution, he recognizes a scale of perfection within the biological world that, if reconfigured as a temporal progression toward higher perfection, provides elements of an evolutionary theory.[34] Moreover, in the *History of Animals*, an impressive catalogue of zoological fieldwork, Aristotle recognizes affinities between animals and man, especially in the emotions and passions:

For even the other animals mostly possess traces of the characteristics to do with the soul, such as present differences more obviously in the case of humans. For tameness and wildness, gentleness and roughness, courage and cowardice, fears and boldnesses, temper and mischievousness are present in many of them together with resemblances of intelligent understanding... For some characters differ by the more-and-less compared with man, as does man compared with a majority of the animals (for certain characters of this kind are present to a greater degree in man, certain others to a greater degree in the other animals), while others differ by analogy.[35]

His remarks on children support the view of sociobiology that human instincts are evident in a primitive form in animals: 'This kind of thing is clearest if we look at the age of childhood; for in children, though one can see as it were traces and seeds of the dispositions that they will have later, yet their soul at this period has practically no difference from that of wild animals, so that it is not illogical if some characters are the same in the other animals, while others are very like, and others are analogous.'[36] Similarities of instinct between children and animals seem to confirm, within an infinitely shorter time frame than that of evolution, the biological affinity between animals and man.

Aristotle recognized the 'social' behaviour of certain species, especially that of hymenoptera (ants, bees, wasps), which sociobiology claims as evidence for primitive altruism. He also documented the social behaviour of cranes as they emigrated from the Scythian steppes to the source of the Nile. As well as a leader, signalers control the flock with whistle calls; when the flock settles and sleeps, the leader keeps watch and cries an alert in case of danger.[37] More importantly he provides an example of mutual utility, of the kind interpreted by sociobiology as 'reciprocal altruism', between the sandpiper and the crocodile: 'When crocodiles gape the sandpipers fly in and clean their teeth, and while they themselves are getting their food the crocodile perceives that he is being benefited and does not harm them, but when he wants them to go he moves his neck so as not to crush them in his teeth.'[38]

SOCIOBIOLOGY AND PHILOSOPHICAL METHOD

The most patent flaw in the approach of sociobiology to moral philosophy is the gratuitous assertion of E.O. Wilson that morality is no longer a matter for philosophy, that its only hope is to be 'biologicized'. Theoretically and historically there is no warrant for this verdict. As a sweeping view it ranks with Wilson's wild assertion: 'The history of philosophy consists largely of failed models of the brain.'[39] Wilson presumes that moral phenomena are no different from biological data, and may be analyzed, interpreted and codified in the same empirical manner. Sociobiology proceeds on the unquestioned assumption that biological evolution is a philosophical panacea. In his popularizing book, *On Human Nature*, Wilson declared: 'Above all, for our own physical well-being if nothing else, ethical philosophy must not be left in the hands of the merely wise.'[40] Peter Singer's reaction is probably typical of philosophers generally: 'Most of my colleagues in university departments of philosophy regard Wilson's invasion of their territory as too absurd to merit a considered response.'[41] Philip Kitcher has remarked: 'Ironically, the very ease with which they come to pronounce on philosophical issues that go beyond their professional expertise tells against their having much influence on our understanding of those issues. Biologists may believe that they have a license to advance views about human freedom and morality without considering what philosophers and other humanists have written about these subjects.'[42]

Theodosius Dobzhansky famously remarked that nothing in biology makes sense except in light of evolution. For sociobiology nothing whatsoever has meaning except in light of evolution: biology itself acquires its value from evolution. In turn it is reduced to physics; despite its nomenclature, the naturalist sociobiology of Wilson, Ruse, and Dawkins assumes that the entire realm of nature is a closed system of material causes and effects, without any possible influence from outside. In his ambition to embrace, harmonize and integrate all scientific approaches into a single synthesis (an approach termed 'consilience'), Wilson advances a strongly materialist position: 'The central idea of the consilience world view is that all tangible phenomena, from the birth of stars to the workings of social institutions, are based on material processes and are ultimately reducible . . . to the laws of physics.'[43]

191

Sociobiology is emphatically and exclusively materialist.[44] As a philosophical doctrine this exceeds the competence of biological science.

One marvels at the confidence with which biologists such as Wilson and Dawkins make grand pronouncements about the ultimate meaning of the biological universe and the purpose of human existence.[45] Science conventionally concerns itself with causes and operations within the observable world.[46] Its methods are empirical, its explanations formulated in theories that appeal to measurable data. Its own validity is a question for philosophy of science. Sociobiology has adopted the ambitious aim of incorporating all knowledge whatsoever under the mantle of consilience, to be measured by the methods of biology. Wilson proclaims: 'Science offers the boldest metaphysics of the age... There is a general explanation of [the] origin and nature of the human condition, proceeding from the deep history of genetic evolution to modern culture.'[47] Evolution supplies, on this view, the answers to the ultimate questions; it is the key to understand human behaviour, and the perspective to unify all knowledge. Wilson makes no distinction between the scientific insights of the biological theory of evolution, and the philosophical implications of the theory for man's nature and origin.[48]

The theory of evolution is indisputably of immeasurable value in the life sciences, but the wider question of its profound meaning goes beyond science. It becomes itself an *explanandum* within the broader context of philosophical reflection. Because of its object and method, science is obliged to adopt a naturalistic viewpoint: it may not affirm any reality that cannot be measured in terms of space and time. It must follow positivist procedures. When the scientist addresses wider questions, she becomes a philosopher and may not apply the same criteria or means of measurement and investigation. She cannot presume that science has all the answers – or, more importantly, that it asks all the questions. Sociobiology ignores the hierarchy of explanation that reflects irreducible levels of reality; Aristotle was keenly aware of this, as noted by Alasdair MacIntyre: 'His is a universe structured in a hierarchical way – that is why the hierarchical structure of the sciences is appropriate for giving a realist account of such a universe – and each level of the hierarchy provides the matter in and through which the forms of the next higher level actualize and perfect themselves. The physical provides the material for biological formation, the biological the material for human formation. Efficient and material causes serve final and formal causes.'[49]

GENETIC FALLACY

Since evolution has to do with origins and development, to approach human nature in light of evolution is doubtless of great value. Aristotle affirmed: 'He who considers things genetically and originatively will obtain the clearest view of them.'[50] For Aristotle, however, γένεσις/*genesis* is more than a temporal beginning; it connotes nature (φύσις) and growth toward a τέλος or goal, so that a complete understanding of a substance refers to all four causes. Evolution, as generally presented, is concerned with material and efficient causes, neglecting the formal and final principles of explanation. In particular evolutionary ethics collapses the final cause into the circumstances of the genesis of qualities and tendencies that constitute the material for moral activity. Explanation in terms of material and efficient causation are incomplete. In the *De Anima*, Aristotle contrasts the respective approaches of the natural philosopher (φυσικός) and the dialectician (διαλεκτικός) in explaining anger. The latter explains it in terms of its purpose, namely the desire for retaliation, whereas the former describes it as a surging of the blood and heat around the heart. 'The one is describing the matter, the other the form or formula of the essence.'[51] Both accounts are required; each responds at a different level, but the formal account is more meaningful.[52] The naturalist approach to phenomena is a valid but incomplete explanation.[53] On the abandonment of final and formal causes by modern philosophy Stephen Clark notes that what was first a methodological precaution quickly became an ontological assumption. But as Clark tellingly remarks, 'Mathematical formulae have usually been exempt, and beauty keeps breaking in.'[54] Evolutionary theorists eagerly formulate development patterns in sophisticated equations.[55]

As well as reducing all aspects of human nature and behaviour to the biological and material, the sociobiological account of morality is seriously flawed by the restriction of its value to the conditions from which it arose. Evolutionary ethics is guilty of the 'genetic fallacy', as described by Nietzsche in the *Genealogy*: 'The cause of the origin of a thing and its eventual utility (*die Ursache der Entstehung eines Dinges und dessen schliessliche Nützlichkeit*), its actual employment and place in a system of purposes (*dessen tatsächliche Verwendung und Einordnung in ein System von Zwecken*), lie worlds apart; whatever exists, having somehow come into being, is again and again reinterpreted to new ends, taken over, transformed, and redirected by some power superior to it.'[56] Sociobiology substitutes causal conditions for moral reasons. The fact that animal behaviour developed in certain ways is no reason why we should adopt their history as a moral norm for our present and future actions.

Accusing them of the genetic fallacy, Daniel Dennett rejects the claim of Wilson and Ruse that 'morality, or more strictly our belief in morality, is merely an adaptation put in place to further our reproductive ends.'[57] Dennett's reply is simple: 'Nonsense. Our reproductive ends may have been the ends that kept us in the running till we could develop culture, and they may still play a powerful – sometimes overpowering – role in our thinking, but that does not license any conclusion at all about our current values. It does not follow from the fact that our reproductive ends were the ultimate historical source of our present values, that they are the ultimate (and still principal) beneficiary of our ethical actions.'[58] Dennett adds that, once persons are on the scene, they are also potential beneficiaries of biological reproduction: 'Hence the truth of an evolutionary explanation would not show that our allegiance to ethical principles or a "higher code" was an "illusion".'[59] Dennett illustrates his point: 'It is also true that we grew from fish, but our reasons aren't the reasons of fish just because fish are our ancestors.'[60]

There is no doubt but that our biological nature evolved from more basic forms of life. It is equally evident that birds, insects and animals engage in collective behaviour. It is not at all directly evident, however, that the ethical impulse that seems to be innate in most members of the human species has its origin in the collective orientation or 'altruistic' behaviour of those life forms from which mankind evolved. While it would be consistent with the overall pattern of evolutionary development and progress to conjecture that the social behaviour of nonhuman species evolved over time, there is nothing contradictory in the assumption that they might have so behaved from their initial emergence as distinct species. The mother-child bond, for instance, is with few exceptions universal among mammals; did it need to evolve? Reciprocal recognition is instinctive in most species. While we observe some animal kinds acting collectively, many do not: should we expect that they also will eventually evolve social tendencies? *E contrario*, if their survival were thus dependent, they should have long since perished.

PERSONAL MORALITY AND FREEDOM

To accept that we have a genetic propensity to behave morally does not yet explain why we are *obliged* to act morally. Applying Aquinas' comment on the individual nature of knowledge (*hic homo intelligit*), we may affirm: *hic homo deliberat et agit*. Moral action is a matter of personal motivation, resolve, action, responsibility and consequence. It requires a sense of personal identity and continued moral commitment over time. The centre of moral behaviour is the individual person, consciously aware of herself or himself as motivated for individual reasons, and aware of the responsibilities and consequences attending one's actions. A difficulty with evolutionary ethics is its failure to give reasons why we should be moral in the first place; it does not provide any compelling motivation, either positive in terms of reward or negative in terms of sanction. It postulates ethics as a persuasatory strategy inherent in evolutionary progress. I am expected to behave correctly because I thus promote the genetic material of humanity. To what purpose? What is my obligation to posterity – more precisely to the genes for which my descendants are nothing more than carriers? What debt have I to my ancestors, that I should obey the epigenetic rules I have inherited? If I am obligated to human life, the question imposes itself: What is the point of life?

Aristotle's ethics, on the contrary, is immediately appealing because it offers personal reasons and incentives why we should be moral; it is centred upon individual happiness. Rather than ground morality on an impersonal process of species propagation, in which we are insignificant instruments, he recognizes that we are self-conscious individuals with a distinct nature, and a rich potentiality to be freely realized. He accepts the tension between elements of personality, hence the need for moral education. It is a matter of immediate self-experience that we deliberate upon conflicting goals and make free and reflective choices. The motivation is happiness; it is pursued naturally and spontaneously, since the good is what the mind recognizes as desirable. With subtle metaphysical insight, Aristotle defines happiness as the perfect activity of our most human powers; its success is virtue. Virtue depends on us, as does also vice.[61] Aristotle's account reflects real-life experience. We are obliged to make moral choices; other animals do not have reason, do not deliberate or choose.[62] They do not have the power to form universal concepts,[63] and they are incapable of action.[64] We are the only animals that can be happy (μὴ μετέχειν τὰ λοιπὰ ζῷα εὐδαιμονίας).[65] The animal's purpose is life (ζῆν), man's is the good life (τὸ εὖ ζῆν). 'Animals have no share in well-being or in purposive life.'[66]

We may say that for Aristotle, man is essentially ethical. This means both that by nature he tends to act morally, and that the norms of ethical behaviour are embedded in the kind of being that he is. His nature is the source for the capacity and necessity for ethics, as well as the standard that constitutes moral behaviour. Central to Aristotle's ethics is the teleology of human nature, a teleology that is both biological and moral. The distinction of act and potency illumines the distance between man's condition and his goal; it explains the dynamism of action and the weight of obligation. The individual is never all that he can or should be. By nature he is equipped with a definite nature, but one that is never fully determined or complete: that is the task of action and freedom. Morality is the corollary of teleology and a condition for happiness. The individual freely and consciously pursues his natural fulfilment. When early in the *Nicomachean Ethics* Aristotle distinguishes between the various levels of life, beginning with the simple act of plant life, and the sentient life of animals, he refers to the 'practical life of the rational part of man (πρακτική τις τοῦ λόγον ἔχοντος)'.[67] Human practice flows from reason; man seeks reasons for what he does. He is a reason-seeking animal, and acts for reasoned ends.

What is, for Aristotle, the human nature that is the basis of morality? It is evidently complex: most obviously material and biological. At this level, evolutionary theory is enlightening. Man, however, is more than his biology. We behave morally, not because we are programmed to obey an impersonal zoological command, but because as rational agents we recognize that by our actions we choose concretely our individual fulfilment in view of permanent and universal values. As moral agents we discern reasons that justify our actions in accord with demands discerned within our nature, and obligations arising from our relationships. The reduction of moral behaviour to an unconscious biological impetus ignores the evidence of immediate experience: our moral deliberation in the face of ineluctable choices, the awareness that we are in control, and that we choose goals for nonbiological purposes. Life in the concrete is always personal. Each one lives in him- or herself as an individual, neither retrospectively in one's ancestors, nor proleptically in one's genes, or vicariously in one's offspring. It is in each case an individual 'I' who lives, acts, and shapes a personal world. Evolutionary accounts ignore the irreducible element of subjective experience. It is the difference between the detached aspect of the third person as publicly observed, and the inalienable first-person experience, which is *sui generis*, but which each of us knows intimately as inner agent.

Aristotle's agent is individual and free, with a self-contained telos. By contrast, for sociobiology 'the organism does not live for itself. Its primary function is not even to reproduce other organisms; it reproduces genes, and it serves as their temporary carrier... The organism is only DNA's way of making more DNA.'[68] The individual has no intrinsic purpose; it is an instrument to replicate and perpetuate the genes. This is a unidimensional reductionism, that views events entirely in terms of their eventual natural consequences. It places human beings within the confines of biological time, precluding any exploration of a possible nontemporal goal or purpose.

The first victim of such a vision is individual liberty: 'The agent itself is created by the interaction of the genes and the environment. It would appear that our freedom is only a self-delusion.'[69] The inadequacy of evolutionary ethics is evident in the first-person experience each one has as a free and responsible agent. It is beyond doubt that at crucial times in our lives individuals experience the unshirkable weight of choice and dilemmas, without signposts from an evolutionary past. With individual rationality we transcend our biological and cultural heredity and enter the world of personal freedom: 'Men at some time are masters of their fates.'[70]

It is difficult to see how evolutionary ethics can avoid the charge of genetic determinism. Ruse writes: 'As a function of our biology, our moral ideas are thrust upon us, rather than being things needing or allowing decision at the individual level. This is the claim. Just as we have no choice about having four limbs, so we have no choice about the nature of our moral awareness.'[71] It is true that in one sense we have no choice in the matter of morality, a fact emphasized by Kantian deontology, according to which, Ruse notes, 'the supreme principle of morality is categorical – it is laid upon us... We are not free to choose what right and wrong are to be.'[72] We should clarify: moral imperatives are imposed, not coercively, but as a condition for the happy life, which we can freely reject. Moreover while morality is imposed – it follows upon our nature – it is not a biological determinant. The analogy of arms and legs leads nowhere: *nec ambulando solvitur*.

Another serious difficulty is sociobiology's derivation of moral norms from inherited social patterns and instincts, the primitive manifestations of which are observed in lower animals. Besides social or communal tendencies, we also observe less desirable instincts such as acquisitiveness and aggression. Should these also be accepted as morally normal? How are we to distinguish between the good and bad instincts that we inherit? Each person is influenced by a variety of physical or biological dispositions that are genetically predetermined. Such predispositions are a necessary starting point for actions: they are the material of moral activity. These may include physical strengths or handicaps, biochemical proclivities (e.g. addictive behaviour, mental imbalance). However, these predispositions do not constitute or predetermine the moral character of the agent's actions. When the agent consciously and freely adopts a conscious attitude, becoming '*dominus sui*', actions become responsible and ethical. For Aristotle the free man is one who exists for his own sake, and not for another.[73] (Aquinas: 'The free man is his own cause: *liber est causa sui*.')[74] Genetics is one among a number of elements affecting an individual's moral life, but not the most decisive.[75] What counts is that I take possession of my biological heritage, place it under my control and shape my moral personality.

I have certain temperamental dispositions resulting from my genetic constitution; I am biologically determined, but not entirely so. In the nature *versus* nurture/culture debate, it is often assumed that natural means biological in the sense of subrational: that is to identify man with his biology. Wilson comments that genes hold culture on a leash.[76] Alasdair MacIntyre conveys the same when he states that 'our biological nature certainly places constraints on all cultural possibility'. He remarks, however: 'Man without culture is a myth… Man who has nothing but a biological nature is a creature of whom we know nothing.'[77] Both agree that nature and culture are both essential, but they differ in their understanding of nature. Human nature is for Wilson biological and ultimately physical; for MacIntyre, as for Aristotle, it is something more. While heredity places constraints upon human nature and keeps it on a leash, it does not fessle it in chains.[78]

Our genetic constitution, evolved over millennia, predisposes us to act in certain definite ways. Such propensities are not unique to members of the human species, but are shared with our evolutionary cousins, primates and chimpanzees. It cannot be doubted that our biology is fundamentally influenced by our genetic makeup, as it interacts with the environment; there is a historic component in our biochemical constitution. Our biology disposes us to react in certain ways to our natural and human environment, without however entirely determining our behaviour. We experience ourselves as independent in some measure, in the choices we make and in the life projects upon which we deliberate and execute over long periods of time with an awareness of freedom, commitment and responsibility. Charles Darwin significantly declared: 'A moral being is one who is capable of comparing his past and future actions or motives, and of approving or disapproving of them. We have no reason to suppose that any of the lower animals have this capacity.'[79] We can explain man's uniqueness, it may be argued, only by accepting that we may not be entirely identified with our biology. Man's biology enters into his nature as a moral being but does not fully constitute or exhaust it. Man is more than his biology; hence morality cannot in principle be fully explained in terms of biology. Man is moral because of the capacity to chose, to think and to reason in universal terms. These are not entirely explicable in biological terms.

Ethics and Biology

In *After Virtue*, Alasdair MacIntyre contended that a weak element in Aristotle's theory of virtue was its reliance upon a biological teleology.[80] Hence the dilemma: 'If we reject that biology, as we must, is there any way in which that teleology can be preserved?'[81] Needless to say, teleology is indispensable, since virtue is linked to function and finality. 'Any adequate teleological account must provide us with some clear and defensible account of the *telos*; and any adequate generally Aristotelian account must supply a teleological account which can replace Aristotle's metaphysical biology.'[82] In place of Aristotle's 'biologically teleological account' MacIntyre proposed a 'socially teleological account' of the virtues.[83] This account happily 'does not require the identification of any teleology in nature, and hence it does not require any allegiance to Aristotle's metaphysical biology'. MacIntyre suggested that the notion of function as applied to man, upon which the notion of virtue depends, 'is far older than Aristotle and it does not initially derive from Aristotle's metaphysical biology. It is rooted in the forms of social life to which the theorists of the classical tradition give expression. For according to that tradition to be a man is to fill a set of roles each of which has its own point and purpose: member of a family, citizen, soldier, philosopher, servant of God. It is only when man is thought of as an individual prior to and apart from all roles that "man" ceases to be a functional concept.'[84] *After Virtue* considered the place of the virtues within social practices, and the lives of individuals within communities. By the time of writing *Dependent Rational Animals* MacIntyre had reversed his position: 'Although there is indeed good reason to repudiate important elements in Aristotle's biology, I now judge that I was in error in suppposing an ethics independent of biology to be possible.'[85]

There is common ground between MacIntyre and sociobiology in the reasons offered for this change of emphasis. First, an account of the moral life and development of biologically constituted beings must take as its starting point 'our initial animal condition'. Second, an account of that development must involve 'comparison between humans and members of other intelligent animal species'. MacIntyre emphasized how important it is 'to attend to and to understand what human beings have in common with members of other intelligent animal species'.[86] While there is little in common between Alasdair MacIntyre and E.O. Wilson, both speak emphatically of 'other intelligent animals'. While this is only one of many fundamental differences with sociobiologists, it is possibly my only major disagreement with MacIntyre. Other species exhibit behaviour suggestive of purposeful activity, but I suggest that it is misleading to interpret this as properly intelligent. Referring to Aristotle, Aquinas presents the following explanation: 'The word *intellectus* implies an innermost knowledge, for *intelligere* is the same as *intus legere* (to read inwardly). This is clear to anyone who considers the difference between intellect and sense, because sensitive knowledge is concerned with external sensible qualities, whereas intellective knowledge penetrates into the very essence of a thing, because "the object of the intellect is what a thing is" as stated in *De Anima* 3, 6.'[87] While Aquinas' etymological explanation is perhaps questionable, his essential point is valid. Intellectual insight is intuitive; it goes beyond appearances and grasps something of the determining inwardness of what is passively given to the senses. (Thoreau remarks: 'The intellect is a cleaver; it discerns and rifts its way into the secret of things.')[88] It is only by analogy with human behaviour that we speak of animal intelligence. Aristotle credits animals with *phronesis* but never with *nous*. Animals display an estimative power (*vis aestimativa*) or 'practical intelligence' that seems akin to human reason. If we overstretch the analogy, however, the term becomes equivocal and results in ambiguity. It is important to point out, of course, that while MacIntyre refers to members of some nonhuman species as intelligent, he nowhere ascribes to them rationality of the kind that we possess.

For Aristotle, it is clear that intelligence is a prerequisite for the exercise of moral actions: 'The terms "self-restrained" and "unrestrained" denote being restrained or not by one's intellect, and thus imply that the intellect is the man himself. Also it is our reasoned acts that are felt to be in the fullest sense our own acts, voluntary acts. It is therefore clear that a man is or is chiefly the dominant part of himself, and that a good man values this part of himself most.'[89] Further, 'The good man does what he ought, since intelligence always chooses for itself that which is best, and the good man obeys his intelligence.'[90]

Given our nature as biological creatures, our morality cannot escape its biological framework. As Aristotle noted, it is the same soul that animates digestion, the passions, sensation, willing, and intellection; these are distinct though related activities. Our morality relies upon our biology, but transcends it; while we are integrally biological, our nature may not be reduced to its biology. As Stephen J. Pope remarks: 'Morality is "natural" but it is not "in the genes," except in the sense that the capacities that allow for morality are based in our biological make-up. Moral codes are transmitted culturally rather than genetically. The body functions in positive ways to support morality.'[91] More important than the role of culture, however, are man's spiritual powers which are prior to culture and beyond his biology; these alone make freedom and morality possible.

Alasdair MacIntyre agrees with sociobiology when he states that an ethics independent of biology is not possible. There can be no ethics that does not take account of the fact that by nature we are biological beings. Human biology makes material demands upon morality. But while ethics may not ignore man's biological nature, moral norms cannot be drawn from biology: such is the essence of sociobiology. We may prescribe respect for each person's biological integrity, but this obligation follows from a general law of respect for the totality of the person. Because man is a biological entity, moral philosophy pronounces upon biological behaviour, but requires a distinct foundation.

MAN AND FELLOW ANIMALS

In an editorial marking the bicentenary of his birth, the *Irish Times* suggested that Darwin's revolutionary biology robbed man of his central uniqueness and apartness from the rest of life.[92] Evolutionary theory offers a detailed account of the manner in which all living beings are fundamentally related, belonging as they do to the common tree of life. Man resembles not just animals, but all living things in his evolutionary origin. The fact that we share 98 percent of our DNA with chimpanzees, and 35 percent with daffodils[93] confirms our continuity with all living creatures. By essence man is an animal – a fact shared with all sentient creatures. It is a gratuitous simplification to suggest, however, that he differs in no way from other animals, or that he can be fully explained in biological and physical terms. Man is related to all living things, but is distinct and separate; he is not confined within biology or immersed in the material world. Human activity manifests spiritual powers that go beyond the biological. The capacity for universal knowledge, the powers of self-reflection, symbolization, conceptualization and reasoning attest to this. There are many reasons to infer that human nature is not fully explained through biological evolution. Human activity manifests properties not to be explained as capacities of matter. Spirit, characterized by its ability to transcend spatio-temporal limitations, simply cannot emerge from matter. To be spiritual is to be immaterial; by definition matter cannot be the origin of spirit.

One of the great discoveries of evolution is our shared solidarity with other species in a common ecology. Evolution confirms our continuity with all life forms, especially the origins and characteristics shared with fellow animals. We have much to learn from animal behaviour. Descartes evaluated the world in terms of introspection, and reductively identified the soul with consciousness; since animals show no evidence of introspection he emptied them of their interiority and reduced them to the mechanical level. Aristotle by contrast observed the autonomous activity of animals and inferred that they too possess an animating soul. His insights cohere perfectly with the biology of evolution; many contemporary scientists recognize in DNA a more accurate version of Aristotelian form (εἶδος). Ψυχή (*psyche*) is for Aristotle the principle of life, the element that characterizes each living being. Diverse levels of perfection indicate distinct types of soul: most perfect is man, whose rational soul incorporates the vegetative and sensitive powers in a unique principle. Evolution confirms the importance of Aristotle's metaphysical biology. This, however, is ignored by sociobiology, which attributes no importance whatsoever to individuals, animals or men: what count are the genes that pass from one generation to another.

Aristotle's acceptance of an immaterial element in human nature, yet his commitment to the unity of the human composite, posed for his successors the question of the relation between the physical body and an immaterial soul. Many attempts to solve the problem simplify and so avoid the reality – which must truly be described as a mysterious relation, an instance of what Aquinas suitably termed the *admirabilis connexio rerum*. I suggest that philosophers pay too little attention to personal lived experience; it is not easy to frame the concrete and rich intensity of selfhood in categories of the measurable: *individuum est ineffabile*. The experience of which each one is immediately and intensively aware cannot be adequately grasped. This is the first datum to be recognized. Blaise Pascal expresses the paradox of the familiar, yet the inscrutable status of self-knowledge:

> Who would not think, seeing us compose all things of mind and body, but that this mixture would be quite intelligible to us? Yet it is the very thing we least understand. Man is to himself the most wonderful object in nature; for he cannot conceive what the body is, still less what the mind is, and least of all how a body should be united to a mind. This is the consummation of his difficulties, and yet it is his very being. *Modus quo corporibus adhaerent spiritus comprehendi ab hominibus non potest, et hoc tamen homo est.* (The manner in which the spirit is united to the body can not be understood by man; and yet it is man).[94]

Pascal rightly declares that we have profound and intimate awareness of human nature. We are aware of the unity of the self as synthesis of body and mind. It may not be clear how this operates; but we do not solve the problem by denying one or another aspect of the given certainty. Man is, Shakespeare notes, 'most ignorant of what he's most assured, his glassy essence'.[95] E.O. Wilson's approach to the question 'Who am I?' reminds one of Pooh-Bah in *The Mikado*: 'I am, in point of fact, a particularly haughty and exclusive person, of pre-Adamite ancestral descent. You will understand this when I tell you that I can trace my ancestry back to a protoplasmal primordial atomic globule.'

The sociobiology of Edward Wilson and the ethology of Konrad Lorenz study animal behaviour to illuminate aspects of human nature, especially social life. This is a valid contribution, to the degree that man resembles other animals: many nonrational tendencies, such as sociability, aggression, lust, fear, and altruism, are studied more easily and objectively at the simpler animal level. The similarities, however, may not be exaggerated or generalized to define the proper essence of man, or to deny his uniqueness. Darwin asserted in *The Descent of Man*: '[T]he difference in mind between man and the higher animals, great as it is, certainly is one of degree and not of kind.'[96] Teilhard de Chardin was correct, I believe, in arguing the exact opposite. Having described at length the human capacity for reflection he wrote: 'We are separated by a chasm – or a threshold – which it cannot cross. Because we are reflective we are not only different but quite another. It is not merely a matter of change of degree, but of a change of nature, resulting from a change of state.'[97] It is axiomatic for sociobiology that there is no essential difference at the metaphysical level between humans and other animals. It is this belief that legitimates the application of conclusions drawn from animal evolution to humans. If there is no difference between us and other biological individuals, it makes sense that the primitive behaviour evident in chimpanzees, ants, and so forth may be projected back to the earliest developmental stages of our ancestors. It is crucial that sociobiology should remove all barriers between us and other animals, and deny exactly what was asserted by de Chardin. Wilson maintains that two traditionally upheld peculiarities of human nature, language and self-awareness, may no longer be regarded as such. He refers to primatologist David Premack's success at training chimpanzees by means of sign language and plastic symbols to learn up to two hundred words and elementary forms of syntax.[98] Wilson concludes: 'Many zoologists now doubt the existence of an unbridgeable linguistic chasm between animals and man.' Further: 'Another chasm newly bridged is self-awareness.'[99] Wilson refers to psychologist Gordon G. Gallup's experiments proving that chimpanzees acquire a sense of self-recognition by observing their reflection in a mirror.

Both of these claims are hasty. It is beyond doubt that chimpanzees have some limited memory and can make certain associations in response to stimuli. They distinguish colours and can separate shapes. But while the chimpanzee responds to the physical shape, it does not have the concept of triangle and will not grasp the theorem of Pythagoras. Dolphins imitate complex acoustic signals in a manner similar to children as they learn to use their speech organs, but they do not engage in concept-based conversation. What is singular to humans is the power of symbolization. We can arbitrarily posit a synnoetic connection between any two events or entities – mental or physical – and assign a meaning to this relationship: it could be mnemonic (wearing my watch on the other wrist reminds me to phone my godson for his birthday), or semantic as in the case of language, which associates thoughts with marks upon a material surface, or with identifiable sound waves. This power of symbolic signification is possible only because the human mind has an unlimited openness to the entirety of reality, and can thus create a connection between any two entities. Aristotle expresses this openness in the *De Anima* when he states, 'The soul is in a sense all things (ἡ ψυχὴ τὰ ὄντα πώς ἐστι πάντα).'[100] The mind has the ability to intentionally receive any reality in mental form and intentionally fabricate countless modalities of meaning. The mind, he states, can *become* everything (πάντα γίνεσθαι), and *make* everything (πάντα ποιεῖν).[101]

Wilson concludes from the fact that chimpanzees respond to their reflection in mirrors that they also possess self-knowledge, a power traditionally considered unique to humans. Again we must distinguish. It is clear that, looking at itself in the mirror, the chimp has an inchoate awareness of itself: this is not the self-knowledge enjoyed by humans. The chimpanzee sees itself in the glass darkly, but its knowledge is not transparently self-reflexive: it does not *know that it knows* itself. It cannot contemplate or investigate the act of self-cognition and distinguish in that act between itself as simultaneously subject and object. Certainly it exhibits what *we interpret* as curiosity, but it cannot resolve its puzzlement. It cannot distance itself from the act of knowing in which it is at once subject and object. Harry Frankfurt distinguishes between first- and second-order desires.[102] Only humans can have desires about desires; this is distinctive of what it is to be a person. The same applies to knowledge: only humans have self-reflexive knowledge of themselves as knowing. I can both know and desire my acts of cognition; I can know and desire my acts of volition. St Augustine perceived an even richer relationship across the diverse powers of the mind: 'For I remember that I have memory and understanding, and will; and I understand that I understand, and will, and remember; and I will that I will, and remember, and understand; and I remember together my whole memory, and understanding, and will.'[103] Other animals are incapable of such interanimation of mental activities.

Having debunked the unique status of human consciousness and communication Wilson arrives at an important conclusion, appealing once more to Premack: 'If consciousness of self and the ability to communicate ideas with other intelligent beings exist, can other qualities of the human mind be far away? Premack has pondered the implications of transmitting the concept of personal death to chimpanzees, but he is hesitant. 'What if, like man,' he asks, 'the ape dreads death and will deal with this knowledge as bizarrely as we have? . . . The desired objective would be not only to communicate the knowledge of death, but more important, to find a way of making sure that the apes' response would not be that of dread, which, in the human case, has led to the invention of ritual, myth and religion. Until I can suggest concrete steps in teaching the concept of death without fear, I have no intention of imparting the knowledge of mortality to the ape.'[104] It is difficult to take this passage seriously. We are asked to believe that we could, if we wished, enlighten the ape about its mortal fate but that out of kindness we should refrain from doing so.[105] Some animals suffer anguish from an instinctive anticipation of imminent death; it stretches the imagination, however, to assume that the ape, or any animal, can be reflectively aware of the implications of death and can ponder the alternatives of survival and extinction. This requires the ability to form universal notions, of which animals are incapable. Man alone among animals is conscious of death. Its ineluctable certainty and uncertain significance elicit fear and fascination; it is a *mysterium tremendum et fascinans*.[106] An animal might be trained to enunciate or sign the phrase 'To be, or not to be: that is the question', but could never grasp its significance. It could not ask whether in confronting the troubles of life it is nobler to end them freely or to seek fulfilment by creatively transforming them in defiant affirmation.

Interestingly the significance of death for humans is addressed by Wilson in the opening lines of *Sociobiology*, only to be dismissed as irrelevant:

> Camus said that the only serious philosophical question is
> suicide. That is wrong, even in the strict sense intended.
> The biologist, who is concerned with questions of
> physiology and evolutionary history, realizes that self-
> knowledge is constrained and shaped by the emotional

control centers in the hypothalamus and limbic system of the brain. These centers flood our consciousness with all the emotions – hate, love, guilt, fear, and others – that are consulted by ethical philosophers who wish to intuit the standards of good and evil. What, we are then compelled to ask, made the hypothalamus and limbic system? They evolved by natural selection. That simple biological statement must be pursued to explain ethics and ethical philosophers, if not epistemology and epistemologists, at all depths.[107]

Wilson rightly associates the question of suicide with that of the existence of the self, but dismisses this as irrelevant, since – from his evolutionist perspective – not the self, but the gene is the prime mover. He asserts:

Self-existence, or the suicide that terminates it, is not the central question of philosophy. The hypothalamic-limbic complex automatically denies such logical reduction by countering it with feelings of guilt and altruism. In this one way the philosopher's own emotional control centers are wiser than his solipsist consciousness, 'knowing' that in evolutionary time the individual organism counts for almost nothing. In a Darwinian sense the organism does not live for itself. Its primary function is not even to reproduce other organisms; it reproduces genes, and it serves as their temporary carrier.[108]

The suggestion is that, since in the long run only genes matter, the self is unimportant.

Wilson's position is inconsistent: suicide kills the bearer, thwarting the propagation process, but that is a minor point. More importantly, sociobiology is incapable of recognizing the central philosophical question of self-existence. (For understandable philosophico-cultural reasons neither did Aristotle pose the question, assuming the eternity of the cosmos and perpetuity of all species). Camus rightly suggests that the fundamental question is whether life is worth living. To ask 'Why should I exist?' cannot be detached from the question why anything should exist. It is difficult to see how feelings of guilt or altruism can pronounce one way or another on the question either of self-existence or of existence generally. Guilt and altruism might intervene if, in response to a nihilistic response, one were tempted to choose suicide, although on Wilson's terms, since the self is of no significance, such feelings make little sense.

Wilson's viewpoint recalls Hume's opinion that 'the life of a man is of no greater importance to the universe than that of an oyster'.[109] From the abstract, impersonal, perspective of universal existence man is of no consequence; and if the self is merely the instrumental vehicle of the genetic molecule, it is of negligible importance. From the irreducible personal subjective point of view, however, it is distinctly the opposite. In his autobiography Somerset Maugham conveys the contrast: 'To myself I am the most important person in the world; though I do not forget that, not even taking into consideration so grand a conception as the Absolute, but from the standpoint of common sense, I am of no consequence whatever. It would have made small difference to the universe if I had never existed.'[110] While my existence is a matter of indifference to the universe on the global impersonal scale, for me it is the most important truth about everything that I am; without that self-experience, the world has no meaning for me. Extrapolating my experience to fellow conscious subjects, without the subjective the world would be devoid of all objective meaning.

Our capacity for universal openness to reality, and our ability to return in reflection upon the self allows the question: Why do I exist? As Augustine concretely illustrates, because we are self-consciously aware, each one becomes a question to himself: *Mihi quaestio factus sum*.[111] Each one may ask: What am I? More radically, one cannot escape the more fundamental question: Why am I? This question, significantly, is inseparable from the wider inquiry: Why does anything exist? Why is there something rather than nothing? Kant famously posed three fundamental questions: 'What can I know?', 'What should I do?', and 'What may I hope?'[112] He replied summarily that I can know nature, should do my duty, and may hope for the realization of the highest good. In their deeper contexts these questions are closely related. To respond to the question 'What should I do?' by invoking duty, however, does not go far enough. The question 'Why be moral?' requires a fuller response, which presumes not only a sure ground for knowledge and a legitimate prospect of hope, but more importantly some tacit response to the basic question: Why do I exist? The questions of action and value are inseparable from those of knowledge and existence: What can I hope to know, and why should I be? It must be presumed that the question of knowledge has been answered to some satisfactory degree, and that the question of existence is not only legitimate, but the most significant and ultimate that I can pose.

In the question of self-existence man questions himself and the totality of the real. One may not *a priori* equate the world of nature with the totality of the real. One may not determine in advance that reality is just what can be measured scientifically. Richard Dawkins makes this fundamental mistake in his challenge to religion: 'A universe with a supernatural presence would be a fundamentally and qualitatively different kind of universe from one without. The difference is, inescapably, a scientific difference. Religions make existence claims, and this means scientific claims.'[113] E.O. Wilson affirms: 'Every part of existence is considered to be obedient to physical laws requiring no external control.'[114] It is interesting to find a similarly reductive position in one of Alasdair MacIntyre's early writings: 'The concept of divine existence is of a highly dubious character. Our concept of existence is inexorably linked to our talk about spatio-temporal objects.'[115] (It hardly needs pointing out that in later writings MacIntyre espouses a much more fundamental and metaphysical notion of existence.)[116] Philosophers have much to learn from the ontology of William Jefferson Clinton: 'It depends on what the meaning of the word "is" is.'[117] The question of being lies outside the range of biology. Lord Martin Rees, president of the Royal Society, begins his book *Our Cosmic Habitat* by asserting: 'The preeminent mystery is why anything exists at all. What breathes life into the equations, and actualized them in a real cosmos? Such questions lie beyond science... They are the province of philosophers and theologians.'[118]

CONCLUSION

The final chapter of Wilson's *On Human Nature*, with its encouraging title 'Hope', proclaims a future project in which the search for values will 'go beyond the utilitarian calculus of genetic fitness'.[119] Wilson prophetically announces his aspiration that the true Promethean spirit of science will liberate man by giving him knowledge and dominion over the physical world, and will respond to the 'deepest needs of human nature, and [be] kept strong by the blind hopes that the journey on which we are now embarked will be farther and better than the one just completed'.[120] This is a grand-sounding ambition that promises little. Values are to be measured by the intensity of emotion; the neuro-physiology of our responses needs to be deciphered, and their evolutionary history awaits reconstruction.[121] What the deepest needs of human nature are remains unsaid. In his subsequent volume *Consilience* Wilson continues to champion a scientific evolutionist materialism: 'Moral reasoning will either remain centered in idioms of theology and philosophy, where it is now, or it will shift toward science-based material analysis.'[122] Available evidence 'favors a purely material origin of ethics'.[123]

In the final analysis, evolutionary ethics is founded upon a biological endless regress in which persons have no ultimacy. Human individuals exist for the exclusive purpose of propagating offspring, whose aim is likewise simply to propagate. To what end? What is the goal of the process in its totality? Aristotle points out that no action is ever complete if its goal is indefinitely deferred. It might be objected that Aristotle is himself guilty of this lacuna, since he also maintains that the highest activity of a living substance is to perpetuate its species. There is, however, for Aristotle a universal final cause, and, having an individual *telos*, the individual transcends the process of generation. The activity of reproduction is not itself the foundation of morality.

It is arguable that the ultimate ground for moral obligation and universal duty is the status of each member of the human species as an individual consciously aware of his or her freedom within the totality of the real, and the inescapable demand to make one's life personally meaningful, with all the possibilities and limits of our common nature. The recognition of this demand in oneself and in others illumines the moral commands arising from our nature as free and rational beings, conscious of the need to make our way in the world, a task that confronts each and every human being.

9

ARISTOTLE AND EVOLUTIONARY ALTRUISM

A ltruism is not an operative concept for Aristotle; he does not list benevolence among the virtues. Commentators debate – anachronistically – whether Aristotelian attitudes towards others, as expounded in his treatment of friendship, are egoistic or altruistic. Conclusions inevitably depend upon the definitions initially adopted and the parameters within which the interpretation unfolds. Aristotle's reflections on friendship are characteristically marked by profound common sense and sympathy with his fellow man; they are supported by subtle analyses of psychological motives and moral values. As the first western philosopher to write systematic treatises in ethics, as well as pioneering works of zoology and biology, Aristotle is a helpful guide in assessing any proposal to relate ethics to biology.

The most sustained attempt in recent decades to ground ethics upon biology, specifically upon the theory of evolution, is that of sociobiology. Defined by its founder E.O. Wilson as 'the systematic study of the biological basis of all social behavior',[1] sociobiology aims to lay bare the biological underpinnings of animal behaviour, and to apply these to man. Other renowned proponents are Michael Ruse and Richard Dawkins. According to sociobiology, the ultimate goal of human life is to propagate the human species. If such is the over-arching purpose of human existence the question arises: What is the role of the individual? What guarantees the morality of our behaviour whose ultimate end is to advance the all-important purpose of promoting our shared genetic material? Is there any moral warrant? Sociobiology grounds ethical obligation in certain altruistic tendencies which it postulates as inherited from our animal origins. It appeals to 'social' structures in the animal kingdom as indicating, analogously, a biological foundation for human morality. Morality is rooted in so-called 'epigenetic' or hereditary rules transmitted from our ancestors, each generation a transitory and transient relay in the onward perpetuation of the genotype.

Sociobiology maintains that the all-embracing goal of human life is to perpetuate the species. It holds that the inherited trait of altruism provides an answer to the question 'Why be moral?' Historically, however, the ideal of cooperation for the sake of the greater goal seems contrary to Darwin's 'general law leading to the advancement of all organic beings – namely, multiply, vary, let the strongest live and the weakest die'.[2] Against early Darwinism, which emphasized survival of the fittest in the struggle for survival, sociobiology points to the need for cooperation within the group to guarantee survival of their *shared* genetic material. According to Wilson, Ruse, and Dawkins, this is attained in the concrete through altruistic behaviour which promotes the continuation and expansion of the gene pool. According to Ruse and Wilson 'the individual individual is altruistic but his genes are "selfish"'.[3] Wilson defines altruism as 'self-destructive behavior performed for the benefit of others'.[4] This occurs principally in two contexts: kin selection and reciprocal altruism. It is supported by the evidence of 'social' structures observed in the animal kingdom, which might be called 'biological altruism'.

Firstly individuals linked through kinship bestow altruistic favours on one another in order to increase the genetic fitness of the group as a whole, even though this may result in the reduced fitness of some individuals.[5] The collective goal is the maximization of shared genes into the next generation; what counts is 'inclusive fitness'. A perfect example of such altruism is the behaviour of hymenoptera (ants, bees, wasps), as studied by William D. Hamilton, who provided sociobiologists with empirical evidence to support their theory: many females do not reproduce but devote themselves instead entirely to the queen, helping her produce as many offspring as possible. Peculiarly females of this insect group are more closely related to their sisters than to their daughters; it is thus genetically more productive to support fertile sisters than fertile daughters.[6]

Kin selection operates within the restricted blood circle. Sociobiology appeals, secondly, to practices of reciprocal altruism within the wider population. It cites studies of Harvard zoologist Robert L. Trivers to conclude that our tendencies toward such behaviour are inherited.[7] While the classic paradigm for *pure* altruism is the Good Samaritan, intuitively it contradicts the model of natural selection and seems overly idealistic. Altruism is more plausible on the wider scale if interpreted not as sheer benevolence, but in the context of generalized reciprocal or mutual benefit. Sociobiology contends that a population marked by an extended spirit of mutual cooperation will be genetically more successful. Wilson concedes: 'The theory of group selection has taken most of the good will out of altruism.' He acknowledges moreover: 'Human behavior abounds with reciprocal altruism consistent with genetic theory, but animal behavior seems to be almost devoid of it.'[8] Nonetheless a variety of examples may be cited. Some small fish clean the mouths of larger species, while simultaneously being fed. This cleaning symbiosis is to the advantage of the larger fish, but can function only on the tacit assumption that it will not make a meal of its dental hygienist. Some birds make warning calls to alert others against a predator, thereby placing themselves in danger. Wilson refers to the trading of food among chimpanzees, African wild dogs and wolves.[9] How is reciprocity established in evolution? Wilson speculates: 'There exists a critical frequency of the altruist gene above which the gene will spread explosively through the population and below which it will slowly recede to the mutational equilibrium. How critical frequencies are attained from scratch remains unknown.'[10]

E.O. Wilson himself acknowledges that altruism is the 'central theoretical problem of sociobiology: how can altruism, which by definition reduces personal fitness, possibly evolve by natural selection?'[11] Leaving aside the serious theoretical weaknesses specifically recognized by its champions with regard to its biological mechanism, it may be remarked in general that, while altruism might plausibly be an attractive ideal, it is unfeasible as a realistic grounding for an effective and convincing universal ethics. It assumes universal good will among all members of the human race; it is a counsel of perfection rather than a practical proposition. Universal altruism makes sense on condition that everyone shares an acceptance of a common independent value recognized by all as deserving love and respect.

Aristotle helpfully distinguishes three kinds of friendship, based respectively on goodness, utility, and pleasure.[12] This, I suggest, is a valid division with which to assess the claims of evolutionary ethics. Importantly Aristotle also distinguishes between the rare commitment between virtuous friends, and a universal goodwill (εὔνοια), which is devoid of moral purchase. The primary friendship of the good, Aristotle notes, 'only occurs in man, for he alone has conscious purpose; but those of utility and pleasure occur also in the lower animals'.[13] According to Aristotle, therefore, genuine altruism could only occur between humans who are independently good. There are friendships of utility and pleasure among men who are not entirely virtuous, and there is even a kind of 'goodwill' among certain animals. In Aristotelian terms we do not observe altruism in animal behaviour; the suggestion of a hereditary altruism on the basis of zoological data, therefore, holds no promise. More importantly the selfless altruism required for the successful propagation of the species is nowhere to be found among humans. The purest altruism we find in humans is that which obtains reciprocally among virtuous individuals, but from an Aristotelian perspective there is no motivation to sacrifice oneself for the propagation of the species.

The term altruism was coined by Auguste Comte (1798–1857). With his proposed new religion dedicated to 'the Great Being, Humanity', he defined altruism as 'vivre pour autrui'. Although Charles Kahn has warned that to discuss altruism with reference to Aristotle 'introduces the risk of anachronistic assumptions and associations',[14] this has not prevented scholars from introducing him to the debate since he provides valuable insights into the nature and status of other-regarding proclivities. We find little evidence in Aristotle's writings either for or against altruism as understood by sociobiologists. We must distinguish between altruism as an actually observed human tendency and its supposed genetic origins: one might validly defend altruism as a feature of morality and reject its evolutionary explanation.

Julia Annas believes that 'Aristotle's discussion in the *Nicomachean Ethics* is often abused as reducing friendship and all apparent altruism to egoism.'[15] As an example of this common view she cites D.J. Allan: 'Every point confirms the impression that Aristotle does not think it psychologically possible for a man to choose otherwise than in his own interest, and is seeking, in one way or another, to say what really happens when men appear to subordinate their interest to that of another.'[16] Richard Kraut rejects the view that Aristotle is an egoist.[17] Arthur Madigan accepts Julia Annas' reading.[18] Annas, however, is working with a mild definition of altruism, which makes no mention of self-sacrifice: 'Now and in what follows, these terms are used without any implication of selfishness versus selflessness; I take egoism to be the doctrine that an agent has no reason for acting unless it can be shown to be in his interests in some way, and altruism to be the doctrine that at least on some occasions the interests of another person can be a reason for his acting, without any reference to his own interests.'[19]

Significantly Aristotle speaks of 'people mutually well-disposed, whom nevertheless we cannot speak of as friends, because they are not aware of each other's regard'.[20] The concept of altruism does not arise for Aristotle. At most we might extrapolate from a passage at the beginning of *Nicomachean Ethics* 8, where he speaks of a natural and instinctive friendship between birds and most animals of the same species. This is strongest of all, he notes, among humans: 'For which reason we praise those who love their fellow men. Even when travelling abroad one can observe that a natural affinity and friendship exist between man and man universally.'[21] The natural affinity universally observed among members of the human race is the closest we find in his writings to altruism as a possible foundation for ethics, but is much too vague.[22] Aristotle speaks enthusiastically of the benevolence that exists between close friends; but what is needed to support sociobiology's case would be impracticable. As Terence Irwin notes:

> The friendship of virtuous people requires highly developed altruistic concerns; but the concerns extend to very few people. We may think that the sort of altruism required by justice and the other virtues of character is so different from

the sort required by friendship that we need a different account for these other virtues. Aristotle, however, seems to offer no defence of the other-regarding aspects of the virtues beyond the defence of friendship; and so he seems to face a serious difficulty in justifying them.[23]

Some elements of Aristotle's friendship are echoed in Wilson's altruism. Charles Kahn remarks: 'If by altruism we mean a concern for the interests of others for their own sake, then for Aristotle true friendship is by definition altruistic.'[24] Sociobiology, however, demands something much more: altruism is '*self-destructive behavior* performed for the benefit of others',[25] a concept foreign to Aristotle. David Hume's position is similar to that of Aristotle; he recognizes that love is firstly centred upon the self, and that men are 'endowed only with a confined generosity'.[26] Aristotle's virtuous man 'wishes his own good (ἑαυτῷ τἀγαθὰ)... desires his own life and security (καὶ ζῆν δὲ βούλεται ἑαυτὸν καὶ σῴζεσθαι)... for existence is good for the virtuous man (ἀγαθὸν γὰρ τῷ σπουδαίῳ τὸ εἶναι); and everyone wishes his own good: no one would choose to possess every good in the world on condition of becoming somebody else'.[27] The last phrase implies that no one would wish to sacrifice himself for the sake of another self, which is the demand of sociobiology's altruism. The natural love of self precedes and supersedes the love of friendship: 'everybody wishes good things for himself most of all'.[28] Without implying any negative connotation, Aristotle's ethics may be characterized as self-centred. While friendship is love of the other as of one's own self, it always remains in some measure a function of self-love.

Alasdair MacIntyre refers in *Dependent Rational Animals* to 'influential accounts of altruism according to which it is either a disguised form of egoism, or in some more sophisticated versions, a transformation of egoism in the interests of satisfying egoism's goals'.[29] The problem arises, however, only if one seeks to ground ethics upon altruistic sentiments. The distinction between egoism and altruism is a false starting point. As MacIntyre points out in *After Virtue*, altruism was proposed in modern philosophy as a solution to the problem of morality when men came to be viewed as by nature dangerously egoistic. Altruism becomes the only solution, but it is 'apparently impossible and, if and when it occurs, inexplicable'. MacIntyre points out:

> On the traditional Aristotelian view such problems do not arise. For what education in the virtues teaches me is that my good as man is one and the same as the good of those others with whom I am bound up in human community. There is no way of my pursuing my good which is necessarily antagonistic to your pursuing yours because *the* good is neither mine peculiarly nor yours peculiarly – goods are not private property. Hence Aristotle's definition of friendship, the fundamental form of human relationship, is in terms of shared goods. The egoist is thus, in the ancient and medieval world, always someone who has made a fundamental mistake about where his own good lies and someone who has thus and to that extent excluded himself from human relationships.[30]

I would add, however, that for Aristotle it is not out of generosity that we share goods. Acknowledging that there is a certain universal friendship among men,[31] Aristotle recognizes with good common sense that all men are selfish (φίλαυτοι) to a greater or lesser degree.[32] In *Politics* Book 1 he notes that some people are consumed by zeal not for the good life, but for the material means needed simply to live; they have a limitless desire (εἰς ἄπειρον) for such goods.[33] Experience has shown him that 'the things people approve of openly are not those which they approve of secretly: openly, their chief praise is given to justice and nobleness; but in their hearts they prefer their own advantage'.[34] Individuals are more interested in private possessions than in what is owned in common.[35] Through practice and moral education we acquire the virtues to counter selfish tendencies. While Aristotle defines friendship in terms of shared goods, friendship is not itself the foundation for justice – even though friendship is preferred by legislators to justice. This is not a contradiction: friendship surpasses justice, but as the foundation for universal political concord it is an unattainable ideal. Justice is grounded rather on the recognition of common, independent and universal values shared by mankind. Diogenes Laertius reports that when his friends expressed surprise when he gave an alms to an unworthy beggar, Aristotle replied that he was not giving to the man but to the humanity in him.[36]

There are two particular reasons why on Aristotle's view altruistic friendship could never be the ultimate foundation for morality. Firstly, true friendship only exists among virtuous persons – friendship already presupposes virtue.[37] Since altruism depends upon virtue, it cannot itself be the motivating origin of virtue. Secondly, friendship of the kind necessary for genuine altruism is possible only within a very small circle of friends. In *Nicomachean Ethics* 9 Aristotle states: 'It is true that one may be friendly with many fellow-citizens… but it is not possible to have many friends whom we love for their virtue and for themselves. We may be glad to find even a few friends of this sort.'[38] He remarks: 'Such friendships are rare, because such men are few.'[39]

Roger Trigg suggests that reciprocal altruism, 'unlike kin selection, involves an appeal to pure self-interest and is very Hobbesian'.[40] Commenting on the inclination of some neo-Darwinians to explain morality wholly in evolutionary terms, Trigg comments:

> Such an enterprise is misconceived. Human reason, as a capacity, may be the product of evolution, but it is sufficiently flexible and free-ranging to detach itself from the direction of our natural inclinations. It can even sit in judgment on them. Certainly evolutionary theory is more adept at dealing with the origin of our natural sympathies and aversions, our likes and dislikes, than in explaining the operation of human reason. Since it is itself the product of the latter, it is wise not to overreach itself.[41]

Evolutionary ethicists postulate a motivational connection between altruism and genetic promulgation. That this is not necessarily the case is obvious from the fact that many sublimely altruistic lifestyles – e.g. poverty or celibacy in the service of one's fellows – exactly preclude the propagation of one's gene material. E.O. Wilson's interpretation of Mother Teresa's care of Calcutta's destitute as self-serving and 'cheerfully subordinate' to her 'biological imperatives' is an extreme case of biological reductionism.[42] Even if we were to dismiss her motives as selfish in pursuit of otherworldly rewards, and such inspiration were illusory, she can only have been motivated by spiritual imperatives.[43] St Paul speaks of the love that 'does not seek its own interest'.[44] Human nature being what it is, it is difficult to imagine a genuine altruism or charity that is not motivated by some noble and lofty ideal, involving commitment to a greater value, whether it be the beauty of the natural universe, the earthly paradise of Marxist socialism, or the love of a transcendent God. Whatever the cause, it involves a universal good perceived as somehow greater than the individual. It must certainly be more than biological in nature and inspiration.

The argument that altruism is rooted in the universal drive to perpetuate one's genes involves many strange suppositions. It implies logically that anyone who has no interest whatsoever in the duplication of his or her genes need not feel bound by any moral imperative. If I have no interest in propagating the genetic material of the group to which I belong, am I bereft of all sense of duty and goodness? Am I supposed to have inherited it as an intrinsically biological element of my constitution, simply because at some distant time in the remote past my ancestors felt the compulsion to secure their family stock. Is it the gene that is selfishly driven to perpetuate itself? The gene is not conscious, deliberative or free. While I am the bearer of my genes, they are distinct from me. Apart from the very general control dependent upon my decision whether or not to mate with a member of the opposite sex, I have no control over my genes. Although, as parasites, they depend upon me to carry them into the future, their identity is distinct from mine.

There is no logical connection between altruistic behaviour towards others and the genetic advantage of my descendants; it will on the contrary result in increased benefit to the beneficiary's offspring rather than mine. While sociobiologists argue that morality obliges me to further the genetic pool rather than promote my own good, the obvious question is: Why? What motivation is there to do so? By the same token, the logic of maximum genetic benefit requires that instead of coming to the aid of 'losers', I should concentrate on my own group, or devote myself to those whose current success augurs well for their descendants. Much is made by evolutionary ethicists of the attachment to familial kinship for the sake of genetic propagation. How should I adjudicate between kin and reciprocal altruism? On a wider scale it is naïve to expect that all humans should in practise assume the universal duty of reciprocal altruism. There are countless incapacitated persons who can never repay any acts of beneficence, but towards whom we have moral obligations. What possible reason could I have to sacrifice myself for the sake of someone who is the carrier of defective genes? If the entire purpose of ethics is to spread the genetic material for the optimal benefit of the human race, this goes counter to its aim. It does not seem possible, therefore, to establish ethics upon the principles of evolution, since the struggle for existence and survival of the fittest inevitably exclude much of what is central to any acceptable ethical system, namely concern for the weaker members of the human species. Peter Singer remarks: 'Kin altruism plus reciprocal altruism with perhaps a little group altruism too, seems a slender basis on which to explain human ethics.'[45]

On an Aristotelian view the extreme selfless demands of sociobiology would be possible only – if at all – for totally virtuous individuals. Aristotle is too much of a pragmatist to accept that humans would universally sacrifice themselves for the sake of the species. While he too maintains (for biological reasons) that the highest human activity is the perpetuation of the species, he attributes significant personal goals to the individual moral agent. If indeed altruism is interpreted as concern for others for their own sake, Aristotelian friendship may be regarded as altruism.

Aristotle's views on friendship, and the motivations and sacrifices it involves, provide a helpful perspective on evolutionary altruism. The incontrovertible evidence is that, contrary to the claims of evolutionary ethics, many people are indifferent to their fellow humans, and pursue anything but the ideals of universal benevolence. Aristotle is too realistic to imagine that humans will devote themselves with total dedication to a selfless ideal. He notes that most men overindulge their appetites and the irrational passions of their souls.[46]

Sociobiology, I suggest, incorrectly interprets one's commitment to one's kith and kin. I act altruistically towards members of my family, not because I have any great concern for the propagation of our common genetic material, or because I am somehow unconsciously committed to our shared genetic inheritance. It is in the first place, and instinctively, from a natural feeling of attachment and affection. Fraternal attachment and goodwill may, however, be destroyed through sibling rivalry or betrayal.

Does morality demand that I sacrifice myself for the sake of the other? In absolute terms, not. I may indeed be required to disadvantage myself in order to obey my moral obligation to defend the life or dignity of another human being. Morality, however, does not require me to totally sacrifice myself for the benefit of another, or even for a multitude of others. If I chose to do so, it will be a moral act, if the cause is right and just; but I will not act immorally if I do not. Altruism goes beyond the demands of morality. Appeals to the inherited bonds of kinship and the indirect benefits of reciprocal altruism are therefore irrelevant as an evolutionary explanation of morality.

Sociobiologists claim that altruism is genetically inherited. They argue that because our ancestors were altruistically minded, their offspring – eventually ourselves – survived. This line of argument, however, assumes part of what it aims to prove, namely that altruism is genetically determined. Human behaviour is patently psychosomatic, and thus affected by physical – especially biochemical – constituents; however it may not be assumed that altruism is exclusively determined by genetic components. It is theoretically plausible that a human trait such as generosity, or intelligence, is a non-biological disposition.[47]

Richard Dawkins is helpfully honest when he departs from the position of fellow sociobiologists Wilson and Ruse: 'Be warned that if you wish, as I do, to build a society in which individuals cooperate generously and unselfishly toward a common good, you can expect little help from biological nature. Let us try to teach generosity and altruism, because we are born selfish.'[48] Dawkins protests that the word 'selfish' in the title of his celebrated bestseller was incorrectly taken to mean that ethics was impossible; in *The God Delusion* he sought to set the record straight. His protest is correct in one respect; the misunderstanding, however, is inevitable: the fault is Dawkins' for not clarifying that, attributed to the gene, 'selfish' is used in a figurative sense. In switching from figurative to literal use, however, he invites the misinterpretation. How are we to understand the following assertion if not literally: 'The logic… is this: Humans and baboons have evolved by natural selection… Anything that has evolved by natural selection should be selfish.

Therefore we must expect that when we go and look at the behaviour of baboons, humans, and all other living creatures, we will find it to be selfish.'[49] The logic is not at all obvious. While Wilson and Ruse seek examples of altruism among the primates, Dawkins states that 'pure, disinterested altruism' has never before humanity existed in the whole history of the world.[50]

In *The God Delusion* Dawkins accounts for so-called altruistic behaviour by explaining it – explaining it away? – as an unconscious strategy of genetic manipulation. Excluding the possibility of higher motivation, however, action becomes depersonalized: it is difficult to see how any real sense of freedom can remain, if the subject is the unwitting instrument in the onward march of impersonal primordial genetic forces. Darwin himself recognized the fatal implications for his theory of natural selection, if such a thing as an overriding altruism were discovered: 'Natural selection cannot possibly produce any modification in any one species exclusively for the good of another species... If it could be proved that any part of the structure of any one species had been formed for the exclusive good of another species, it would annihilate my theory, for such could not have been produced through natural selection.'[51]

The revised view is that human nature is not essentially egotistical; through natural selection we have inherited an inclination towards altruism, a tendency to help others at a cost to ourselves. Evolution thus offers a solution to the problem of egoism, which was a hurdle for Darwin. Collective hunting, shared defence, and provision of shelter etc. promote the more likely survival of those who cooperate, before that of the egotistical, who will remain isolated and perish. The logic is impeccable: only those who cooperate will survive to produce offspring.[52] The implied interpretation, however, is anything but logical: continued survival of the lineage is assured due to an instinctive altruism, repeatedly inherited and transmitted. In essence the claim is that humans are ethical because they would not exist in the first place unless their ancestors were altruistic; such altruism is genetically ingrained, constituting the very core and foundation of moral behaviour. A crucial question ensues: Who is moral – is it I who am moral, or my genes? Who or what is responsible for my actions? If it is my genes, can I be responsible?

Altruism, which it claims is genetically motivated, is the figleaf providing sociobiology with the appearance of an ethics hitherto difficult to justify within the context of Darwinism. The scandal for traditional ethics has been the problem of evil; the challenge for evolutionary ethics is the fact of goodness, which makes little sense within the struggle for survival. Intuitively and implicitly we associate morality with service and benevolence rather than strife and the struggle for survival. Altruism fulfils a double function for sociobiology. As well as providing a ground for ethics, it is also important that naturalistic evolutionists can assign an evolutionary role to altruistic behaviour, explaining how it serves the biological imperative of genetic transmission. Otherwise it might potentially embarrass the theory by unmasking itself as a cipher for some (possibly transcendent) value or origin of non-biological inspiration.

10

Joyce and Aristotle

It is arguable that Aristotle – next to Homer – was Joyce's greatest master. Without the *Odyssey*, Joyce could never have conceived *Ulysses*; had he not written the book celebrating his first rendezvous with a beautiful girl from Galway, whatever he wrote would, however, have been profoundly marked by the philosopher of Stagira. There is, I suggest, a profound affinity of mind between Joyce and Aristotle; perhaps part of this kinship may be explained by its Homeric parentage. Aristotle too was profoundly influenced by Homer; he cites him over one hundred times, second in frequency only to Plato. Many of these citations are in those works of Aristotle which Joyce would read. One of the most moving documents which we possess from the entire corpus of ancient philosophy is the fragment of a letter written by Aristotle toward the end of his life: 'The more solitary and isolated I am, the more I have come to love myths.'[1] One recalls Rembrandt's famous painting of Aristotle contemplating the bust of Homer.

It is noteworthy that in *Gulliver's Travels*, Jonathan Swift places Homer and Aristotle in the same company: 'Having a desire to see those ancients, who were most renowned for wit and learning, I set apart one day on purpose. I proposed that Homer and Aristotle might appear at the head of all their commentators... I had a whisper from a ghost, who shall be nameless, that these commentators always kept in the most distant quarter from their principals, in the lower world, through a consciousness of shame and guilt, because they had so horribly misrepresented the meaning of those authors to posterity'.[2] Joyce would bear no such guilt in the company of Homer and Aristotle.

Joyce set out to emulate Homer and his success is beyond dispute. He was also a true and sympathetic follower of Aristotle. He regarded Aristotle as the greatest of all philosophers, declaring: 'In the last two hundred years we have had no great thinker. My assertion is bold, since Kant is included. All the great thinkers of recent centuries from Kant to Benedetto Croce have only recultivated the garden. The greatest thinker of all times, in my opinion, is Aristotle. He defines everything with wonderful clarity and simplicity. Later, volumes were written to define the same things.'[3]

How did Joyce came to know Aristotle? Why such great esteem? I will presently assess the most obvious source of influence – his Jesuit education – but would first like to mention one which is perhaps overlooked. For generations in Ireland, the name of Aristotle has been associated in the popular tradition with wisdom and erudition. The German travel writer Johann Georg Kohl, visiting Ireland in September 1842, reported that he twice heard Irish people 'speak of Aristotle as a wise and mighty king of Greece, as if they had the same conception of him as of King Solomon'.[4] Aristotle's renown was alive *i mbéal an phobail*. My own great-grandmother from West Cork, born a generation later, spoke reverently of 'Harry Stakle'. The Irish, however, by no means regarded Aristotle as omniscient; Joyce copied in *Scribbledehobble*, his workbook for *Finnegans Wake*, the widespread traditional Irish triad, '3 things Aristotle didn't know: labour of bees, flow of tide, mind of women'.[5]

Joyce was unwittingly exposed to the categories of Aristotle throughout his Catholic education. Catholic theology has for centuries made use of Aristotelian concepts and terminology. Consider the traditional vocabulary of the catechism. The sacraments are explained in terms of Aristotelian principles: each has its matter and form. The Eucharist is described in the vocabulary of substance and accident. Joyce, like many Irish youngsters before and since, imbibed the practicality of Aristotle's metaphysics. There is less sympathy, it may be noted, in the Protestant tradition of Luther, who did not disguise his contempt for 'that cursed heathen': 'What will they not believe who have credited that ridiculous and injurious blasphemer Aristotle? His propositions are so absurd that an ass or a stone would cry out at them… My soul longs for nothing so ardently as to expose and publicly shame that Greek buffoon, who like a spectre has befooled the Church… If Aristotle had not lived in the flesh I should not hesitate to call him a devil.'[6]

It may be fairly presumed that under the Jesuits Joyce was likewise exposed to the scholastic mode of deliberation, which owed much to the logic of Aristotle. Joyce rejected much of his Jesuit education, but was in many ways grateful. Buck Mulligan remarks to Stephen: '[Y]ou have the cursed jesuit strain in you, only it's injected the wrong way'.[7] Asked by the sculptor August Suter what he retained from his Jesuit education, he replied: 'I have learnt to arrange things in such a way that they become easy to survey and to judge.'[8] Commenting on Aristotle, Aquinas defines wisdom as the discovery of order: *Sapientis est ordinare*. The opening words of a translation of Aquinas which Joyce himself later owned, and which could not have failed to attract his attention on publication in 1905, read: 'According to established popular usage, which the Philosopher [Aristotle] considers should be our guide in the naming of things, they are called "wise" who put things in their right order and control them well.'[9] Curiously, AE remarked to the young Joyce: 'I do not see in your beginnings enough chaos to make a world.'[10] It was precisely this confrontation with chaos which spurred him on. In *Stephen Hero* we read: 'And over all the chaos of history and legend, of fact and supposition, he strove to draw out a line of order, to reduce the abysses of the past to order by diagram.'[11]

Order was the hallmark of Aristotle's mind; his investigations were a comprehensive attempt not only to analyse and differentiate the full entirety of given reality, but more importantly to integrate and unify. This fixity upon order is formulated in the mind of Bloom: 'The necessity of order, a place for everything and everything in its place'.[12] This is repeated in the essay title associated with Aristotle in 'Night Lessons' in *Finnegans Wake*: 'A Place for Everything and Everything in its Place'.[13] Joyce had occasionally, in Wallace Stevens's phrase, a 'blessed rage for order'. When Frank Budgen inquired of the progress of Ulysses, Joyce replied: 'I have been working hard on it all day.' 'Does that mean that you have written a great deal?', Budgen asked. 'Two sentences,' said Joyce, in all seriousness. 'You have been seeking the *mot juste*?' 'No. I have the words already. What I am seeking is the perfect order of words in the sentence. There is an order in every way appropriate. I think I have it.'[14] The words in question referred to the seductive effect of women's silk petticoats hanging in a shop window: 'Perfume of embraces all him assailed. With hungered flesh obscurely, he mutely craved to adore.' 'You can see for yourself', said Joyce, in how many different ways they might be arranged.' This is echoed in *Finnegans Wake*: 'The ring man in the rong shop but the rite words by the rote order.'[15]

Joyce began to discover the philosophy of Aristotle in a formal academic manner, if not before, then certainly from his early days at university. He graduated in English, French and Italian, taking courses also in Mathematics, Physics, and Logic. His studies, however, took place within an atmosphere permeated by Aristotelian scholasticism. It is worth recalling that for the founder of the university, John Henry Newman, Aristotle was the 'oracle of nature and of truth'; he declared: 'to think correctly, is to think like Aristotle.'[16] Herbert Gorman, author of a biography written very much under Joyce's own direction, refers to Joyce's readings of Aristotle in Paris as 'rereadings', which, he says, 'were but a continuance of the road he had naturally found and followed under Jesuitical direction.'[17] Constantine Curran recalls the first lecture in the English Literature course: 'The professor was Father Darlington, the Dean of Studies, and his opening words were from Aristotle's *Poetics*.'[18] The following year Darlington moved from English to a chair in Philosophy.

Philosophy, doubtless that of Aristotle and St Thomas, also dominated Italian classes with Fr Ghezzi, who in all likelihood introduced Joyce to many notions of aesthetics. Eugene Sheehy depicts the scene: 'Joyce and I both attended the same class for Italian. Our lecturer was an Italian Jesuit named Father Ghezzi ... My function in the class was to listen to Father Ghezzi and Joyce discuss philosophy and literature in Italian, and, for all I could understand of the dialogue, I would have been more profitably engaged in taking high dives from the spring-board at the Forty-foot Hole in Sandycove.'[19]

William Dawson, auditor of the College Literary & Historical Society in 1902–1903, and also a past pupil of Belvedere recalled: 'The influences strongest upon us in those young days were Father Delany, Father Tom Finlay and Professor Magennis. And the greatest of those was Finlay. We strove to talk like him; perhaps, even, to think like him.'[20] Interestingly, in my own copy of the Logic handbook used in the College at the time, the first owner recorded the following quotation from Fr Finlay: 'I look upon scholasticism as the most perfect training for the mind that can be perceived.'

Of the broader picture Felix E. Hackett, another classmate of Joyce, writes as follows (playing on the original sense of the Greek word 'peripatetic', 'to walk', and its transferred meaning, referring to Aristotle who lectured as he strolled):

> Dublin at that time could well have been described as a city of peripatetic discourse. The university atmosphere around 86 St. Stephen's Green was indeed peripatetic also in the philosophic sense, as is evident from the description given by Joyce in A Portrait of the Artist as a Young Man. The aesthetic discussion with Father Darlington may be an idealised or a synthetic version of many such talks but it conveys the essence of the spirit of reference to Aristotle, which was the salient characteristic of Father Darlington's interventions in the discussions of the L. & H. and other societies such as the Library Conference and the Academy of St. Thomas Aquinas.[21]

For Joyce's commitment to Aristotle we have ample evidence. Stanislaus Joyce, James's younger brother, informs us in his diary: 'He upholds Aristotle against his friends, and boasts himself an Aristotelian.'[22] In Portrait of the Artist, Stephen declares: 'For my purpose I can work on at present by the light of one or two ideas of Aristotle and Aquinas.'[23]

Shortly after his arrival in Paris Joyce abandoned plans to study medicine, on learning that fees were to be paid in advance. He turned his attention, as it were, from physic to metaphysic, applying himself seriously to the study of Aristotle. On 8 February 1903 he wrote to Stanislaus: 'I am feeling very intellectual these times and up to my eyes in Aristotle's Psychology.'[24] The following month, on 20 March 1903, he wrote to his mother: 'I read every day in the Bibliotheque Nationale and every night in the Bibliotheque Sainte Genevieve ... I am at present up to my neck in Aristotle's *Metaphysics* and read only him and Ben Jonson.'[25] The following year, on 19 November 1904, he wrote to Stanislaus from Pola: 'I think that after a short course in Aristotle I will shut up the books and examine for myself in a cafe.'[26]

Joyce's Paris experiences are faithfully reflected, as we shall see, in Stephen's reflections in *Ulysses*. The quotations from Aristotle in his Paris Notebook of 1903–1904 are a valuable insight into what Joyce found significant in the writings of Aristotle, and into the way Joyce's understanding of the world was formed. The choice of passages, confirmed by his effort to transcribe them, attest to a tacit sympathy of mind. All aspects of Joyce's life and experience find expression in his work, either as material transmuted through artistic creation, or as principles of that very creation. This is particularly the case with Joyce's assimilation of Aristotle: the principles of the Philosopher are put to work in the construction, but also provide multiple elements of content.

Joyce's first published pronouncement on Aristotle was a review sent from Paris and published in the *Daily Express* on 3 September 1903 of John Burnet's book *Aristotle on Education*, a compilation drawn from Aristotle's *Ethics* and *Politics*. What is revealing in an otherwise unenthusiastic review is the conclusion: 'This book can hardly be considered a valuable addition to philosophical literature, but it has a contemporary value in view of recent developments in France, and at the present time, when the scientific specialists and the whole cohort of Materialists are cheapening the good name of philosophy, it is very useful to give heed to one who has been wisely named *maestro di color che sanno*.'[27] In a forceful declaration Joyce affirms the power of Aristotle's timeless wisdom against the emergent materialism of his day.

Aristotle also appears as an authority in *The Holy Office*, the famous satirical poem written by Joyce shortly before he left Dublin in 1904 lampooning Yeats and other leading figures of the Irish literary revival; he criticises in particular their spurious spirituality and false ethereal Celtic mysticism. He asks: 'Ruling one's life by commonsense / How can one fail to be intense?' In a literal interpretation of the doctrine of catharsis, Joyce sees it as his task to cleanse literary Ireland, appealing to Aristotle even in the most inauspicious surroundings:

> Myself unto myself will give
> This name, Katharsis-Purgative.
> I, who dishevelled ways forsook
> To hold the poets' grammar-book,
> Bringing to tavern and to brothel
> The mind of witty Aristotle,
> Lest bards in the attempt should err
> Must here be my interpreter:
> Wherefore receive now from my lip
> Peripatetic scholarship.

Anyone who has read Aristotle may well wonder about the phrase 'witty Aristotle'. He is not exactly the most light-hearted; I can think only of two or three passages where there might be the hint of intellectual playfulness. Hugh Kenner points out however that Joyce is translating Dante's description of Aristotle as *maestro di color che sanno* ('master of those who know') into a Saxon idiom; from the verb 'witan', 'witty' means 'knowing'.[28] As noted earlier, Swift also refers in *Gulliver's Travels* to Aristotle as 'renowned for wit and learning'.[29]

Joyce's natural sympathy with Aristotle also comes across in his review of a book by one of those figures targeted in 'The Holy Office', Lady Gregory's *Poets and Dreamers*. One might wonder why he should start a review with the name of Aristotle. The review was published on 26 March 1903, six days after he wrote that he was up to his neck in Aristotle's *Metaphysics*; drawing out the essence of the early pages of that treatise, he sketches the trajectory from childhood wonder to the wisdom of old age. He writes: 'Aristotle finds at the beginning of all speculation the feeling of wonder, a feeling proper to childhood, and if speculation be proper to the middle period of life it is natural that one should look to the crowning period of life for the fruit of speculation, wisdom itself.'[30]

Before proceeding to consider some of the more particular aspects of Aristotle's philosophy referred to in Joyce's writings, I would like to single out a principle of fundamental importance which indicates how hard-steeled Joyce is in the spirit of Aristotle. According to Richard M. Kain, the two basic themes of *Ulysses* were social criticism and philosophical relativity.[31] The following declaration from *Stephen Hero* is indicative: 'It is a mark of the modern spirit to be shy in the presence of all absolute statements. However sure you may be now of the reasonableness of your convictions you cannot be sure that you will always think them reasonable'.[32] In a review of Ibsen's *Catalina*, published in March 1903, Joyce wrote: 'As the breaking-up of tradition, which is the work of the modern era, discountenances the absolute, and as no writer can escape the spirit of his time, the writer of dramas must remember now more than ever a principle of all patient and perfect art which bids him express his fable in terms of his characters'.[33] Here in his recipe for the role of art in counteracting the relativism of the day, Joyce invokes Aristotle's use of character as exemplar.[34] Typical of this general frame of mind to which Joyce refers is the empiricist attitude, according to which we live in a world not of realities but of relativities. Aristotle's stance was diametrically opposed. Concerning his brother's passing curiosity in Pragmatism, Stanislaus Joyce noted: 'The asserted relativity of truth and the practical test of knowledge by its usefulness to an end ran counter not only to his Aristotelian principles of logic, but still more to his character'.[35]

To borrow a phrase from Descartes, founder of the modern philosophic spirit, Aristotle also sought the *fundamentum inconcussum veritatis*: the unshaken ground of truth. This is recognised by Stephen Dedalus: 'Aristotle's entire system of philosophy rests upon his book of psychology and that, I think, rests on his statement that the same attribute cannot at the same time and in the same connection belong to the same subject'.[36] In fact Stephen is mistaken – perhaps this is intentional on Joyce's part; it is in the *Metaphysics*, not his treatise on the soul, that Aristotle declares: 'The same thing cannot at the same time both belong and not belong to the same object and in the same respect'.[37] Aristotle wanted an absolute, necessary, non-hypothetical principle which would guarantee all discourse. Thus he formulated the famous law of non-contradiction. Stephen is clearly struck by the luminosity of this fundamental law governing all thought and pervading all reality: insofar as something is, it cannot not-be; insofar as we affirm, we cannot simultaneously deny. It is rigorous and compelling; it is absolutist. According to Aristotle, whoever denies it reduces himself to the status of the plant. Stanislaus, Joyce's brother, interestingly, invokes the evidence of the principle of non-contradiction when scorning the idea of belief in mystery: 'One would laugh at the ridiculous idea of Aristotle covering his face with his hands and praying to God in agony of spirit to remove the temptation to disbelieve in the principle that at the same time and in the same connection the same attribute cannot belong and not belong to the same object.'[38]

Joyce remarked to Mary Colum: 'The equation in mathematics and the syllogism in logic are the great intellectual inventions.'[39] Joyce was required to treat of syllogistic forms in his second year Logic examination at UCD. The first question on that paper asked: 'What position in Logic is assigned to the principles of Contradiction and Identity? Can these principles be said to constitute the Criteria of Truth?' The principle of non-contradiction reappears, appropriately reformulated, in *Finnegans Wake*:

> ...dime *is* cash and the cash system (you must not be allowed to forget that this is all contained, I mean the systems in the dogmarks of origen on spurios) means that I cannot now have or nothave a piece of cheeps in your pocket at the same time and with the same manners as you can now nothalf or half the cheek apiece I've in mind unless Burrus and Caseous have not or not have seemaultaneously sysentangled themselves, selldear to soldthere, once in the dairy days of buy and buy.[40]

In *Stephen Hero* the protagonist likewise expresses a criticism of the modern intellectual and moral climate: 'The modern spirit is vivisective. Vivisection itself is the most modern process one can conceive.'[41] Cranly rejoins presently: 'I suppose you know that Aristotle founded the science of biology.' (Joyce knew this from John Burnet's book *Aristotle and Education*).[42] Stephen replies: 'I would not say a word against Aristotle for the world but I think his spirit would hardly do itself justice in treating of the "inexact" sciences.'[43] Joyce may have been familiar with

Aristotle's comment that it is the mark of the wise person to only seek the degree of exactness which the subject allows;[44] this is quoted by Aquinas in the *Summa Contra Gentiles*,[45] which, on Gogarty's evidence, Joyce read continuously while in the Martello Tower.[46]

Richard Ellmann put it well when he stated that for Joyce, 'What the universe was had been laid down by Aristotle.'[47] One might well respond that in this he was no exception to the majority of the human race. Henri Bergson – of Irish-Jewish extraction, who died in the same year as Joyce – wrote that if we remove from Aristotle's philosophy everything derived from poetry and religion, as well as from a rudimentary physics and biology, we are left with a solid framework which is the 'natural metaphysic of the human intellect'.[48] What is this natural metaphysics of the human intellect? It is the spontaneous urge to accept the visible world around us as real and intelligible; most of us do not hold with Plato that the things we see are but images of higher essences, which abide in separation beyond our experience. We are accustomed, moreover, by our Western education to interpret the world through the categories first elaborated by Aristotle.

Stephen proclaims 'a genuine predisposition in favour of all but the "premisses" of scholasticism'.[49] Speaking of Joyce, Harry Levin sharply remarked: 'He lost his faith, but he kept his categories.'[50] These were none other than the categories of Aristotle, i.e. the philosophical concepts of scholasticism viewed independently of the theological premises upon which they were ultimately founded. The very term 'category' (meaning accusation or attribution) was borrowed by Aristotle from the law courts to express the diverse ways we interpret things. These categories, first named by Aristotle, are the labels of our daily discourse: substances, accidents, quality, quantity, relation, and so on: they are, in a phrase coined by Sidney Hook and beloved of Arthur Koestler, the 'grammar of existence'.[51] Aristotle's vocabulary has shaped our daily concepts, and the ways we view the world; Roget's *Thesaurus*, for example, broadly follows the outlines of Aristotle's metaphysics.

What makes Joyce unique in his Aristotelianism is that he made it reflectively his own, and applied it to his own art – either as material for its content, or as a principle of organization. There are many aspects of Aristotelian doctrine which enter into Stephen's consciousness, but I wish first to point out an influence which has not been adequately recognised. This is the notion of analogy as the principle of order which joins diversity and unity. Here, I suggest, is an Aristotelian doctrine consciously adopted by Joyce as a principle of artistic organization. In a letter to Ezra Pound, Joyce writes: 'I wonder if you will like the book I am writing? I am doing it, as Aristotle would say, by different means in different parts.'[52] In a critical essay on Joyce, Pound wrote in turn: 'He expresses himself differently in the different parts of his book (as even Aristotle permits), but it is not a case, as the distinguished Larbaud says, of abandoning the unity of style.'[53] Pound did not appreciate that this diversity of means for distinct ends is precisely the unity of style demanded, and not merely permitted, by Aristotle: the unity of analogy. The *principium operis* is made explicit in another letter by Joyce: 'It is also a kind of encyclopedia. My intention is not only to render the myth *sub specie temporis nostri* but also to allow each adventure (that is, every hour, every organ, every art being interconnected and interrelated in the somatic scheme of the whole) to condition and even to create its own technique.'[54] Joyce shared with Aristotle the recognition of analogy as fundamental to our understanding of nature. Analogy is intrinsic to the human mode of cognition, discovery and creativity. It is required most of all to unify disparate elements within the totality. Again it is interesting to note that a question in Joyce's Second Year Logic examination at University College Dublin concerned Aristotelian analogy.

Analogy is the key to Aristotle's synthesising mind, yielding rich results in many areas of his system but particularly in his biological works, poetics, and metaphysics. It is the organizing principle of his zoological investigations, allowing the discovery of order among disparate species on the basis of a similarity of function or operation. Put simply: birds have wings, fishes have fins; the study of a function in one species will cast light upon the corresponding function in a separate species, thus making for economy of research.[55] In the *Poetics* Aristotle understands metaphor as analogy of proportionality; it rests upon the ability to perceive likeness in the most unlikely places, and is the most important element in poetry. Most far-reaching is Aristotle's use of analogy in metaphysics. 'There is', he declares, 'analogy between all the categories of being.'[56] He states: 'In one sense, the causes and principles are different for different things; but in another, if one is to speak universally and analogically, they are all the same.'[57]

In the final paragraph of his important essay '*Ulysses*: A Short History', Richard Ellmann has written: '*Ulysses* may be seen to conduct its affirmation by discovery of kinship among disparate things, whether these are mind and body, casual and important, contemporary and Homeric, or Bloom and Stephen. The universe is, if nothing else, irrevocably interpenetrating.'[58] This all-universal interconnectedness of the universe is summed up in one of the phrases which Joyce copied by hand in the Bibliothèque Sainte-Geneviève in Paris from the work of Aristotle: 'Nature, it seems, is not a collection of unconnected episodes, like a bad tragedy.'[59] This line from the *Metaphysics* is re-echoed in Stephen's reference to 'The playwright who wrote the folio of this world and wrote it badly.'[60] Such is not the cosmos of Aristotle, who states: 'All things are ordered together somehow, but not all alike – both fishes and fowl and plants; and the world is not such that one thing has nothing to do with another, but they are all connected. For all are ordered together to one end.'[61] The perception of such pervasive unity which allows the convergence of relations between widely divergent realities and experiences is likewise one of the most fundamentally characteristic structures of Joyce's *oeuvre*. Herbert Gorman, his first biographer, remarked: 'There is an Aristotelean leaning toward the unities in Joyce.'[62] Analogical insight, the capacity to perceive unities of similarity across diverse or seemingly disparate contexts, was for Aristotle the greatest sign of genius.[63] It is a gift of nature which cannot be learned from another. Joyce was certainly familiar with this declaration from the *Poetics*, and he himself appreciated the importance of analogy; this is confirmed by his many references to analogy throughout *Ulysses*. In a phrase which rivals Johnson's celebrated description of metaphor as 'two ideas for one',[64] Joyce provides an analogy which conveys the very essence of analogy: 'Though they didn't see eye to eye in everything, a certain analogy there somehow was, as if both their minds were travelling, so to speak, in the one train of thought.'[65]

In June 1921 Joyce wrote to Harriet Shaw Weaver: 'My head is full of pebbles and rubbish and broken matches and lots of glass picked up "most everywhere". The task I set myself technically in writing a book from eighteen different points of view and in as many styles, all apparently unknown or undiscovered by my fellow tradesmen, that and the nature of the legend chosen would be enough to upset anyone's mental balance.'[66] Joyce, however, maintained his equipoise; besides the magpie's beak, which gathered the detritus and discarded debris of everyday living, Joyce had the eagle eye to grasp the grand majestic design. The Greek poet Archilochus contrasted the wiles of the fox who knows many things, with the single-mindedness of the hedgehog who knows one big thing.[67] True genius discerns both the singularity of the grand unity and the minutiae of multiplicity; for that reason it is exceedingly rare. The brilliance of *Ulysses* is that of a universal panorama woven from the torn shreds and broken shards of multifarious living; its success derives from the writer's mastery of creative analogy. Joyce is himself proof of Aristotle's conviction that analogy is a sign of unique genius, a natural gift that cannot be acquired. Joyce effected in art a fundamental insight gained from his study of Aristotle. One recalls Sartre's remark: 'The novelist's aesthetic always sends us back to his metaphysic.'[68]

Allied to this appreciation of analogy Joyce had moreover, unusually for his time, a proper understanding of Aristotle's famous principle governing the relation between art and nature. He correctly rejects a superficial interpretation, according to which art simply aims to copy nature as its original. '*E tekhne mimeitai ten physin* – This phrase is falsely rendered as "Art is an imitation of Nature". Aristotle does not here define art; he says only, "Art imitates Nature" and means that the artistic process is like the natural process.'[69] This is another example of a fundamental affinity between Aristotle and Joyce. In *Stephen Hero*, we gain the following insight from Stephen's reflection on his conversation with his professor: 'It must have been a surprise for him to find in such latitudes a young man who could not conceive a divorce between art and nature and that not for reasons of climate or temperament but for intellectual reasons. For Stephen art was neither a copy nor an imitation of nature: the artistic process was a natural process.'[70] Joyce's choice of phrase captures Aristotle's parallel, i.e. analogy, between the natural and artistic process. Intimately active in all her works nature resembles, Aristotle suggests, the artist who models in clay rather than the carpenter, since she shapes her product not at arm's length through an intermediate tool, but by palpably touching it herself in direct action.[71] This analogy, nevertheless, as Aristotle admits, fails to express the full power of nature, since 'the final cause and the beautiful are more fully present in the works of nature than in the works of art.'[72]

Joyce assimilated many elements of Aristotelian construction, most noticeably the unity of action. Both *Exiles* and *Ulysses* are acted out in a single day. He accepted Aristotle's demand for a certain magnitude in drama. Joyce considered Synge's *Riders to the Sea* (which he helped translate into Italian) too short to have a tragic scope.[73] When Synge showed him the manuscript in Paris in March 1903, he was ungenerous, referring to it as a 'dwarf-drama'.[74] Beauty requires, according to Aristotle, not only an orderly arrangement of parts, but must also be of a certain magnitude.[75] Synge had been encouraged by Yeats' praise that the play was 'quite Greek'; Joyce wrote to Stanislaus in 1903: 'Thanks be to God Synge isn't an Aristotelian.'[76] Presumably he wished to preserve that stronghold for himself, preferring to count Synge among his Celtic platonizing rivals.[77] His view changed, however, over the years, since in the programme notes for the play, performed by his own troupe in Zurich in June 1918, he wrote: 'Whether a brief tragedy be possible or not (a point on which Aristotle had some doubts) the ear and the heart mislead one gravely if this brief scene from "poor Aran" be not the work of a tragic poet.'[78]

Having suggested a general architectonic principle of *Ulysses*, I wish to consider some elements of Aristotle's philosophy which feature throughout the work, either as artistic technique or material content. Stephen comes across with the naïve and admirable enthusiasm of one who names the world for the first time, having discovered the illuminating language of the philosopher. He is not yet the doctrinaire Aristotelian: there is an element of parody, perhaps even a touch of caricature. He brings to bear all the mentality and jargon of Aristotle in his encounter with the world in the 'Nestor' and 'Proteus' episodes. Aristotle too provides the stylistic wherewithal for 'Aeolus', which relies heavily on Aristotle's *Rhetoric*. 'Scylla and Charybdis' throws up perilous dilemmas which lurk within the deep. Stephen is set adrift as his Aristotelianism is confronted by the radical alternative of Platonism; as he clings to the rock of Aristotelian realism he is challenged by the modern rejection of self which threatens to unsettle the traditional solidity of substance.

Aristotelian metaphysics and psychology provide Stephen in *Ulysses* with the vocabulary and categories he needs to understand himself and to interpret the world. Aristotle inspires Stephen's musings upon a series of enigmas presented to his consciousness throughout the course of the day. We are privy to his thoughts on the meaning of history (in the classroom), the nature of perception and knowledge (Sandymount strand), and the identity of the self (National Library). To appreciate the Aristotelian context for these reflections, it will be helpful to first outline some few elementary concepts from both Aristotle's metaphysics and psychology.

The greatest challenge faced by Aristotle in metaphysics was the declaration by Parmenides that change was impossible. Fixated with the overwhelming logic which rules the stark separation between being and non-being, this giant of Presocratic philosophy argued that for something to become other than what it is, requires that it necessarily pass to its only alternative, i.e. nonbeing. Aristotle's greatest merit was to discern that 'being is said in many ways'.[79] He recognized the distinction between actual and potential being. Change is, in language with which we are all familiar and which we owe to Aristotle, the actualization of that which is potential; in his lapidary definition, change or movement is 'the act of the potential as potential'.

Aristotle further distinguished two related meanings of actuality. There is the word '*energeia*' (our word 'energy'), meaning to be active, or literally 'at work'; he also coined the term '*entelecheia*' to denote the fully actualized perfection of something once it has attained its goal and completed its action.[80] 'Entelechy' denotes the actuality of an individual insofar as it is fundamentally determined as a definite kind of substance; another word used to describe this is essence or 'form' (Greek *eidos*). Both terms, as we shall see, are central to Stephen's theorizing. Unfortunately the word 'form' suggests to the ordinary ear the meaning of external or superficial: 'outline' or 'shape'. Form or *eidos* is for Aristotle the most intrinsic actualising principle which determines the very essence of things. It is the basic perfection or actualization of an individual as itself – its first determination. The most significant instance of form for Aristotle is the soul, which he defines as 'the first actuality (*entelechy*) of a natural body endowed with organs'.[81] The body will act, and further actualize itself by means of its organs, but in order to do so, these must first be determined and co-ordinated as the organs of this particular body. Before it can do anything whatsoever, the body must itself be actualized as such. Aristotle's notion of form is well conveyed by Edmund Spenser: 'For of the soul the body form doth take / For soul is form and doth the body make'.[82] With the rise of the scientific method and its influence in modern philosophy the Aristotelian principle of form was abandoned, as evidenced by the preface to Newton's *Principia*: 'the moderns, rejecting substantial forms and occult qualities, have endeavoured to subject the phenomena of nature to the laws of mathematics'.[83] Substance was rejected by the British empiricists, prompting doubts regarding self-identity such as those that trouble Stephen in 'Scylla and Charybdis'.

Moving on to Aristotle's psychology we note how these same concepts are exploited by Aristotle to explain the nature of the soul and its cognitive activity. The human soul is for Aristotle a unique kind of form, *eidos* or entelechy: whereas the form of every other kind of living thing is limited to itself, the human form has the capacity to receive immaterially into itself, in both sensation and intellection, the forms of everything that it knows.[84] Aristotle thus calls it the 'form of forms' – as the hand is the 'tool of tools', because it literally '*manu*-factures' every other tool or instrument. Although for Aristotle all intellectual knowledge depends for its content upon sensation, its activity is to some degree independent of the senses; in this mode of separation it is, according to Aristotle,[85] 'immortal and eternal' – incorrectly (perhaps intentionally) transcribed by Joyce in his Paris notebook as 'immortal and *divine*'.[86]

We may now proceed to observe how these notions are interlaced in Stephen's reflections. Stephen's school colleague and headmaster, Mr Deasy, views history *sub specie aeternitatis*: his perspective is eschatological – not merely Christian but Hegelian in the extreme: 'All human history moves towards one great goal, the manifestation of God'.[87] Stephen experiences history differently. Subjectively it is the nightmare from which he is trying to awake; objectively it is the actualization of possible contingencies, and in this regard, his interpretation is Aristotelian. Past events are simply happenings which have taken place and are thus removed from the world of possible contingency – excised from time, and forever inscribed on the scroll of history: 'Had Pyrrhus not fallen by a beldam's hand in Argos or Julius Caesar not been knifed to death? They are not to be thought away. Time has branded them and fettered they are lodged in the room of the infinite possibilities they have ousted'.[88] Aristotle himself declares: 'What has happened cannot be made not to have happened'.[89]

Stephen provides a summary definition of history, and explains his source: 'It must be a movement then, an actuality of the possible as possible. Aristotle's phrase formed itself within the gabbled verses and floated out into the studious silence of the library of Sainte Genevieve where he had read, sheltered from the sin of Paris, night by night'.[90] This is one of the phrases that Joyce copied into his Paris notebook: 'Movement is the actuality of the possible as possible'. Joyce's reliance here on Aristotle calls for comment. The translation which he used, that of J. Barthélemy-Saint-Hilaire,[91] was, in the words of a later French translator, 'très deféctueuse'.[92] Correctly the text reads: 'Movement is the actuality of the potential as potential'. Aristotle defines motion or change as the actuality, or actualization, not of the possible as the possible, but of the potential as potential. The correct French equivalent is 'puissance' or 'potentialité', not 'possibilité'.[93] What difference could this simple difference between 'potency' and 'possibility' have made to the composition of Ulysses? What are the consequences of Joyce's mistake regarding one of the most fundamental doctrines of Aristotle's metaphysics? Perhaps none, other than a change of word that re-occurs throughout the book. The phrase 'actuality of the potential as the potential', it must be said, does not have the same flowing cadence, so perhaps the error is bien trouvé.

This same paragraph from 'Nestor' is rich in Aristotelian allusion and association. Having theorized about history in the light of Aristotle's metaphysics, Stephen progresses to reflections upon knowledge, thought and the soul, based upon both Aristotle's Metaphysics and De Anima: 'Thought is the thought of thought. Tranquil brightness. The soul is in a manner all that is: the soul is the form of forms. Tranquillity sudden, vast, candescent: form of forms'.[94] Joyce once more draws from his treasury of quotations, taking licence, however, in fusing – if not indeed confusing – aspects of Aristotle's psychology with his metaphysics and theology. As we have seen, the soul is for Aristotle the 'form of forms', because it uniquely has the power to assimilate in an immaterial mode the essences or forms of everything it knows. God is defined by Aristotle as the 'thought of thought'. Thinking is the highest act of which humans are capable, hence the best activity we can ascribe to the Prime Mover. And since the only proper object of God's thinking can be God himself, i.e. the being whose nature is itself the plenitude of thought, God is defined as *noesis noeseos*.

Joyce here applies the phrase 'thought of thought' to the activity of intellect. There is no need to suggest, as does Sheldon Brivic, that 'form of forms' is 'clearly a definition of godhead, the first cause of everything else', and that Joyce equates mind with God.[95] 'Form of forms' is Aristotle's definition of soul; 'thought of thought' is his description of the prime mover. Stephen merely assimilates both phrases – a natural association, but there can be no identification of the human mind with God. The self-reflection of intellectual knowledge (the 'form of forms' reflecting upon its contents), while clearly different from the self-thinking thought of god, may equally be described as thought of thought. In his intellectual activity man most resembles the nature of divinity; Aristotle remarks that we sometimes do what God does always. There is no reason, however, to read this identification into Stephen's musings.

The opening paragraphs of 'Proteus' are a farrago of philosophic reflection drawing upon a wide diversity of sources: Aristotle, Boehme, Berkeley and Weininger. The Aristotelian allusions are well known, including two of the most famous phrases from the entire work: 'ineluctable modality of the visible'[96] and 'ineluctable modality of the audible'.[97] They summarize with accuracy Aristotle's fundamental teaching regarding the infallibility of sense knowledge, as outlined in *De Anima*, which Joyce had studied in the Bibliothèque Sainte Geneviève. While it is possible that scholars may yet discover that Joyce borrowed the phrase 'ineluctable modality', I am inclined to believe it to be of his own coinage. Robert McAlmon spotted in Joyce what he himself recognised as the professional malady of young writers, and from which Joyce never recovered, namely a penchant towards particular words. McAlmon mentioned in particular the words 'ineluctable' and 'metempsychosis' – 'grey, clear, abstract, fine-sounding words that are "ineluctable" a bit themselves'.[98] The common French word '*modalité*' is another such fine-sounding word which strikes the Anglophone visitor as lending extraordinary elegance to everyday French conversation. It is unnecessary to seek Joyce's penchant for the word in the Kantian transcendental deduction of the categories.

The meaning and source of 'ineluctable modality' are straightforward. According to Aristotle, each of the sense faculties is infallible within its particular, very restricted, domain. The eye perceives colour, the ear perceives sound; in the simple apprehension of their respective objects they cannot err. Joyce copied from Aristotle's book *On the Soul*: 'The sensation of particular things is always true.'[99] This follows by definition from the very nature of the sense faculty itself: the eye is the organ equipped exclusively to grasp colour; the ear is the faculty which necessarily and inevitably grasps sound. 'Ineluctable' is Joyce's choice word for the necessity and inevitability of sense knowledge. Aristotle makes the important distinction between the proper and the common objects of perception; colour is the proper sensible of the eye, sound the proper sensible of the ear. Size, shape, speed and distance, on the other hand, are among what he calls the 'common perceptibles', which may be grasped by more than one sense faculty. I am open to error if I judge the perceived object by relying on only one of my senses.

For Aristotle sensation thus provides a secure foundation for knowledge. The phrase 'thought through my eyes'[100] confirms the Aristotelian doctrine that the intellect is itself barren and void of content; it must be activated by the senses, from which it receives its material. This reflection on sensation and thought is repeated later in the work, where Stephen considers the difficulty of seeing correctly with defective eyes: 'Distance. The eye sees all flat. Brain thinks. Near: far. Ineluctable modality of the visible.'[101] The eye necessarily perceives according as it is equipped; erroneous impressions are corrected by the judgment of intellect. We find this reflection also in 'Scylla and Charybdis', in the debate between Platonism and Aristotelianism: 'God: noise in the street: very peripatetic. Space: what you damn well have to see'.[102]

The contrast between Aristotle and Plato is dramatised by Joyce in 'Scylla and Charybdis'. 'The brain', he told Frank Budgen, 'is the organ presiding over Scylla and Charybdis. The Aristotelian and Platonic philosophies are the monsters that lie in wait in the narrows for the thinker.'[103] The German romantic philosopher Friedrich Schlegel (1772–1829) remarked that every man is born either a Platonist or an Aristotelian; Joyce probably knew this aphorism via Coleridge (1772–1834). He was himself very much the Aristotelian; Yeats was very much the Platonist, represented in this episode by Eglington and Russell: 'Art has to reveal to us ideas, formless spiritual essences. The supreme question about a work of art is out of how deep a life does it spring . . . Plato's world of ideas. All the rest is the speculation of schoolboys for schoolboys'.[104] He becomes impassioned: 'Upon my word it makes my blood boil to hear anyone compare Aristotle with Plato'.[105] Stephen, the empirically grounded Aristotelian is steadfast: 'Hold to the now, the here, through which all future plunges to the past'.[106] The reality is here and now, the instant when history occurs. In the spirit of the young Stephen Hero, who aims 'to pierce to the significant heart of everything',[107] in *Ulysses* he resolves: 'Unsheathe your dagger definitions. Horseness is the whatness of allhorse'.[108]

Soon Stephen begins to ponder his own self-identity as he recalls the pound he once borrowed from Russell: with the passage of time does he, as lender, still exist? Put crassly, have not all his molecules changed? More subtly: is he still the same individual, despite his discrete memories: is he the same enduring 'I' – indicated punctually: 'I, I' – or are there different successive selves: 'I. I'?.[109] The dilemma is clarified with the help of Aristotle: Stephen endures in his identity by virtue of his personal entelechy – persisting under the ever-changing forms that pass and are remembered, because the soul is the primordial 'form of forms'. Contemplating his debt to Russell, whose pseudonym was 'Æ', Stephen concludes his musings with one of the most brilliant literary jokes in any language, a sentence consisting entirely of the vowels 'A.E.I.O.U.'[110]

According to William James, whose pragmatist theories held brief interest for Joyce,[111] 'The passing Thought is the only Thinker which Psychology requires.'[112] This is essentially the narrative technique employed by Joyce the author: consciousness itself abides within the flowing stream. It could not, however, satisfy Stephen, who briefly entertains Locke's theory of self-identity as grounded in memory, but holds fast to a belief in soul, the primary entelechy governing the exchange of molecules and giving actuality to memory. In one of his metaphysical insights in 'Nighttown', Stephen brilliantly describes first entelechy, the soul, as 'the structural rhythm'.[113] With this principle, Aristotle could respond to the *panta rhei* ('all is flux') of Heraclitus; one could step twice into the same stream, indeed step out of it, as the stream itself flows on: 'human nature was a constant quantity', we read in *Stephen Hero*.[114]

We may well ask: how can Joyce the 'Aristotelian' reconcile the ineluctable modalities not only of the audible, visible, and other sensibles, but more crucially the ineluctability of the laws of thought, with his technique of free association? Can the analytic/synthetic/dialectic mentality of Aristotle host the idiosyncratic idiom of the *monologue intérieur*? One recalls Coleridge's remark about 'the streamy nature of association, which thinking-reason curbs and rudders'.[115] Does not the flow of consciousness, as Anthony Burgess suggests, follow 'subterranean laws of association rather than logic'?[116] Joyce's technique exemplifies the problem of identity posed by Stephen. But Aristotle too recognizes the power of association, which is equally indispensable for metaphor; it is likewise a gift of nature, free and spontaneous, which cannot be learned from another but is a sign of genius. For Aristotle there is no conflict, only the difference between two levels of human activity: the primary order of natural reality and the derivative order of creative imitation. There is no reason to believe Joyce would disagree.

Whereas *Ulysses* is the book which celebrates daytime life and existence, *Finnegans Wake* ponders the brooding world of nocturnal obscurity. In *Ulysses* what Mario Vargas Llosa calls the 'metaphysical greyness of Dublin'[117] becomes lambent in the epiphanies of Stephen, illuminated by the categories of Aristotle. In *Finnegans Wake* the shadows of darkness prevail; the lucid grammar of existence is no longer valid. In a letter to Joyce, Harriet Weaver referred to the 'darkness and unintelligibilities of your deliberately-entangled language system'.[117] This was possibly in reply to what Joyce had written to her some weeks earlier: 'One great part of every human existence is passed in a state which cannot be rendered sensible by the use of wideawake language, cutanddry grammar and goahead plot'.[119] As Sheldon Brivic remarks,

'Causality is carried beyond Aristotle in the *Wake*.'[120] The logic of identity, of 'either/or', ruled by the law of non-contradiction, is subsumed into a unity of opposites governed by the paradox of 'both/and'. Aristotle gives way to Nicholas of Cusa, alias Micholas de Cusack: dichotomies 'by the coincidance of their contraries reamalgamerge in that indentity of indiscernibles'.[121] Florry Talbot, lady of Nighttown, proclaims the profound axiom of psychoanalytic theory: 'Dreams go by contraries.'[122]

Seamus Deane remarks: 'In the *Wake*, the Greeks don't get a look-in',[123] which makes my present task much simpler. Aristotle is given his correct name only once, in connection with the law of universal order: 'A Place for Everything and Everything in its Place'.[124] We have seen how his formulation of the principle of non-contradiction is the subject of parody. Also parodied is his statement in the *Poetics* that 'a probable impossibility is to be preferred to a thing improbable and yet possible'.[125] With oblique allusion to John Pentland Mahaffy's clever quip that 'in Ireland the inevitable never happens, the unexpected always', the author of the *Wake* writes:

> in this madh vaal of tares . . . where the possible was the improbable and the improbable the inevitable . . . we are in for a sequentiality of improbable possibles though possibly nobody after having grubbed up a lock of cwold cworn above his subject probably in Harrystotalies or the vivle will go out of his way to applaud him on the onboiassed back of his remark for utterly impossible as are all these events they are probably as like those which may have taken place as any others which never took person at all are ever likely to be. Ahahn![126]

Joyce pokes fun here at Aristotle, as well as the Bible. Later we are told that the polymorphic protagonist is a 'conformed aceticist and aristotaller'.[127] These few references would seem to be the extent of Aristotle's presence in Joyce's final masterpiece. I suspect, however, in a phrase favoured by one Irish politician, that we may find in *Finnegans Wake* further 'vestigial evidence' of Joyce's favourite philosopher.

NOTES

INTRODUCTION

1   See Louise Johncox, 'Trip To The Top', *The Times*, 28 October 1995.

2   See the remarkable passage from Coleridge, p. 149 below.

3   William Norris Clarke, *The Universe as Journey. Conversations with W. Norris Clarke, S.J.* (New York: Fordham University Press, 1988), p. 53.

4   *Pol.* 3, 11, 1282a22–3.

5   *Pol.* 6, 6, 1320b35–7, trans. Jowett, *CW* 2, p. 2096.

6   *Pol.* 3, 2, 1276b24–5, trans. Rackham, p. 187.

7   *Rhet.* 2, 20, 1393b6–8.

8   *Pol.* 7, 4, 1326a35–1326b2, trans. Jowett, *CW* 2, p. 2105.

9   *De Motu An.* 2, 698b8–699a12.

10   *Insomn.* 2, 460b26–7.

11   *De Motu An.* 7, 701b25–8.

12   *EN* 2, 9, 1109a30–4.

13   *EN* 3, 3, 1112b5.

14   *EN* 3, 1, 1110a8–11.

15   *EN* 9, 6, 1167b6–9.

16   *Rhet.* 2, 5, 1383a29–32.

17   *Phys.* 4, 4, 212a8–20.

18   See *Protrepticus*, ed. D.S. Hutchinson & Monte Ransome Johnson, www.protrepticus.info, p. 53. Accessed 15 August 2015. See Anton-Hermann Chroust, *Aristotle. New Light on his Life and on Some of his Works* (Notre Dame: University of Notre Dame Press, 1973), vol. 2, p. 106. Also Ingemar Düring, *Aristotle's Protrepticus. An Attempt at Reconstruction* (Gothenburg: Acta Universtitatis, 1961), p. 69.

19   *EN* 7, 2, 1146a35.

20   *Ath. Const.* 16.

21   *EN* 10, 5, 1175b11–12.

22   *EN* 8, 2, 1155b29.

23   J.G. Kohl, *Travels in Ireland* (London: Bruce and Wyld, 1844), pp. 70–1. Similar reverence for the philosopher is evident in the devotion of the Clerk (probably an ecclesiastical student) in Chaucer's *Canterbury Tales*:

A clerk from Oxford was there also,

Who'd studied philosophy, long ago.

As lean was his horse as is a rake,
And he too was not fat, that I take,
But he looked emaciated, moreover, abstemiously.
Very worn off was his overcoat; for he
Had got him yet no churchly benefice,
Nor he was worldly to accept secular office.
For he would rather have at his bed's head
Some twenty books, all bound in black or red,
Of Aristotle and his philosophy
Than rich robes, fiddle, or gay psaltery.
Yet, and for all he was philosopher in base,
He had but little gold within his suitcase.
(Geoffrey Chaucer, *The Canterbury Tales*, ed. Sinan Kökbugur, http://www.librarius.
com/cantales.htm. Accessed 22 October 2015).
The original text:
A clerk ther was of Oxenford also,
That unto logyk hadde longe ygo.
As leene was his hors as is a rake,
And he nas nat right fat, I undertake,
But looked holwe and therto sobrely.
Ful thredbare was his overeste courtepy;
For he hadde geten hym yet no benefice,
Ne was so worldly for to have office.
For hym was levere have at his beddes heed
Twenty bookes, clad in blak or reed,
Of Aristotle and his philosophie,
Than robes riche, or fithele, or gay sautrie.
But al be that he was a philosophre,
Yet hadde he but litel gold in cofre.

24 Johann Wolfgang von Goethe, *Sämtliche Werke*, vol. 3 (Stuttgart: Cotta'scher Verlag,
1840), p. 160: 'Wir würden gar vieles besser kennen, wenn wir es nicht zu genau
erkennen wollten.'

25 *EN* 6, 7, 1141a33; 6, 7, 1141a21.

26 *Phys.* 1, 1, 184a20, trans. Hardie & Gaye, *CW* 1, p. 315. Here is the full paragraph
in another translation: 'The path of investigation must lie from what is more
immediately cognizable and clear to us, to what is clearer and more intimately
cognizable in its own nature; for it is not the same thing to be directly accessible to
our cognition and to be intrinsically intelligible. Hence, in advancing to that which
is intrinsically more luminous and by its nature accessible to deeper knowledge,
we must needs start from what is more immediately within our cognition, though

in its own nature less fully accessible to understanding.' Trans. Wicksteed & Cornford, p. 11.

27   *EN* 1, 7, 1098b2.

28   *Met.* 3, 1, 995a29–30: λύειν δ' οὐκ ἔστιν ἀγνοοῦντας τὸν δεσμόν.

29   *EN* 6, 7, 1141b6–8.

30   *De Caelo* 2, 13, 294a12, trans. Stocks modified, *CW* 1, p. 484.

31   Jonathan Barnes, *Aristotle. A Very Short Introduction* (Oxford: Oxford University Press, 2000), p. 137.

32   Barnes, ibid.

33   Pythian Ode 2, 72: γένοι᾿, οἷος ἐσσὶ μαθών. *Olympian Odes, Pythian Odes,* ed. William H. Race (Cambridge, MA: Harvard University Press, 1997), p. 244.

34   Thomas Speed Mosby, *Little Journeys to Parnassus* (Jefferson City, MO: Hugh Stephens, 1922), p. 32. Johannes Scottus Eriugena, the Irish giant of medieval philosophy, referred to Aristotle as 'the shrewdest among the Greeks in discovering the way of distinguishing natural things'. (*Periphyseon* I, 463A: 'Aristoteles acutissimus apud Graecos, ut aiunt, naturalium rerum discretionis repertor omnium rerum.') Alfred North Whitehead accorded to Aristotle 'the position of the greatest metaphysician', remarking about Aristotle's God, that 'in his consideration of this metaphysical question [Aristotle] was entirely dispassionate; and he is the last European metaphysician of first-rate importance for whom this claim can be made… It may be doubted whether any properly general metaphysics can ever, without the illicit introduction of other considerations, get much farther than Aristotle.' *Science and the Modern World* (New York: Macmillan, 1967), p. 173. Gilbert Highet, the renowned modern classicist, described Aristotle as 'probably the best and broadest single mind the human species has yet produced'. *The Art of Teaching* (New York: Vintage, 1950), p. 161.

35   *De An.* 3, 8, 431b21: ἡ ψυχὴ τὰ ὄντα πώς ἐστι πάντα.

36   *Part. An.* 1, 3, 643a25.

37   The alternative to something's existence is total nothingness; the alternative to its essence is for it to be the essence of something else: existence and essence belong to different orders. See Fran O'Rourke, *Pseudo-Dionysius and the Metaphysics of Aquinas* (Notre Dame, IN: University of Notre Dame Press, 2005), especially pp. 174–87. See pp. 180–1 above.

38   *De Spiritualibus Creaturis*, art. 5: Proprium philosophiae eius fuit a manifestis non discedere.

39   Henri Bergson, *Creative Evolution* (London: Macmillan, 1922), p. 344.

40   See Ingemar Düring, *Aristotle's Protrepticus*, pp. 78–85.

Chapter One

1   From 'Incantation' by Czesław Miłosz. Trans. Robert Pinsky, *The Figured Wheel* (New York: Farrar, Straus & Giroux, 1966), p. 32, by kind permission of the translator.

2   Valentin Rose (ed.), *Fragmenta* (Stuttgart: Teubner, 1967), p. 420, no. 668: ὅσῳ γὰρ αὐτίτης καὶ μονώτης εἰμί, φιλομυθότερος γέγονα.

3   Werner Jaeger, *Aristotle. Fundamentals of the History of his Development* (Oxford: Oxford University Press, 1934), p. 321.

4   *Poet.* 9, 1451b5–7: διὸ καὶ φιλοσοφώτερον καὶ σπουδαιότερον ποίησις ἱστορίας ἐστίν: ἡ μὲν γὰρ ποίησις μᾶλλον τὰ καθόλου, ἡ δ᾽ ἱστορία τὰ καθ᾽ ἕκαστον λέγει. Trans. Stephen Halliwell, *The Poetics of Aristotle. Translation and Commentary* (Chapel Hill: University of North Carolina Press, 1987), p. 41. Depending on the version which best fits the discussion, I also cite translations by Bywater, Hamilton Fyfe, as well as Halliwell's version published in the Loeb series. Remaining quotations from Halliwell in this chapter are from the Loeb translation. References to the *Poetics* are according to Rudolf Kassel, *Aristotelis de Arte Poetica Liber* (Oxford: Clarendon Press, 1966).

5   See Stephen Halliwell, 'Aristotelian Mimesis and Human Understanding', in Øivind Andersen and Jon Haarberg (eds), *Making Sense of Aristotle. Essays in Poetics* (London: Duckworth, 2001), pp. 87–107.

6   *Met.* 1, 1, 980a22: πάντες ἄνθρωποι τοῦ εἰδέναι ὀρέγονται φύσει.

7   *Met.* 1, 2, 982b12–13: διὰ γὰρ τὸ θαυμάζειν οἱ ἄνθρωποι καὶ νῦν καὶ τὸ πρῶτον ἤρξαντο φιλοσοφεῖν.

8   See *Met.* 1, 2, 982b17–19, trans. W.D. Ross, *CW* 2, p. 1554.

9   *Rhet.* 1, 11, 1371b27–8: ἔστιν δ᾽ ἡ σοφία πολλῶν καὶ θαυμαστῶν ἐπιστήμη. References are according to R. Kassel, *Ars Rhetorica* (Berlin: de Gruyter, 1976).

10   *De An.*, 3, 8, 431b21; *De An.*, 3, 5, 430a14–15.

11   See Josef Pieper, *Leisure the Basis of Culture* (New York: Mentor, 1963), pp. 103–4.

12   See Gabriel Marcel, *Being and Having* (Westminster: Dacre Press, 1949), p. 117: 'A problem is something which I meet, which I find completely before me, but which I can therefore lay siege to and reduce. But a mystery is something in which I am myself involved, and it can therefore only be thought of as a sphere where the distinction between what is in me and what is before me loses its meaning and initial validity.' See also Noam Chomsky, *Reflections on Language* (London: Fontana, 1976), p. 137.

13   *Gen. An.* 5, 8, 788b20–2: 'Nature is neither lacking in providing what is necessary, nor does it work anything which is superfluous or in vain.' (ἐπεὶ δὲ τὴν φύσιν ὑποτιθέμεθα, ἐξ ὧν ὁρῶμεν ὑποτιθέμενοι, οὔτ᾽ ἐλλείπουσαν οὔτε μάταιον οὐθὲν ποιοῦσαν τῶν ἐνδεχομένων περὶ ἕκαστον). *De Caelo*, 1, 4, 271a33: 'Nature and God

do nothing in vain' (ὁ δὲ θεὸς καὶ ἡ φύσις οὐδὲν μάτην ποιοῦσιν). See James G. Lennox, 'Nature does nothing in vain…', in H.-Chr. Günther & A. Rengakos (eds), *Beiträge zur antiken Philosophie, Festschrift für Wolfgang Kullmann* (Stuttgart: Franz Steiner, 1997), pp. 199–214.

14 *Rhet.* 1, 1, 1355a15–17, trans. Roberts, *CW* 2, p. 2154.

15 *Rhet.* 1, 1, 1355a21–22, trans. Roberts, ibid.; *Rhet.* 1, 1, 1355a37–8: 'Things that are true and things that are better are, by their nature, practically always easier to prove and more persuasive.' Trans. Roberts, ibid.; *Rhet.* 3, 2, 1404b19–20: 'What is natural (πεφυκότως) is persuasive (πιθανόν); what is artificial the opposite.' My trans. *Rhet.* 1, 7, 1365b1: 'What aims at reality is better than what aims at appearance.' Trans. Roberts, *CW* 2, p. 2172.

16 *Met.* 1, 2, 982b17–18: ὁ δ᾽ ἀπορῶν καὶ θαυμάζων οἴεται ἀγνοεῖν.

17 See *Phys.* 1, 1, 184a16–21; *EN* 1, 4, 1095b2–3; *Met.* 7, 3, 1029b11.

18 *Met.* 2, 1, 993b7–11.

19 *Rhet.* 1, 11, 1370a16–18: καὶ οὗ ἂν ἡ ἐπιθυμία ἐνῇ, ἅπαν ἡδύ· ἡ γὰρ ἐπιθυμία τοῦ ἡδέος ἐστὶν ὄρεξις. Trans. Freese modified, p. 117.

20 *Rhet.* 1, 11, 1371a31–34: καὶ τὸ μανθάνειν καὶ τὸ θαυμάζειν ἡδὺ ὡς ἐπὶ τὸ πολύ· ἐν μὲν γὰρ τῷ θαυμάζειν τὸ ἐπιθυμεῖν μαθεῖν ἐστιν, ὥστε τὸ θαυμαστὸν ἐπιθυμητόν, ἐν δὲ τῷ μανθάνειν <τὸ> εἰς τὸ κατὰ φύσιν καθίστασθαι. My trans.

21 *Poet.* 24, 1460a17–18. Aristotle states also at *Rhet.* 3, 2, 1404b12 that what is marvellous is pleasant. See pp. 35-6 below.

22 *Poet.* 24, 1460a13–14.

23 *Poet.* 24, 1460a26–7. See *Poet.* 25, 1461b11–12: 'For poetic effect a convincing impossibility (πιθανὸν ἀδύνατον) is preferable to that which is unconvincing though possible (ἀπίθανον καὶ δυνατόν).' Trans. Fyfe, p. 111.

24 *Poet.* 25, 1461b14.

25 *Poet.* 25, 1460b10.

26 Stephen Halliwell refers to 'a discrepancy between the intrinsically rational and secular standards of probability or plausibility on which Aristotle's theory as a whole depends, and the fundamentally religious outlook embodied in the traditional myths of tragedy'. *The Poetics of Aristotle*, p. 175.

27 *Poet.* 9, 1451b33–5.

28 *Poet.* 24, 1460a27–9, trans. Halliwell, p. 125. See also 1454b6–7.

29 *Poet.* 15, 1454a33–6.

30 *Poet.* 24, 1460a34–5, trans. Halliwell, p. 125.

31 *Poet.* 15, 1454b1–6, trans. Halliwell, p. 81.

32 *Poet.* 9, 1451a37–8.

33 *Poet.* 25, 1460b23–6.

34 *Poet.* 25, 1460b13–15.

35 *Poet.* 25, 1461b9–10.

36 *Poet.* 25, 1461b14–15: πρὸς ἅ φασιν τἄλογα· οὕτω τε καὶ ὅτι ποτὲ οὐκ ἄλογόν ἐστιν· εἰκὸς γὰρ καὶ παρὰ τὸ εἰκὸς γίνεσθαι. Trans. Halliwell, p. 135.

37 *Rep.* 533c.

38 See Søren Kierkegaard: 'One should not think slightingly of the paradoxical; for the paradox is the source of the thinker's passion, and the thinker without a paradox is like a lover without feeling, a paltry mediocrity.' *Philosophical Fragments* (Oxford: Oxford University Press, 1936), p. 29.

39 *Poet.* 9, 1452a4–7, trans. Bywater, *CW* 2, p. 2323.

40 *Poet.* 11, 1452a30–1: ἐξ ἀγνοίας εἰς γνῶσιν μεταβολή.

41 *Poet.* 16, 1455a16–17, trans. Bywater, *CW* 2, p. 2328.

42 As Aristotle explains in the *Physics*, so-called 'chance' events may be unintended, unforeseen or unpredicted; they are, however, caused and may be explained. Chance and fortune (τὸ αὐτόματον καὶ ἡ τύχη) imply the antecedent activity of mind and nature as causes. See *Phys.* 2, 6, 198a5–12. Chance is thus properly coincidence, i.e. the accidental concurrence of a sequence normally due to natural teleology. *Phys.* 2, 5, 197a32–5: 'Both luck and chance, then, are causes that come into play incidentally and produce effects that possibly, but not necessarily or generally, follow from the purposeful action to which in this case they are incident, though the action might have been taken directly and primarily for their sake.' Trans. Wicksteed & Cornford, p. 155. See also *Phys.* 2, 6, 197b18–21.

43 Jonathan Lear, 'Katharsis', in Amélie Oksenberg Rorty (ed.), *Essays on Aristotle's Poetics* (Princeton: Princeton University Press, 1992), p. 324.

44 Perfect knowledge is the privilege of the gods (*Met.* 1, 2, 982b28–983a10). Human nature, according to Aristotle, is in many ways servile. It is because he does not enjoy perfect σοφία that man engages in φιλοσοφία.

45 *EN* 6, 12, 1144a4–6.

46 See *EN*, Bk 10, chaps 7–8.

47 *Met.* 9, 8, 1050a35–b1.

48 *Poet.* 4, 1448b13–15, trans. Fyfe modified, p. 15. For a wide-ranging discussion see Stephen Halliwell, 'Pleasure, Understanding, and Emotion in Aristotle's *Poetics*', in Amélie Oksenberg Rorty (ed.), *Essays in Aristotle's Poetics*, pp. 241–60. For a comprehensive treatment of all relevant passages, see Basileios A. Kyrkos, *Die Dichtung als Wissensproblem bei Aristoteles* (Athen: Gesellschaft für Thessalische Forschung, 1972), pp. 95–108.

49 *Rhet.* 1, 10, 1369b15–16: δι' ἐπιθυμίαν δὲ πράττεται ὅσα φαίνεται ἡδέα.

50 *Rhet.* 1, 11, 1370a3–4: ἀνάγκη οὖν ἡδὺ εἶναι τό τε εἰς τὸ κατὰ φύσιν ἰέναι ὡς ἐπὶ τὸ πολύ. Φύσις is that which each thing is in its complete state, when its coming-to-be (γένεσις) is complete. *Pol.* 1, 2, 1252b32–34: ἡ δὲ φύσις τέλος ἐστίν· οἷον γὰρ ἕκαστόν ἐστι τῆς γενέσεως τελεσθείσης, ταύτην φαμὲν τὴν φύσιν εἶναι ἑκάστου, ὥσπερ ἀνθρώπου ἵππου οἰκίας.

51 *Rhet.* 1, 11, 1371b12: τὸ κατὰ φύσιν ἡδύ.

52 *Rhet.* 1, 10, 1369b33–5: ὑποκείσθω δὴ ἡμῖν εἶναι τὴν ἡδονὴν κίνησίν τινα τῆς ψυχῆς καὶ κατάστασιν ἀθρόαν καὶ αἰσθητὴν εἰς τὴν ὑπάρχουσαν φύσιν. Ἀθρόαν can also mean 'all at once' or 'suddenly'.

53 See *Rhet.* 1, 11, 1370a27–28: Pleasure is the sensation of a certain kind of emotion (πάθος), namely the attainment of that which we desire (ἐστὶν τὸ ἥδεσθαι ἐν τῷ αἰσθάνεσθαί τινος πάθους).

54 *Rhet.* 1, 11, 1371b8–10, trans. Freese, p. 125.

55 *Poet.* 4, 1448b15–17: 'The reason of the delight in seeing the picture is that one is at the same time learning – gathering the meaning of things, e.g. that the man there is so-and-so (ὅτι οὗτος ἐκεῖνος).' Trans. Bywater, *CW* 2, p. 2318.

56 *Poet.* 4, 1448b6–7. At *Problems* 30, 6, 956a11–14 the question is asked why man should be obeyed more than other animals: 'Is it because he is the most imitative (for it is for this reason that he can learn)?' Trans. Forster, *CW* 2, p. 1504.

57 *Rhet.* 3, 10, 1410b19.

58 Nature is the primordial and principal origin of poetry in every respect, endowing all men with a natural inclination for imitation, rhythm and harmony (*Poet.* 4, 1448b20–2: κατὰ φύσιν δὲ ὄντος ἡμῖν τοῦ μιμεῖσθαι καὶ τῆς ἁρμονίας καὶ τοῦ ῥυθμοῦ … ἐξ ἀρχῆς οἱ πεφυκότες). *Poet.* 4, 1448b22–4: 'Starting with these instincts men very gradually developed them until they produced poetry out of their improvisations.' Trans. Fyfe, p. 15. Poetry, in the strict sense of an original literary creation, must still be explained. Nature, Aristotle suggests, selects some individuals for special favour, bestowing the gifts of the muses upon poets, not uniformly but in accordance with their *individual* nature; this accounts for the different genres of poetry (διεσπάσθη δὲ κατὰ τὰ οἰκεῖα ἤθη ἡ ποίησις). More serious poets represent 'noble actions and the doings of fine men' in hymns and eulogies, while those of less exalted nature depict the deeds of inferior men, starting first with satire (*Poet.* 4, 1448b24–7).

59 *Rhet.* 3, 2, 1404b9–12: ὥσπερ γὰρ πρὸς τοὺς ξένους οἱ ἄνθρωποι καὶ πρὸς τοὺς πολίτας, τὸ αὐτὸ πάσχουσιν καὶ πρὸς τὴν λέξιν· διὸ δεῖ ποιεῖν ξένην τὴν διάλεκτον· θαυμασταὶ γὰρ τῶν ἀπόντων εἰσίν, ἡδὺ δὲ τὸ θαυμαστόν ἐστιν. My trans. See *Rhet.* 3, 3, 1406a15–16: ἐξαλλάττει γὰρ τὸ εἰωθὸς καὶ ξενικὴν ποιεῖ τὴν λέξιν.

60 *Rhet.* 3, 2, 1405a8–9, my trans.

61 *Poet.* 22, 1459a5–7: πολὺ δὲ μέγιστον τὸ μεταφορικὸν εἶναι. μόνον γὰρ τοῦτο οὔτε παρ' ἄλλου ἔστι λαβεῖν εὐφυΐας τε σημεῖόν ἐστι. See *Rhet.* 3, 2, 1405a9–10.

62 See *Rhet.* 3, 10, 1410b14; *Rhet.* 3, 10, 1410b21.

63 *Rhet.* 3, 10, 1410b10–12, trans. Freese, pp. 397–9.

64 E.M. Cope, *The 'Rhetoric' of Aristotle, with a Commentary*, vol. 3, J.E. Sandys (ed.) (Cambridge: Cambridge University Press, 1877), p. 20.

65 *Part. An.* 1, 5, 644b22–645a26, trans. William Ogle, *CW* 1, pp. 1003–4. See text, viii above.

66   *Part. An.* 1, 5, 645a16–17.

67   *Part. An.* 1, 5, 644b31–644b35.

68   See the opening lines of *De Anima* (*De An.* 1, 1, 402a1–4), where Aristotle also contrasts the accuracy of knowledge with the excellence of its object.

69   *Met.* 12, 10, 1075a16–18.

70   *Met.* 4, 1, 1003a21: ἔστιν ἐπιστήμη τις ἣ θεωρεῖ τὸ ὂν ἧ ὄν.

71   Of course, this is not the case for Aristotle, for whom the eternity of the world is axiomatic.

72   This is admirably dealt with by Josef Pieper, in the lecture 'The Philosophical Act', published in *Leisure the Basis of Culture* (New York: Mentor, 1963).

73   *Erläuterungen zu Hölderlins Dichtung* (Frankfurt am Main: Klostermann, 1971), p. 42: 'Voll Verdienst, doch dichterisch wohnet / Der Mensch auf dieser Erde.' Heidegger comments: 'Was der Mensch wirkt und betreibt, ist durch eigenes Bemühen erworben und verdient. "Doch" – sagt Hölderlin in harter Entgegensetzung dazu – all das berührt nicht das Wesen seines Wohnens auf dieser Erde, all das reicht nicht in den Grund des menschlichen Daseins.'

74   *Poet.* 9, 1451b8–9, trans. Halliwell, p. 59.

75   *Rhet.* 3, 8, 1408b27–8. See also *Rhet.* 3, 9, 1409a31; *Gen. An.* 1, 1, 715b14–16: ἡ δὲ φύσις φεύγει τὸ ἄπειρον· τὸ μὲν γὰρ ἄπειρον ἀτελές, ἡ δὲ φύσις ἀεὶ ζητεῖ τέλος. In *Phys.* 3, 6, 207a 7–10, Aristotle contrasts ἄπειρον ('amorphous', 'boundless') with τέλειον καὶ ὅλον ('complete and whole'), the qualities required in the action of tragedy. See S.H. Butcher, *Aristotle's Theory of Poetry and Fine Art* (London: Macmillan, 1902), p. 275. Also Humphry House, *Aristotle's Poetics* (London: Rupert Hart-Davis, 1956), pp. 48–51.

76   William James, *The Principles of Psychology* (New York: Dover, 1950), vol. 2, p. 353.

77   Siger of Brabant, *Quaestiones in IV Metaphysicam*, ed. William Dunphy (Louvain-la-Neuve: Éditions de l'Institut Supérieur de Philosophie, 1981), pp. 169–70: Si enim quaeratur quare est magis aliquid in rerum natura quam nihil. See Friedrich Schelling, *Werke* 13, p. 242: 'If I go to the limits of all thought, I must recognize is as possible that there were nothing at all. The last question is always, Why is there anything at all, why is there not nothing?' (Wenn ich bis an die Grenze alles Denkens gehen will, so muß ich ja auch als möglich anerkennen, daß überall nichts wäre. Die letzte Frage ist immer: warum ist überhaupt etwas, warum ist nicht nichts?). *Sämtliche Werke* 13 (Stuttgart: Cotta, 1858), p. 242. See p. 7: 'Weit entfernt also, daß der Mensch und sein Thun die Welt begreiflich mache, ist er selbst das Unbegreiflichste, und treibt mich unausbleiblich zu der Meinung von der Unseligkeit alles Seyns, einer Meinung, die in so vielen schmerzlichen Lauten aus alter und neuer Zeit sich kundgegeben. Gerade Er, der Mensch, treibt mich zur letzten verzweiflungsvollen Frage: warum ist überhaupt etwas? warum ist nicht nichts?' See *The Grounding of Positive Philosophy*, trans. Bruce Matthews (Albany:

SUNY Press, 2007), p. 94: 'Thus far from man and his endeavors making the world comprehensible, it is man himself that is the most incomprehensible and who inexorably drives me to the belief in the wretchedness of all being, a belief that makes itself known in so many bitter pronouncements from both ancient and recent times. It is precisely man that drives me to the final desperate question: Why is there anything at all? Why is there not nothing?'

78   *Poet.* 25, 1460b9–13, trans. Fyfe modified, p. 101.

79   *Poet.* 9, 1451a36–8.

80   See Malcolm Heath, 'The Universality of Poetry in Aristotle's *Poetics*', *Classical Quarterly* 41 (1991), p. 400: 'The universals which are embodied in poetry need not tell us the truth about the world; …what is said or believed to be true is an admissible object of imitation as well as what is in fact true. In other words, it is consistent with the nature of poetry that the possibilities which it discloses to us are those not of the real world but of commonly believed falsehood.'

81   *Rhet.* 2, 20, 1394a2–6.

82   *Rhet.* 3, 2, 1405a9–10, *Poet.* 22, 1459a4–7.

83   *Rhet.* 3, 11, 1412a11–12, trans. Roberts, *CW* 2, p. 2253.

84   Gerald F. Else, *Aristotle's Poetics: The Argument* (Leiden: Brill, 1957), p. 306. Else continues: 'The ultimate never confronts us in the *Poetics*, any more than it does in the *Ethics* or the *Politics* – except in the form of Chance or the marvellous, τὸ θαυμαστόν.' However, it is precisely in its experience of τὸ θαυμαστόν, in the perfect act of θεωρία, that human nature at its most sublime resembles divine nature, whose life is 'like the best which we temporarily enjoy'. (*Met.* 12, 7, 1072b16). Hannah Arendt remarks: '*Theoria* in fact, is only another word for *thaumazein*; the contemplation of truth at which the philosopher ultimately arrives is the philosophically purified speechless wonder with which he began.' *The Human Condition* (Chicago: University of Chicago Press, 1998), p. 302. Aristotle declares: 'If the happiness which God always enjoys is as great as that which we enjoy sometimes, it is marvellous; and if it is greater, this is still more marvellous.' (*Met.* 12, 7, 1072b24–6, trans. Tredennick, p. 151).

85   *Poet.* 1, 1447a8–9, trans. Halliwell.

86   Cf. Stephen Halliwell, *The Poetics of Aristotle. Translation and Commentary*, p. 177: 'Poetry had for long been regarded as a repository of wisdom, knowledge and moral insight, capable of exhibiting the finest values and ideals of human life (particularly through heroic myth) and of conveying both explicit and implicit injunctions to human conduct.'

87   *Poet.* 1, 1447a12–13, trans. Halliwell, p. 29.

88   Shakespeare, Sonnet 44.

89   Pindar, *Pythian Ode* 4, 247–8: καί τινα οἶμον ἴσαμι βραχύν· πολλοῖσι δ᾽ ἄγημαι σοφίας ἑτέροις.

90   Pindar, *Pythian Ode* 9, 54: ἐπ' ἄλλοτ' ἄλλον ὥτε μέλισσα θύνει λόγον.

91   Martin Heidegger, *Erläuterungen zu Hölderlins Dichtung*, p. 17.

92   Plutarch, *De Audiendis Poetis* 35f: οὕτως ὅ τι ἂν ἀστεῖον εὕρωμεν παρ' αὐτοῖς καὶ χρηστόν, ἐκτρέφειν χρὴ καὶ αὔξειν ἀποδείξεσι καὶ μαρτυρίαις φιλοσόφοις ... καὶ γὰρ δίκαιον καὶ ὠφέλιμον, ἰσχὺν τῆς πίστεως καὶ ἀξίωμα προσλαμβανούσης, ὅταν τοῖς ἀπὸ σκηνῆς λεγομένοις καὶ πρὸς λύραν ᾀδομένοις καὶ μελετωμένοις ἐν διδασκαλείῳ τὰ Πυθαγόρου δόγματα καὶ τὰ Πλάτωνος ὁμολογῇ. *Moralia*, vol. 1 (Cambridge, MA: Harvard University Press, 1927), trans. Frank Cole Babbitt, p. 189.

CHAPTER TWO

1   *The Prose Works of Sir Philip Sidney*, vol. 3, ed. Albert Feuillerat (Cambridge: Cambridge University Press, 1963), p. 26.

2   Herodotus, 1, 30. There is evidence, however, that Pythagoras had already used the word a century earlier, and more than likely had coined the word. Cicero gives the most complete account of the circumstances, citing the fourth century (BC) philosopher Heraclides of Pontus. It is worth including his opening remark: 'While we see that philosophy is something very ancient, we admit that its name is of recent origin... [Pythagoras] is said to have visited Phlius and to have spoken learnedly and eloquently with Leon, the ruler of the Phlisians. Leon, admiring his genius and eloquence, asked him what skill he professed; but he replied that he knew no skill but was a philosopher. Leon wondered at the novel word and asked what philosophers were and how they differed from other men; but Pythagoras replied that life seemed to him like the gathering where the great games were held, which were attended by the whole of Greece. For some men sought to win fame and the glory of the crown by exerting their bodies, others were attracted by the gain and profit of buying and selling, but there was one kind of man, the noblest of all, who sought neither applause nor profit but came in order to watch and wanted to see what was happening and how: so too among us, who have migrated into this life from a different life and mode of being as if from some city to a crowded festival, some are slaves to fame, others to money; but there are some rare spirits who, holding all else as nothing, eagerly contemplate the universe; these he called lovers of wisdom, for that is what philosopher means; and as at the festival it most becomes a gentleman to be a spectator without thought of personal gain, so in life the contemplation and understanding of the universe is far superior to all other pursuits.' Trans. H.B. Gottschalk, *Heraclides of Pontus* (Oxford: Clarendon Press, 1980), pp. 23–4. Diogenes Laertius states explicitly that Pythagoras 'was the first to give philosophy its name and to call himself a philosopher' (1, 12: Φιλοσοφίαν δὲ πρῶτος ὠνόμασε Πυθαγόρας καὶ ἑαυτὸν φιλόσοφον.) As the source for his more

succinct account he cites Sosicrates: Σωσικράτης δ' ἐν Διαδοχαῖς φησιν αὐτὸν ἐρωτηθέντα ὑπὸ Λέοντος τοῦ Φλιασίων τυράννου τίς εἴη, φιλόσοφος εἰπεῖν. καὶ τὸν βίον ἐοικέναι πανηγύρει· ὡς οὖν εἰς ταύτην οἱ μὲν ἀγωνιούμενοι, οἱ δὲ κατ' ἐμπορίαν, οἱ δέ γε βέλτιστοι ἔρχονται θεαταί, οὕτως ἐν τῷ βίῳ οἱ μὲν ἀνδραποδώδεις, ἔφη, φύονται δόξης καὶ πλεονεξίας θηραταί, οἱ δὲ φιλόσοφοι τῆς ἀληθείας (8, 8). See also Iamblichus, *De Vita Pythagorica* 44, 58, 59, 159.

3   Herodotus 2, 53: οὗτοι δέ εἰσι οἱ ποιήσαντες θεογονίην Ἕλλησι καὶ τοῖσι θεοῖσι τὰς ἐπωνυμίας δόντες καὶ τιμάς τε καὶ τέχνας διελόντες καὶ εἴδεα αὐτῶν σημήναντες.

4   *Rhet.* 2, 9, 1387a16–17.

5   Hermann Broch: 'So stand Homer an der Wiege des Griechentums, Sprachschöpfer, Mythenbildner, Dichter und Philosoph. Und in seiner Hand hielt er den Keim des Künftigen.' *Gesammelte Werke* 10 (Zürich, Rhein-Verlag, 1967), p. 304.

6   Strabo, 1, 2, 3: οἱ παλαιοὶ φιλοσοφίαν τινὰ λέγουσι πρώτην τὴν ποιητικήν, εἰσάγουσαν εἰς τὸν βίον ἡμᾶς ἐκ νέων καὶ διδάσκουσαν ἤθη καὶ πάθη καὶ πράξεις μεθ' ἡδονῆς.

7   Plutarch, *De audiendis poetis*, 36d: ἔτι δὲ προανοίγει καὶ προκινεῖ τὴν τοῦ νέου ψυχὴν τοῖς ἐν φιλοσοφίᾳ λόγοις.

8   Porphyry, *Quaestiones Homericae*, ed. H. Schrader (Leipzig: Teubner, 1882). Werner Jaeger perhaps overstates Homer's importance for Neoplatonism: 'The pupils of the Neoplatonists, partly of Oriental (Near Eastern) origin, needed the study of Homer very badly in order to understand Plato against his own Hellenic background, as do modern philosophers. As a matter of fact, Homer was taught in the Neoplatonic school by Proclus and Iamblichus also, and could hardly ever have been entirely dropped from it even at the time of Porphyry, who had written several works on the great poet. For ages Homer had been the equivalent of what the average Greek understood by "paideia," as we can see from the Greek novels written in Hellenistic times.' Werner Jaeger, *Early Christianity and Greek Paideia* (Oxford: Oxford University Press, 1962), p. 126.

9   My favourite example of myth providing an allegorical explanation for a natural phenomenon refers to the origin of the Milky Way. Zeus seduces Alcmene, wife of Amphytrion, who becomes pregnant with Hercules. Hera, wife of Zeus, is tricked into suckling the child, who bites too hard on the nipple, causing Hera to pull away and her milk to spray across the sky. Details of the story vary but the essentials remain the same. The word 'galaxy' is derived from γάλα, Greek for milk.

10   *Rep.* 607b: παλαιὰ μέν τις διαφορὰ φιλοσοφίᾳ τε καὶ ποιητικῇ.

11   Fragment 40: πολυμαθίη νόον ἔχειν οὐ διδάσκει. Hermann Diels & Walter Kranz, *Die Fragmente der Vorsokratiker* I (Zürich: Weidmann, 1992), p. 160.

12   Hesiod, *Theogony* 124.

13   Fragment 57. Diels/Kranz I, p. 163.

14   Fragment 42. Diels/Kranz I, p. 160.

15   J.W.H. Atkins, *Literary Criticism in Antiquity. A Sketch of its Development*, vol. 1 (London: Methuen, 1952), p. 14.

16   Liddell and Scott, *An Intermediate Greek-English Lexicon* (Oxford: Clarendon Press, 1975. First edition 1889), p. 759.

17   Ibid., p. 37. The standard large edition simply gives: 'interpret allegorically', 'speak figuratively or metaphorically', 'veiled language'. See Lidl & Aldi, *Greek-English Lexicon*, 9th edition with Revised Supplement (Oxford: Clarendon Press, 1996), p. 69.

18   *Odyssey*, XIX, 203; Cf. Hesiod, *Theogony*, 27–8.

19   *Patrologia Latina* 210, 451C: At, in superficiali litterae cortice falsum resonat lyra poetica, sed interius, auditoribus secretum intelligentiae altioris eloquitur, ut exteriore falsitatis abjecto putamine, dulciorem nucleum veritatis secrete intus lector inveniat. Trans. Marie-Dominique Chenu, *Nature, Man, and Society in the Twelfth Century* (Chicago: University of Chicago Press, 1957), p. 99.

20   Plutarch, *De Iside et Osiride* 358f–359a.

21   *Rep.* 401c: ἰχνεύειν τὴν τοῦ καλοῦ τε καὶ εὐσχήμονος φύσιν.

22   *Meno* 99d.

23   *Ion* 533e, trans. W.R.M. Lamb (Cambridge, MA: Harvard University Press, 2001). In the *Apology* (22bc), Socrates declares that 'poets do not compose their poems with knowledge, but by some inborn talent and by inspiration, like seers and prophets who also say many fine things without any understanding of what they say'. Trans. G.M.A. Grube, *Plato. Complete Works*, ed. John M. Cooper (Indianapolis: Hackett, 1997), p. 22.

24   J.W.H. Atkins, *Literary Criticism in Antiquity*, vol. 1, p. 12. Cf. *Odyssey* 8, 44–5; 8, 62–4.

25   Cf. *Theogony* 2, 22–34.

26   *Works and Days* 662: μοῦσαι γάρ μ' ἐδίδαξαν ἀθέσφατον ὕμνον ἀείδειν.

27   *Ion* 534b, trans. Paul Woodruff, *Plato. CW*, p. 942.

28   *Phaedrus* 245a, trans. H.N. Fowler (Cambridge, MA: Harvard University Press, 1966) modified.

29   *Lysis* 214a: οὗτοι γὰρ ἡμῖν ὥσπερ πατέρες τῆς σοφίας εἰσὶν καὶ ἡγεμόνες.

30   *Meno* 81a.

31   *Rep.* 595a–608b. I present here a standard summary of Plato's position. For a detailed examination, see Stephen Halliwell, *The Aesthetics of Mimesis. Ancient Texts and Modern Problems* (Princeton: Princeton University Press, 2002), pp. 37–147. See also Jos Mertens, 'De Artistieke Mimèsis bij Plato', *Tijdschrift voor Filosofie* 43 (1981), pp. 642–98.

32   *Ion*, 530b.

33   *Rep.* 599d.

34   *Rep.* 596d, 601b.

35   *Rep.* 608a.

36   *Rep.* 607a.

37   *Poet.* 9, 1451b5–7, trans. Stephen Halliwell, *The Poetics of Aristotle. Translation and Commentary* (Chapel Hill: University of North Carolina Press, 1987), p. 41.

38   Cf. *EN* 6, 3, 1139b28–9: ἡ μὲν δὴ ἐπαγωγὴ ἀρχῆς ἐστι καὶ τοῦ καθόλου, ὁ δὲ συλλογισμὸς ἐκ τῶν καθόλου.

39   *Met.* 7, 7, 1032a32–b2: ἀπὸ τέχνης δὲ γίγνεται ὅσων τὸ εἶδος ἐν τῇ ψυχῇ· εἶδος δὲ λέγω τὸ τί ἦν εἶναι ἑκάστου καὶ τὴν πρώτην οὐσίαν.

40   S.H. Butcher, *Aristotle's Theory of Poetry and Fine Art* (London: Macmillan, 1902), p. 192.

41   *Poet.* 7, 1450b23–1451a15.

42   *Poet.* 23, 1459a17–21, trans. Malcolm Heath, *Arisotle. Poetics* (London: Penguin, 1996), p. 38. Butcher (p. 188), erroneously in my view, maintains that in both passages ζῷον refers to the *picture* of a ζῷον. This is indicative of a certain Platonic tendency in his interpretation of Aristotle's approach to poetry. The notion of organic unity recurs repeatedly as a leitmotif in Aristotle's analysis of art, poetry and tragedy. Paramount in tragedy is the plot (μῦθος); it is the 'principle and, as it were, the soul (ψυχή) of the tragedy' (1450a37: ἀρχὴ μὲν οὖν καὶ οἷον ψυχὴ ὁ μῦθος τῆς τραγῳδίας). Tragedy is principally an imitation of action (1450b3: μίμησις πράξεως). Hence its most important aspect is the combination or arrangement of actions (1452a15: ἡ τῶν πραγμάτων σύστασις). Integral to unity are wholeness and completeness, which is why Aristotle stresses the importance of beginning, middle and end in the representation of action. (1450b26: ὅλον δέ ἐστιν τὸ ἔχον ἀρχὴν καὶ μέσον καὶ τελευτήν: 'A whole is that which has a beginning, middle and end.') The unity of the μῦθος comes from the fact that it deals with a single, continuous action in its entirety (1451a28–32: περὶ μίαν πρᾶξιν . . . ἐπεὶ πράξεως μίμησίς ἐστι, μιᾶς τε εἶναι καὶ ταύτης ὅλης. 1452l5: συνεχοῦς καὶ μιᾶς.) A bad drama is one which lacks the proper sequence and development of episodes (1451b34).

43   *Met.* 14, 3, 1090b19–20: οὐκ ἔοικε δ' ἡ φύσις ἐπεισοδιώδης οὖσα ἐκ τῶν φαινομένων, ὥσπερ μοχθηρὰ τραγῳδία.

44   *Phys.* 2, 2, 194a21–2

45   *EN* 6, 4, 1140a10–16, trans. Rackham (Cambridge, MA: Harvard University Press, 1947), p. 335.

46   Liberato Santoro, *The Tortoise and the Lyre* (Dublin: Irish Academic Press, 1993), p. 25. Φύσις is the 'principle of that which has within itself its own source of motion and change.' (*Phys.* 2, 1, 192b13–14). Cf. *Phys.* 2, 1, 192b20–23; *Phys.* 2, 1, 192b28–9: An artefact 'does not have within itself the principle of its own making'.

47   *Part. An.* 1, 1, 639 b 19–21: μᾶλλον δ' ἐστὶ τὸ οὗ ἕνεκα καὶ τὸ καλὸν ἐν τοῖς τῆς φύσεως ἔργοις ἢ ἐν τοῖς τῆς τέχνης. Trans. Peck, amended.

48   *Gen. An.* 1, 22, 730b29–32.

49   *Poet.* 9, 1451b4–7, trans. Heath.

50   *Met.* 7, 13,1038b11–12.

51   According to Nicolai Hartmann, 'The poet must bring to light the ideal dimension of what is beyond the given reality.' Cited by Liberato Santoro, *Tortoise and the Lyre*, p. 39. See Nicolai Hartmann, *Aesthetics*, trans. Eugene Kelly (Berlin: De Gruyter, 2014), p. 291: 'It is always the poets – that is, the epic poets – who hold the ideal image of man and virtue before the people's eyes that define the ethos against which the people must measure themselves, and, in fact, do so measure themselves.' John Henry Newman: 'Biography and history represent individual characters and actual facts; poetry, on the contrary, generalizing from the phenomena of nature and life, supplies us with pictures drawn not after an existing pattern, but after the creation of the mind... Moreover, by confining the attention to one series of events and scene of action, it bounds and finishes off the confused luxuriance of real nature; while, by a skilful adjustment of circumstances, it brings into sight the connection of cause and effect, completes the dependence of the parts one on another, and harmonizes the proportions of the whole.' John Henry Newman, 'Poetry with reference to Aristotle's Poetics', in Edmund D. Jones (ed.), *English Critical Essays (Nineteenth Century)* (Oxford: Oxford University Press, 1959), p. 199.

52   *Poet.* 15, 1454b8–15.

53   *Poet.* 25, 1461b13: τὸ γὰρ παράδειγμα δεῖ ὑπερέχειν.

54   *Phys.* 2, 8, 199a15–17. See Ficino: 'Non servi [sumus] naturae, sed aemuli.' *Theologia Platonica*, 13, 3 (Hildesheim: Olms, 1975), p. 220.

55   *Pol.* 3, 11, 1281b10–15, trans. B. Jowett, *CW* 2, p. 2034.

56   *Poet.* 25, 1460b32.

57   *Poet.* 2, 1448a11–12.

58   S.H. Butcher, *Aristotle's Theory of Poetry*, p. 153; italics in original. See also pp. 150, 161, 184.

59   According to Butcher, poetry is the highest form of imitative art, which creates according to a true idea (*EN* 6, 4, 1140a10); the latter he identifies with εἶδος, 'an ideal form which is present in each individual phenomenon but imperfectly manifested'. The artist seeks 'to bring to light the ideal which is only half revealed in the world of reality' (p. 153). Poetry is an expression of the universal element in human life, eliminating the transient, revealing the essential features of the original. 'It discovers the "form" (*eidos*) towards which an object tends, the result which nature strives to attain, but rarely or never can attain. Beneath the individual it finds the universal. It passes beyond the bare reality given by nature, and expresses a purified form of reality disengaged from accident, and freed from conditions which thwart its development' (p. 150). See also pp. 161, 184.

60   *Phys.* 2, 1, 193b3–4.

61   *Phys.* 2, 1, 193a30–31.

62 Butcher, *Aristotle's Theory of Poetry*, p. 153.

63 *Poet.* 9, 1451b8–9, trans. Halliwell, *The Poetics of Aristotle*, p. 41. Halliwell's italics.

64 Butcher, *Aristotle's Theory of Poetry*, p. 153.

65 *Top.* 8, 14, 164a10–11; Cf. *An. Post.* 2, 19, 100 a3–b5.

66 *Poet.* 2, 1448a1; *Poet.* 9, 1451b27–9: 'It is clear … that the poet should be more a maker of plots than of verses, in so far as he is a poet by virtue of mimesis, and his mimesis is of actions.' Trans. Stephen Halliwell, *Aristotle. Poetics* (Cambridge, MA: Harvard University Press, 1995), p. 61.

67 Martha Nussbaum, *The Fragility of Goodness. Luck and Ethics in Greek Tragedy and Philosophy* (Cambridge: Cambridge University Press, 1986), p. 386.

68 *EN* 3, 1, 1110b6–7: αἱ γὰρ πράξεις ἐν τοῖς καθ' ἕκαστα.

69 Cf. Stephen Halliwell, 'Pleasure, Understanding, and Emotion in Aristotle's *Poetics*', in Amélie Oksenberg Rorty (ed.), *Essays on Aristotle's Poetics* (Princeton, NJ: Princeton University Press, 1992), p. 250: 'Universals are related to causes, reasons, motives, and patterns of intelligibility in the action and characters as a whole.' See also Stephen Halliwell, 'Aristotelian Mimesis Reevaluated', in Lloyd Gerson (ed.), *Aristotle. Critical Assessments*, vol. 4 (London: Routledge, 1999), p. 318: 'A poem which incorporates historical details is not for that reason mimetic, but only insofar as it works these into a dramatized pattern of action which exhibits "universals".'

70 Malcolm Heath, 'The Universality of Poetry in Aristotle's Poetics', *Classical Quarterly* 41 (1991), p. 390.

71 See Francis Bacon, *De Augmentis Scientiarum* 2. 13: 'Res gestae et eventus qui verae historiae subjiciuntur non [sunt] eius amplitudinis in qua anima humana sibi satisfaciat.' *Works of Francis Bacon*, vol. 1, ed. James Spedding et al. (New York: Garrett Press, 1968), p. 518. Trans. vol. 4, p. 316: 'The acts and events which are the subjects of real history are not of sufficient grandeur to satisfy the human mind.' Cited by Butcher, *Aristotle's Theory of Poetry*, p. 185: 'The acts or events of true history have not that magnitude which satisfieth the mind of man.'

72 Martha Nussbaum, *Fragility of Goodness*, p. 386.

73 Jonathan Lear, 'Katharsis', in Amélie Oksenberg Rorty (ed.), *Essays on Aristotle's Poetics* (Princeton, NJ: Princeton University Press, 1992), p. 339, n 63. According to G.E.M. de Ste Croix, while Aristotle was probably thinking of Thucydides, the latter was 'the one historian who is least open to the charge of merely relating particular events and failing to deal with universals, with "what might happen"'. G.E.M. de Ste Croix, 'Aristotle on History and Poetry' in Amélie Oksenberg Rorty (ed.), *Essays on Aristotle's Poetics*, p. 27.

74 Thucydides 1, 10, 3: ἦν εἰκὸς ἐπὶ τὸ μεῖζον μὲν ποιητὴν ὄντα κοσμῆσαι.

75 Thucydides 1, 20, 3.

76 Thucydides 1, 21, 1.

77 Thucydides 1, 22, 4, trans. Charles Foster Smith (Cambridge, MA: Harvard

University Press, 1956), p. 41. Aristotle also remarks that 'for the most part, the future resembles the past'. (*Rhet.* 2, 20, 1394a8–9: ὅμοια γὰρ ὡς ἐπὶ τὸ πολὺ τὰ μέλλοντα τοῖς γεγονόσιν).

78   *Met.* 1, 1, 981a15–17: ἡ μὲν ἐμπειρία τῶν καθ' ἕκαστόν ἐστι γνῶσις ἡ δὲ τέχνη τῶν καθόλου, αἱ δὲ πράξεις καὶ αἱ γενέσεις πᾶσαι περὶ τὸ καθ' ἕκαστόν εἰσιν.

79   *Poet.* 9, 1451b9.

80   *Met.* 6, 2, 1026b35: τὸ μὲν ἀεὶ ἢ ὡς ἐπὶ τὸ πολύ. See also *Post. An.* 2, 12, 96a10; *Rhet.* 1, 11, 1371b14; *Rhet.* 2, 20, 1394a8–9.

81   *Poet.* 9, 1451b33–35: τῶν δὲ ἁπλῶν μύθων καὶ πράξεων αἱ ἐπεισοδιώδεις εἰσὶν χείρισται· λέγω δ' ἐπεισοδιώδη μῦθον ἐν ᾧ τὰ ἐπεισόδια μετ' ἄλληλα οὔτ' εἰκὸς οὔτ' ἀνάγκη εἶναι.

82   Gottfried Wilhelm Leibniz, *Philosophical Writings* (London: Dent, 1973), p. 24.

83   *Poet.* 6, 1450a38–9.

84   *Part. An.* 1, 5, 644b22–645a26, trans. William Ogle, *CW* 1, pp. 1003–4. See page viii above.

85   *Phys.* 2, 2, 194a21–2: ἡ τέχνη μιμεῖται τὴν φύσιν.

86   The text uses the word εἰκόνας, referring to γραφικὴ ἢ πλαστικὴ τέχνη. However, there can be no doubt but that Aristotle is here speaking of μίμησις.

CHAPTER THREE

1   On the comprehensive and multifarious character of Aristotle's thought, Hegel remarked: 'He penetrated into the whole universe of things, and subjected its scattered wealth to intelligence; and to him the greater number of philosophical sciences owe their origin and distinction.' Trans. George Henry Lewes, *Aristotle. A Chapter from the History of Science* (London: Smith, Elder & Co, 1864), p. 18. See *Vorlesungen über die Geschichte der Philosophie* 2 (Frankfurt am Main: Suhrkamp, 1986), p. 132: 'Aristoteles ist in die ganze Masse und alle Seiten des realen Universums eingedrungen und hat ihren Reichtum und Zerstreuung dem Begriffe unterjocht; und die meisten philosophischen Wissenschaften haben ihm ihre Unterscheidung, ihren Anfang zu verdanken.'

2   *Hist. An.* 1, 6, 491a20–3, trans. Peck, p. 37.

3   *Part. An.* 2, 10, 656a9–10, trans. Peck, p. 173. In many of the quotations that follow I have slightly modified Peck's translation.

4   *Gen. An.* 5, 1, 780b4–5 (on hair going grey); *Part. An.* 3, 10, 673a7–9 (on laughter and response to tickling).

5   *Hist. An.* 1, 9, 492a5–6 (on eye colours); *Part. An.* 2, 14, 658a15–16 (on eyelashes).

6   *Hist. An.* 2, 1, 497b31–2 (on use of both hands): μόνον δὲ καὶ ἀμφιδέξιον γίγνεται τῶν ἄλλων ζῴων ἄνθρωπος. *Hist. An.* 1, 11, 492a 22–3 (on inability to move ears). See H.C. Baldry, *The Unity of Mankind in Greek Thought* (Cambridge: Press, 1965), p. 89.

7   *Part. An.* 2, 1, 662b20–2.

8   *Pol.* 1, 2, 1253a9–10, trans. Rackham, p. 11.

9   *Part. An.* 2, 10, 655b37–656a8, my translation after Peck, p. 173.

10   *Part. An.* 2, 10, 656a10–13; 4, 10, 686a25–7. On man defined as 'upward gazer', see Plato, *Cratylus* 399c: 'The word ἄνθρωπος implies that other animals never examine, or consider, or look up at what they see, but that man not only sees but considers and looks up at that which he sees, and hence he alone of all animals is rightly called ἄνθρωπος, because he looks up at (ἀναθρεῖ) what he has seen (ὄπωπε)'. Trans. B. Jowett, *The Dialogues of Plato* (New York: Random House, 1937), vol. 1, p. 198, modified after H.N. Fowler, *Cratylus* (Cambridge, MA: Harvard University Press, 1977), p. 59.

11   *Part. An.* 4, 10, 686a27–31, trans. Peck, p. 367.

12   *Part. An.* 2, 13, 658a8–9: οὐδὲν γὰρ ἡ φύσις ποιεῖ μάτην. For an excellent treatment of this principle see James G. Lennox, Chapter 9, 'Nature does nothing in Vain..', in *Aristotle's Philosophy of Biology. Studies in the Origins of Life Science* (Cambridge: Cambridge University Press, 2001), pp. 205–23.

13   *Part. An.* 2, 14, 658a23–4.

14   *Part. An.* 3, 1, 662b18–22, trans. Peck, p. 217.

15   *Part. An.* 2, 10, 656b26–32, trans. Peck, p. 179.

16   *Part. An.* 2, 16, 659b33–660a2, trans. Ogle, *CW* 1, p. 1028.

17   *Part. An.* 2, 16, 660a2–13, trans. Ogle, ibid.

18   *Part. An.* 2, 17, 660a17–18, trans. Ogle, ibid.

19   *Part. An.* 2, 17, 660a22–5, trans. Peck, p. 201.

20   *De An.* 2, 8, 420b5–7: ἡ δὲ φωνή ψόφος τίς ἐστιν ἐμψύχου· τῶν γὰρ ἀψύχων οὐθὲν φωνεῖ, ἀλλὰ καθ' ὁμοιότητα λέγεται φωνεῖν. Trans. Hett modified, pp. 115–17.

21   *Part. An.* 4, 10, 687a9–12, trans. Peck, p. 371.

22   *Part. An.* 4, 10, 687a15–23, trans. Peck, pp. 371–3, modified.

23   *Part. An.* 4, 10, 687a28–9, trans. Peck, p. 373.

24   *Part. An.* 4, 10, 687b2–5, trans. Peck, p. 373.

25   *Pol.* 1, 8, 1256b20–2, trans. Jowett, *CW* 2, pp. 1993–4.

26   *Pol.* 7, 15, 1334b14–15.

27   *Pol.* 7, 15, 1334b17–28, trans. Rackham modified, p. 617.

28   *Pol.* 1, 2, 1253a9–10: οὐθὲν γάρ, ὡς φαμέν, μάτην ἡ φύσις ποιεῖ, λόγον δὲ μόνον ἄνθρωπος ἔχει τῶν ζῴων.

29   *Pol.* 1, 2, 1253a15–18, trans. Rackham, p. 11.

30   *Pol.* 1, 2, 1253a31–7, trans. Jowett modified, *CW* 2, p. 1988.

31   *Hist. An.* 8, 1, 588a16–31.

32   *Hist. An.* 9, 1, 608a21–608b4.

33   *Hist. An.* 9, 1, 608b4–8, trans. Balme, p. 219.

34   *De An.* 2, 2, 413a21–2: διωρίσθαι τὸ ἔμψυχον τοῦ ἀψύχου τῷ ζῆν. Trans. Hett, p. 75.

35   *De An.* 1, 2, 405b10–12: ὁρίζονται δὲ πάντες τὴν ψυχὴν τρισὶν ὡς εἰπεῖν, κινήσει, αἰσθήσει, τῷ ἀσωμάτῳ.

36   *De An.* 1, 2, 403b25–7: τὸ ἔμψυχον δὴ τοῦ ἀψύχου δυοῖν μάλιστα διαφέρειν δοκεῖ, κινήσει τε καὶ τῷ αἰσθάνεσθαι. My translation.

37   *De An.* 2, 2, 413b2: τὸ δὲ ζῷον διὰ τὴν αἴσθησιν πρώτως. See *Part. An.* 3, 4, 666a34: τὸ μὲν γὰρ ζῷον αἰσθήσει ὥρισται.

38   Fragment 45: ψυχῆς πείρατα ἰὼν οὐκ ἂν ἐξεύροιο, πᾶσαν ἐπιπορευόμενος ὁδόν οὕτω βαθὺν λόγον ἔχει. Hermann Diels & Walther Kranz, *Die Fragmente der Vorsokratiker* I (Zürich: Weidmann, 1964), p. 161.

39   *Met.* 12, 9, 1074b15: τὰ δὲ περὶ τὸν νοῦν ἔχει τινὰς ἀπορίας.

40   *De An.* 1, 1, 402a1–7, trans. Hett modified, p. 9.

41   *De An.* 1, 3, 406a17: ἐστὶν ἡ οὐσία τῆς ψυχῆς τὸ κινεῖν ἑαυτήν.

42   *De An.* 1, 3, 406a30: φαίνεται κινοῦσα τὸ σῶμα.

43   *De An.* 2, 2, 2, 414a12–14: ἡ ψυχὴ δὲ τοῦτο ᾧ ζῶμεν καὶ αἰσθανόμεθα καὶ διανοούμεθα πρώτως. Trans. Smith modified, *CW* 1, p. 659. For a comprehensive account, see *De An.* 2, 4, 415a14–415b28.

44   *De An.* 1, 5, 411b7–9: δοκεῖ γὰρ τοὐναντίον μᾶλλον ἡ ψυχὴ τὸ σῶμα συνέχειν. ἐξελθούσης γοῦν διαπνεῖται καὶ σήπεται. Trans. Smith modified, *CW* 1, p. 655.

45   *De An.* 2, 1, 412a27–8: ψυχή ἐστιν ἐντελέχεια ἡ πρώτη σώματος φυσικοῦ δυνάμει ζωὴν ἔχοντος. See the entire passage 412a20–412b6.

46   *De An.* 2, 1, 412b8–9.

47   *De An.* 2, 4, 415b13–14: τὸ δὲ ζῆν τοῖς ζῶσι τὸ εἶναί ἐστιν, αἰτία δὲ καὶ ἀρχὴ τούτων ἡ ψυχή. Trans. Hett modified, p. 87.

48   *De An.* 2, 1, 412b5–6: ἐντελέχεια ἡ πρώτη σώματος φυσικοῦ ὀργανικοῦ.

49   *De An.* 2, 4, 415b7–8: ἔτι δὲ ἡ ψυχὴ τοῦ ζῶντος σώματος αἰτία καὶ ἀρχή. Also 2, 1, 412b11: τοῦτο δὲ τὸ τί ἦν εἶναι τῷ τοιῷδι σώματι.

50   *Part. An.* 3, 4, 667b21–3: τοῦ μὲν οὖν εἰς μίαν ἀρχὴν συντελεῖν καὶ ἀπὸ μιᾶς αἴτιον τὸ μίαν ἔχειν πάντα τὴν αἰσθητικὴν ψυχὴν ἐνεργείᾳ.

51   *Pol.* 1, 5, 1254a33.

52   *Pol.* 1, 5, 1254a34, my trans.

53   *Pol.* 1, 5, 1254a36–1254b15. See *Pol.* 1, 5, 1254b23–4 τὰ γὰρ ἄλλα ζῷα οὐ λόγῳ αἰσθανόμενα ἀλλὰ παθήμασιν ὑπηρετεῖ. I am leaving aside Aristotle's justification of slavery, which is the context of these remarks.

54   *De An.* 1, 4, 408b25–7.

55   *De An.* 1, 4, 408b13–15: βέλτιον γὰρ ἴσως μὴ λέγειν τὴν ψυχὴν ἐλεεῖν ἢ μανθάνειν ἢ διανοεῖσθαι, ἀλλὰ τὸν ἄνθρωπον τῇ ψυχῇ.

56   *De An.* 1, 1, 403a5–25, trans. Smith modified, *CW* 1, pp. 642–3.

57   *De An.* 2, 2, 414a19–20: μήτ᾽ ἄνευ σώματος εἶναι μήτε σῶμά τι ἡ ψυχή. See *Juv.* 1, 467b14: 'It is clear that the soul's substance cannot be corporeal' (δῆλον ὅτι οὐχ οἷον τ᾽ εἶναι σῶμα τὴν οὐσίαν αὐτῆς).

58 *Part. An.* 1, 3, 643a24–5: οὔτε γὰρ ἄνευ ὕλης οὐδὲν ζῴου μόριον, οὔτε μόνη ὕλη ἡ ὕλη.

59 *De An.* 2, 1, 412b6–8, trans. Hett, p. 69.

60 *De An.* 1, 1, 403a7–12, trans. Smith, *CW* 1, p. 642.

61 *De An.* 1, 4, 408b18–19: ὁ δὲ νοῦς ἔοικεν ἐγγίνεσθαι οὐσία τις οὖσα, καὶ οὐ φθείρεσθαι.

62 *De An.* 1, 4, 408b21–2.

63 *De An.* 1, 4, 408b25–7: τὸ δὲ διανοεῖσθαι καὶ φιλεῖν ἢ μισεῖν οὐκ ἔστιν ἐκείνου πάθη, ἀλλὰ τουδὶ τοῦ ἔχοντος ἐκεῖνο.

64 *De An.* 1, 4, 408b24, 408b27–8.

65 *De An.* 1, 4, 408b29–30.

66 *De An.* 2, 2, 413b24–7, trans. Hett, p. 77.

67 *De An.* 2, 2, 413b29–31, trans. Hett modified, p. 77.

68 Howard Robinson comments: 'Right from the beginning of the *De Anima* Aristotle affirms that the soul is the form of the body and that it remains to be discovered whether all faculties of the soul are embodied. It never seems to cross Aristotle's mind that the doctrine of the soul as form of the body strictly requires that the soul is embodied in all its parts. It follows that either Aristotle was very obtuse about the basic features of his own concept of form, or that that concept is fundamentally different from that attributed to him by those who deny that any part of a bodily form could be non-bodily.' 'Form and the Immateriality of the Intellect from Aristotle to Aquinas', *Aristotle and the Later Tradition: Studies in Ancient Philosophy*, Supp. Vol. 2 (1991), p. 210.

69 Enrico Berti, 'Aristote était-il un penseur dualiste?', *Thêta-Pi* 2 (1973), p. 97.

70 H.M. Robinson, 'Aristotelian Dualism', *Studies in Ancient Philosophy* 1 (1983), p. 123.

71 Christopher Shields, 'Some Recent Approaches to Aristotle's *De Anima*', in Aristotle. *De Anima, Books II and III*, trans. D.W. Hamlyn, rev. Christopher Shields (Oxford: Clarendon Press, 1993), p. 165.

72 *De An.* 2, 12, 424a17–19, trans. Hett, p. 137; see also *De An.* 3, 2, 425b23–4: τὸ γὰρ αἰσθητήριον δεκτικὸν τοῦ αἰσθητοῦ ἄνευ τῆς ὕλης ἕκαστον.

73 *De An.* 3, 2, 425b24–5.

74 *De An.* 2, 12, 424a26–8.

75 *De An.* 3, 4, 429a13–15.

76 *De An.* 2, 5, 417b22–8.

77 *De An.* 3, 4, 429a18: ἀνάγκη ἄρα, ἐπεὶ πάντα νοεῖ, ἀμιγῆ εἶναι.

78 *De An.* 3, 4, 429a24–5: διὸ οὐδὲ μεμῖχθαι εὔλογον αὐτὸν τῷ σώματι.

79 *De An.* 2, 4, 429a25–6.

80 *De An.* 3, 4, 429b23: ὁ νοῦς ἁπλοῦν ἐστὶ καὶ ἀπαθές.

81 *De An.* 3, 4, 429a27–8.

82   *De An.* 3, 8, 432a2.

83   *De An.* 2, 5, 417b22–3: τῶν καθ' ἕκαστον ἡ κατ' ἐνέργειαν αἴσθησις, ἡ δ' ἐπιστήμη τῶν καθόλου.

84   *De An.* 3, 4, 429a30–429b5; 3, 13, 435b7–16.

85   *De An.* 3, 4, 429b4–5: τὸ μὲν γὰρ αἰσθητικὸν οὐκ ἄνευ σώματος, ὁ δὲ χωριστός. Trans. Hett, p. 167.

86   *De An.* 1, 3, 407a2–3: οὐ καλῶς τὸ λέγειν τὴν ψυχὴν μέγεθος εἶναι.

87   *De An.* 1, 3, 407a6–11, trans. Hett modified, p. 39.

88   Thomas Aquinas, *In Aristotelis Librum De Animae* (Turin: Marietti, 1959) I, lect. 8, n111, p. 31: Unde, cum obiectum intellectus sint intelligibilia, haec autem, scilicet intelligibilia, non sunt unum ut magnitudo seu continuum, sed sicut numerus, eo quod consequenter se habeant, manifestum est, quod intellectus non est magnitudo, sicut Plato dicebat. See *Commentary on Aristotle's De Anima*, eds Kenelm Foster and Sylvester Humphries (Notre Dame: Dumb Ox, 1994), p. 41.

89   *De An.* 3, 5, 430a14–15: καὶ ἔστιν ὁ μὲν τοιοῦτος νοῦς τῷ πάντα γίνεσθαι, ὁ δὲ τῷ πάντα ποιεῖν, ὡς ἕξις τις, οἷον τὸ φῶς.

90   *De An.* 3, 5, 430a17–18: καὶ οὗτος ὁ νοῦς χωριστὸς καὶ ἀπαθὴς καὶ ἀμιγὴς τῇ οὐσίᾳ ὢν ἐνεργείᾳ.

91   *De An.* 3, 5, 430a22–3: χωρισθεὶς δ' ἐστὶ μόνον τοῦθ' ὅπερ ἐστι, καὶ τοῦτο μόνον ἀθάνατον καὶ ἀΐδιον.

92   *De An.* 3, 5, 430a24.

93   *De An.* 3, 5, 430a24–5.

94   *De An.* 3, 5, 430a18–19.

95   *De An.* 3, 7, 431a16–17: διὸ οὐδέποτε νοεῖ ἄνευ φαντάσματος ἡ ψυχή. *De An.* 3, 7, 431b2: 'The thinking faculty thinks of its forms in mental images' (τὰ μὲν οὖν εἴδη τὸ νοητικὸν ἐν τοῖς φαντάσμασι νοεῖ).

96   *In De An.* III, 7, 699, p. 167: Mirum est autem quomodo tam leviter erraverunt, ex hoc quod dicit quod intellectus est separatus, cum ex litera sua huius rei habeatur intellectus, dicit enim separatus intellectus, quia non habet organum, sicut sensus. Et hoc contingit propter hoc, quia anima humana propter suam nobilitatem supergreditur facultatem materiae corporalis, et non potest totaliter includi ab ea. Unde remanet ei aliqua actio, in qua materia corporalis non communicat. Et propter hoc potentia eius ad hanc actionem non habet organum corporale, et sic est intellectus separatus. Trans. Foster and Humphries, p. 210.

97   Gérard Verbeke, 'Comment Aristote conçoit-il l'immatériel?', *Revue philosophique de* , 44 (1946), pp. 227–8.

98   *De An.* 3, 5, 430a12.

99   *De An.* 3, 5, 430a14–15.

100   *Gen. An.* 2, 3.736b5–7, trans. Platt, *CW* 1, p. 1143.

101　*Gen. An.* 2, 3, 736b27–9: λείπεται δὲ τὸν νοῦν μόνον θύραθεν ἐπεισιέναι καὶ θεῖον εἶναι μόνον· οὐθὲν γὰρ αὐτοῦ τῇ ἐνεργείᾳ κοινωνεῖ σωματικὴ ἐνεργεία. Trans. Platt, ibid.

102　*De An.* 3, 5, 430a17. See R.D. Hicks, ed. and trans. *De Anima* (Cambridge: Cambridge University Press, 1907), p. 502.

103　Martin Luther, 'An Open Letter to The Christian Nobility of the German Nation Concerning the Reform of the Christian Estate' (1520), in *Works of Martin Luther* (Philadelphia: A.J. Holman, 1915), vol. 2, p. 25.

104　*De An.* 2, 1, 413a4–5, trans. Hett, p. 73.

105　*De An.* 1, 1, 403a16–25.

106　*De An.* 3, 2, 425b12.

107　*Sens.* 7, 448a26–8: εἰ γὰρ ὅτε αὐτὸς αὑτοῦ τις αἰσθάνεται ἢ ἄλλου . . . μὴ ἐνδέχεται τότε λανθάνειν ὅτι ἐστίν.

108　*De An.* 3, 2, 425b16.

109　*Somn.* 2, 455a17. *CW* 1, p. 723.

110　*De An.* 3, 8, 431b21: ἡ ψυχὴ τὰ ὄντα πώς ἐστι πάντα.

111　*De An.* 3, 4, 429b5–6, 429b9–10.

112　*De An.* 3, 4, 430a2–5, trans. Hamlyn, p. 59.

113　An interesting application of this doctrine is to be found at *Physics* 3, 3, 202b6–8: 'It is not absurd that the actualization of one thing should be in another. Teaching is the activity of a person who can teach, yet the operation is performed in something – it is not cut adrift from a subject, but is of one thing in another.' Trans. R. Hardie & R. Gaye, *CW* 1, p. 345.

114　See Gérard Verbeke, 'Comment Aristote conçoit-il l'immatériel?', p. 226.

115　*De An.* 3, 4, 429b29–430a2.

116　Cf. *Met.* 12, 9, 1074b36–37: φαίνεται δ' ἀεὶ ἄλλου ἡ ἐπιστήμη καὶ ἡ αἴσθησις καὶ ἡ δόξα καὶ ἡ διάνοια, αὑτῆς δ' ἐν παρέργῳ.

117　*De An.* 3, 4, 429a21–24, trans. Hett modified, p. 165.

118　Joseph Owens, 'The Self in Aristotle', *Review of Metaphysics* 41 (1988), p. 707.

119　*De An.* 1, 4, 408b13–15.

120　*De An.* 1, 4, 408b25–7: τὸ δὲ διανοεῖσθαι καὶ φιλεῖν ἢ μισεῖν οὐκ ἔστιν ἐκείνου πάθη, ἀλλὰ τουδὶ τοῦ ἔχοντος ἐκεῖνο. Trans. Hett modified, p. 49.

121　*Sens.* 2, 438a8.

122　*EN* 1, 1, 1094a3.

123　*EN* 1, 7, 1097a34.

124　*EN* 1, 7, 1097b28–33, trans. Rackham modified, p. 31.

125　*EN* 1, 7, 1098a13–14.

126　*EN* 1, 7, 1098a14–16, trans. Rackham, p. 33.

127　*EN* 1, 8, 1099a7.

128　*EN* 1, 8, 1099a24–5: ἄριστον ἄρα καὶ κάλλιστον καὶ ἥδιστον ἡ εὐδαιμονία.

129 *EN* 9, 4, 1166a31–2: ἔστι γὰρ ὁ φίλος ἄλλος αὐτός.

130 *EN* 9, 4, 1166a13–14, trans. Rackham, p. 533.

131 *EN* 9, 4, 1166a16–17, trans. Ross, *CW* 2, p. 1843.

132 *EN* 9, 4, 1166a19–23, trans. Rackham, p. 535.

133 *EN* 10, 7, 1177b34–1178a4, trans. Rackham, pp. 617–19.

134 *EN* 8, 12, 1161b28–29.

135 *EN* 9, 4, 1166a23–29, trans. Rackham, p. 535.

136 *EN* 9, 6, 1167b6–9, trans. Rackham, p. 543.

137 *EN* 9, 7, 1168a5–8, trans. Rackham, p. 547. In *Pol.* 1, 2, 1254a7, Aristotle stresses: 'Life is a doing, not a making' (ὁ δὲ βίος πρᾶξις, οὐ ποίησίς ἐστιν).

138 *EN* 9, 7, 1168a8–9, trans. Rackham, p. 547.

139 See pp. 149–50 in Chapter 8 above.

140 *EN* 9, 7, 1168a13–15, trans. Rackham, p. 547.

141 *EN* 9, 8, 1168b28–30, trans. Rackham, p. 553.

142 *EN* 9, 8, 1168b35–1169a1, trans. Rackham, p. 553.

143 *EN* 10, 4, 1175a12.

144 *EN* 10, 7, 1177a12.

145 *EN* 10, 6, 1176b5–6; *EN* 10, 6, 1176b31.

146 *EN* 9, 9, 1170a16–17.

147 *EN* 9, 9, 1170a17–19, trans. Rackham, pp. 561–3.

148 *EN* 9, 9, 1170a35.

149 *De An.* 2, 4, 415b13.

150 *EN* 9, 9, 1169b30–1.

151 *EN* 9, 9, 1169b32–3: τοῦ δ' ἀγαθοῦ ἡ ἐνέργεια σπουδαία καὶ ἡδεῖα καθ' αὑτήν.

152 *EN* 9, 9, 1170b7.

153 *EN* 9, 9, 1170b8–10: τὸ δ' εἶναι ἦν αἱρετὸν διὰ τὸ αἰσθάνεσθαι αὑτοῦ ἀγαθοῦ ὄντος, ἡ δὲ τοιαύτη αἴσθησις ἡδεῖα καθ' ἑαυτήν. trans. Rackham, p. 565.

154 *EN* 9, 9, 1170a29–33, trans. Rackham, p. 563.

155 *EN* 9, 9, 1170b1, trans. Rackham, p. 563.

156 *EN* 9, 9, 1170b4.

157 *EN* 9, 9, 1170b10–11 and *EN* 9, 12, 1171b33–5: καὶ ὡς πρὸς ἑαυτὸν ἔχει, οὕτω καὶ πρὸς τὸν φίλον, περὶ αὑτὸν δ' ἡ αἴσθησις ὅτι ἔστιν αἱρετή· καὶ περὶ τὸν φίλον δή.

158 *EN* 10, 6, 1177a2.

159 *EN* 10, 7, 1177a12–18.

160 *EN* 10, 7, 1177a19–22, trans. Rackham, p. 613.

161 See *EN* 10, 7, 1177a22–1177b6; *EN* 10, 7, 1177b19–23.

162 *EN* 10, 7, 1177b21–5, trans. Rackham, p. 617.

163 *EN* 10, 7, 1177b26–31, trans. Rackham, p. 617.

164 Pindar, *Isthm.* 4, 16.

165 *EN* 10, 7, 1177b33–1178a2, trans. Rackham, p. 617.

166 *EN* 10, 7, 1178a2–4, trans. Rackham, p. 619.

167 *EN* 10, 7, 1178a5–8, trans. Rackham, p. 619.

168 *EN* 10, 8, 1178a20–22.

169 *EN* 10, 8, 1178b7–8, trans. Rackham, p. 623.

170 *EN* 10, 8, 1178b18–21.

171 *EN* 10, 8, 1178b21–3, trans. Rackham, p. 623.

172 *Met.* 12, 9, 1074b35.

173 *Met.* 12, 9, 1074b16.

174 *EN* 10, 8, 1178b24–32, trans. Rackham, pp. 623–5.

175 *EN* 10, 8, 1179a23–31, trans. Rackham, p. 627.

176 *Gen. An.* 2, 1, 731b24–732a1: 'Now some existing things are eternal and divine whilst others admit of both existence and non-existence. But that which is noble and divine is always, in virtue of its own nature, the cause of the better in such things as admit of being better or worse, and what is not eternal does admit of existence and non-existence, and can partake in the better and the worse. And soul is better than body, and the living, having soul, is thereby better than the lifeless which has none, and being is better than not being, living than not living. These, then, are the reasons of the generation of animals. For since it is impossible that such a class of things as animals should be of an eternal nature, therefore that which comes into being is eternal in the only way possible. Now it is impossible for it to be eternal as an individual – for the substance of the things that are is in the particular; and if it were such it would be eternal – but it is possible for it as a species. This is why there is always a class of men and animals and plants.' Trans. Platt, *CW* 1, p. 1136.

177 *De An.* 2, 4, 415a26–415b1, trans. Smith, *CW* 1, p. 661.

178 *De An.* 2, 4, 415b3–415b8.

CHAPTER FOUR

1 Brand Blanshard, *Reason and Analysis* (London: George Allen & Unwin, 1962), p. 493.

2 *Met.* 1, 6, 987b1–4: Σωκράτους δὲ περὶ μὲν τὰ ἠθικὰ πραγματευομένου περὶ δὲ τῆς ὅλης φύσεως οὐθέν, ἐν μέντοι τούτοις τὸ καθόλου ζητοῦντος καὶ περὶ ὁρισμῶν ἐπιστήσαντος πρώτου τὴν διάνοιαν. Trans. Tredennick modified, p. 43.

3 Albert Camus, *L'homme révolté* (Paris: Gallimard, 1951), p. 39: 'Si les hommes ne peuvent pas se référer à une valeur commune, reconnue par tous en chacun, alors l'homme est incompréhensible à l'homme.'

4 Suzanne Mansion, *Le jugement d'existence chez Aristote* (Louvain: Éditions de l'Institut Supérieur de Philosophie, 1976), p. 17: 'La science est une connaissance *universelle* et *nécessaire*, elle atteint *l'essence* des choses et les explique par leur *cause*.

Telles sont les quatre propriétés les plus apparentes de l'ἐπιστήμη aristotélicienne.'
Emphases in original.

5   *Met.* 5, 5, 1015a20–b15.

6   *Part. An.* 1, 1, 642a10.

7   Sophocles, *Electra* 256: ἀλλ' ἡ βία γὰρ ταῦτ' ἀναγκάζει μέ δρᾶν.

8   See also *An. Post.* 1, 3, 71b9–72b4.

9   Cf. *An. Pr.* 1, 10, 30b33–4 on the distinction between simple and conditional necessity: ἀναγκαῖον ἁπλῶς, ἀλλὰ τούτων ὄντων ἀναγκαῖον.

10 Joseph Owens, *Cognition. An Epistemological Inquiry* (Houston: Center for Thomistic Studies, 1992), p. 98.

11 *De An.* 3, 1, 424b26–7: ἀνάγκη τ', εἴπερ ἐκλείπει τις αἴσθησις, καὶ αἰσθητήριόν τι ἡμῖν ἐκλείπειν.

12 *De An.* 3, 3, 428b18–19: ἡ αἴσθησις τῶν μὲν ἰδίων ἀληθής ἐστιν.
    Cf. also 3, 3, 427b11–12: ἡ μὲν γὰρ αἴσθησις τῶν ἰδίων ἀεὶ ἀληθής.

13 James Joyce, *Ulysses* (New York: Vintage, 1986), p. 31 (*U* 3.1 and 3.13). See pp. 243-4 above. The entire passage (*U* 3.1–15) is a dramatization of Aristotle's theory of sensation, combined with elements from Boehme, Berkeley and Weininger: 'Ineluctable modality of the visible: at least that if no more, thought through my eyes. Signatures of all things I am here to read, seaspawn and seawrack, the nearing tide, that rusty boot. Snotgreen, bluesilver, rust: coloured signs. Limits of the diaphane. But he adds: in bodies. Then he was aware of them bodies before of them coloured. How? By knocking his sconce against them, sure. Go easy. Bald he was and a millionaire, *maestro di color che sanno*. Limit of the diaphane in. Why in? Diaphane, adiaphane. If you can put your five fingers through it, it is a gate, if not a door. Shut your eyes and see. Stephen closed his eyes to hear his boots crush crackling wrack and shells. You are walking through it howsomever, I am, a stride at a time. A very short space of time through very short times of space. Five, six: the *Nacheinander*. Exactly: and that is the ineluctable modality of the audible. Open your eyes. No. Jesus! If I fell over a cliff that beetles o'er his base, fell through the *Nebeneinander* ineluctably!'

14 *Met.* 4, 4, 1006a8–9. Cf. C.S. Lewis, *The Abolition of Man* (London: Macmillan 1947), p. 31: 'If nothing is self-evident, nothing can be demonstrated.'

15 *Met.* 4, 3, 1005b11–12, 18.

16 *Met.* 4, 3, 1005b19–20.

17 Avicenna, *Liber de philosophia prima sive scientia divina*, ed. Simone Van Riet (Louvain: Peeters / Leiden: Brill, 1977) I, 5, pp. 31–2: Dicemus igitur quod res et ens et necesse talia sunt quod statim imprimuntur in anima prima impressione, quae non acquiritur ex aliis notioribus se.

18 *Met.* 4, 3, 1005b13–17: γνωριμωτάτην τε γὰρ ἀναγκαῖον εἶναι τὴν τοιαύτην (περὶ γὰρ ἃ μὴ γνωρίζουσιν ἀπατῶνται πάντες) καὶ ἀνυπόθετον. ἣν γὰρ ἀναγκαῖον ἔχειν

τὸν ὁτιοῦν ξυνιέντα τῶν ὄντων, τοῦτο οὐχ ὑπόθεσις· ὃ δὲ γνωρίζειν ἀναγκαῖον τῷ ὁτιοῦν γνωρίζοντι, καὶ ἥκειν ἔχοντα ἀναγκαῖον. Trans. Apostle, p. 58.

19 *Met.* 9, 10, 1051b1.

20 *De Int.* 9, 19a23–4: τὸ μὲν οὖν εἶναι τὸ ὂν ὅταν ᾖ, καὶ τὸ μὴ ὂν μὴ εἶναι ὅταν μὴ ᾖ, ἀνάγκη. Trans. Ackrill, *CW* 1, p. 30.

21 *De Int.* 13, 23a18–20: καὶ ἔστι δὴ ἀρχὴ ἴσως τὸ ἀναγκαῖον καὶ μὴ ἀναγκαῖον πάντων ἢ εἶναι ἢ μὴ εἶναι, καὶ τὰ ἄλλα ὡς τούτοις ἀκολουθοῦντα ἐπισκοπεῖν δεῖ. Trans. Ackrill, *CW* 1, p. 36.

22 Fragment 8. Hermann Diels & Walter Kranz, *Die Fragmente der Vorsokratiker* I (Zürich: Weidmann, 1992), p. 237. Trans. Kathleen Freeman, *Ancilla to the Pre-Socratic Philosophers* (Oxford: Basil Blackwell, 1962), pp. 43–4. The primordial necessity of Being, first wrought in language by Parmenides, is faithfully captured in the following passage from *The Friend* by Samuel Taylor Coleridge: 'Hast thou ever raised thy mind to the consideration of EXISTENCE, in and by itself, as the mere act of existing? Hast thou ever said to thyself thoughtfully, IT IS! heedless in that moment whether it were a man before thee, or a flower, or a grain of sand? Without reference, in short, to this or that particular mode or form of existence? If thou hast indeed attained to this, thou wilt have felt the presence of a mystery, which must have fixed thy spirit in awe and wonder. The very words, There is nothing! or, There was a time, when there was nothing! are self-contradictory. There is that within us which repels the proposition with as full and instantaneous light, as if it bore evidence against the fact in the right of its own eternity. Not TO BE, then, is impossible: TO BE, incomprehensible. If thou hast mastered this intuition of absolute existence, thou wilt have learnt likewise that it was this, and no other, which in the earlier ages seized the nobler minds, the elect among men, with a sort of sacred horror. This it was which first caused them to feel within themselves a something ineffably greater than their own individual nature.' S.T. Coleridge, *The Friend*, Collected Works 4, vol. 1, ed. Barbara E. Rooke (London: Routledge & Kegan Paul, 1993), p. 514. Emphases in original.

23 *EN* 6, 2, 1139b8–11: τὸ δὲ γεγονὸς οὐκ ἐνδέχεται μὴ γενέσθαι· διὸ ὀρθῶς Ἀγάθων μόνου γὰρ αὐτοῦ καὶ θεὸς στερίσκεται, ἀγένητα ποιεῖν ἅσσ' ἂν ᾖ πεπραγμένα.

24 *An. Post.* 2, 9, 94a20–3: 'We only think that we have knowledge of a thing when we know its cause. There are four kinds of cause: the essence, the necessitating conditions, the efficient cause which started the process, and the final cause' (ἐπεὶ δὲ ἐπίστασθαι οἰόμεθα ὅταν εἰδῶμεν τὴν αἰτίαν, αἰτίαι δὲ τέτταρες, μία μὲν τὸ τί ἦν εἶναι, μία δὲ τὸ τίνων ὄντων ἀνάγκη τοῦτ' εἶναι, ἑτέρα δὲ ἡ τί πρῶτον ἐκίνησε, τετάρτη δὲ τὸ τίνος ἕνεκα). Trans. Tredennick, p. 209. See also *An. Post.* 1, 2, 71b9–12: 'We consider that we have unqualified knowledge (ἐπίστασθαι ἁπλῶς) of anything (as contrasted with the accidental knowledge of the sophist) when we believe that we know (i) that the cause from which the fact results is the cause of

that fact, and (ii) that the fact cannot be otherwise (μὴ ἐνδέχεσθαι τοῦτ' ἄλλως ἔχειν).' Trans. Tredennick, p. 29. In an excellent study Robert Bolton considers Aristotle's problematic claim that 'scientific truths are without qualification necessary truths'. See Robert Bolton, 'Aristotle on Essence and Necessity in Science', *Proceedings of the Boston Area Colloquium in Ancient Philosophy* 13 (1997), p. 114.

25 *Phys.* 7, 1, 241b34.

26 W.V. Quine, *Ontological Relativity and other Essays* (New York: Columbia University Press, 1969), p. 72.

27 *EN* 6, 6, 1140b31-2: ἡ ἐπιστήμη περὶ τῶν καθόλου ἐστὶν ὑπόληψις καὶ τῶν ἐξ ἀνάγκης ὄντων.

28 *De An.* 3, 8, 431b2; cf. 431b29–432a1.

29 Cf. *EN* 6, 3, 1139b28-9: ἡ μὲν δὴ ἐπαγωγὴ ἀρχή ἐστι καὶ τοῦ καθόλου, ὁ δὲ συλλογισμὸς ἐκ τῶν καθόλου.

30 Cf. Brian Ellis, *Scientific Essentialism* (Cambridge: Cambridge University Press, 2001). Also *The Philosophy of Nature. A Guide to the New Essentialism* (Chesham: Acumen, 2002).

31 Ellis, *The Philosophy of Nature*, p. 15.

32 Ibid., p. 12.

33 William A. Wallace, *The Modeling of Nature, Philosophy of Science and Philosophy of Nature in Synthesis* (Washington, DC: Catholic University of America Press, 1996), p. 19.

34 *EN* 6, 3, 1139b19–24: πάντες γὰρ ὑπολαμβάνομεν, ὃ ἐπιστάμεθα, μηδ' ἐνδέχεσθαι ἄλλως ἔχειν· τὰ δ' ἐνδεχόμενα ἄλλως, ὅταν ἔξω τοῦ θεωρεῖν γένηται, λανθάνει εἰ ἔστιν ἢ μή. ἐξ ἀνάγκης ἄρα ἐστὶ τὸ ἐπιστητόν. ἀίδιον ἄρα· τὰ γὰρ ἐξ ἀνάγκης ὄντα ἁπλῶς πάντα ἀίδια, τὰ δ' ἀίδια ἀγένητα καὶ ἄφθαρτα. Trans. Rackham, p. 333.

35 Wallace, *The Modeling of Nature*, p. 20.

36 Ellis, *The Philosophy of Nature*, p. 13.

37 Wallace, *The Modeling of Nature*, p. 20.

38 See pp. 96 and 158 above.

39 *Part. An.* 1, 1, 642a1-2: εἰσὶν ἄρα δύ' αἰτίαι αὗται, τό θ' οὗ ἕνεκα καὶ τὸ ἐξ ἀνάγκης. Trans. William Ogle, *CW* 1, p. 999.

40 *Part. An.* 1, 1, 642a11–13, trans. Peck. At 3, 1, 663b22-4, he states that ἡ κατὰ τὸν λόγον φύσις makes use of the products of ἀναγκαία φύσις in order to serve a purpose. See *Part. An.* 1, 1, 640a33–640b4: '*Because* the essence of man is what it is, *therefore* a man has such and such parts, since there cannot be a man without them... There cannot be a man at all otherwise than with them... *Because* man is such and such, *therefore* the process of his formation must of necessity be such and such and take place in such a manner; which is why first this part is formed, then that. And thus similarly with all the things that are constructed by Nature.' Peck's translation and emphases.

41   *Phys.* 7, 1, 242a53–4: ἀνάγκη εἶναί τι τὸ πρῶτον κινοῦν, καὶ μὴ βαδίζειν εἰς ἄπειρον.

42   *In de Anima* 3, 2, 586, p. 148: Impossibile [est] compleri actionem quae dependet ab actionibus infinitis. See *Commentary on Aristotle's De Anima*, trans. Kenelm Foster and Sylvester Humphries (Notre Dame: Dumb Ox, 1994), p. 182.

43   *Met.* 5, 5, 1015b9–1015b11: τῶν μὲν δὴ ἕτερον αἴτιον τοῦ ἀναγκαῖα εἶναι, τῶν δὲ οὐδέν, ἀλλὰ διὰ ταῦτα ἕτερά ἐστιν ἐξ ἀνάγκης.

44   See Terence Irwin, *Aristotle's First Principles* (Oxford: Clarendon Press, 1990), p. 157. Plotinus employs Aristotle's phrase when referring to the Stoics, who 'are themselves driven by the truth to bear witness that there must be a form of soul prior to bodies and stronger than they are'. *Enneads* IV 7[2], 4: μαρτυροῦσι δὲ καὶ αὐτοὶ ὑπὸ τῆς ἀληθείας ἀγόμενοι ὡς δεῖ. Trans. A.H. Armstrong, *Plotinus* IV (Cambridge, MA: Harvard University Press, 1984), p. 347.

45   *Met.* 1, 5, 986b31.

46   *Part. An.* 1, 1, 642a19: ἐνιαχοῦ δέ που αὐτῇ καὶ Ἐμπεδοκλῆς περιπίπτει, ἀγόμενος ὑπ' αὐτῆς τῆς ἀληθείας, καὶ τὴν οὐσίαν καὶ τὴν φύσιν ἀναγκάζεται φάναι τὸν λόγον εἶναι.

47   *Phys.* 1, 5, 188b28–30: πάντες γὰρ τὰ στοιχεῖα καὶ τὰς ὑπ' αὐτῶν καλουμένας ἀρχάς, καίπερ ἄνευ λόγου τιθέντες, ὅμως τἀναντία λέγουσιν, ὥσπερ ὑπ' αὐτῆς τῆς ἀληθείας ἀναγκασθέντες.

48   *Met.* 1, 3, 984b8–11: μετὰ δὲ τούτους καὶ τὰς τοιαύτας ἀρχάς, ὡς οὐχ ἱκανῶν οὐσῶν γεννῆσαι τὴν τῶν ὄντων φύσιν, πάλιν ὑπ' αὐτῆς τῆς ἀληθείας, ὥσπερ εἴπομεν, ἀναγκαζόμενοι τὴν ἐχομένην ἐζήτησαν ἀρχήν. Trans. Tredennick, p. 25. See also *Met.* 1, 3, 984a16–19: ἐκ μὲν οὖν τούτων μόνην τις αἰτίαν νομίσειεν ἂν τὴν ἐν ὕλης εἴδει λεγομένην· προϊόντων δ' οὕτως, αὐτὸ τὸ πρᾶγμα ὡδοποίησεν αὐτοῖς καὶ συνηνάγκασε ζητεῖν.

49   These occurences may be easily located in the online version of the *Index Thomisticum*. See the excellent study by Cristina D'Ancona, '*Quasi ab ipsa veritate coacti*: Histoire gréco-arabe d'un thème aristotélicien' in Caroline Noirot & Nuccio Ordine (eds), *Omnia in uno. Hommage à Alain-Philippe Segonds* (Paris: Les Belles Lettres, 2012), pp. 223–41.

50   *ST* I, 9, 1: Et inde est quod quidam antiquorum, quasi ab ipsa veritate coacti, posuerunt primum principium esse immobile. *Contra Gentiles* 1, 43: Huic etiam veritati attestantur antiquissimorum philosophorum dicta, qui omnes infinitum posuerunt primum rerum principium, quasi ab ipsa veritate coacti.

51   *In I Sent.*, d. 36 q. 2 a. 1 ad 1: Plato et alii antiqui philosophi, quasi ab ipsa veritate coacti, tendebant in illud quod postmodum Aristoteles expressit, quamvis non pervenerint in ipsum: et ideo Plato ponens ideas, ad hoc tendebat, secundum quod et Aristoteles posuit, scilicet eas esse in intellectu divino; unde hoc improbare philosophus non intendit; sed secundum modum quo Plato posuit formas naturales per se existentes sine materia esse.

52 *In I Meta.*, lect. 5, n 93, p. 28: Sed et ipsa rei evidens natura dedit viam ad veritatis cognitionem.

53 *In I de Anima*, lect. 4, n 43, p. 14: Ipsi antiqui philosophi, quasi ab ipsa veritate coacti, somniabant quodammodo veritatem. See *Commentary on Aristotle's De Anima*, trans. Foster and Humphries, p. 18.

CHAPTER FIVE

1 *Met.* 4, 4, 1006b8: τὸ γὰρ μὴ ἓν σημαίνειν οὐθὲν σημαίνειν ἐστίν.

2 John Middleton Murry, *Countries of the Mind. Essays in Literary Criticism.* Second Series (London: Oxford University Press, 1937), p. 2.

3 Herodotus 1, 64.2–3: τοὺς νεκροὺς μετεφόρεε ἐς ἄλλον χῶρον τῆς Δήλου.

4 Herodotus 2, 125.

5 Isocrates, Evagoras 190D, trans. W.B. Stanford, *Greek Metaphor. Studies in Theory and Practice* (Oxford: Blackwell, 1936), p. 3.

6 See Stanford, pp. 3–4. An excellent account of Plato's use of metaphor may be found in E.E. Pender, *Images of Persons Unseen* (Sankt Augustin: Akademia, 2002).

7 U. Eco, *Semiotics and the Philosophy of Language* (London: Macmillan, 1984), p. 88.

8 P. Swiggers, 'Cognitive Aspects of Aristotle's Theory of Metaphor', *Glotta* 62 (1984) p. 40.

9 *Poet.* 21, 1457b7.

10 *Poet.* 21, 1457b9.

11 *Rhet.* 3, 10, 1410b36–1411a1: τῶν δὲ μεταφορῶν τεττάρων οὐσῶν εὐδοκιμοῦσι μάλιστα αἱ κατ᾽ ἀναλογίαν.

12 See J.T. Kirby, 'Aristotle on Metaphor', *American Journal of Philology* 118 (1997), p. 532.

13 *EN* 5, 3, 1131a31–2: ἡ γὰρ ἀναλογία ἰσότης ἐστὶ λόγων, καὶ ἐν τέτταρσιν ἐλαχίστοις.

14 *Poet.* 21, 1457b16–19: τὸ δὲ ἀνάλογον λέγω, ὅταν ὁμοίως ἔχῃ τὸ δεύτερον πρὸς τὸ πρῶτον καὶ τὸ τέταρτον πρὸς τὸ τρίτον· ἐρεῖ γὰρ ἀντὶ τοῦ δευτέρου τὸ τέταρτον ἢ ἀντὶ τοῦ τετάρτου τὸ δεύτερον. Trans. Bywater modified, *CW* 2, p. 2332.

15 *Rhet.* 3, 4, 1407a15–17: οἷον εἰ ἡ φιάλη ἀσπὶς Διονύσου, καὶ τὴν ἀσπίδα ἁρμόττει λέγεσθαι φιάλην Ἄρεως. See *Poet.* 21, 1457b20–2.

16 *Poet.* 21, 1457b22–5.

17 *Rhet.* 3, 11, 1412a9–12: δεῖ δὲ μεταφέρειν, καθάπερ εἴρηται πρότερον, ἀπὸ οἰκείων καὶ μὴ φανερῶν, οἷον καὶ ἐν φιλοσοφίᾳ τὸ ὅμοιον καὶ ἐν πολὺ διέχουσι θεωρεῖν εὐστόχου. Trans. Roberts, *CW* 2, p. 2253.

18 *Rhet.* 3, 2, 1405a8–10: καὶ τὸ σαφὲς καὶ τὸ ἡδὺ τὸ ξενικὸν ἔχει μάλιστα ἡ μεταφορά, καὶ λαβεῖν οὐκ ἔστιν αὐτὴν παρ᾽ ἄλλου.

19 *EN* 3, 5, 1114b9–10: τὸ γὰρ μέγιστον καὶ κάλλιστον, καὶ ὃ παρ᾽ ἑτέρου μὴ οἷόν τε λαβεῖν μηδὲ μαθεῖν.

20 *Poet.* 22, 1459a4–8, trans. Bywater, *CW* 2, pp. 2334–5. Aristotle remarks elsewhere that in the case of things that greatly diverge, much practice is needed; in other things, similarities are more easily seen. (*Top.* 1, 17, 108a12–14: μάλιστα δ' ἐν τοῖς πολὺ διεστῶσι γυμνάζεσθαι δεῖ· ῥᾷον γὰρ ἐπὶ τῶν λοιπῶν δυνησόμεθα τὰ ὅμοια συνορᾶν.)

21 George Eliot, *The Mill on the Floss* (Oxford: Clarendon Press, 1980), p. 123.

22 *Rhet.* 3, 2, 1404b34–5: πάντες γὰρ μεταφοραῖς διαλέγονται καὶ τοῖς οἰκείοις καὶ τοῖς κυρίοις.

23 Benedetto Croce, *The Philosophy of Giambattista Vico*, trans. R.G. Collingwood (New York: Russell & Russell, 1964), p. 48.

24 *Pol.* 1, 5, 1254b38–39: ἀλλ' οὐχ ὁμοίως ῥᾴδιον ἰδεῖν τό τε τῆς ψυχῆς κάλλος καὶ τὸ τοῦ σώματος. Trans. Jowett, *CW* 2, p. 1991.

25 Porphyry, *On Aristotle's Categories*, trans. Steven K. Strange (Ithaca: Cornell University Press, 1992), pp. 29–31.

26 Simplicius, *In Aristotelis Categorias Commentarium* (Berlin: Reimer, 1907), p. 74.

27 We chew on ideas, swallow and digest them, put them in our pipe and smoke them. An idea can be bright, dull or dumb, be up to scratch, have an upside or a downside. We can have sharp ideas – with a point, unless they are dull, blunt and rigid. We put a spin or a slant on an idea, iron it out, hammer away at it and drive it home; we focus on an idea, underline it, or have it up our sleeve. We toy with the grain of an idea, get to the kernel, but may find it hard to crack. Ideas emerge or spring to mind; they percolate and trickle down; an idea might make a splash or cause a ripple; we can be flooded by a spate of ideas; we channel, float and filter; fish and trawl for ideas. We warm to an idea, put a damper, or throw cold water on it; we put it on ice or on the back burner. An idea may be threadbare or redundant; if it has a silver lining we may cash it in – unless it has become bankrupt. We convey ideas, ditch them, drop and dump them, throw them out the window. An idea can be a red herring, which we ram down someone's throat. It can be pregnant and bear fruit – prematurely if it's before its time. If an idea adds up, we can break it down; it can measure up and outweigh the opposition. We can run it up the flagpole; it may take off, or sink like a lead balloon. It may be a milestone, perhaps even pioneering. An idea may be in the pipeline, or coming down the track. We can map it out; if it is explosive it will break new ground. An idea sometimes takes on legs and does the rounds; but occasionally it comes home to roost. Consider the language of violence attached to ideas: an idea can grab, strike and stun us; we hit on an idea; we can be floored or flattened by an idea; it can hit us like a ton of bricks. We can seize upon an idea, come to grips with it, get a handle on it, grasp it, hold it, pull it asunder, jump at it, grapple with it, toss it about, push it too far, pick it up and run with it. We struggle with ideas, pin them down, knock them on the head, bounce them off one other and take them apart – it sounds just like wrestling!

28 Ralph Walter Emerson, *Selected Writings*, ed. Brooks Atkinson (New York: Modern Library, 1950), p. 18. See p. 15: 'Man is an analogist, and studies relations in all objects'; p. 130: 'Nature is full of a sublime family likeness throughout her works, and delights in startling us with resemblances in the most unexpected quarters.' Also p. 293: 'Nature shows all things formed and bound. The intellect pierces the form, overleaps the wall, detects intrinsic likeness between remote things and reduces all into a few principles.'

29 *EN* 10, 7, 1177b28–9; *EN* 10, 8, 1178a20.

30 *EN* 5, 3, 1131a31–2.

31 A. MacIntyre, 'Analogy in Metaphysics', *The Downside Review* 69 (1950), p. 45. M. Heidegger, *Wegmarken* (Frankfurt am Main: Klostermann, 1976), p. 348.

32 *Top.* 1, 7, 103a7–14: 'In general, "sameness" would seem to fall into three divisions; for we usually speak of numerical, specific and generic sameness. There is numerical sameness when there is more than one name for the same thing, e.g., "mantle" and "cloak". There is specific sameness when there are several things but they do not differ in species, e.g., one man and another man, one horse and another horse; for such things as fall under the same species are said to be specifically the same. Similarly things are generically the same when they fall under the same genus, e.g., horse and man.' Trans. Forster, p. 289.

33 *Top.* 1, 17, 108a8–12, my trans.

34 The relationship between these is the basis for the first three kinds of metaphor noted by Aristotle at *Poet.* 21, 1457b7–16.

35 *Met.* 5, 6, 1017a2–3: ὅσα δὲ ἓν ἀναλογίᾳ, οὐ πάντα γένει. Trans. Ross, *CW* 2, p. 1605.

36 G.E.R. Lloyd, *Aristotelian Explorations* (Cambridge: Cambridge University Press, 1996), p. 138. I have benefited greatly from Chapter 7 ('The Unity of Analogy'), and Chapter 10 ('The Metaphors of *Metaphora*') of this excellent volume.

37 *Met.* 5, 6, 1016b31–5, trans. Lloyd, *Aristotelian Explorations*, p. 140.

38 *Part. An.* 1, 4, 644a21–2.

39 *Hist. An.* 1, 1, 486b17–22, trans. Thompson, *CW* 2, p. 775.

40 *An. Post.* 2, 14, 98a20–3.

41 *Part. An.* 1, 5, 645a36–645b13; *Part. An.* 2, 2, 647b14–15; *Part. An.* 2, 2, 648a4–5; *Part. An.* 2, 6, 652a3; *Part. An.* 2, 7, 652b24–5.

42 *Top.* 1, 18, 108b13: ἔνδοξόν ἐστι, ὡς ποτε ἐφ' ἑνὸς τῶν ὁμοίων ἔχει, οὕτως καὶ ἐπὶ τῶν λοιπῶν. Trans. Pickard-Cambridge, *CW* 1, p. 180.

43 *An. Post.* 1, 10, 76a37–40.

44 *Met.* 14, 6, 1093b18–19, trans. Tredennick, p. 303.

45 *Met.* 12, 4, 1070a31–3, trans. Apostle, p. 200.

46 *Met.* 9, 6, 1048a35–b9.

47 Analogy makes the knowledge of prime matter possible (*Phys.* 1, 7, 191a8: ἡ δ' ὑποκειμένη φύσις ἐπιστητὴ κατ' ἀναλογίαν).

48 *Met.* 14, 3, 1090b19–20: οὐκ ἔοικε δ᾽ ἡ φύσις ἐπεισοδιώδης οὖσα ἐκ τῶν φαινομένων, ὥσπερ μοχθηρὰ τραγῳδία.

49 *Met.* 12, 10, 1075a16–19, trans. Ross, *CW* 2, p. 1699.

50 Thomas de Vio (Cardinal Cajetan), *Scripta Philosophica* (*De Nominum Analogia, De Conceptu Entis*), ed. P. Zammit (Rome: Angelicum, 1952), p. 3: 'Est siquidem eius notitia necessaria adeo, ut sine illa non possit metaphysicam quispiam discere, et multi in aliis scientiis ex eius ignorantia errores procedant.' See p. 29: 'Unde sine huius analogiae notitia, processus metaphysicales absque arte dicuntur.' For translation see *The Analogy of Names*, trans. E.A. Bushinski (Pittsburgh: Duquesne University Press, 1953), pp. 9, 29.

51 M.-D. Philippe, '*Analogon* and *Analogia* in the Philosophy of Aristotle', *The Thomist* 33 (1969), p. 1.

52 *EN* 6, 10, 1137b30–2.

53 *Rhet.* 1, 4,1360a25–30

54 *Rhet.* 2, 9, 1387a27–1387b2.

55 See *EN* 8, 7, 1158b23–8.

56 See *Rhet.* 3, 10, 1411b21–33.

57 *Rhet.* 3, 11, 1412a4–6, trans. Freese, p. 407.

58 Hugh Kenner, *Dublin's Joyce* (London: Chatto and Windus, 1955), p. 117.

59 Plutarch, *Isis and Osiris* 358f–359a: καθάπερ οἱ μαθηματικοὶ τὴν Ἶριν ἔμφασιν εἶναι τοῦ ἡλίου λέγουσι ποικιλλομένην τῇ πρὸς τὸ νέφος ἀναχωρήσει τῆς ὄψεως, οὕτως ὁ μῦθος ἐνταῦθα λόγου τινὸς ἔμφασίς ἐστιν ἀνακλῶντος ἐπ᾽ ἄλλα τὴν διάνοιαν. Trans. Frank Cole Babbitt, Plutarch, *Moralia*, vol. 5 (Cambridge, MA: Harvard University Press, 1936), p. 51: 'Just as the rainbow, according to the account of the mathematicians, is a reflection of the sun, and owes its many hues to the withdrawal of our gaze from the sun and our fixing it on the cloud, so the somewhat fanciful accounts here set down are but reflections of some true tale which turns back our thoughts to other matters.'

60 'Villanelle for an Anniversary', written for the 350th anniversary of Harvard.

61 *Insomn.* 1, 459a15–16: καὶ ἔστι μὲν τὸ αὐτὸ τῷ αἰσθητικῷ. Trans. Beare, *CW* 1, p. 730.

62 *Rhet.* 1, 11, 1370a28–9: ἡ δὲ φαντασία ἐστιν αἴσθησις τις ἀσθενής.

63 *Top.* 6, 2, 139b34–35: πᾶν γὰρ ἀσαφὲς τὸ κατὰ μεταφορὰν λεγόμενον.

64 Cecil Day-Lewis, *The Poetic Image* (London: Jonathan Cape, 1947), p. 35.

65 *Met.* 1, 9, 991a20–2.

66 *Meteor.* 2, 3, 357a 24–8, trans. Webster modified, *CW* 1, p. 581.

67 *Top.* 4, 3, 123a33–7: 'You must also see whether your opponent has assigned as a genus a term used metaphorically, speaking, for example, of "temperance" as a "harmony"; for every genus is predicated of its species in its proper sense, but "harmony" is predicated of temperance not in its proper sense but metaphorically; for a harmony consists always of sounds.' Trans. Forster, p. 441.

68   *Top.* 6, 2, 139b35–6.

69   *An. Post.* 2, 13, 97b37–9, trans. Tredennick, p. 241.

70   *Rhet.* 3, 2, 1405b17–19, trans. Roberts, *CW* 2, p. 2241.

71   *Poet.* 21, 1457b2; *Poet.* 22, 1458a33. Referring to iambic verse, which most resembles spoken language, he states: 'Only those words are allowed which might be used in speech. These are the ordinary word, metaphor, and ornament (ἔστι δὲ τὰ τοιαῦτα τὸ κύριον καὶ μεταφορὰ καὶ κόσμος).' *Poet.* 22, 1459a12–14, trans. Fyfe modified, p. 91.

72   *Rhet.* 3, 2, 1404b10–11.

73   *Rhet.* 3, 2, 1404b11–12: θαυμασταὶ γὰρ τῶν ἀπόντων εἰσίν, ἡδὺ δὲ τὸ θαυμαστόν ἐστιν.

74   *Rhet.* 3, 10, 1410b10–13, trans. Freese, pp. 395–7.

75   Nicolas Malebranche, *Oeuvres complètes* 12, ed. A. Robinet (Paris: Vrin, 1965), p. 30: 'Non, je ne vous conduirai point dans une terre étrangère; mais je vous apprendrai peut-être que vous êtes étranger vous-même dans votre propre pays.'

76   *Poet.* 21, 1457b25–30. Aristotle's example is the poet's analogy between the casting forth of seed-corn, i.e. sowing, and the casting forth by the sun of its flame, for which there is no word.

77   *Rhet.* 3, 2, 1405a35–7: 'In using metaphors to give names to nameless things, we must draw them not from remote but from kindred and similar things, so that the kinship is clearly perceived as soon as the words are said.' Trans. Roberts, *CW* 2, p. 2241. Clearly such metaphor does not give rise to obscurity: 'A metaphor in a way adds to our knowledge of what is indicated on account of the similarity, for those who use metaphors always do so on account of some similarity.' *Top.* 6, 2, 140a8–11, trans. Forster, p. 567.

78   *Rhet.* 3, 11, 1412a20–1: ὡς ἀληθῶς, ἐγὼ δὲ ἥμαρτον.

79   *Rhet.* 3, 10, 1410b10, 21.

80   *Rhet.* 3, 10, 1410b14.

81   *Rhet.* 3, 10, 1410b19.

82   *Rhet.* 3, 4, 1406b20: ἔστι δὲ καὶ ἡ εἰκὼν μεταφορά· διαφέρει γὰρ μικρόν.

83   *Rhet.* 3, 10, 1410b15–21.

84   Max Black, *Models and Metaphors. Studies in Language and Philosophy* (Ithaca: Cornell University Press, 1962); 'More about metaphor', *Dialectica* 31 (1977), pp. 432–57; 'How Metaphors Work: A Reply to Donald Davidson', *Critical Inquiry* 6/1 (Autumn 1979), pp. 131–43.

85   I.A. Richards, *The Philosophy of Rhetoric* (London: Oxford University Press, 1936), p. 96.

86   Ernan McMullin, 'The Motive for Metaphor', *Proceedings of the American Catholic Philosophical Association* 55 (1981), p. 39.

87   The full phrase is worth citing: 'And, Sir, as to metaphorical expression, that is a

great excellence in style, when it is used with propriety, for it gives you two ideas in one; – conveys the meaning more luminously, and generally with a perception of delight.' George Birkbeck Hill (ed.), *Boswell's Life of Johnson* (Oxford: Clarendon Press,1934), vol. 3, p. 174.

88   James Joyce, *Ulysses*, ed. Hans Walter Gabler (New York: Vintage, 1984), p. 536 (*U* 16.1579–81).

89   *Rhet.* 3, 11, 1412a10–12.

90   *Rhet.* 3, 10, 1410b12–13.

91   *De Caelo* 1, 1, 268b1.

92   *An. Post.* 1, 7, 75a38–9.

93   *De An.* 3, 8, 431b21: ἡ ψυχὴ τὰ ὄντα πώς ἐστι πάντα.

94   *De An.* 3, 2, 426b17–23.

95   G. Frege, *Begriffsschrift und andere Aufsätze* (Hildesheim: Olms, 1964), p. 107: 'Die Zeichen sind für das Denken von derselben Bedeutung wie für die Schifffahrt die Erfindung, den Wind zu gebrauchen, um gegen den Wind zu segeln.'

96   C. Day-Lewis, *The Poetic Image*, pp. 29, 34, 35.

97   C. Spurgeon, *Shakespeare's Imagery and What It Tells Us* (Cambridge: Cambridge University Press, 1936), p. 6.

98   Henri Bergson, *Creative Evolution* (London: Macmillan, 1922), p. 344.

CHAPTER SIX

1   See *EN* 9, 9, 1181b12–15.

2   *Pol.* 1, 1, 1252a1–7. While page and line numbers follow the standard Bekker text, chapter numbers are cited according to the revised Oxford translation, ed. Jonathan Barnes.

3   The similarity of my title to Otfried Höffe's excellent chapter 'Aristoteles' Politische Anthropologie' is coincidental. See Otfried Höffe (ed.), *Aristoteles. Politik* (Berlin: Akademie Verlag, 2001), pp. 21–35.

4   While I will use the terms 'description' and 'definition' interchangeably, one should not take Aristotle as offering here a strict definition.

5   I have substituted 'polis' for 'state' in all translated quotations.

6   Referring to *Pol.* 1, 2, 1252b27–1253a38, Alasdair MacIntyre remarks: 'This is a passage whose importance for the interpretation of everything that Aristotle wrote about human life cannot be underrated, and it is peculiarly crucial for understanding his claims about justice, practical reasoning, and their relationship.' *Whose Justice? Which Rationality?* (Notre Dame: University of Notre Dame Press, 1988), pp. 96–7.

7   *Pol.* 1, 2, 1252a24–5: ἐξ ἀρχῆς τὰ πράγματα φυόμενα βλέψειεν. Aristotle adopts a different approach at *Part. An.* 1, 1, 640a10–640b4.

8   *Pol.* 1, 2, 1252a26–7: ἀνάγκη δὴ πρῶτον συνδυάζεσθαι τοὺς ἄνευ ἀλλήλων μὴ δυναμένους εἶναι.

9   *Pol.* 1, 2, 1252b12–14: ἡ μὲν οὖν εἰς πᾶσαν ἡμέραν συνεστηκυῖα κοινωνία κατὰ φύσιν οἶκός ἐστιν. Trans. Jowett, *CW* 2, p. 1987.

10   *Pol.* 1, 2, 1252b15–16: ἡ δ᾽ ἐκ πλειόνων οἰκιῶν κοινωνία πρώτη χρήσεως ἕνεκεν μὴ ἐφημέρου κώμη.

11   *Pol.* 7, 4, 1326b7–9: διὸ πρώτην μὲν εἶναι πόλιν ἀναγκαῖον τὴν ἐκ τοσούτου πλήθους ὃ πρῶτον πλῆθος αὔταρκες πρὸς τὸ εὖ ζῆν ἐστι κατὰ τὴν πολιτικὴν κοινωνίαν. Trans. Jowett, *CW* 2, p. 2105.

12   *EN* 8, 12, 1162a16–19: ἀνδρὶ δὲ καὶ γυναικὶ φιλία δοκεῖ κατὰ φύσιν ὑπάρχειν· ἄνθρωπος γὰρ τῇ φύσει συνδυαστικὸν μᾶλλον ἢ πολιτικόν, ὅσῳ πρότερον καὶ ἀναγκαιότερον οἰκία πόλεως. Trans. Terence Irwin, Aristotle, *Nicomachean Ethics* (Indianapolis: Hackett, 1999), p. 133.

13   *EN* 8, 12, 1162a20–2: οἱ δ᾽ ἄνθρωποι οὐ μόνον τῆς τεκνοποιίας χάριν συνοικοῦσιν, ἀλλὰ καὶ τῶν εἰς τὸν βίον.

14   *EE* 7, 10, 1242a40–1242b1: διὸ ἐν οἰκίᾳ πρῶτον ἀρχαὶ καὶ πηγαὶ φιλίας καὶ πολιτείας καὶ δικαίου. Trans. Rackham.

15   *Pol.* 1, 2, 1252b27–30: ἡ δ᾽ ἐκ πλειόνων κωμῶν κοινωνία τέλειος πόλις, ἤδη πάσης ἔχουσα πέρας τῆς αὐταρκείας ὡς ἔπος εἰπεῖν, γινομένη μὲν τοῦ ζῆν ἕνεκεν, οὖσα δὲ τοῦ εὖ ζῆν.

16   Christopher J. Rowe, 'Aristotle for and against Democracy', in D.N. Koutras (ed.), *Political Equality and Justice in Aristotle and the Problems of Contemporary Society* (Athens: To Lykeion, 2000), p. 408. See *Pol.* 3, 9, 1280b38–9: ἡ γὰρ τοῦ συζῆν προαίρεσις φιλία. τέλος μὲν οὖν πόλεως τὸ εὖ ζῆν.

17   Otherwise, he states, 'a collection of slaves or of lower animals would be a polis, but as it is, it is not a polis, because slaves and animals have no share in well-being or in purposive life'. *Pol.* 3, 9, 1280a31–4: εἰ δὲ μήτε τοῦ ζῆν μόνον ἕνεκεν ἀλλὰ μᾶλλον τοῦ εὖ ζῆν (καὶ γὰρ ἂν δούλων καὶ τῶν ἄλλων ζῴων ἦν πόλις· νῦν δ᾽ οὐκ ἔστι, διὰ τὸ μὴ μετέχειν εὐδαιμονίας μηδὲ τοῦ ζῆν κατὰ προαίρεσιν). Trans. Rackham, p. 213.

18   *Pol.* 1, 2, 1252b30–1: διὸ πᾶσα πόλις φύσει ἔστιν, εἴπερ καὶ αἱ πρῶται κοινωνίαι.

19   *Pol.* 1, 2, 1252b32–1253a1: οἷον γὰρ ἕκαστόν ἐστι τῆς γενέσεως τελεσθείσης, ταύτην φαμὲν τὴν φύσιν εἶναι ἑκάστου, ὥσπερ ἀνθρώπου ἵππου οἰκίας. ἔτι τὸ οὗ ἕνεκα καὶ τὸ τέλος βέλτιστον.

20   *Pol.* 1, 2, 1253a1–3: ἡ δ᾽ αὐτάρκεια καὶ τέλος καὶ βέλτιστον. ἐκ τούτων οὖν φανερὸν ὅτι τῶν φύσει ἡ πόλις ἐστί, καὶ ὅτι ὁ ἄνθρωπος φύσει πολιτικὸν ζῷον.

21   *Pol.* 1, 2, 1253a4; also *Pol.* 1, 2, 1253a26–9.

22   *Iliad* 9. 63: ἀφρήτωρ ἀθέμιστος ἀνέστιός. See *Pol.* 1, 2, 1253a5.

23   Sophocles, *Philoctetes*, 1018: ἄφιλον ἔρημον ἄπολιν, ἐν ζῶσιν νεκρόν. See Jean Roberts, 'Political Animals in the *Nicomachean Ethics*', *Phronesis* 34 (1989), p. 200, n 20.

24   *EN* 1, 7, 1097b7–11, trans. Rackham, p. 29.

25   *Pol.* 1, 2, 1253a7–10: διότι δὲ πολιτικὸν ὁ ἄνθρωπος ζῷον πάσης μελίττης καὶ παντὸς ἀγελαίου ζῴου μᾶλλον, δῆλον. οὐθὲν γάρ, ὡς φαμέν, μάτην ἡ φύσις ποιεῖ· λόγον δὲ μόνον ἄνθρωπος ἔχει τῶν ζῴων. Trans. Rackham, p. 11.

26   *Pol.* 1, 2, 1253a10–18: ἡ μὲν οὖν φωνὴ τοῦ λυπηροῦ καὶ ἡδέος ἐστὶ σημεῖον, διὸ καὶ τοῖς ἄλλοις ὑπάρχει ζῴοις μέχρι γὰρ τούτου ἡ φύσις αὐτῶν ἐλήλυθε, τοῦ ἔχειν αἴσθησιν λυπηροῦ καὶ ἡδέος καὶ ταῦτα σημαίνειν ἀλλήλοις, ὁ δὲ λόγος ἐπὶ τῷ δηλοῦν ἐστι τὸ συμφέρον καὶ τὸ βλαβερόν, ὥστε καὶ τὸ δίκαιον καὶ τὸ ἄδικον· τοῦτο γὰρ πρὸς τὰ ἄλλα ζῷα τοῖς ἀνθρώποις ἴδιον, τὸ μόνον ἀγαθοῦ καὶ κακοῦ καὶ δικαίου καὶ ἀδίκου καὶ τῶν ἄλλων αἴσθησιν ἔχειν· ἡ δὲ τούτων κοινωνία ποιεῖ οἰκίαν καὶ πόλιν. Trans. Rackham, p. 11.

27   M.I. Finley, *Politics in the Ancient World* (Cambridge: Cambridge University Press, 1991), p. 24: 'In the *Politics* Aristotle defined man as a *zoön politikon*, and what that meant is comprehensible only in the light of his metaphysics.'

28   *Hist. An.* 1, 1, 488a7–8: πολιτικὰ δ' ἐστὶν ὧν ἕν τι καὶ κοινὸν γίγνεται πάντων τὸ ἔργον.

29   Aristotle refers to the social behaviour of cranes, which emigrate from the steppes of Scythia to the source of the Nile in the marshes of Egypt. As well as a leader, signallers patrol the flock for cohesion with whistle calls that are heard by all; when they settle and sleep (head under wing), the leader keeps watch and cries an alert in the event of danger. See *Hist An.* 8, 12, 597a3–6; 9, 10, 614b18–26. Plato had already noted the 'political' character of bees, wasps and ants. See *Phaedo* 82b5–8: ὅτι τούτους εἰκός ἐστιν εἰς τοιοῦτον πάλιν ἀφικνεῖσθαι πολιτικὸν καὶ ἥμερον γένος, ἤ που μελιττῶν ἢ σφηκῶν ἢ μυρμήκων, καὶ εἰς ταὐτόν γε πάλιν τὸ ἀνθρώπινον γένος, καὶ γίγνεσθαι ἐξ αὐτῶν ἄνδρας μετρίους.

30   *Hist. An.* 7, 1, 588a29–31, trans. Balme, p. 61.

31   Fred D. Miller, Jr., *Nature, Justice, and Rights in Aristotle's Politics* (Oxford: Clarendon Press, 1997), p. 3. For an exhaustive treatment of the word's origins see Chapter 2, 'Excursus on the Ancient Meanings of the word Πόλις', in M.B. Sakellariou, *The Polis-State. Definition and Origin* (Athens/Paris: National Hellenic Research Foundation/De Boccard, 1989), pp. 155–211.

32   Wolfgang Kullmann, 'Man as a Political Animal in Aristotle', in David Keyt and Fred D. Miller, Jr (eds), *A Companion to Aristotle's Politics* (Oxford: Blackwells, 1991), p. 99. For an exhaustive treatment of this principle, see James G. Lennox, 'Nature does nothing in vain...', in *Aristotle's Philosophy of Biology* (Cambridge: Cambridge University Press, 2001), pp. 205–23. Kullman warns against an idealizing interpretation (*idealisierende Ausdeutung*) of Aristotle's definition, as presented by some classical philologists for whom the *paideia*-ideal is achieved through the education of the πολιτικὸν ζῷον. Aristotle's definition, Kullmann insists, refers to man's nature, to *what he is* and not to an ideal. See *Aristoteles und*

die moderne Wissenschaft [hereafter *Aristoteles*] (Stuttgart: Steiner, 1998), p. 334.

33 Kullmann, 'Man as a Political Animal in Aristotle', p. 100.

34 Ibid., pp. 100–1. Fred D. Miller also states: 'In this argument "political animal" can be understood in terms of the broader, biological sense.' Miller, *Nature, Justice, and Rights in Aristotle's Politics*, p. 32 See John M. Cooper, *Reason and Emotion. Essays on Ancient Moral Psychology and Ethical Theory* (Princeton: Princeton University Press, 1999), p. 362. The chapter 'Political Animals and Civic Friendship' was originally published under the same title in Günther Patzig (ed.), *Aristoteles' Politik* (Göttingen: Vandenhoeck & Ruprecht, 1990), pp. 221–48. Also David J. Depew, 'Humans and Other Political Animals in Aristotle's *History of Animals*', *Phronesis* 40 (1995), p. 163, n 16: 'In the matter of literal predications and salient explanations, the zoological sense is basic.' See Kullmann, *Aristoteles*, p. 337: 'Der Mensch wird als "Lebewesen" (ζῷον) bezeichnet und insofern in eine Reihe mit den Tieren gestellt, und durch die Herausstellung der ursprünglichen Gemeinschaft der Paarung von Mann und Frau, die durch Vergleich mit den übrigen Lebewesen und den Pflanzen als ein triebhaftes, nicht auf rationaler Entscheidung (προαίρεσις) beruhendes, auf Fortpflanzung zielendes Verhalten charakterisiert wird, macht er ebenfalls auf ein biologisches Grundfaktum aufmerksam.' Also p. 340: 'Es kommt ihm also wiederum darauf an, den Menschen, insofern er ein biologisches Wesen ist, als von Natur aus politisch zu charakterisieren. Der Satz, daß die Natur nichts umsonst macht, ist eine Art biologisches Axiom, das in diesem Zusammenhang unterstreicht, daß der Mensch in seinem Bauplan durch die psychosomatische Eigentümlichkeit des Logos auf die von ihm im politischen Bereich ausgeführten Leistungen und Funktionen hin angelegt ist. Auch die Sprache ist hier rein als biologische Eigentümlichkeit betrachtet und wird allein von ihrer Leistung im Rahmen des menschlichen Sozialverhaltens aus gesehen.'

35 *Pol.* 1, 2, 1253a7–8, trans. Rackham, p. 11.

36 Richard Bodéüs, 'L'animal politique et l'animal économique', in André Motte & Christiaan Rutten (eds) *Aristotelica. Mélanges offerts à M. De Corte* (Bruxelles: Éditions Ousia / Liège: Presses Universitaires, 1985), p. 66: 'La remarque ne vise pas, nous semble-t-il, une différence du plus ou moins. Aristote n'entend pas dire vraiment que l'espèce humaine possède un caractère politique plus marqué que toute autre espèce du même genre, mais que c'est elle, plutôt que n'importe quelle espèce d'abeille ou d'animal grégaire, qui possède ce caractère. La remarque est donc de grande portée.' Bodéüs adds: 'Conformément à l'usage du grec, il eût alors écrit πολιτικώτερον, comme dans *Hist. des an.*, VIII, 1, 589a 1–2 à propos des animaux qui élèvent plus ou moins longtemps leur progéniture.' (Ibid., n 10.) Kullmann (*Aristoteles*, p. 339, n 70) argues in favour of a comparative reading: 'Auch das Wort "jede" spricht dafür, daß die Worte μᾶλλον πολιτικόν in komparativischem Sinne verstanden werden müssen.'

37 Kullmann's article (published originally as 'Der Mensch als Politisches Lebewesen bei Aristoteles', *Hermes* 108 (1980), pp. 419–43) has been greatly extended in *Aristoteles und die moderne Wissenschaft*, pp. 334–63, where account is taken of more recent literature (Miller, Labarrière, Annas, Depew, Keyt, Berti). Much of the content of this section appears, in reorganized form and with minor additions, as Chapter 2 of a shorter book, published in Italian as *Il pensiero politico di Aristotele* (Milano: Guerini, 1992), and in Greek as *Η Πολιτική Σκέψη του Αριστοτέλη* (Αθήνα: Μορφωτικό Ίδρυμα Εθνικής Τραπέζης, 2003).

38 Kullmann, *Aristoteles*, p. 354: 'Auf jeden Fall zeigt die Stelle eindeutig, daß ζῷον πολιτικόν eine biologische Bestimmung ist. Zwar is der Begriff "politisch" selbst kein biologischer Begriff. Seine Herübernahme is die Biologie, erklärt sich aber aus dem Darlehnungsprinzip der aristotelischen Biologie, die Unterschiede der einzelnen Tierarten am Maßstab der am höchsten entwickelten Tierart zu messen, und dies ist der Mensch.'

39 Gérard Verbeke, *Moral Education in Aristotle* (Washington, DC: Catholic University of America Press, 1990), p. 76.

40 *De An.* 3, 9, 432b21–2 and 3, 12, 434a31. Aristotle notes that since the goal of politics is human excellence and happiness, the student of politics should study the activities of the soul. See *EN* 1, 13, 1102a24–6.

41 *EN* 1, 13, 1102a18–23.

42 *EN* 1, 7, 1097b28–30.

43 *EN* 1, 2, 1094a21: ὥστ᾽ εἶναι κενὴν καὶ ματαίαν τὴν ὄρεξιν.

44 *De An.* 3, 8, 431b21.

45 *Rhet.* 1, 1, 1355a15–17, trans. Roberts, *CW* 2, p. 2154.

46 Kullmann, *Aristoteles*, p. 341: 'Die starke biologische Komponente ist keine Eigentümlichkeit der *Politik* allein.'

47 Ibid., p. 339.

48 *Inc. An.* 4, 706a19–20: διὰ τὸ κατὰ φύσιν ἔχειν μάλιστα τῶν ζῴων. Trans. Farquharson, *CW* 1, p. 1099. See *Inc. An.* 4, 706b10: μάλιστα γὰρ κατὰ φύσιν ἐστι δίπους. Aristotle suggests that as the final member of the series man best realizes the nature of the animal.

49 Kullmann correctly states (*Aristoteles*, p. 338): 'Aristoteles war überzeugt, daß die Sozialstrukturen bestimmter Tiere mit denen der Menschen Ähnlichkeiten haben.' The question, however, is whether such similarities point to a political capacity in the full sense of the term: whether 'political' is affirmed of other animals literally or figuratively.

50 John M. Cooper, *Reason and Emotion*, p. 357. Cooper considers 'animal that lives in cities' to be a less misleading translation of *zoön politikon* than 'political animal'.

51 R.G. Mulgan, 'Aristotle's Doctrine that Man is a Political Animal', *Hermes* 120 (1974), p. 439.

52 David J. Depew, 'Humans and Other Political Animals in Aristotle's *History of Animals*', *Phronesis* 40 (1995), p. 162. Joachim Ritter (*Metaphysik und Politik*, Frankfurt: Suhrkamp, 1969, p. 76) and Günther Bien (*Die Grundlegung der politischen Philosophie bei Aristoteles*, Freiburg/München: Alber, 1973) 'are among those who take "political" to name the human essence'.

53 Hannah Arendt, *The Human Condition* (Chicago: University of Chicago Press, 1958), p. 27. For similar criticisms of German interpretations, largely inspired by Hegel, see Kullmann, pp. 342–3.

54 Kullmann, *Aristoteles*, p. 351.

55 Kullmann's criticism (*Aristoteles*, p. 343) of Günther Bien is therefore not to the point.

56 *Part. An.* 4, 10, 687a23–6. Aristotle's point is that through manual dexterity and intelligence man more than compensates.

57 *Pol.* 1, 10, 1258a21–3: ὥσπερ γὰρ καὶ ἀνθρώπους οὐ ποιεῖ ἡ πολιτική, ἀλλὰ λαβοῦσα παρὰ τῆς φύσεως χρῆται αὐτοῖς. Trans. Rackham, p. 49.

58 *EN* 9, 9, 1170b8–14: τὸ δ᾽ εἶναι ἦν αἱρετὸν διὰ τὸ αἰσθάνεσθαι αὐτοῦ ἀγαθοῦ ὄντος, ἡ δὲ τοιαύτη αἴσθησις ἡδεῖα καθ᾽ ἑαυτήν. συναισθάνεσθαι ἄρα δεῖ καὶ τοῦ φίλου ὅτι ἔστιν, τοῦτο δὲ γίνοιτ᾽ ἂν ἐν τῷ συζῆν καὶ κοινωνεῖν λόγων καὶ διανοίας· οὕτω γὰρ ἂν δόξειε τὸ συζῆν ἐπὶ τῶν ἀνθρώπων λέγεσθαι, καὶ οὐχ ὥσπερ ἐπὶ τῶν βοσκημάτων τὸ ἐν τῷ αὐτῷ νέμεσθαι. Trans. Rackham, p. 565.

59 *Pol.* 3, 9, 1280b38–9: τὸ δὲ τοιοῦτον φιλίας ἔργον· ἡ γὰρ τοῦ συζῆν προαίρεσις φιλία. *Pol.* 4, 11, 1295b24: ἡ γὰρ κοινωνία φιλικόν.

60 *EN* 8, 1, 1155a22–8: ἔοικε δὲ καὶ τὰς πόλεις συνέχειν ἡ φιλία, καὶ οἱ νομοθέται μᾶλλον περὶ αὐτὴν σπουδάζειν ἢ τὴν δικαιοσύνην: ἡ γὰρ ὁμόνοια ὅμοιόν τι τῇ φιλίᾳ ἔοικεν εἶναι, ταύτης δὲ μάλιστ᾽ ἐφίενται καὶ τὴν στάσιν ἔχθραν οὖσαν μάλιστα ἐξελαύνουσιν· καὶ φίλων μὲν ὄντων οὐδὲν δεῖ δικαιοσύνης, δίκαιοι δ᾽ ὄντες προσδέονται φιλίας, καὶ τῶν δικαίων τὸ μάλιστα φιλικὸν εἶναι δοκεῖ. Trans. Rackham p. 453.

61 *EN* 9, 9, 1169b16–22: ἄτοπον δ᾽ ἴσως καὶ τὸ μονώτην ποιεῖν τὸν μακάριον· οὐδεὶς γὰρ ἕλοιτ᾽ ἂν καθ᾽ αὑτὸν τὰ πάντ᾽ ἔχειν ἀγαθά· πολιτικὸν γὰρ ὁ ἄνθρωπος καὶ συζῆν πεφυκός. καὶ τῷ εὐδαίμονι δὴ τοῦθ᾽ ὑπάρχει· τὰ γὰρ τῇ φύσει ἀγαθὰ ἔχει, δῆλον δ᾽ ὡς μετὰ φίλων καὶ ἐπιεικῶν κρεῖττον ἢ μετ᾽ ὀθνείων καὶ τῶν τυχόντων συνημερεύειν. δεῖ ἄρα τῷ εὐδαίμονι φίλων. Translation Ross modified, *CW* 2, p. 1848.

62 *Pol.* 3, 6, 1278b19–30: φύσει μέν ἐστιν ἄνθρωπος ζῷον πολιτικόν. διὸ καὶ μηδὲν δεόμενοι τῆς παρὰ ἀλλήλων βοηθείας οὐκ ἔλαττον ὀρέγονται τοῦ συζῆν· οὐ μὴν ἀλλὰ καὶ τὸ κοινῇ συμφέρον συνάγει, καθ᾽ ὅσον ἐπιβάλλει μέρος ἑκάστῳ τοῦ ζῆν καλῶς. μάλιστα μὲν οὖν τοῦτ᾽ ἐστὶ τέλος, καὶ κοινῇ πᾶσι καὶ χωρίς· συνέρχονται δὲ καὶ τοῦ ζῆν ἕνεκεν αὐτοῦ καὶ συνέχουσι τὴν πολιτικὴν κοινωνίαν, ἴσως γὰρ ἔνεστί τι τοῦ καλοῦ μόριον καὶ κατὰ τὸ ζῆν αὐτὸ μόνον· ἂν μὴ τοῖς χαλεποῖς κατὰ

τὸν βίον ὑπερβάλῃ λίαν, δῆλον δ᾽ ὡς καρτεροῦσι πολλὴν κακοπάθειαν οἱ πολλοὶ τῶν ἀνθρώπων γλιχόμενοι τοῦ ζῆν, ὡς ἐνούσης τινὸς εὐημερίας ἐν αὐτῷ καὶ γλυκύτητος φυσικῆς. Trans. Rackham, pp. 201–3.

63 Jean-Louis Labarrière, 'Aristote penseur de la différence entre l'homme et l'animal', *Anthropozoologica*, 33–34 (2001), p. 108.

64 At *Hist. An.* 8, 1, 589a1–2, Aristotle uses the term 'more political' as a comparative term among non-human animals. He notes that while some animals terminate contact with their offspring after birth or first nourishment and have no further association with them, 'those that have more understanding and possess some memory continue their association, and have a more political (πολιτικώτερον) relationship with their offspring.' Trans. Balme modified, p. 67.

65 See *Pol.* 1, 2, 1253a16–18.

66 The view of Hermann Bengston, as discussed by Kullmann, 'Man as a Political Animal in Aristotle', p. 94, n2. Despite its common usage, the term 'city-state' is unsatisfactory. It is itself a literal translation of the German *Stadtstaat*, used first in 1765 by Herder to translate *Polis*. *Stadtstaat* distinguished a city that was also a state in the German empire from the *Stadt* or city-settlement. The acceptance of the English equivalent was largely due to the classical scholar William Warde Fowler. See M.B. Sakellariou, *The Polis-State. Definition and Origin*, pp. 19–20.

67 The assumption that in ancient Greece 'Mensch-Sein' is equivalent to 'Bürger-Sein' is criticized by Olof Gigon, *Aristoteles. Politik* (München: Deutscher Taschenbuch Verlag, 1973), p. 13.

68 *Pol.* 1, 2, 1253a27–9. In Alasdair MacIntyre's phrase, 'Separated from the polis, what could have been a human being becomes instead a wild animal.' *Whose Justice? Which Rationality?*, p. 98.

69 *Pol.* 1, 2, 1253a32–3, trans. Jowett, *CW* 2, p. 1988.

70 Kullmann, *Aristoteles*, p. 341: 'Die starke biologische Komponente ist keine Eigentümlichkeit der *Politik* allein.'

71 Kullmann, *Aristoteles*, p. 349: 'Der menschliche Staat ist also für Aristoteles weder im Sinne der Hegelianer ein reines Vernunftgebilde noch ein bloßer Bienenstaat. Er hat gewissermaßen von beiden etwas.'

72 *Met.* 12, 7, 1072b29.

73 Kullmann, *Aristoteles*, p. 338: 'Dem steht aber entgegen, daß der ganze Kontext in der Politik von der Beziehung zur (biologischen) Naturwissenschaft ausgeht.'

74 *Pol.* 1, 2, 1252b30: πᾶσα πόλις φύσει ἔστίν. Olof Gigon suggests that Aristotle appears so intent on demonstrating the natural character of the polis, that he may have been polemically motivated. Gigon refers to the Socratic traditions that discouraged all practical political activity, and maintained that political community is a product of convention (*nomos*). He cites Aristippus of Cyrene (Cf. Xenophon, *Mem.* 2, 1, 8–13), who influenced Epicurus and the Cynics. See Gigon, *Aristoteles*.

Politik, p. 267. He may have also had Democritus in mind. See Kullmann, *Aristoteles*, pp. 339 and 355.

75 *Pol.* 1, 2, 1253a2: φανερὸν ὅτι τῶν φύσει ἡ πόλις ἐστί. *Pol.* 7, 8, 1328a22: τῶν κατὰ φύσιν συνεστώτων.

76 *Pol.* 4, 4, 1291a24.

77 *Pol.* 1, 2, 1252b32–1253a1. See footnote 18 above.

78 *Phys.* 2, 1, 192b13–14. See also *Phys.* 2, 1, 193a29–30. Nature is the 'principle of that which has within itself its own source of motion and change'. My translation.

79 *Pol.* 7, 4, 1326a3–5, trans. Rackham, p. 553. For further references see David Keyt, 'Three Fundamental Theorems in Aristotle's Politics', *Phronesis* 32 (1987), p. 55.

80 See Fred D. Miller, Jr., *Nature, Justice, and Rights in Aristotle's Politics* (Oxford: Clarendon Press, 1997), p. 29. Aristotle was familiar with the view, later championed famously by Hobbes, that citizenship was a matter of choice and convention. See Miller p. 31.

81 Any polis worthy of the name must be concerned with virtue. See *Pol.* 3, 9, 1280b5: δεῖ περὶ ἀρετῆς ἐπιμελὲς εἶναι.

82 *EN* 1, 3, 1094b14–16: τὰ δὲ καλὰ καὶ τὰ δίκαια, περὶ ὧν ἡ πολιτικὴ σκοπεῖται, πολλὴν ἔχει διαφορὰν καὶ πλάνην, ὥστε δοκεῖν νόμῳ μόνον εἶναι, φύσει δὲ μή. Miller speaks of Aristotle's 'political naturalism', p. 37.

83 *EN* 5, 7, 1134b18–20: τοῦ δὲ πολιτικοῦ δικαίου τὸ μὲν φυσικόν ἐστι τὸ δὲ νομικόν, φυσικὸν μὲν τὸ πανταχοῦ τὴν αὐτὴν ἔχον δύναμιν, καὶ οὐ τῷ δοκεῖν ἢ μή.

84 *EN* 5, 7, 1134b25–7: τὸ μὲν φύσει ἀκίνητον καὶ πανταχοῦ τὴν αὐτὴν ἔχει δύναμιν, ὥσπερ τὸ πῦρ καὶ ἐνθάδε καὶ ἐν Πέρσαις καίει.

85 *EN* 5, 7, 1134b29–30: παρ᾽ ἡμῖν δ᾽ ἔστι μέν τι καὶ φύσει, κινητὸν μέντοι πᾶν, ἀλλ᾽ ὅμως ἐστὶ τὸ μὲν φύσει τὸ δ᾽ οὐ φύσει.

86 *Pol.* 8, 1, 1337a27–30: ἅμα δὲ οὐδὲ χρὴ νομίζειν αὐτὸν αὑτοῦ τινα εἶναι τῶν πολιτῶν, ἀλλὰ πάντας τῆς πόλεως, μόριον γὰρ ἕκαστος τῆς πόλεως· ἡ δ᾽ ἐπιμέλεια πέφυκεν ἑκάστου μορίου βλέπειν πρὸς τὴν τοῦ ὅλου ἐπιμέλειαν. Trans. Rackham, pp. 635–7.

87 *Pol.* 1, 2, 1253a20: τὸ γὰρ ὅλον πρότερον ἀναγκαῖον εἶναι τοῦ μέρους. Trans. Rackham, p. 11.

88 *Pol.* 1, 2, 1253a18–20: καὶ πρότερον δὲ τῇ φύσει πόλις ἢ οἰκία καὶ ἕκαστος ἡμῶν ἐστιν. τὸ γὰρ ὅλον πρότερον ἀναγκαῖον εἶναι τοῦ μέρους. 1253a25–26: ἡ καὶ φύσει πρότερον ἢ ἕκαστος. Trans. Rackham modified, p. 11.

89 *Pol.* 1, 2, 1253a20–7: ἀναιρουμένου γὰρ τοῦ ὅλου οὐκ ἔσται ποὺς οὐδὲ χείρ, εἰ μὴ ὁμωνύμως, ὥσπερ εἴ τις λέγοι τὴν λιθίνην διαφθαρεῖσα γὰρ ἔσται τοιαύτη, πάντα δὲ τῷ ἔργῳ ὥρισται καὶ τῇ δυνάμει, ὥστε μηκέτι τοιαῦτα ὄντα οὐ λεκτέον τὰ αὐτὰ εἶναι ἀλλ᾽ ὁμώνυμα. ὅτι μὲν οὖν ἡ πόλις καὶ φύσει πρότερον ἢ ἕκαστος, δῆλον· εἰ γὰρ μὴ αὐτάρκης ἕκαστος χωρισθείς, ὁμοίως τοῖς ἄλλοις μέρεσιν ἕξει πρὸς τὸ ὅλον. Trans. Rackham, p. 11. Aristotle convincingly employs the analogy to illustrate the

strength of democracy in the collective wisdom of its citizens: 'Where there are many, each individual, it may be argued, has some portion of virtue and wisdom, and when they have come together, just as the multitude becomes a single man (ὥσπερ ἕνα ἄνθρωπον τὸ πλῆθος) with many feet and many hands and many senses, so also it becomes one personality as regards the moral and intellectual faculties. This is why the general public is a better judge of the works of music and those of the poets, because different men can judge a different part of the performance, and all of them all of it.' *Pol.* 3, 11, 1281b4–10, trans. Rackham, p. 223. See also *Pol.* 3, 11, 1281b34–8.

90   See *Part. An.* 1, 1, 640b33–5: 'A corpse has the same shape and fashion as a living body; and yet it is not a man.' Trans. Peck, p. 67. See *Part. An.* 1, 1, 641a17–21: 'Now it may be that the form of any living creature is soul, or some part of soul, or something that involves soul. At any rate, when its soul is gone, it is no longer a living creature, and none of its parts remains the same, except only in shape, just like the animals in the story that were turned into stone.' Trans. Peck, p. 69. See *Gen. An.* 2, 1, 734b24–5: 'There is no face without the soul.' (οὐ γάρ ἐστι πρόσωπον μὴ ἔχον ψυχήν).

91   *Pol.* 3, 4, 1277b7–8: ἀλλ᾽ ἔστι τις ἀρχὴ καθ᾽ ἣν ἄρχει τῶν ὁμοίων τῷ γένει καὶ τῶν ἐλευθέρων. See Höffe, 'Aristoteles᾽ Politische Anthropologie', p. 23. Höffe points out that Aristotle already had the recently revived concept of subsidiarity: higher organs of society support the independence of its inferiors. See p. 25.

92   Fred D. Miller, Jr, *Nature, Justice and Right in Aristotle's Politics*, p. 30.

93   See W.L. Newman, *The Politics of Aristotle*, vol. 2 (Oxford: Clarendon Press, 1887), p. 230: 'There was a real difference of opinion between Aristotle and Plato on this subject. The State is less of a σύμφυσις (2. 4. 1262b14sqq) to Aristotle than to Plato; the individual counts for more with him, and is less lost and swallowed up in the State.'

94   *Pol.* 3, 1, 1274b41: ἡ γὰρ πόλις πολιτῶν τι πλῆθός ἐστιν. *Pol.* 2, 2, 1261a18: πλῆθος γάρ τι τὴν φύσιν ἐστὶν ἡ πόλις. See M.B. Sakellariou, *The Polis-State. Definition and Origin*, pp. 229–32.

95   *Pol.* 2, 2, 1261a20–1: μᾶλλον γὰρ μίαν τὴν οἰκίαν τῆς πόλεως φαίημεν ἄν, καὶ τὸν ἕνα τῆς οἰκίας.

96   *Pol.* 7, 8, 1328b16–17: ἡ γὰρ πόλις πλῆθός ἐστιν οὐ τὸ τυχὸν ἀλλὰ πρὸς ζωὴν αὔταρκες.

97   *Pol.* 2, 2, 1261a22–4: οὐ μόνον δ᾽ ἐκ πλειόνων ἀνθρώπων ἐστὶν ἡ πόλις, ἀλλὰ καὶ ἐξ εἴδει διαφερόντων. *Pol.* 2, 2, 1261a29–30: ἐξ ὧν δὲ δεῖ ἓν γενέσθαι εἴδει διαφέρειν.

98   *Pol.* 7, 8, 1328a35–7: ἡ δὲ πόλις κοινωνία τίς ἐστι τῶν ὁμοίων, ἕνεκεν δὲ ζωῆς τῆς ἐνδεχομένης ἀρίστης.

99   See *Pol.* 3, 3, 1276a34–1276b1. See W.L. Newman, *The Politics of Aristotle* I, pp. 41–4.

100 Peter L. Phillips Simpson, *A Philosophical Commentary on the Politics of Aristotle* (Chapel Hill: The University of North Carolina Press, 1998), p. 134.

101 *Pol.* 3, 9, 1280b5–10. περὶ δ᾽ ἀρετῆς καὶ κακίας πολιτικῆς διασκοποῦσιν ὅσοι φροντίζουσιν εὐνομίας. ᾗ καὶ φανερὸν ὅτι δεῖ περὶ ἀρετῆς ἐπιμελὲς εἶναι τῇ γ᾽ ὡς ἀληθῶς ὀνομαζομένῃ πόλει, μὴ λόγου χάριν. γίγνεται γὰρ ἡ κοινωνία συμμαχία, τῶν ἄλλων τόπῳ διαφέρουσα μόνον, τῶν ἄπωθεν συμμάχων. Trans. Rackham modified, p. 215.

102 See *Pol.* 3, 9, 1280b29–35: φανερὸν τοίνυν ὅτι ἡ πόλις οὐκ ἔστι κοινωνία τόπου, καὶ τοῦ μὴ ἀδικεῖν σφᾶς αὐτοὺς καὶ τῆς μεταδόσεως χάριν· ἀλλὰ ταῦτα μὲν ἀναγκαῖον ὑπάρχειν, εἴπερ ἔσται πόλις, οὐ μὴν οὐδ᾽ ὑπαρχόντων τούτων ἁπάντων ἤδη πόλις, ἀλλ᾽ ἡ τοῦ εὖ ζῆν κοινωνία καὶ ταῖς οἰκίαις καὶ τοῖς γένεσι, ζωῆς τελείας χάριν καὶ αὐτάρκους.

103 *Pol.* 3, 9, 1280b38–1281a4: τὸ δὲ τοιοῦτον φιλίας ἔργον· ἡ γὰρ τοῦ συζῆν προαίρεσις φιλία. τέλος μὲν οὖν πόλεως τὸ εὖ ζῆν, ταῦτα δὲ τοῦ τέλους χάριν. πόλις δὲ ἡ γενῶν καὶ κωμῶν κοινωνία ζωῆς τελείας καὶ αὐτάρκους, τοῦτο δ᾽ ἐστίν, ὡς φαμέν, τὸ ζῆν εὐδαιμόνως καὶ καλῶς. τῶν καλῶν ἄρα πράξεων χάριν θετέον εἶναι τὴν πολιτικὴν κοινωνίαν ἀλλ᾽ οὐ τοῦ συζῆν.

104 *Pol.* 2, 5, 1263b31–2: δεῖ μὲν γὰρ εἶναί πως μίαν καὶ τὴν οἰκίαν καὶ τὴν πόλιν, ἀλλ᾽ οὐ πάντως.

105 *Pol.* 3, 4, 1279a21: ἡ δὲ πόλις κοινωνία τῶν ἐλευθέρων ἐστίν.

106 *Pol.* 2, 5, 1263b36–7: ἀλλὰ δεῖ πλῆθος ὄν, ὥσπερ εἴρηται πρότερον, διὰ τὴν παιδείαν κοινὴν καὶ μίαν ποιεῖν. Trans. Jowett modified, *CW* 2, p. 2005.

107 Fragment 95, *Lyra Graeca* II, ed. J.M. Edmonds (Cambridge, MA: Harvard University Press, 1958), p. 337.

108 *Pol.* 8, 1, 1337a21–7: ἐπεὶ δ᾽ ἓν τὸ τέλος τῇ πόλει πάσῃ, φανερὸν ὅτι καὶ τὴν παιδείαν μίαν καὶ τὴν αὐτὴν ἀναγκαῖον εἶναι πάντων, καὶ ταύτης τὴν ἐπιμέλειαν εἶναι κοινὴν καὶ μὴ κατ᾽ ἰδίαν, ὃν τρόπον νῦν ἕκαστος ἐπιμελεῖται τῶν αὐτοῦ τέκνων ἰδίᾳ τε καὶ μάθησιν ἰδίαν, ἣν ἂν δόξῃ, διδάσκων. δεῖ δὲ τῶν κοινῶν κοινὴν ποιεῖσθαι καὶ τὴν ἄσκησιν. Trans. Rackham, p. 635

109 *Pol.* 2, 5, 1263b31–35.

110 See *EN* 1, 1, 1094a1–b6.

111 *EN* 1, 2, 1094b6–1, 3, 1094b15: ὥστε τοῦτ᾽ ἂν εἴη τἀνθρώπινον ἀγαθόν. εἰ γὰρ καὶ ταὐτόν ἐστιν ἑνὶ καὶ πόλει, μεῖζόν γε καὶ τελειότερον τὸ τῆς πόλεως φαίνεται καὶ λαβεῖν καὶ σῴζειν· ἀγαπητὸν μὲν γὰρ καὶ ἑνὶ μόνῳ, κάλλιον δὲ καὶ θειότερον ἔθνει καὶ πόλεσιν. ἡ μὲν οὖν μέθοδος τούτων ἐφίεται, πολιτική τις οὖσα. ... τὰ δὲ καλὰ καὶ τὰ δίκαια, περὶ ὧν ἡ πολιτικὴ σκοπεῖται. (This latter remark resembles *Pol.* 1, 2, 1253a15–18, where Aristotle says that it is partnership in goodness and justice that makes the household and polis.) The *Politics* also opens with the declaration that the city or political community (ἡ καλουμένη πόλις καὶ ἡ κοινωνία ἡ πολιτική) aims at the supreme human good (*Pol.* 1, 1, 1252a1–7). In the *Nicomachean Ethics*

Aristotle compares the *ad hoc* and sectional partnerships that arise among humans: 'But all these associations seem to be subordinate to the association of the polis, which aims not at a temporary advantage but at one covering the whole of life (εἰς ἅπαντα τὸν βίον) ... All these associations then appear to be parts of the association of the polis.' *EN* 8, 9, 1160a20–3, 28–30. A different perspective is offered at *EN* 6, 7, 1141a20–2, 1141a33–b1: 'It is absurd to think that Political Science or Prudence is the loftiest kind of knowledge, inasmuch as man is not the highest thing in the world... It may be argued that man is superior to the other animals, but this makes no difference: since there exist other things far more divine in their nature than man.' Trans. Rackham, pp. 343–5.

112 *EN* 6, 8, 1142a9–10: ἴσως οὐκ ἔστι τὸ αὑτοῦ εὖ ἄνευ οἰκονομίας οὐδ' ἄνευ πολιτείας.

113 *Pol.* 7, 2, 1324a5–8.

114 *Pol.* 3, 13, 1283b40–2.

115 *Pol.* 7, 2, 1324a12–13.

116 *Pol.* 7, 2, 1324a23–5, trans. Jowett, *CW* 2, p. 2101.

117 *Pol.* 3, 18, 1288a38–9.

118 *Pol.* 7, 13, 1332a32–8: ἀλλὰ μὴν σπουδαία γε πόλις ἐστὶ τῷ τοὺς πολίτας τοὺς μετέχοντας τῆς πολιτείας εἶναι σπουδαίους· ἡμῖν δὲ πάντες οἱ πολῖται μετέχουσι τῆς πολιτείας. τοῦτ' ἄρα σκεπτέον, πῶς ἀνὴρ γίνεται σπουδαῖος. καὶ γὰρ εἰ πάντας ἐνδέχεται σπουδαίους εἶναι, μὴ καθ' ἕκαστον δὲ τῶν πολιτῶν, οὕτως αἱρετώτερον· ἀκολουθεῖ γὰρ τῷ καθ' ἕκαστον καὶ τὸ πάντας.

119 See *EN* 5, 11, 1138a4–14.

120 *EN* 1, 5, 1095b16–19.

121 See *EN* 10, 7, 1177a12–1177b4.

122 *Hist. An.*1, 1, 487b34–488a7: τὰ μὲν γὰρ αὐτῶν ἐστιν ἀγελαῖα τὰ δὲ μοναδικά ... ὁ δ' ἄνθρωπος ἐπαμφοτερίζει. See Stephen R.L. Clark. *Aristotle's Man. Speculations upon Aristotelian Anthropology* (Oxford: Clarendon Press, 1983), p. 98; John M. Cooper, *Reason and Emotion*, pp. 359–60.

123 See Kullman, *Aristoteles*, p. 360: 'So transzendiert das eigentliche Telos des Menschen den Bereich des Politischen.'

124 *EN* 9, 9, 1170a5–6: μονώτῃ μὲν οὖν χαλεπὸς ὁ βίος· οὐ γὰρ ῥάδιον καθ' αὑτὸν ἐνεργεῖν συνεχῶς, μεθ' ἑτέρων δὲ καὶ πρὸς ἄλλους ῥᾷον.

CHAPTER SEVEN

1 Ἀριστοτέλης τῆς φύσεως γραμματεὺς ἦν, τόν κάλαμον ἀποβρέχων εἰς νοῦν. See Ingemar Düring, *Aristotle in the Ancient Biographical Tradition* (Göteborg: Elanders Boktryckeri Aktiebolag, 1957), p. 327.

2 Letter to William Ogle on the publication of his translation of *Parts of Animals*,

1882. See *The Life and Letters of Charles Darwin III*, ed. Francis Darwin, vol. 3 (London: John Murray, 1888), p. 251. For a reproduction of the Ogle-Darwin letters and a full discussion, see Allan Gotthelf, 'Darwin on Aristotle', *Journal of the History of Biology* 32 (1999), pp. 3–31.

3   J.L. Ackrill, *Essays on Plato and Aristotle* (Oxford: Clarendon Press, 1997), p. 7.

4   W.K.C. Guthrie, *A History of Philosophy VI, Aristotle: an Encounter* (Cambridge: Cambridge University Press, 1981), p. 222.

5   *Part. An.* 1, 5, 644b22–645a26. *CW* 1, pp. 1003–4. See page viii above. On its publication William Ogle sent a gift of his translation to Charles Darwin.

6   It is agreed that Aristotle carried out his natural researches during his middle years; A.L. Peck therefore suggested that 'we might legitimately proceed to interpret Aristotle's more strictly philosophical work in the light of his work in natural history.' A.L. Peck, Preface, *Generation of Animals* (Cambridge, MA.: Harvard University Press, 1942), p. viii. Sophia M. Connell, however, has noted more recently that 'since such works as the *Generation of Animals* and the *Movement of Animals* exhibit an intellectual sophistication on a par with much of the *Metaphysics* and the *Ethics*, it is generally thought that the biology was not systematized and recorded until later on. This implies that Aristotle was thinking about biology for much of his life; and as Balme has suggested, there was likely to have been a "reciprocal influence" between the biology and those texts which are traditionally considered to be more central to his thought ... Because Aristotle himself does not attempt to distinguish the biological from the philosophical, it makes sense to read all Aristotelian texts as potentially representative of the same philosophical outlook.' Sophia M. Connell, 'Toward an Integrated Approach to Aristotle as a Biological Philosopher', *The Review of Metaphysics* 55/2 (December 2001), pp. 301–2. Aristotle himself emphasizes the need for careful observation of the physical world as a preparation for any general interpretation of the cosmos: 'Lack of experience diminishes our power of taking a comprehensive view of the admitted facts. Hence those who dwell in intimate association with nature and its phenomena are more able to lay down principles such as to admit of a wide and coherent development; while those who through much abstract discussion have lost sight of the facts are more likely to dogmatize on the basis of a few observations.' *De Gen. et Corr.* 1, 2, 316a5–10, trans. Joachim, *CW* 1, p. 515.

7   See J.L. Ackrill: 'There were parts even of Aristotle that were hardly known to exist by most mid-century philosophers. Aristotle's biological works form a large part of his preserved work, and were clearly for him an important, integral part of philosophy.' Ackrill, *Essays on Plato and Aristotle*, p. 7.

8   *Hist. An.* 2, 3, 501b19–20.

9   *Hist. An.* 9, 45, 630b8–14. David Balme has remarked: 'Much of this criticism [of Aristotle's biological writings] arose in the nineteenth and early twentieth centuries

from armchair naturalists who disbelieved Aristotle's reports and thought them too silly for a great philosopher . . . I confess that I was still blaming Aristotle for swallowing the story about buffaloes projecting their dung at enemies, until in 1983 I saw a picture on television of hippopotamuses doing just that.' 'The Place of Biology in Aristotle's Philosophy', in Allan Gotthelf and James G. Lennox (eds), *Philosophical Issues in Aristotle's Biology* (Cambridge: Cambridge University Press, 1987), pp. 16–17.

10   See Georg Wöhrle, 'Aristoteles' biologische Schriften heute lesen?', in H.-Ch. Günther & A. Rengatos (eds), *Beiträge zur antiken Philosophie* (Stuttgart: Franz Steiner, 1997), p. 233.

11   *Hist. An.* 8, 28, 606b4–5; *Gen. An.* 2, 8, 748a25–6.

12   *Part. An.* 3, 6, 669a19–21.

13   Ingemar Düring, *Aristoteles. Darstellung und Interpretation seines Denkens* (Heidelberg: Carl Winter, 1966), pp. 521–2: 'Die Verdienste des Aristoteles als Beobachter von Tatsachen, besonders meeresbiologischer, sind unstreitbar... Jene Gelehrten, von G.H. Lewes bis zu Bertrand Russell, die sich daraus ein Vergnügen machen, alle Irrtümer des Aristoteles zu registrieren, übertreiben deren Bedeutung; die überwältigende Mehrzahl der in seinen Schriften verzeichneten Beobachtungen ist richtig, und viele sind genial. In das entgegengesetze Extrem verfallen jene, die wie W. Ogle alle Irrtümer als Textfehler oder spätere Interpretationen wegerklären. Konstatieren wir ruhig, daß Aristoteles sich zuweilen von seinen Gewährsmännern irreführen ließ.'

14   Jonathan Barnes, *Aristotle. A Very Short Introduction* (Oxford: Oxford University Press, 2000), pp. 20, 23. The scope of Aristotle's investigations is breathtaking, including in its wide range detailed and minute descriptions of countless varieties of insects, birds, fish and animals. It incurred the criticism of Proclus, who laments that Aristotle 'neglected theological principles and spent too much time on physical matters'. Proclus, *In Platonis Timaeum Commentarii*, ed. E. Diehl (Leipzig: Teubner, 1903), 1, 295, 26: τῶν μὲν θεολογικῶν ἀρχῶν ἀφιστάμενος τοῖς δὲ φυσικοῖς λόγοις πέρα τοῦ δέοντος ἐνδιατρίβων. Aristotle's justification is to be found at *De Gen. et Corr.* 1, 2, 316a5–10, quoted in footnote 6 above.

15   See George Wöhrle, 'Aristoteles' biologische Schriften', p. 233: 'Auch im 20. Jahrhundert hat man Aristoteles, soweit zu sehen ist, weitgehend als Begründer der Biologie gewürdigt.' George Henry Lewes (1817–1878), one of Aristotle's severest critics, wrote concerning *Generation of Animals*: 'It is an extraordinary production. No ancient work, and few modern works, equal it in comprehensiveness of detail and profound speculative insight. We find there some of the obscurest problems of biology treated with a mastery which, when we consider the condition of science at that day, is truly astounding.' *Aristotle: A Chapter from the History of Science* (London: Smith, Elder and Co, 1864), p. 325. Joseph Needham wrote: 'The depth

of Aristotle's insight into the generation of animals has not been surpassed by any subsequent embryologist, and, considering the width of his other interests, cannot have been equalled.' *A History of Embryology* (Cambridge: Cambridge University Press, 1959), p. 42.

16 Jason A. Tipton, 'Aristotle's Study of the Animal World. The Case of the *kobios* and *phucis*', *Perspectives in Biology and Medicine* 49/3 (Summer 2006), pp. 369–83; 'Aristotle's Observations of the Foraging Interactions of the Red Mullet (Mullidae: *Mullus* spp) and the Sea Bream (Sparidae: *Diplodus* spp)', *Archives of Natural History* 35/1 (2008), pp. 164–71.

17 Wolfgang Kullmann, *Aristoteles und die moderne Wissenschaft* (Stuttgart: Franz Steiner, 1998), p. 23. All translations from Kullmann are mine; further references to Kullmann are to this work.

18 Kullmann, p. 29. In similar vein John Herman Randall Jr. writes: 'The temporary eclipse of Aristotle's physics [from the age of Newton through the end of the nineteenth century] is emerging as a kind of adolescent stage in the development of our own physical theory, a mere passing blindness. Today it is Aristotle who often seems strikingly modern, and Newton who appears "of mere historical interest." Newton, despite his epoch-making contributions to "natural philosophy", that is, to the science of dynamics, seems in his notions and concepts of his more general "philosophy of nature" to have been confused, in many of his ideas barren, and even wrong in his aim. It is Aristotle who strikes the present-day student as suggestive, enlightening, and sound.' John Herman Randall Jr., *Aristotle* (New York: Columbia University Press, 1960), pp. 167–8. A.L. Peck suggests that the works of Aristotle suffered by association from an anti-scholastic prejudice: '[D]uring the seventeenth century, the authority of Aristotle and the scholastic doctrine with which he was identified were being combated in the name of freedom, and thus it came about that the zoological works also, which had been brought to light by the dark ages, were allowed to pass back into oblivion by the age of enlightenment. They were not discovered until the end of the eighteenth century by Cuvier (1769–1832) and Saint-Hilaire (1805–1895) in the nineteenth.' A.L. Peck, Introduction to Aristotle, *Parts of Animals* (Cambridge, MA: Harvard University Press, 1945), p. 44.

19 See Kullmann, p. 284: 'Wohl die bedeutendste naturwissentschaftliche Leistung des Aristoteles ist seine Embryologie. Das beruht darauf, daß ihm auf diesem Gebiet einzigartige empirische zoologische Beobachtungen gelungen sind und daß es ihm möglich war, diese Beobachtungen theoretisch und begrifflich in einer Weise zu formulieren, die bis in die Gegenwart hinein diese Disziplin terminologisch bestimmt hat.'

20 Max Delbrück, 'Aristotle – totle – totle', in *Of Microbes and Life*, Jacques Monod and Ernst Borek (eds), (New York: Columbia University Press, 1971), p. 55.

21   *Gen. An.* 1, 19, 726b15–24: 'Thus, the semen of the hand or of the face or of the whole animal really is hand or face or a whole animal though in an undifferentiated way; in other words, what each of those is in actuality, such the semen is potentially, whether in respect of its own bulk, or because it has some dynamis within itself ... since neither a hand nor any other part of the body whatsoever is a hand or any other part of the body if it lacks soul or some other dynamis; it has the same name, but that is all.' Trans. Peck, pp. 91–3. In chapters 17 and 18 of *Gen. An.* 1, Aristotle outlines in detail the various arguments in favour of pangenesis, and rejects each in turn. According to Kullmann, by a strange irony of history, Aristotle's objections against Democritus are still valid against Darwin's [hypothesis of] preformationism; see *Aristoteles*, pp, 31 and 311. See G.E.R. Lloyd, 'Empirical Research in Aristotle's Biology', in Allan Gotthelf and James Lennox (eds), *Philosophical Issues in Aristotle's Biology* (Cambridge: Cambridge University Press, 1987), pp. 59–61. See David Depew's brief but incisive remarks in 'Etiological Approaches to Biological Aptness in Aristotle and Darwin', in Wolfgang Kullmann and Sabine Föllinger (eds), *Aristotelische Biologie. Intentionen, Methoden, Ergebnisse*, hereafter *Aristotelische Biologie* (Stuttgart: Franz Steiner, 1997), pp. 219–20; also Montgomery Furth, *Substance, Form and Psyche: an Aristotelian Metaphysics* (Cambridge: Cambridge University Press, 1988), pp. 113–17.

22   See *Gen. An.* 2, 1, 733b23–735a26. See Kullmann, p. 285: 'Die sukzessive Entstehung der Organe steht für ihn also fest, eine Präformation aller Teile ist ausgeschlossen.'

23   The term was made popular by William Harvey in *Exercitationes de generatione animalium* (1651) and Caspar Friedrich Wolff in *Theoria generationis* (1759). A.L. Peck notes: 'The discussion which follows shows that Aristotle fully appreciated the greatest problem of embryological theory, a problem which gave rise to centuries of controversy. Does the embryo contain all its parts in little from the beginning, unfolding like a Japanese paper flower in water ("preformation"), or is there a true formation of new structures as it develops ("epigenesis")? Aristotle was an epigenesist, but he was not vindicated till the time of C.F. Wolff and K.E. von Baer, at the end of the 18th and the beginning of the 19th century.' A.L. Peck, *Aristotle. Generation of Animals* (Cambridge, MA: Harvard University Press, 1990), p. 144. See G.E.R. Lloyd, *Aristotle: The Growth and Structure of his Thought* (Cambridge: Cambridge University Press, 1968), p. 84: 'While the controversy remained a live issue well into the nineteenth century, the epigenesis view eventually prevailed, thanks largely to the work first of Caspar Friedrich Wolff and then of K.E. von Baer.'

24   See Charles Darwin, *The Variation of Animals and Plants under Domestication* (London: John Murray, 1868), vol. 2, pp. 357–404. According to Darwin's hypothesis, small particles or atoms (*gemmules*) are transmitted from all cells of the entire body; these are contained in the smallest egg or semen and control

reproduction and heredity. See Kullmann, pp. 31, 310–11. Having published his views as a 'provisional hypothesis', Darwin wrote to J.D. Hooker: 'I feel *sure* that if Pangenesis is now still-born it will, thank God, at some future time re-appear, begotten by some other father, and christened by some other name.' *Letters* pp. 3, 78. In March 1870, he wrote to E. Ray Lankester: 'I was pleased to see you refer to my much despised child "Pangenesis", who I think will some day, under some better nurse, turn out a fine stripling.' Ibid. p. 120. David Depew argues that, according to recent scholarship, Darwin 'held an epigenetic (rather than a preformationist or proto-Mendelian) conception of development. He believed that variation, albeit undirected, arose when normal epigenetic systems were stressed by the same competitive ecological pressures that would differentially determine the fate of this variation, and indeed that variation would not exist unless normal development had been interrupted by such stresses. Darwin's hypothesis of pangenesis was intended to show how this information could be gathered together and passed on. Pangenesis was not, therefore, an alternative to epigenesis so much as a modification of it designed to show how the process described by Aristotle and his modern successors could slowly and gradually give rise to changing descriptions of lineages. When Darwin is read in his own terms, accordingly, the similarities between him and Aristotle ... become even more salient.' 'Etiological Approaches', p. 227, n 39. For an extensive treatment, see M.J.S. Hodge, 'Darwin as a Lifelong Generation Theorist', in David Kohn (ed.), *The Darwinian Heritage* (Princeton: Princeton University Press, 1985), pp. 207–44.

25 See Kullmann, pp. 32, 284, and 308–9. Kullmann notes (p. 309) Driesch's later espousal of vitalism – the belief in the existence of an immaterial element, also called '*Entelechie*', but understood quite differently to Aristotle.

26 Kullmann, p. 312.

27 What Kullmann calls 'abstract model' may well be taken as the basic metaphysical insight guiding Aristotle's interpretive inquiry into biological reality.

28 Kullmann, p. 32 (emphasis in original). See p. 287: 'Erst die Methoden der modernen Molekularbiologie konnten auf diesem Gebiet eine größere empirische Basis erarbeiten. Gleichwohl ist die Ausgewogenheit und Aktualität der aristotelischen Position erstaunlich.' Also p. 309. It is worth noting that, having been regarded for centuries as a 'finalist' – whether positively or negatively – in the conflict between 'vitalists' and 'mechanists', it is now recognized that with his concept of finality, according to which a living thing reproduces its own eidos, Aristotle had basically the same thing in mind as today's biologist who speaks of chemically-coded programs, such as those contained by a chicken egg for it to become a hen, guaranteeing all her necessary functions and operations. See Wöhrle, 'Aristoteles' biologische Schriften', p. 237.

29 Delbrück, 'Aristotle – totle – totle', p. 55. Delbrück justifies his surprising suggestion

as follows: 'What strikes the modern reader most forcibly is his insistence that in the generation of animals the male contributes, in the semen, a *form principle*, not a mini-man… Put into modern language: The form principle is the information which is stored in the semen. After fertilization it is read out in a preprogrammed way; the readout alters the matter upon which it acts, but it does not alter the stored information, which is not, properly speaking, part of the finished product.' pp. 53–4.

30   Guthrie, *A History of Philosophy* VI, p. 243.

31   *Enneads* 5.5.8.

32   Samuel Taylor Coleridge, *Biographia Literaria* 1, Collected Works, vol. 7 (London: Routledge and Kegan Paul, 1983), pp. 241–2; emphasis in original.

33   *Met.* 9, 3, 1047a30–2.

34   John Herman Randall, Jr., Introduction, Frederick J.E. Woodbridge, *Aristotle's Vision of Nature*, eds John Herman Randall, Jr., Charles H. Kahn and Harold A. Larrabee (New York: Columbia University Press, 1965), p. xx. Charles H. Kahn states: 'The standard etymology of ἐντελέχεια, referred to by Woodbridge [coined from ἐν, τέλος and ἔχειν], which dates from the Renaissance, is linguistically impossible: ἔχεια has nothing to do with ἔχειν, to have. The term seems to be an abstract noun derived from the adjective, ἐντελής "perfected" or "completed".' Ibid. p. 36.

35   *Met.* 9, 6, 1048b18–34. See John Wild, *Plato's Theory of Man* (New York: Octagon Books, 1964), p. 292. On the meaning of κίνησις and ἐνέργεια, see John Dudley, *Dio e contemplazione in Aristotele. Il fondamento metafisico dell' Etica Nicomachea* (Milano: Vita e Pensiero, 1999), pp. 155–64.

36   *Phys.* 3, 2, 201b31–2: ἥ τε κίνησις ἐνέργεια μὲν εἶναί τις δοκεῖ, ἀτελὴς δέ. See *De An.* 2, 5, 417a16.

37   *Met.* 9, 8, 1050b2–3, my trans.

38   The following lines from the poem 'Flowers do not ask questions' by Greek poet George Thémelis contain a suggestion of such self-contained fullness:
Perhaps they drive on toward the point of the origin of origins to close the circumference,
To end the adventure of the long escape and to exclude
From the province of the completed all eventualities and all vain flights,
Casting themselves out, canceling themselves out,
Having no beginning and no end within the immobility of fulfillment,
Sealing the perfect movement in the fullest immobility,
Like a statue, like a ship in bas-relief that sails on and on …
Flowers will reach perfection by returning to their fullest reality
And their glory shall be to give themselves without hesitation to our fullest gaze.
Modern Greek Poetry, trans. Kimon Friar (New York: Simon Schuster, 1973), p. 319.

39   *De An.* 2, 1, 412b5–6: ἐντελέχεια ἡ πρώτη σώματος φυσικοῦ ὀργανικοῦ.

40   *De An.* 2, 1, 414a12–14, my trans. For a comprehensive account, see *De An.* 2, 4, 415a14–415b28.

41   *Part. An.* 1, 1, 640b33–5. See 1, 1, 641a17–21: 'Now it may be that the form of any living creature is soul, or some part of soul, or something that involves soul. At any rate, when its soul is gone, it is no longer a living creature, and none of its parts remains the same, except only in shape, just like the animals in the story that were turned into stone.' Trans. Peck, p. 69.

42   William Shakespeare, *Julius Caesar* III, i, 254–7.

43   *Phys.* 2, 1, 193a29–30, my trans. Cf. *Phys.* 2, 1, 192b13–14.

44   *Phys.* 2, 1, 192b21–3: 'For nature is the principle and cause of motion and rest to those things, and those things only, in which she inheres primarily, as distinct from incidentally.' Trans. Wicksteed & Cornford, p. 109.

45   *Phys.* 2, 1, 192b28–9.

46   *Phys.* 2, 1, 193b4.

47   *Phys.* 2, 1, 193a30–1.

48   Joseph Owens, 'Aristotelian Ethics, Medicine, and the Changing Nature of Man', in John R. Catan (ed.), *Aristotle. The Collected Papers of Joseph Owens* (Albany: SUNY Press, 1981), p. 173.

49   *Phys.* 2, 1, 193b12–18, trans. Wicksteed & Cornford modified, pp. 115–17.

50   *Pol.* 1, 1, 1252b32–1253a1: ἡ δὲ φύσις τέλος ἐστίν· οἷον γὰρ ἕκαστόν ἐστι τῆς γενέσεως τελεσθείσης, ταύτην φαμὲν τὴν φύσιν εἶναι ἑκάστου, ὥσπερ ἀνθρώπου ἵππου οἰκίας. ἔτι τὸ οὗ ἕνεκα καὶ τὸ τέλος βέλτιστον. Trans. Jowett modified, *CW* 2, p. 1987.

51   *Part. An.* 1, 1, 639b11–17, trans. Peck, p. 57. For a detailed study see Alan Code, 'The Priority of Final Causes over Efficient Causes in Aristotle's PA', in Kullmann & Föllinger (eds), *Aristotelische Biologie*, pp. 127–43.

52   *Met.* 4, 4, 1006a8–9.

53   *Phys.* 2, 1, 193a3: ὡς δ' ἔστιν ἡ φύσις, πειρᾶσθαι δεικνύναι γελοῖον. My trans.

54   *Gen. An.* 1, 22, 730b29–32.

55   *Part. An.* 1, 1, 639b19–21: μᾶλλον δ' ἐστὶ τὸ οὗ ἕνεκα καὶ τὸ καλὸν ἐν τοῖς τῆς φύσεως ἔργοις ἢ ἐν τοῖς τῆς τέχνης. Trans. Peck modified, p. 57.

56   *Phys.* 2, 2, 194a28–30, my trans.

57   Cf. *Phys.* 8, 4, 255a1–b24.

58   *Gen. An.* 2, 1, 731b24–732a1.

59   *Phys.* 2, 8, 199a7–8, *Phys.* 2, 8, 199b26–33.

60   *Inc. An.* 8, 708a9–12, my trans.

61   *Inc. An.* 2, 704b11–18, trans. Forster, p. 487.

62   *Met.* 4, 3, 1005b18.

63   James G. Lennox has provided a most helpful study of the use and status of this assertion in his article 'Nature does nothing in vain...', in Günther & Rengatos (eds),

Beiträge, pp. 199–214, reprinted in James G. Lennox, *Aristotle's Philosophy of Biology. Studies in the Origins of Life Science* (Cambridge: Cambridge University Press, 2001), pp. 205–23. The following passages will suffice to illustrate the variety of articulations: 'Nature never makes anything without a purpose, nor omits anything that is necessary' (*De An.* 3, 9, 432b21–2: ἡ φύσις μήτε ποιεῖ μάτην μηθὲν μήτε ἀπολείπει τι τῶν ἀναγκαίων); 'Nature is neither neglectful, nor does it work anything in vain.' (*Gen. An.* 5, 8, 788b21–2: οὔτ' ἐλλείπουσαν οὔτε μάταιον οὐθὲν ποιοῦσαν); 'Everything which Nature does is done either because it is necessary or else because it is better.' (*Gen. An.* 1, 4, 717a15–16: πᾶν ἡ φύσις ἢ διὰ τὸ ἀναγκαῖον ποιεῖ ἢ διὰ τὸ βέλτιον); 'It is what occurs generally that is most in accord with the course of Nature.' (*Gen. An.* 1, 19, 727b29–30: τὰ δ' ὡς ἐπὶ τὸ πολὺ γιγνόμενα μάλιστα κατὰ φύσιν ἐστίν.); 'Nature and God do nothing in vain.' (*De Caelo*, 1, 4, 271a33: ὁ δε θεὸς καὶ ἡ φύσις οὐδὲν μάτην ποιοῦσιν). He uses also the formula: ταῦτα πάντα εὐλόγως ἡ φύσις δημιουργεῖ (*Gen. An.* 1, 23, 731a24). See also *Gen. An.* 5, 2, 781b22–3.

64 *Gen. An.* 2, 6, 744b16.

65 See the text of Pittendrigh's letter to Ernst Mayr, *Toward a New Philosophy of Biology*, hereafter *Toward a New Philosophy* (Cambridge, MA: Harvard University Press, 1988), pp. 63–4. Pittendrigh remarks: 'The more I thought about that, it ocurred to me that the whole thing was nonsense – that what it was the biologist couldn't live with was not the illegitimacy of the relationship, but the relationship itself... What it was the biologist could not escape was the plain fact – or rather the fundamental fact – which he must (as scientist) explain: that the objects of biological analysis are organizations (he calls them organisms) and, as such, are end-directed. Organization is more than mere order; order lacks end-directedness; organization *is* end-directed.' For the first use of the word 'teleonomy', see C.S. Pittendrigh, 'Adaptation, natural selection, and behavior', in A. Roe & G.G. Simpson (eds), *Behavior and Evolution* (New Haven: Yale University Press, 1958), p. 394. Decades earlier J.H. Woodger had in fact remarked: 'It would doubtless be desirable in biology to avoid the term "teleology" if a suitable substitute could be found.' *Biological Principles* (London: Kegan Paul, Trench, Trubner & Co., 1929), p. 453, n 1. See Kullmann, pp. 301–2: '[Die moderne Biologie] unterscheidet zwischen wirklichen teleologischen Prozessen, die von einem Bewußtsein intendiert sind, und scheinbar teleologisch ablaufenden Prozessen, wie sie in der lebenden Natur ständig vorkommen.' For a detailed account of Aristotle's teleology, see ibid., pp. 255–312. The term *'teleologia'* was coined in 1728 by Christian Wolff (1679–1754), who in his *Logica*, chapter 3 (*Discursus Praeliminaris*, no. 85), wrote of '... still another part of natural philosophy, which sets forth the purposes of things (*quae fines rerum explicat*). So far it is without name, though it is most noble and most useful. It could be called "Teleology".' Trans. Joseph Owens, *Collected Papers*, p. 216,

n 1. The OED dates its first use in English to 1807 (*Edin. Rev.* 10, 151), as referring to the 'doctrine of final causes'. See James G. Lennox, 'Teleology', in Evelyn Fox Keller and Elisabeth A. Lloyd (eds), *Keywords in Evolutionary Biology* (Cambridge, MA: Harvard University Press: 1992), p. 324. Karl Popper dismisses the term 'teleonomy': 'The old fear of teleology, which led people, Monod for example, to introduce the term "teleonomy" is, let us say, somewhat silly. The fear of using teleological terms reminds me of the Victorian fear of speaking about sex, because teleological terms are constantly used in biology and are utterly unavoidable.' Karl Popper, 'A New Interpretation of Darwinism', in Hans-Joachim Niemann (ed.), *Karl Popper and the Two New Secrets of Life* (Tübingen: Mohr Siebeck, 2014), p. 124.

66 See William A. Wallace, 'Is Finality Included in Aristotle's Definition of Nature?', in Richard F. Hassing (ed.), *Final Causality in Nature and Human Affairs* (Washington, DC: Catholic University of America Press, 1997), pp. 61–2: 'Much of the difficulty with teleology in nature arises from conceiving all final causality as intentional or cognitive and not sufficiently distinguishing the cognitive from the terminative and the perfective. St. Albert the Great gave expression to this mentality with the aphorism: *opus naturae est opus intelligentiae*, the work of nature is the work of intelligence.'

67 Kullmann, p. 302: 'So kann man nur zu der Aussage kommen, daß die aristotelische Teleologie in Wirklichkeit nicht teleologisch, sondern in hohem Maße teleonomisch ist. Die Zweckmäßigkeit, die konstatiert wird, ist nicht intendiert.'

68 Kullmann (pp. 288–9) indicates that it is clearly erroneous to interpret Aristotle in any sense anthropomorphically.

69 Edmund Spenser, 'An Hymne in Honour of Beautie', *Shorter Poems of Edmund Spenser*, ed. William A. Oram et al. (New Haven: Yale University Press, 1989), p. 712.

70 Isaac Newton, *Mathematical Principles of Natural Philosophy* (Berkeley: University of Calfifornia Press, 1960), xvii. I owe this reference to Terence Nichols, 'Aquinas' Concept of Substantial Form and Modern Science', *International Philosophical Quarterly* 36/3 (September 1996), p. 304; emphasis added.

71 *The New Organon* Bk 1, Aph. 51, *The Works of Francis Bacon*, vol. 4, eds James Spedding, Robert Leslie Ellis & Douglas Denon Heath (New York: Garrett Press, 1968), p. 58. For Latin original, see *Works* 1, p. 168–9.

72 *De Augmentis Scientiarum*, Bk 3, chap. 5, *Works* 1, p. 571: Causarum finalium inquisitio sterilis est et, tamquam virgo Deo consecrata, nihil parit. For translation, see *Works* 4, p. 365. A contrary view concerning the perennial role of finality is given by D'Arcy Wentworth Thompson (translator of Aristotle's *History of Animals*), in his classic *On Growth and Form*, a work which has received exceptional praise from many Darwinian adherents: 'Time out of mind it has been by way of the "final cause", by the teleological concept of end, of purpose or of "design", in one of its many forms … that men have been chiefly wont to explain the phenomena of the

living world; and it will be so while men have eyes to see and ears to hear withal. With Galen, as with Aristotle, it was the physician's way; with John Ray as with Aristotle it was the naturalist's way; with Kant as with Aristotle it was the philosopher's way... It is a common way, and a great way; for it brings with it a glimpse of a great vision, and it lies deep as the love of nature in the hearts of men.' D'Arcy Wentworth Thompson, *On Growth and Form* (Cambridge: Cambridge University Press, 1942), p. 3. On Bacon's attitude to Aristotle, Jonathan Barnes remarks: 'It is worth adding that our modern notion of scientific method is thoroughly Aristotelian. Scientific empiricism – the idea that abstract argument must be subordinate to factual evidence, that theory is to be judged before the strict tribunal of observation – now seems a commonplace; but it was not always so, and it is largely due to Aristotle that we understand science to be an empirical pursuit. The point needs emphasizing, if only because Aristotle's most celebrated English critics, Francis Bacon and John Locke, were both staunch empiricists who thought that they were thereby breaking with the Aristotelian tradition. Aristotle was charged with preferring flimsy theories and sterile syllogisms to the solid, fertile facts. But the charge is outrageous; and it was brought by men who did not read Aristotle's own works with sufficient attention and who criticized him for the faults of his successors.' Jonathan Barnes, *Aristotle. A Very Short Introduction*, p. 137.

73   See Desmond Connell, *Essays in Metaphysics* (Dublin: Four Courts, 1996), p. 47. Wolfgang Wieland writes: 'Scientists today consider Aristotle's teleological interpretation of nature to be at best an interesting mistake, perhaps explicable in historical terms. They hold it responsible for delaying the progress of science some two thousand years, and for obscuring the first steps Democritus took on what they hold to be a more fruitful path. It cannot be denied that modern science was right to criticize what it rejected when it abandoned traditional teleology. For because its guiding principle had been used far too narrowly and mechanically, the teleology associated with traditional Aristotelianism had already reduced itself to near-absurdity. It was a less important question whether this traditional teleology could justifiably claim Aristotle's authority, and one in which there was little interest at the beginning of the modern era – even if Galileo, for example, had some inkling of the discrepancies between Aristotle and Aristotelianism.' Wolfgang Wieland, 'The Problem of Teleology', in Jonathan Barnes, Malcolm Schofield, Richard Sorabji (eds), *Articles on Aristotle*, vol. 1, *Science* (Duckworth: London, 1975), p. 142.

74   Marjorie Grene, *The Understanding of Nature* (Dordrecht: Reidel, 1974), p. 141.

75   Aristotle would doubtless agree with the definition of species generally accepted by Neo-Darwinians, that is, a group of interbreeding individuals. Ernst Mayr states: 'Species are groups of interbreeding natural populations that are reproductively isolated from other such groups.' *Toward a New Philosophy. Observations of an Evolutionist.* (Cambridge, MA: Harvard University Press, 1988), p. 318. Aristotle

maintained that an essential characteristic of a proper species is the ability to produce fertile offspring; hybrids, on the other hand, are normally sterile and are unable to perpetuate a constant and identifiable line of propagation.

76 *Aristotle's De Partibus Animalium* I *and De Generatione Animalium* I, trans. with notes by D.M. Balme (Oxford: Clarendon Press, 1972), p. 97.

77 James G. Lennox, 'Are Aristotelian Species Eternal?' in Allan Gotthelf (ed.), *Aristotle on Nature and Living Things* (Pittsburgh: Mathesis Publications, 1985), p. 90; reprint, *Philosophy of Biology*, p. 155. I express my gratitude to Professor Lennox for graciously offering a comment on an earlier version of my text; my interpretation of his position goes beyond our exchange, and I do not wish to ascribe to him any particular view in the matter.

78 Lennox, ibid.

79 Letter, 26 May 1999; I am most grateful to Professor MacIntyre for an extremely helpful exchange of views, both in conversation and correspondence. I do not wish to attribute to him any opinions expressed elsewhere in this essay.

80 See *Met.* 6, 2, 1026b35: τὸ μὲν ἀεὶ ἢ ὡς ἐπὶ τὸ πολύ. Also *Post. An.* 2, 12, 96a10; *Rhet.* 1, 11, 1371b14; *Rhet.* 2, 20, 1394a8–9.

81 *Part. An.* 4, 10, 687a16–17: ἡ δὲ φύσις ἐκ τῶν ἐνδεχομένων ποιεῖ τὸ βέλτιστον. Note the following comment by Francis Bacon: 'So does the wisdom of God shine forth more admirably when nature intends one thing and Providence draws forth another.' *De Augmentis*, 3, 4, *Works* 1, p. 570.

82 From the perspective of his discipline, Ernst Mayr sharply states the question: 'The so-called species problem in biology can be reduced to a simple choice between two alternatives: Are species realities of nature or are they simply theoretical constructs of the human mind?' *The Growth of Biological Thought. Diversity, Evolution, and Inheritance* (Cambridge, MA: The Belknap Press, 1982), p. 285. He notes that attacks on the concept of biological species come either from mathematicians who have only a limited acquaintance with species in nature, or from botanists, whose 'myopic preoccupation' with 'messy' situations has prevented them from seeing that 'the concept species describes natural diversity in plants quite adequately in most cases'.

83 Lennox, *Philosophy of Biology*, p. 155.

84 See Gotthelf's first, highly influential, article, 'Aristotle's Conception of Final Causality', *The Review of Metaphysics* 30/2 (1976–7), pp. 226–54, reprinted with a postscript in Gotthelf and Lennox, *Philosophical Issues*, pp. 204–42, hereafter 'Final Causality', with page reference to both versions.

85 Allan Gotthelf, 'Understanding Aristotle's Teleology', in R.F. Hassing (ed.), *Final Causality in Nature and Human Affairs* (Washington, DC: Catholic University of America Press, 1997), pp. 75–6. Gotthelf's article presents an excellent account of the divergent positions, together with an exhaustive relevant bibliography. For

another comprehensive discussion of the respective positions, see Fred D. Miller, Jr, 'Aristotelian Natural Form and Theology – Reconsidered', *Proceedings of the American Catholic Philosophical Association* 49 (1995): pp. 69–79. Robert Bolton remarks: 'Recent commentators have nearly all followed the earlier tradition in supposing that for goal-oriented entities, on Aristotle's view, the securing of goals, or the tendency to do so, is theoretically *primitive* in the sense that this feature is not itself capable of explanation by reference to anything scientifically more basic while it itself serves as the starting point for the scientific explanation of the other features of the entities in question, such as, for instance, their material constitutions.' Robert Bolton, 'The Material Cause: Matter and Explanation in Aristotle's Natural Science', in Kullmann & Föllinger (eds), *Aristotelische Biologie*, p. 97.

86 Gotthelf ascribes what he calls 'The Pragmatic View' to Wolfgang Wieland, Martha Nussbaum and Richard Sorabji: 'Living organisms and their parts *do* come to be by simple material necessity alone; material-efficient causes are the only actual *causes* involved.' 'Aristotle's Teleology', p. 76, emphases in original. On such accounts, teleological explanantions fulfil an epistemological function.

87 This has been the subject of an engaging debate between James Lennox and Michael Ghiselin, indicated by the titles of their respective articles: 'Darwin *was* a Teleologist', *Biology and Philosophy* 8 (1993), pp. 409–21, and 'Darwin's Language may Seem Teleological, but his Thinking is Another Matter', *Biology and Philosophy* 9 (1994), pp. 489–92). See also T.L. Short, 'Darwin's concept of final cause: neither new nor trivial', *Biology and Philosophy* 17 (2002), pp. 323–40.

88 Terence L. Nichols, 'Aquinas' Substantial Form', p. 309.

89 *Gen. An.* 2, 3, 736b5–7, trans. Platt, *CW* 1, p. 1143.

90 According to Aristotle, in what Randall terms 'a dubious etymology' (*Aristotle*, p. 183), τὸ αὐτόματον is derived from μάτην, that is, the thing itself happens in vain: αὐτὸ μάτην γένηται (*Phys.* 2, 6, 197b22–3). Aristotle himself uses αὐτόματον at *Gen. An.* 2, 1, 734b10 in the sense of something which moves of itself. The terms διὰ τύχην ('by chance') and διὰ τὸ αὐτόματον ('of itself'), are somewhat fluid; both have variously, together and separately, been translated as 'chance'.

91 *Phys.* 2, 6, 197b18–22. See *Phys.* 2, 4, 196b5–7: 'Some, moreover, hold that fortune is a genuine cause of things, but one that has a something divine and mysterious about it, that makes it inscrutable to the human intelligence.' Trans. Wicksteed & Cornford, p. 147.

92 *Phys.* 2, 6, 198a7–10, trans. Wicksteed & Cornford, p. 163.

93 See Randall, *Aristotle*, p. 183.

94 *Phys.* 2, 5, 197a32–5, trans. Wicksteed & Cornford, p. 155; see *Phys.* 2, 6, 197b18–20.

95 Wolfgang Wieland, 'Teleology', p. 146; see pp. 144–5: 'For Aristotle chance is not an independent force which could frustrate or disturb a universal cosmic teleology.

Aristotle seeks rather to show that quite generally, where we speak of chance, teleological structures are already presupposed. With chance, an apparent, 'as if' teleology is involved; this is present *if a goal is reached, although* there was *no intention* to reach it as such. So this goal proves to be accidental, as it were: i.e., reached *via* the intention to reach another goal. Consequently we never leave the realm of teleology in our talk of chance.' For a detailed study, see John Dudley, *The Evolution of Chance in the Physics and Ethics of Aristotle* (Amersfoort: Acco, 1997).

96   *Met.* 14, 3, 1090b19–20.

97   Stephen Jay Gould, *The Panda's Thumb. More Reflections in Natural History* (New York: Norton, 1982), p. 79.

98   Mayr, *Toward a New Philosophy*, pp. 98–9. A similar point is made rhetorically by Aristotle at *Phys.* 2, 8, 199b13–14.

99   Charles Darwin, *The Origin of Species* (London: Penguin, 1985), p. 219.

100   Richard Dawkins, *The Blind Watchmaker* (London: Penguin, 1991), 91.

101   Mayr, *Toward a New Philosophy*, p. 43. Gould remarks: 'If temperatures are dropping and a hairier coat would aid survival, genetic variation for greater hairiness does not begin to arise with increased frequency. Selection works upon unoriented variation and changes a population by conferring greater reproductive success upon advantageous variants.' *Panda's Thumb*, p. 79.

102   Ayala, Francisco J. 'Teleological Explanations in Evolutionary Biology', *Philosophy of Science* 37/1 (March 1970), p. 10.

103   *Part. An.* 1, 1, 642a1–2: εἰσὶν ἄρα δύ' αἰτίαι αὗται, τό θ' οὗ ἕνεκα καὶ τὸ ἐξ ἀνάγκης.

104   *Part. An.* 1, 1, 642a11–13, trans. Peck, p. 77. At *Part. An.* 1, 1, 663b22–4, he states that ἡ κατὰ τὸν λόγον φύσις makes use of the products of ἀναγκαία φύσις in order to serve a purpose. See *Part. An.* 1, 1, 640a33–640b4: '*Because* the essence of man is what it is, *therefore* a man has such and such parts, since there cannot be a man without them… There cannot be a man at all otherwise than with them… *Because* man is such and such, *therefore* the process of his formation must of necessity be such and such and take place in such a manner; which is why first this part is formed, then that. And thus similarly with all the things that are constructed by Nature.' Peck's translation and emphasis. See also *Phys.* 2, 9, 200a5–10: 'No doubt it is a fact that the building cannot dispense with these materials [stones and bricks], and in that sense they "must be there"; but they do not of themselves "make" the building in the sense of constructing it, but only in that of constituting its material. What causes the building to be made is the purpose of protecting and preserving certain goods. And so in all other cases where a purpose can be traced. It cannot be accomplished without materials that have the required nature; but it is not they that "make" the purpose-filling instrument, except materially.' Trans. Wicksteed & Cornford, p. 181.

105 *Part. An.* 1, 1, 642a17.

106 *Part. An.* 1, 1, 641b23–6.

107 Guthrie, *A History of Philosophy* VI, p. 291.

108 'Among School Children' in W.B.Yeats, *The Poems*, ed. Daniel Albright (London: Everyman's Library, 1992), p. 262. Another Irish poet, Louis MacNeice, expresses the contrast between Aristotle and Plato as follows:

Aristotle was better who watched the insect breed,

The natural world develop,

Stressing the function, scrapping the Form in Itself,

Taking the horse from the shelf and letting it gallop;

('Autumn Journal'). From the same poem:

And look for the formal as well as the efficient cause.

Aristotle's pedantic phraseology

Serves better than common sense or hand-to-mouth psychology.

ἔσχε τὴν φύσιν – 'found its nature'; the crude

Embryo rummages every latitude

Looking for itself, its nature, its final pattern.

109 F.H. Bradley, *The Principles of Logic*, vol. 2 (Oxford: Oxford University Press, 1967), p. 591.

110 *Met.* 12, 3, 1070a27–9, trans. Ross, *CW* 2, p. 1690.

111 Guthrie, *A History of Philosophy* VI, p. 222, emphasis added.

112 Mayr, *Toward a New Philosophy*, p. 172.

113 David Balme, 'Aristotle's Biology was not Essentialist', *Archiv für Geschichte der Philosophie* 62 (1980): pp. 1–12.

114 Ibid. p. 1.

115 David Balme, 'Aristotle's Biology was not Essentialist', in Gotthelf and Lennox (eds), *Philosophical Issues*, p. 306; this is a reprint of the 1980 article augmented by two appendices.

116 Anthony Preus aptly labels this 'Noah's Ark Essentialism'. See his excellent article 'Eidos as Norm in Aristotle's Biology', in John P. Anton & Anthony Preus (eds), *Essays in Ancient Greek Philosophy*, vol. 2 (Albany: SUNY Press, 1983), pp. 340–63.

117 *Met.* 12, 10, 1075a16–19, trans. Ross, *CW* 2, p. 1699.

118 N.J.T.M. Needham, *Science and Civilisation in China*, vol. 1 (Cambridge: Cambridge University Press, 1954), p. 155. Once more, Guthrie's comment is less favourable: 'It was, one must admit, Aristotle who burdened science for centuries with the dogma of the fixity of species. It is strange to have to say this of the man who emphasized so strongly the difficulty of drawing a line between living and non-living. He wrote that nature exhibits a continuous progression between the two, and that the border is imperceptible. Yet he saw no need to convert this static continuity, in which one form of existence differs only minutely from the next, into

a dynamic progression or evolution in time. This conviction of the immutability of species, like that of the eternity of the cosmos, was bound up for him with wider philosophical questions, doctrines of form and substance in which he developed and crystallized the Platonic elements in his intellectual heritage.' *In the Beginning. Some Greek Views on the Origin of Life and the Early State of Man* (London: Methuen, 1957), p. 62.

119 *Hist. An.* 8, 1, 588b4–6, trans. Balme, pp. 61–3.

120 *Part. An.* 4, 5, 681a12–15, trans. Peck, p. 333.

121 *Gen. An.* 2, 1, 732b15, trans. Peck, p. 137.

122 For his interpretation of the sponge as plant, see *Part. An.* 4, 5, 681a15–17; as animal, due to its apparent sensation, *Hist. An.* 1, 1, 487b9–10 and *Hist. An.* 5, 16, 548b10–14.

123 *Hist. An.* 2, 8, 502a16–18; trans. Peck, p. 103.

124 *Part. An.* 4, 10, 689b31–3, trans. Peck, p. 387.

125 *Phys.* 2, 2, 194b13, trans. Hardie & Gaye, *CW* 1, p. 332, my emphasis. In the context of our discussion, it is interesting that in the Loeb translation Cornford renders this passage as follows: 'In Nature man generates man; but the process presupposes and takes place in natural material already organized by the solar heat and so forth.' He explains in a footnote: 'There appears to be a hiatus in the original after ἥλιος, but the meaning, as I have tried to restore it, is obvious.' (p. 126).

126 *Pol.* 5, 3, 1302b38–40, trans. Jowett, *CW* 2, pp. 2068–9. On the role of quantity as determining substance Pierre Pellegrin, in his outstanding study of Aristotle's biology, comments: 'there is here a kind of return to a form of Pythagoreanism, a doctrine that Aristotle nevertheless fought'. Pierre Pellegrin, *Aristotle's Classification of Animals. Biology and the Conceptual Unity of the Aristotelian Corpus* (Berkeley: University of California Press, 1986), p. 193.

127 *Phys.* 2, 8, 198b29–31, my trans.

128 See *Part. An.* 1, 1, 640a19–27.

129 Guthrie, *A History of Philosophy* VI, p. 110, n 1.

130 *Gen. An.* 5, 1, 778b2–6, trans. Guthrie, ibid.

131 *Part. An.* 1, 1, 640a19–27, trans. Peck.

132 See Michael Boylan, *Method and Practice in Aristotle's Biology* (Washington, DC: University Press of America, 1983), p. 224.

133 Guthrie's assessment of Aristotle is no doubt influenced by his own view on the matter ('Knowing as we do'), that 'man has evolved from lower types of life'. *The Greek Philosophers from Thales to Aristotle* (London: Methuen, 1978), p. 127.

134 Cf. *Gen. An.* 5, 1, 778a16–778b1. This text immediately precedes the passage considered by Guthrie to be 'anti-evolutionary'.

135 See *De An.* 1, 1, 403a24–403b16.

136 According to Mayr, consistent with essentialism is the theory that 'an existing species could give rise to a new species, by a sudden leap. This, however, is not

evolution. The diagnostic criterion of evolutionary transformation is gradualness.' Ernst Mayr, *Toward a New Philosophy*, p. 173.

137   *De Gen. et Corr.* 1, 1, 10.327b29–31.

138   *De mixtione elementorum*, in *Opuscula Philosophica*, ed. Raymund M. Spiazzi (Turin: Marietti, 1954), p. 156, no. 439: 'Sunt igitur formae elementorum in mixtis non actu, sed virtute.' Trans. V. Larkin, 'On the Combining of the Elements', *Isis* 51 (1960), p. 72, my emphasis; see also *Summa Theologiae* 1, 76, 4, ad 4. See Nichols, 'Aquinas' Substantial Form', p. 315.

139   William A. Wallace, *The Modeling of Nature, Philosophy of Science and Philosophy of Nature in Synthesis* (Washington, DC: Catholic University of America Press, 1996), p. 10.

140   Charles Darwin, *The Variation of Animals and Plants under Domestication*, p. 404.

141   *Gen. An.* 1, 21, 729b5–6.

142   Montgomery Furth, *Substance, Form and Psyche: An Aristotelian Metaphysics* (Cambridge: Cambridge University Press, 1988), p. 117; see *Gen. An.* 2, 1, 734b33; *Gen. An.* 2, 1, 735a2; *Gen. An.* 2, 4, 740b32; *Gen. An.* 4, 3, 767b20. Furth remarks that although Aristotle's account 'is by present-day lights quite crude and childlike compared to the actual mechanisms involved, which are more complicated and more indirect as between the nature of the genetic material itself and the form manifested in the eventual offspring ... the correctness of these ideas on some significant matters of principles is notable also ... The genetic material carries specific form, not by containing little whole animals or parts of animals, but as *information* that under the proper circumstances can proceed to direct the stepwise construction of co-specific offspring ... The affinities with some more recent findings in this area are quite striking.' Ibid., p. 119.

143   Alan Gotthelf, 'Final Causality', p. 239/216; see note 83 above.

144   Cf. Robert Russell, 'Special Providence and Genetic Mutation', in R.J. Russell, W.R. Stoeger, F. Ayala (eds), *Evolutionary and Molecular Biology. Scientific Perspectives on Divine Action* (Vatican City: Vatican Observatory Publications, 1998), p. 205.

145   *Gen. An.* 2, 1, 731b28–30: βέλτιον ... τὸ εἶναι τοῦ μὴ εἶναι καὶ τὸ ζῆν τοῦ μὴ ζῆν. Trans. Peck, p. 131. See *De An.* 2, 4, 415a26–415b1: 'For any living thing that has reached its normal development... the most natural act is the production of another like itself, an animal producing an animal, a plant a plant, in order that, as far as its nature allows it, it may partake in the eternal and divine.' Trans. Smith, *CW* 1, p. 661.

146   See William Wordsworth: 'Still glides the Stream and shall for ever glide; / The Form remains, the Function never dies.' ('The River Duddon: After-Thought', *Poetical Works*, p. 261). The experience of Leibniz provides an interesting historical parallel: 'In the beginning when I had freed myself from the yoke of Arisotle, I had taken to the void and the atoms, for they best fill the imagination; but on recovering

from that, after many reflections, I realised that it is impossible to find the principles of *a true unity* in matter alone or in that which is only passive, since everything in it is only a collection or mass of parts to infinity. Now multitude can only get its reality from *true unities* which come from elsewhere and are quite different from points (it is known that the continuum cannot be composed of points). Therefore to find these *real unities* I was compelled to have recourse to a formal atom, since a material being cannot be both material and perfectly indivisible or endowed with a true unity. It was necessary, hence, to recall and, so to speak, rehabilitate the *substantial forms* so descried today, but in a way which would make them intelligible and which would separate the use we should make of them from the abuse that has been made of them. I thence found that their nature consists in force, and that from that there ensues something analogous to feeling and apppetite; and that accordingly they must be conceived in imitation of the idea we have of Souls. But as the soul should never be used to explain any detail of the economy of the animal's body, I judged likewise that these forms must not be used to explain the particular problems of nature though they are necessary to establish true general principles. Aristotle calls them *first Entelechies.* I call them perhaps more intelligibly, *primitive Forces* which do not contain only the *act* or the complement of possibility, but further an *original activity.*' 'New System of Nature and of the Communication of Substances, as well as of the Union of Soul and Body', in Philip P. Wiener (ed.), *Selections* (New York: Scribner, 1951), pp. 107–8, emphasis in original.

147 Ernst Mayr, *Toward a New Philosophy*, pp. 56–7, emphasis in original. Mayr remarks: 'No other ancient philosopher has been as badly misunderstood and mishandled by posterity as Aristotle.... Although the philosophers of the last forty years acknowledge quite generally the inspiration which Aristotle derived from the study of living nature, they still express his philosophy in words taken from the vocabulary of Greek dictionaries that are hundreds of years old. The time would seem to have come for the translators and interpreters of Aristotle to use a language appropriate to his thinking, that is, the language of biology, and not that of the sixteenth-century humanists.... Much of Aristotle's discussion becomes remarkably modern if one inserts modern terms to replace obsolete sixteenth- and seventeenth-century vocabulary.' Ibid., pp. 55–6.

148 *Part. An.* 1, 5, 645a30–6, trans. Ogle, *CW* 1, p. 1004.

149 I am grateful to Terence Nichols for drawing my attention to the relevant literature. See *The Sacred Cosmos* (Grand Rapids: Brazos Press, 2003) for an expanded treatment of holism in recent biology. Besides those authors referred to here, one may also mention Brian Goodwin, *How the Leopard Changed its Spots: The Evolution of Complexity* (New York: Charles Scribner's Sons, 1994); Mae Won Ho & Peter Saunders (eds), *Beyond Neo-Darwinism: An Introduction to the New Evolutionary Paradigm* (London: The Academic Press, 1984); David J. Depew &

Bruce H. Weber (eds), *Darwinism Evolving* (Cambridge: MIT Press, 1995); Robert G. Wesson, *Beyond Natural Selection* (Cambridge: MIT Press, 1991).

150 See Steven Rose, *Lifelines. Biology, Freedom, Determinism* (London: Penguin, 1998), pp. x, 302. See p. 7: '[My main task] is to offer an alternative vision of living systems, a vision which recognizes the power and role of genes withoug subscribing to genetic determinism, and which recaptures an understanding of living organisms and their trajectories through time and space as lying at the centre of biology.'

151 Stephen Jay Gould, 'Self-Help for a Hedgehog Stuck on a Molehill', *Evolution* 51/3 (1997), p. 1023. Natural selection is, he suggests, 'a necessary but by no means sufficient, principle for explaining the full history of life'. Ibid., p. 1022.

152 Rose, *Lifelines*, p. 93.

153 Rose, *Lifelines*, p. 296.

154 Rose, *Lifelines*, pp. 306–7.

155 Karl Popper, 'A New Interpretation of Darwinism'. The First Medawar Lecture to The Royal Society, 12 June 1986, cited by Rose, *Lifelines*, pp. 75, 96. For Rose's view, see p. 309. Popper's lecture is published as an appendix in Hans-Joachim Niemann (ed.), *Karl Popper and the Two New Secrets of Life*, pp. 115–28. See p. 120.

156 Rose, *Lifelines*, p. 75.

157 Stuart Kaufmann, *At Home in the Universe* (New York: Oxford, 1995), p. 25. See Rose, *Lifelines*, p. 270: 'Life is inevitably autopoietic, self-generating, self-developing, self-evolving.'

158 Arthur Koestler, *The Ghost in the Machine* (London: Picador, 1967), pp. 48–54; see diagram, ibid. p. 60; Arthur Koestler, 'Beyond Atomism and Holism – the Concept of the Holon', in Arthur Koestler (ed.), *Beyond Reductionism. New Perspectives in the Life Sciences* (London: Hutchinson, 1969), pp. 192–232.

159 See Steven Rose, *Lifelines*, pp. 304–5: 'The divisions between [different levels of organization of matter] are confused. In part they are ontological, and relate to scale and complexity, in which successive levels are nested one within another. Thus atoms are less complex than molecules, molecules than cells, cells than organisms, and organisms than populations and ecosystems. So at each level different organizing relations appear, and different types of description and explanation are required. Hence each level appears as a holon – integrating levels below it, but merely a subset of the levels above. In this sense, levels are fundamentally irreducible; ecology cannot be reduced to genetics, nor biochemistry to chemistry.'

160 Steven Rose, *Lifelines*, p. 94.

161 Barry G. Hall, 'Evolution on a Petri Dish', *Evolutionary Biology* 15 (1982), pp. 85–150; 'Evolution of New Metabolic Functions in Laboratory Organisms', in Masatoshi Nei and R.K. Koehn (eds), *Evolution of Genes and Proteins* (Sunderland, MA: Sinauer Associates, 1983), pp. 234–57. For references to this literature I am again gratefully indebted to Terence Nichols, upon whose presentation of this topic I rely

here. See also Kenneth R. Miller, *Finding Darwin's God. A Scientist's Search for Common Ground Between God and Evolution* (New York: Harper Collins, 1999), pp. 145–7; D.J. Futuyama, *Evolution* (Sunderland, MA: Sinauer Associates, 1986), pp. 477–8.

162 Like the fast-breeding fruit fly (*drosophila*), the *Escherichia coli*, or common gut bug, has the advantage that it replicates and mutates rapidly, thus allowing scientists to accelerate the accumulation of data from which to extrapolate the patterns of evolution. Ironically, as Steven Rose remarks, despite the diversity of life forms – estimated between 14 and 30 million – 'most biochemical and genetic generalizations are still derived from just three organisms: the rat, the fruit fly and the common gut bug'. Rose, *Lifelines*, pp. 2, 4.

163 Hall, 'Evolution on a Petri Dish', p. 143.

164 See Richard E. Lenski and John E. Mittler, 'The Directed Mutation Controversy and Neo-Darwinism', *Science* 259/5092 (Jan 8, 1993), pp. 188–94.

165 For the theoretical problems associated with such knowledge, see the excellent article by William A. Wallace, 'Are Elementary Particles Real?', in *From a Realist Point of View. Essays on the Philosophy of Science* (Washington, DC: University Press of America, 1979), pp. 187–99. Highly pertinent to our entire discussion of the role of form is the following remark by Wallace: 'One can only be struck by the outstanding contribution made by genetics to the understanding of evolutionary processes, particularly in terms of DNA–RNA molecular groups, genes, chromosomes, and so on. And what is most remarkable about this development is that the causal explanations it supplies are made, not in terms of efficient or final causality, but rather in terms of material and formal causality.' William Wallace, *Causality and Scientific Explanation*, vol. 2, *Classical and Contemporary Science* (Ann Arbor: University of Michigan Press, 1974), pp. 317–18.

166 William A. Wallace notes: 'Natures are a shorthand way of indicating the intelligible aspects of things in terms of which they can be understood and defined. Thus the concept of nature is not exclusively an empirical concept, if by empirical one means whatever can be measured or photographed or otherwise presented directly to the senses. It is transempirical, for although it takes its origin from sense experience it still requires going beyond the world of sense for its proper comprehension. To refer to the nature of a thing is therefore to designate an inner dimension that makes the thing be what it is, serves to differentiate it from other things, and at the same time accounts for its distinctive activities and responses. This inner dimension is not transparent to the intellect, for we usually do not achieve distinct and comprehensive knowledge of a nature the first time we encounter it in experience. Rather we grasp it in a general and indeterminate way that is open to progressive development and refinement on the basis of additional information.' Wallace, *The Modeling of Nature*, pp. 4–5.

167 W.V. Quine, 'Three Grades of Modal Involvement' in *The Ways of Paradox* (New York, 1966), pp. 175–6. See David Charles's remarks on Quine's position in *Aristotle on Meaning and Essence* (Oxford University Press, 2001), pp. 354–7. The validity of 'natural kinds', as defended by Quine, is of course a pre-requisite in our present discussion, both for Aristotle's notion of φύσις and evolutionary species. See 'Natural Kinds' in *Ontological Relativity and Other Essays* (New York: Columbia University Press, 1969), pp. 114–38. See William A. Wallace, 'A Place for Form in Science: The Modeling of Nature', *Proceedings of the American Catholic Philosophical Association* 49 (1995), p. 39.

168 *De An.* 3, 8, 431b2: τὰ μὲν οὖν εἴδη τὸ νοητικὸν ἐν τοῖς φαντάσμασι νοεῖ. See 431b29–432a1.

169 Jonathan Barnes writes: 'Some modern philosophers have rejected – and ridiculed – Aristotle's talk of essences. But Aristotle shows himself the better scientist; for an important part of the scientific endeavour consists in explaining the various quirks and properties of substances and stuffs in terms of their fundamental natures – that is to say, in terms of their essences. Aristotle's axiomatic sciences will start from essences and successively explain derivative properties. The theorems of animal biology, say, will express the derived properties of animals, and the deduction of the theorems from the axioms will show how those properties are dependent upon the relevant essences.' Barnes, *Aristotle. A Very Short Introduction*, p. 56.

170 Johannes Hübner, 'Die Aristotelische Konzeption der Seele als Aktivität in *de Anima* II 1', *Archiv für Geschichte der Philosophie* 81 (1999), pp. 1–32.

171 D.W. Hamlyn, *Aristotle. De Anima* (Oxford: Clarendon Press, 1993), p. 82.

172 James Lennox, *Philosophy of Biology*, p. 128; see p. xx: 'Animals are unities of matter and form – souls are simply forms (read "functional capacities") of animate bodies.'

173 *De An.* 2, 4, 415b13–14.

174 *Met.* 12, 7, 1072b26–7, my trans.

175 *Met.* 9, 8, 1050b2–3.

176 *De An.* 2, 1, 412b9.

177 I am introducing here a distinction not found in Aristotle. According to the profound novel insight of Aquinas, essence is of itself powerless to be, and requires actualization by the deeper principle of existence. Essence is related to existence as potency to act; whereas Aristotelian essence determines what something is, existence (*esse*) as primary act radically confers reality, elevating a potential being out of nothingness. Emphasizing the active sense of 'being' conveyed by the verbal form of the infinitive *esse* ('to be'), Aquinas states that being or existence is the 'act of all acts and the perfection of all perfections'. See Fran O'Rourke, *Pseudo-Dionysius and the Metaphysics of Aquinas* (Notre Dame, IN: University of Notre Dame Press, 2005), pp. 174–87.

178 Leibniz's letter to Gabriel Wagner (1696) in Leroy E. Loemker (ed.), *Philosophical Papers and Letters* 2 (Chicago: University of Chicago Press, 1956), p. 758. Bacon's

aim is to 'dissect nature': 'Melius autem est naturam secare, quam abstrahere.' *Novum Organon* 1.51, *Works* 1, p. 168.

179 Johann Wolfgang von Goethe, *Maximen und Reflexionen*, Werke 12 (Hamburg: Wegner, 1967), nr 498, p. 434: 'Die Natur verstummt auf der Folter.'

180 Letter to Jakob Thomasius, April 1669: 'Quae Aristoteles enim de materia, forma, privatione, natura, loco, infinito, tempore, motu, ratiocinatur, pleraque certa et demonstrata sunt.' *Sämtliche Schriften und Briefe* 2, 1 (Berlin: Akademie Verlag, 1987), p. 15.

181 Henri Bergson, *Creative Evolution* (London: Macmillan, 1922), p. 344.

182 *De Spiritualibus Creaturis*, art. 5: Proprium philosophiae eius fuit a manifestis non discedere.

183 *Met.* 7, 17, 1041b17.

CHAPTER EIGHT

1 John Dewey, *The Influence of Darwin on Philosophy and Other Essays* (New York: Henry Holt and Company, 1910), p. 2.

2 Ludwig Wittgenstein, *Tractatus Logico-Philosophicus* (London: Routledge & Kegan Paul, 1969), p. 49, n 4.1122.

3 James Joyce, *Finnegans Wake* (London: Penguin, 1992), p. 252.

4 Michael Ruse and E.O. Wilson, 'The Evolution of Ethics', *New Scientist* 108/1478 (17 October 1985), p. 52, also in James E. Huchingson (ed.), *Religion and the Natural Sciences. The Range of Engagement* (Orlando: Harcourt Brace Jovanovich, 1993), p. 311.

5 Stephen Pope remarks: 'The most significant level of interchange concerns more fundamental questions about the nature of reality (metaphysics, and especially ontology) and God (theology), rather than practical moral questions.' Stephen J. Pope, *Human Evolution and Christian Ethics* (Cambridge: Cambridge University Press, 2007), p. 5. See p. 6: 'The deepest moral disagreements are rooted in competing presuppositions about what is most real, how we can come to understand what is most real, and how this knowledge provides guidance for leading good lives and developing good communities.' The dispute, notes Pope, is between moral realism 'which holds that the world is intrinsically morally meaningful and evolutionary ontological naturalism, which denies that it has any meaning other than what we human beings choose to make of it'.

6 As presented throughout his various publications Dawkins' position has not been entirely consistent. In *The Selfish Gene*, he stated that if one wants 'to build a society in which individuals cooperate generously and unselfishly toward a common good, you can expect little help from biological nature'. Richard Dawkins, *The Selfish Gene* (Oxford: Oxford University Press, 2009), p. 3. In his later books he appeals to the evidence from biology in defence of altruism.

7   Edward O. Wilson, *Sociobiology: The New Synthesis* (Cambridge, MA.: Harvard
        University Press, 1978), pp. 4, 595. According to Daniel Dennett, Hobbes and
        Nietzsche were the first sociobiologists. See Daniel Dennett, *Darwin's Dangerous
        Idea: Evolution and the Meanings of Life* (New York: Simon and Schuster, 1996), pp.
        453, 461.

8   Tom Wolfe, 'Sorry, But Your Soul Just Died', *Forbes ASAP* (2 December 1996), p.
        212.

9   Wilson, *Sociobiology*, p. 562.

10   See Peter Singer, 'Ethics and Sociobiology', *Philosophy and Public Affairs*, 11 (1982),
        p. 44: 'Wilson writes as an enthusiast for his subject, occasionally overstepping the
        bounds of his evidence as enthusiasts often do.'

11   Edward O. Wilson, *On Human Nature* (Cambridge, MA: Harvard University Press,
        1978), pp. 1–3. William James similarly wrote: 'Taking a purely naturalistic view of
        the matter, it seems reasonable to suppose that, unless consciousness served some
        useful purpose, it would not have been superadded to life.' William James, review
        of Wilhelm Wundt, *Grundzüge der physiologischen Psychologie*, in *North American
        Review* 121 (1875), p. 201.

12   Michael Ruse, *The Darwinian Paradigm: Essays on its History, Philosophy, and
        Religious Implications* (London: Routledge, 1989), pp. 261–2, 268. See also
        'Evolutionary Ethics: A Phoenix Arisen', in Paul Thompson (ed.), *Issues in
        Evolutionary Ethics* (Albany: State University of New York Press, 1995), p. 230: 'Our
        moral sense, our altruistic nature, is an adaptation – a feature helping us in the
        struggle for existence and reproduction – no less than hands and eyes, teeth and
        feet. It is a cost-effective way of getting us to cooperate, which avoids both the
        pitfalls of blind action and the expense of a superbrain of pure rationality.'

13   Wilson, *Sociobiology*, p. 4. Altruism is defined (p. 578) as 'self-destructive behavior
        performed for the benefit of others'.

14   Wilson, *On Human Nature*, p. 201.

15   Wilson, ibid., p. 2

16   Wilson, ibid., p. 1.

17   Wilson, *Sociobiology*, p. 3.

18   Michael Ruse, *Taking Darwin Seriously* (Oxford: Basil Blackwell, 1989), p. 206.

19   Wilson, *On Human Nature*, p. 2.

20   Wilson, ibid., p. 3.

21   Dawkins, *The Selfish Gene*, pp. xxi, 2.

22   Richard Dawkins, 'God's Utility Function', *Scientific American*, 273/5 (November
        1995), p. 67. For a slightly different version see *A River Out of Eden* (London:
        Weidenfeld & Nicholson, 1995), p. 133.

23   Dawkins, *The Selfish Gene*, p. 19.

24   Dawkins, ibid., pp. 34–5.

25   Michael Ruse and E.O. Wilson, 'The Evolution of Ethics', *New Scientist* 108/1478

(17 October 1985), pp. 51–2, also in James E. Huchingson (ed.), *Religion and the Natural Sciences*, p. 310.

26 Michael Ruse, 'Evolutionary Ethics. A Defence', in Holmes Rolston III (ed.), *Biology, Ethics, and the Origins of Life* (Boston: Jones & Bartlett, 1995), p. 93.

27 Ruse, *Taking Darwin Seriously*, p. 206.

28 Edward O. Wilson, *Consilience* (London: Little, Brown, 1998), p. 164.

29 Ruse, *Taking Darwin Seriously*, p. 155.

30 Ruse, ibid., p. 163.

31 Wilson, *On Human Nature*, p. 167.

32 Dawkins, *The Selfish Gene*, p. 267. He is referring to a quotation from the zoologist G.G. Simpson which he has quoted (p. 1): 'The point I want to make now is that all attempts to answer that question before 1859 are worthless and that we will be better off if we ignore them completely.'

33 On Dawkins' knowledge of the philosophical tradition, Michael Ruse has remarked: 'Frankly, I doubt he has ever read a philosophical work all the way through.' Review of Holmes Rolston's *Genes, Genesis, and God*, Metanexus Institute website: http://www.metanexus.net/book-review/review-holmes-rolstons-genes-genesis-and-god. (1 September 2011, accessed 1 September 2015). Peter Singer is equally forthright in his criticism of E.O. Wilson: 'Though defending Rawls is not a role that comes easily to me, it has to be said that Wilson's criticisms are a mess.' Peter Singer, 'Ethics and Sociobiology', *Philosophy and Public Affairs* 11/1 (Winter, 1982), p. 50.

34 See Chapter 8, 'Aristotle and the Metaphysics of Evolution' above, especially pp. 167–8.

35 *Hist. An.* 7, 1.588a19–28, trans. Balme, pp. 57–61.

36 *Hist. An.* 7, 1, 588a31–588b3, trans. Balme, p. 61.

37 See *Hist An.* 8, 12, 597a4–5; *Hist An.* 9, 10, 614b18–26. Plato had already noted the 'political' character of bees, wasps and ants. See Phaedo 82b5–8, cited p. 282, n 29 above.

38 *Hist. An.* 8, 6, 612a21–4, trans. Balme, slightly modified. Herodotus, 2, 68, says that this bird, also called 'crocodile bird', picks leeches from the crocodile's throat. H. Rackham states: 'In reality it picks gnats from the crocodile's open mouth.' Aristotle, *Eudemian Ethics* (Cambridge, MA: Harvard University Press, 1992), trans. H. Rackham, p. 372.

39 Edward O. Wilson, *Naturalist* (New York: Warner 1995), p. 224.

40 Wilson, *On Human Nature*, p. 7.

41 Peter Singer, *The Expanding Circle. Ethics and Sociobiology* (Oxford: Oxford University Press, 1983), p. xi. Singer remarks: 'It is true that the sociobiological approach to ethics often involves undeniable and crude errors. Nevertheless, I believe that the sociobiological approach to ethics does tell us something important

about ethics, something we can use to gain a better understanding of ethics than has hitherto been possible' (ibid.).

42 Philip Kitcher, *Vaulting Ambition* (Cambridge, MA: MIT Press, 1985), p. 395.

43 Wilson, *Consilience*, p. 297. Wilson refers to his 'deeper agenda that also takes the name of reductionism: to fold the laws and principles of each level of organization into those at more general, hence more fundamental levels. Its strong form is total consilience, which holds that nature is organized by simple universal laws of physics to which all other laws and principles can eventually be reduced. This transcendental world view is the light and way for many scientific materialists. (I admit to being among them.)' Ibid., p. 59. Wilson paradoxically admits that he might well be wrong: 'At least it is surely an oversimplification. At each level of organisation, especially the living cell and above, phenomena exist that require new laws and principles... Perhaps some of them will remain forever beyond our grasp... That would not be at all bad. I will confess with pleasure: The challenge and the crackling of thin ice are what give science its metaphysical excitement.' Ibid.

44 Ruse and Wilson, 'Evolution of Ethics', p. 51.

45 As Philip Kitcher notes, their pronouncements are short on specifics: 'Ruse and Wilson are surprisingly reticent in expressing substantive moral principles, apparently preferring to discuss general features of human evolution and results about the perception of colors.' *Vaulting Ambition*, p. 447.

46 The American Association for the Advancement of Science, in its 'Program of Dialogue between Science and Religion' (1995) declared: 'Science is about causes, religion about meaning. Science deals with how things happen in nature, religion with why there is anything rather than nothing. Science answers specific questions about the workings of nature, religion addresses the ultimate ground of nature.' Quoted in Dorothy Nelkin, 'Less Selfish Than Sacred? Genes and the Religious Impulse in Evolutionary Psychology', in Hilary Rose and Stephen Rose (eds), *Alas, Poor Darwin, Arguments against Evolutionary Psychology* (London: Vintage, 2000), p. 14.

47 Wilson, *Consilience*, pp. 10–11.

48 For a convincing statement of the need for multiple, layered, complementary explanations in biology, see Steven Rose, *Lifelines: Biology, Freedom, Determinism* (London: Penguin, 1998), pp. 10–13.

49 Alasdair MacIntyre, *Whose Justice? Which Rationality?* (London: Duckworth, 1988), p. 101.

50 *Pol.* 1, 2, 1252a24, my trans.

51 *De An.* 1, 1, 403a–403b2.

52 In the *Phaedo* (98c–99c) Socrates likewise offers alternative explanations for his presence in the prison cell: one refers to his muscles and limbs, the other to his respect for the laws and values of the state.

53 When asked if everything could be expressed scientifically, Einstein replied that it could, but that it would make no sense: 'It would be a description without meaning – as if you described a Beethoven symphony as a variation of wave pressure.' See Ronald William Clark, *Einstein: The Life and Times* (New York: Wings Books, 1995), p. 32.

54 Stephen R.L. Clark, *Biology and Christian Ethics* (Cambridge: Cambridge University Press, 2000), p. 80. See Horace, *Letters* 1, 10, 24: *Naturam expellas furca, tamen usque recurret, et mala perrumpet furtim fastidia victrix*: 'Drive out nature with a pitchfork, she will hurry back with furtive victory to break your evil scorn.'

55 See Wilson, *Naturalist*, p. 242: 'I felt certain that the future principles of evolutionary biology would be written in equations, with the deepest insights expressed by quantitative models.'

56 Friedrich Nietzsche, *On the Genealogy of Morals* (New York: Vintage Books, 1967), p. 77.

57 Ruse and Wilson, 'The Evolution of Ethics', p. 51.

58 Dennett, *Darwin's Dangerous Idea*, p. 470.

59 Dennett, ibid. Dennett assigns an important role also to memes; I regard the latter neologism as a superfluous and fanciful synonym for popular ideas which may be readily explained by Aristotelian categories applied to the contents of mind.

60 Dennett, *Darwin's Dangerous Idea*, p. 472.

61 *EN* 3, 4, 1113b6: ἐφ' ἡμῖν δὴ καὶ ἡ ἀρετή, ὁμοίως δὲ καὶ ἡ κακία.

62 *De An.* 3, 3, 428a25; *De An.* 3, 11, 434a7; *EN* 3, 1, 1111b9–11.

63 *EN* 7, 3, 1147b5.

64 *EN* 6, 2, 1139a20.

65 *EN* 10, 8, 1178b24.

66 *Pol.* 3, 9, 1280a34: διὰ τὸ μὴ μετέχειν εὐδαιμονίας μηδὲ τοῦ ζῆν κατὰ προαίρεσιν.

67 *EN* 1, 7, 1098a4, trans. Rackham, p. 31.

68 Wilson, *Sociobiology*, p. 3.

69 Wilson, *On Human Nature*, p 71.

70 *Julius Caesar* I. ii. 139.

71 Ruse, *Taking Darwin Seriously*, p. 259.

72 Ibid.

73 *Met.* 1, 2, 982b26: ἄνθρωπος ἐλεύθερος ὁ αὑτοῦ ἕνεκα καὶ μὴ ἄλλου ὤν.

74 *Summa Theologiae* I, 96, 4.

75 Cf. Stephen Pope: 'Sociobiologists mistakenly suggest that all people share the same genetic and biological motivations, and that these are dominant over and constitute the underlying causes of all other motivations, however much these seem to be chosen consciously by the agent. Individuals have distinctive genotypes and therefore the genetic factors underlying motivation cannot be identical for all people, yet sociobiologists speak at times as if all human beings have the same fixed

motivational characteristics. A non-reductionistic reading of motivation, on the other hand, holds that the genetic basis of motivation is one among a variety of factors that can influence an individual's particular motivational structure.' Pope, *Human Evolution and Christian Ethics*, p. 223.

76 Wilson, *On Human Nature*, p. 167.

77 Alasdair MacIntyre, *After Virtue* (London: Duckworth, 1981), p. 150–1.

78 See Anthony O'Hear, *Beyond Evolution: Human Nature and the Limits of Evolutionary Explanation* (Oxford: Clarendon Press, 1997), p. vii: 'We are prisoners neither of our genes nor of the ideas we encounter as we each make our personal and individual way through life.'

79 Charles Darwin, *The Descent of Man, and Selection in Relation to Sex* (London: Penguin, 2004), p. 135.

80 I believe that the term 'biological teleology' more accurately conveys the meaning of his more frequently used term 'metaphysical biology'. See, e.g., MacIntyre, *After Virtue*, p. 139: 'Hence Aristotle's ethics, expounded as he expounds it, presupposes his metaphysical biology.' To the best of my knowledge MacIntyre nowhere clarifies what he criticizes as 'metaphysical biology'; presumably he had in mind, *inter alia*, Aristotle's views on slavery and women.

81 MacIntyre, *After Virtue*, p. 152.

82 MacIntyre, ibid.

83 MacIntyre, ibid., p. 183.

84 MacIntyre, ibid., p. 56.

85 Alasdair MacIntyre, *Dependent Rational Animals* (Chicago: Open Court, 2008), p. x.

86 MacIntyre, ibid., p. ix.

87 *ST* II–II, 8, 1: Respondeo dicendum quod nomen intellectus quandam intimam cognitionem importat, dicitur enim intelligere quasi intus legere. Et hoc manifeste patet considerantibus differentiam intellectus et sensus, nam cognitio sensitiva occupatur circa qualitates sensibiles exteriores; cognitio autem intellectiva penetrat usque ad essentiam rei, obiectum enim intellectus est quod quid est, ut dicitur in III de anima.

88 Henry David Thoreau, *Walden, or Life in the Woods* (Harmondsworth: Penguin, 1938), p. 86.

89 *EN* 9, 8, 1168b34–1169a2: καὶ ἐγκρατὴς δὲ καὶ ἀκρατὴς λέγεται τῷ κρατεῖν τὸν νοῦν ἢ μή, ὡς τούτου ἑκάστου ὄντος· καὶ πεπραγέναι δοκοῦσιν αὐτοὶ καὶ ἑκουσίως τὰ μετὰ λόγου μάλιστα.

90 *EN* 9, 8, 1169a16: ὁ δ' ἐπιεικής, ἃ δεῖ, ταῦτα καὶ πράττει· πᾶς γὰρ νοῦς αἱρεῖται τὸ βέλτιστον ἑαυτῷ, ὁ δ' ἐπιεικὴς πειθαρχεῖ τῷ νῷ.

91 Pope, *Human Evolution and Christian Ethics*, p. 256.

92 *Irish Times*, 14 February 2009.

93 See Jonathan Marks, *What It Means to Be 98% Chimpanzee: Apes, People, and Their Genes* (Berkeley: University of California Press, 2003), p. 29: 'In the context of a 35% similarity to a daffodil, the 99.44% similarity of the DNA of human to chimp doesn't seem so remarkable. After all, humans are obviously a heck of a lot more similar to chimpanzees than to daffodils. More than that, to say that humans are over one-third daffodil is more ludicrous than profound. There are hardly any comparisons you can make to a daffodil in which humans are 33% similar. DNA comparisons thus overestimate similarity at the low end of the scale ... and underestimate comparisons at the high end.'

94 *Pensées* 72. The quotation is from St. Augustine, *De Civ. Dei*, 21, 10.

95 *Measure for Measure* II. ii. 119–20.

96 Charles Darwin, *The Descent of Man, and Selection in Relation to Sex*, p. 151. A little further on in the same paragraph he states: 'The moral sense perhaps affords the best and highest distinction between man and the lower animals.' See also Singer, *Expanding Circle*, pp. 27–8: 'Attempts to draw sharp lines between ourselves and other animals have always failed. We thought we were the only beings capable of language, until we discovered that chimpanzees and gorillas can learn more than a hundred words in sign language, and use them in combinations of their own devising. Scientists are now laboriously discovering what many dog owners have long accepted; we are not the only animals that reason.'

97 Teilhard de Chardin, *The Phenomenon of Man* (London: Collins, 1960), p. 166. De Chardin's lengthy remarks (pp. 164–6) are by far the best I have read anywhere on the implications of reflection for the distinction between humans and other animals; unfortunately it is one of the few philosophical insights in his work that I find fully convincing. On the failure to appreciate the uniqueness of human cognition, Keith Ward has commented, 'It is rather ironic that it is through the use of those intellectual powers which are so well developed in the human species that thinkers have come to deny any special significance to human life.' See Keith Ward, *The Battle for the Soul: The End of Morality in a Secular Society* (London: Hodder and Stoughton, 1985), p. 57.

98 For a discussion of the reasons why chimpanzees are not capable of language, see O'Hear, *Beyond Evolution*, pp. 38–9.

99 Wilson, *On Human Nature*, p. 26.

100 *De An.* 3, 8, 431b21.

101 *De An.* 3, 5, 430a15.

102 Harry G. Frankfurt, 'Freedom of the Will and the Concept of a Person', *Journal of Philosophy* 68 (1971), pp. 5–20.

103 Augustine, *De Trinitate* 9, 11, 18: 'Memini enim me habere memoriam, et intelligentiam, et voluntatem; et intelligo me intelligere, et velle, atque meminisse; et volo me velle, et meminisse, et intelligere, totamque meam memoriam, et

intelligentiam, et voluntatem simul memini.' This text was taken up later by Alcuin and Anselm.

104 Wilson, *On Human Nature*, p. 27. The quote is from David Premack, 'Language and Intelligence in Ape and Man', *American Scientist* 64 (1976), pp. 681–2.

105 A more realistic approach is offered by Wilson in *Consilience*, p. 250: 'The great apes have the power of self-recognition, but there is no evidence that they can reflect on their own birth and eventual death. Or on the meaning of existence – the complexity of the universe means nothing to them.'

106 In his poem 'Death', William Butler Yeats contrasts the human anticipation of death with the absence of any such animal experience:

Nor dread nor hope attend

A dying animal;

A man awaits his end

Dreading and hoping all;

Many times he died,

Many times rose again.

A great man in his pride

Confronting murderous men

Casts derision upon

Supersession of breath;

He knows death to the bone –

Man has created death.

W.B.Yeats, *The Poems*, ed. Daniel Albright (London: Everyman's Library, 1992), p. 284.

107 Wilson, *Sociobiology*, p. 3. Peter Singer comments: 'If ethical judgments were nothing but the outflow of our emotional control centers, it would be as inappropriate to criticize ethical judgment as it is to criticize gastronomic preferences. Endorsing capital punishment would be as much an expression of our feelings as taking our tea with lemon, rather than milk.' Singer, *Expanding Circle*, p. 85.

108 Wilson, *Sociobiology*, p. 3.

109 David Hume, 'Of Suicide' [1755], in Stephen Copley and Andrew Edgal (eds), *David Hume: Selected Essays* (Oxford: Oxford University Press, 1993), p. 319.

110 W. Somerset Maugham, *The Summing Up* (New York: Mentor, 1957), p. 11.

111 Augustine, *Confessions* 9, 33.

112 Immanuel Kant, *Critique of Pure Reason*, A805/B833.

113 Richard Dawkins, 'You Can't Have It Both Ways: Irreconcilable Differences?', *Skeptical Inquirer* (July 1999), p. 64.

114 Wilson, *On Human Nature*, p. 192.

115 Alasdair MacIntyre, 'The Logical Status of Religious Belief', in Stephen Toulmin,

Ronald W. Hepburn, and Alasdair MacIntyre, *Metaphysical Beliefs. Three Essays* (London: SCM, 1970), p. 192.

116 See Alasdair MacIntyre, *God, Philosophy, Universities: A Selective History of the Catholic Philosophical Tradition* (Lanham, MD: Rowman and Littlefield, 2009), pp. 40–1, 84–5.

117 Starr Report to Congress, available http://www.washingtonpost.com/wp-srv/politics/special/clinton/icreport/icreport.htm (Accessed 20 October 2015).

118 Martin Rees, *Our Cosmic Habitat* (Princeton: Princeton University Press, 2001), p. xi.

119 Wilson, *On Human Nature*, p. 199.

120 Wilson, ibid., p. 209.

121 Wilson, ibid., p.199.

122 Wilson, *Consilience*, p. 267–8.

123 Wilson, ibid., p. 268.

Chapter Nine

1 Edward O. Wilson, *Sociobiology: The New Synthesis* (Cambridge, MA.: Harvard University Press, 1978), pp. 4, 595.

2 Charles Darwin, *On the Origin of Species* (London: Penguin, 1985), p. 263.

3 Edward O. Wilson & Michael Ruse, 'The Evolution of Ethics', *New Scientist* 108, 1478 (17 October 1985), p. 50.

4 Wilson, *Sociobiology*, p. 578. Ruse and Wilson define it as 'self-sacrifice for the benefit of others'. 'The Evolution of Ethics', p. 50.

5 See Wilson, *Sociobiology*, p. 117.

6 See Michael Ruse, *Taking Darwin Seriously* (Oxford: Blackwells, 1989), p. 225.

7 Robert L. Trivers, 'The Evolution of Reciprocal Altruism', *The Quarterly Review of Biology* 46 (1971), pp. 35–57.

8 Wilson, *Sociobiology*, p. 120.

9 Wilson, ibid.

10 Wilson, ibid.

11 Wilson, ibid., p. 3.

12 *EN* 8, 3, 1156a6–8, 4,1157b5.

13 *EE* 7, 2, 1236b5–7, trans. Rackham, p. 373.

14 Charles H. Kahn, 'Aristotle and Altruism', *Mind* 90 (1981), p. 20.

15 Julia Annas, 'Plato and Aristotle on Friendship and Altruism', *Mind* 86 (1977), p. 539.

16 D.J. Allan, *The Philosophy of Aristotle* (Oxford Press, 1952), p. 138.

17 Richard Kraut, *Aristotle on the Human Good* (Princeton: Press, 1989), pp. 9–11, 78–90.

18   Arthur Madigan, 'Eth. Nic. 9.8: Beyond Egoism and Altruism?', in John P. Anton and Anthony Preus (eds), *Essays in Ancient Greek Philosophy IV, Aristotle's Ethics* (Albany: State University of New York Press, 1991), pp. 73–94.

19   Annas, 'Plato and Aristotle on Friendship and Altruism', p. 535.

20   *EN* 8, 2, 1156a2–3, trans. Rackham, p. 457.

21   *EN* 8, 1, 1155a20–2: ὅθεν τοὺς φιλανθρώπους ἐπαινοῦμεν. ἴδοι δ᾽ ἄν τις καὶ ἐν ταῖς πλάναις ὡς οἰκεῖον ἅπας ἄνθρωπος ἀνθρώπῳ καὶ φίλον.

22   As Anthony Preus points out, the passage 'is summarizing common opinions about friendship, and cannot be taken as directly stating Aristotle's opinions'. See 'Aristotle and Respect for Persons', in John P. Anton and Anthony Preus (eds), *Essays in Ancient Greek Philosophy IV, Aristotle's Ethics* (Albany: State University of New York Press, 1991), p. 221.

23   T.H. Irwin, *Aristotle's First Principles* (Oxford: Clarendon Press, 1990), p. 397.

24   Kahn, 'Aristotle and Altruism', p. 21.

25   E.O. Wilson, *Sociobiology*, p. 578, emphasis added.

26   The entire passage presents a clear statement of the fundamental weakness of sociobiological altruism, and why it can never work: 'Men being naturally selfish, or endowed only with a confined generosity, they are not easily induced to perform any action for the interest of strangers, except with a view to some reciprocal advantage, which they had no hope of obtaining but by such a performance. Now as it frequently happens, that these mutual performances cannot be finished at the same instant, it is necessary, that one party be contented to remain in uncertainty, and depend upon the gratitude of the other for a return of kindness. But so much corruption is there among men, that, generally speaking, this becomes but a slender security; and as the benefactor is here supposed to bestow his favours with a view to self-interest, this both takes off from the obligation, and sets an example to selfishness, which is the true mother of ingratitude. Were we, therefore, to follow the natural course of our passions and inclinations, we should perform but few actions for the advantage of others, from disinterested views; because we are naturally very limited in our kindness and affection; and we should perform as few of that kind, out of regard to interest; because we cannot depend upon their gratitude.' David Hume, *A Treatise on Human Nature* (Oxford: Clarendon Press, 1973), pp. 519–20.

27   *EN* 9, 4, 1166a14–21, trans. Rackham, pp. 533–5.

28   *EN* 8, 7, 1159a12, trans. Rackham, p. 481. *EN* 8, 2, 1155b23–4: 'It appears that each person loves what is good for himself.' Trans. p. 455.

29   Alasdair MacIntyre, *Dependent Rational Animals* (Chicago: Open Court, 2008), p. 160. See MacIntyre's entry 'Egoism and Altruism' in the *Encyclopedia of Philosophy*, vol. 2 (New York: Macmillan, 1967), pp. 462–6.

30 Alasdair MacIntyre, *After Virtue* (London: Duckworth, 1981), pp. 212–13.

31 *EN* 8, 1, 1155a20–2.

32 See *Rhet.* 1, 11, 1371b18–23.

33 *Pol.* 1, 3, 1257b40–58a1: αὔξειν τὴν τοῦ νομίσματος οὐσίαν εἰς ἄπειρον. αἴτιον δὲ ταύτης τῆς διαθέσεως τὸ σπουδάζειν περὶ τὸ ζῆν, ἀλλὰ μὴ τὸ εὖ ζῆν· εἰς ἄπειρον οὖν ἐκείνης τῆς ἐπιθυμίας οὔσης.

34 *Rhet.* 2, 23, 1399a28–31: ἄλλος, ἐπειδὴ οὐ ταὐτὰ φανερῶς ἐπαινοῦσι καὶ ἀφανῶς, ἀλλὰ φανερῶς μὲν τὰ δίκαια καὶ τὰ καλὰ ἐπαινοῦσι μάλιστα, ἰδίᾳ δὲ τὰ συμφέροντα μᾶλλον βούλονται. Trans. Roberts, *CW* 2, p. 2230.

35 *Pol.* 2, 3, 1261b34–5.

36 Diogenes Laertius, *Lives of Eminent Philosophers*, trans. R.D. Hicks (Cambridge, MA: Harvard University Press, 1995), vol. 1, p. 465.

37 *EN* 8, 3, 1156b7–11.

38 *EN* 9, 10, 1171a17–20: πολιτικῶς μὲν οὖν ἔστι πολλοῖς εἶναι φίλον καὶ μὴ ἄρεσκον ὄντα, ἀλλ᾽ ὡς ἀληθῶς ἐπιεικῆ· δι᾽ ἀρετὴν δὲ καὶ δι᾽ αὐτοὺς οὐκ ἔστι πρὸς πολλούς, ἀγαπητὸν δὲ καὶ ὀλίγους εὑρεῖν τοιούτους. Trans. Rackham, p. 569.

39 *EN* 8, 3, 1156b24–25.

40 Roger Trigg, *Ideas of Human Nature. An Historical Introduction* (Oxford: Basil Blackwell, 1988), p. 99.

41 Trigg, ibid. In a separate volume dealing specifically with Sociobiology, Trigg offers the following summary judgment: 'The self-centred position of sociobiology would refuse to accept that one can love a mere neighbour merely for his sake. From the moral point of view, however, I should accept that my neighbour's interests are as important as mine and that he matters as much as I do… Our instinctive likes and dislikes are a totally different matter from the question of a morality with a rational basis. In attacking the possibility of the latter, sociobiology is ruling out any genuine concern for those who are not related to us, or who give us no expectation of future benefits if we benefit them. Talk of extrapolation of our sympathies merely begs the question how this is possible. Sociobiology will certainly not allow appeals to the survival of the species to bridge the gap.' Roger Trigg. *The Shaping of Man. Philosophical Aspects of Sociobiology* (Oxford: Basil Blackwell, 1982), p. 144.

42 Edward O. Wilson, *On Human Nature* (Cambridge, MA: Harvard University Press, 2004) p. 166.

43 Stephen J. Pope, *Human Evolution and Christian Ethics* (Cambridge: Cambridge University Press, 2007), p. 225: 'The entire sociobiological project of attempting to "explain" human behavior in strictly behavioral terms, then, cripples its analysis of genuine human altruism.'

44 1 Cor. 13:5.

45 Peter Singer, 'Ethics and Sociobiology', *Philosophy and Public Affairs* 11/1 (Winter 1982), p. 48.

46 *EN* 9, 8 1168b19–21.

47 We may in this light read Triver's comment: 'Models that attempt to explain altruistic behavior in terms of natural selection are models designed to take the altruism out of altruism.' 'The Evolution of Reciprocal Altruism', p. 35.

48 Richard Dawkins, *The Selfish Gene* (Oxford: Oxford University Press, 1989), p. 3.

49 Dawkins, ibid., p. 4.

50 Dawkins, ibid., p. 215.

51 Charles Darwin, *On the Origin of Species* (London: Penguin, 1985), pp. 228–9.

52 Stephen Pope summarizes: 'The logic of evolution implies that phenotypes engaged in cooperative and caring behavior toward organisms who can reciprocate (as well as those who are close kin) are more likely to leave behind copies of their own genes than are phenotypes who act selfishly, that is, who neither cooperate nor care about others.' *Human Evolution and Christian Ethics*, p. 217.

Chapter Ten

1 Valentin Rose (ed.), *Fragmenta* (Stuttgart: Teubner, 1967), no. 668, p. 420.

2 *The Works of Jonathan Swift* (Edinburgh: William P. Nimmo, 1869), p. 180.

3 Georges Borach, 'Conversations with James Joyce', *College English* 15/6 (Mar. 1954), p. 325. Translation Joseph Prescott, modified. See William T. Noon, S. J., *Joyce and Aquinas* (New Haven: Yale University Press, 1957), p. 92. See Georges Borach, 'Gespräche mit James Joyce', in James Joyce, *Die Toten* (Zürich: Diogenes, 1948), p. 331: 'In den letzten zweihundert Jahren haben wir keinen großen Denker gehabt. Mein Ausspruch ist gewagt, denn Kant ist inbegriffen. Alle großen Denker der letzten Jahrhunderte von Kant bis Benedetto Croce haben nur den Garten umgearbeitet. Der größte Denker aller Zeiten ist meines Erachtens Aristoteles. Alles ist bei ihm wunderbar klar und einfach definiert. Später hat man Baende geschrieben, um das Gleiche zu definieren.'

4 J.G. Kohl, *Travels in Ireland* (London: Bruce and Wyld, 1844), p. 71. See p. 16 above.

5 Thomas E. Connolly (ed.), *Scribbledehobble, the Ur-Workbook for* Finnegans Wake (Evanston: Northwestern University Press, 1961), p. 99 [512]. Joyce copied the triad from Thomas F. O'Rahilly, *A Miscellany of Irish Proverbs* (Dublin: Talbot Press, 1922). He does not include this in *Finnegans Wake*; there is, however, the following scene in *Stephen Hero*: 'The nights before the examination were spent sitting outside under the porch of the Library. The two young men gazed up into the tranquil sky and discussed how it was possible to live with the least amount of labour. Cranly suggested bees: he seemed to know the entire economy of bee-life and he did not seem as intolerant towards bees as towards men. Stephen said it would be a good arrangement if Cranly were to live on the labour of the bees and allow him (Stephen) to live on the united labour of bees and of their keeper' James Joyce, *Stephen Hero*, eds Theodore Spencer, John J. Slocum, and Herbert Cahoon (New

York: New Directions, 1963), p. 128.

6   Preserved Smith (ed.), *Life and Letters of Martin Luther* (Boston: Houghton Mifflin, 1911), p. 26.

7   James Joyce, *Ulysses*, ed. Hans Walter Gabler with Wolfhard Steppe and Claus Melchior (New York: Vintage, 1986), 1.209. Cited by episode and line number.

8   August Suter interview with Richard Ellmann in 1956; see Richard Ellmann, *James Joyce* (Oxford: Oxford University Press, 1982), p. 27. Frank Budgen quotes this as follows: 'How to gather, how to order, and how to present a given material.' *James Joyce and the Making of Ulysses* (Oxford: Oxford University Press, 1991), p. 352.

9   Joseph Rickaby, *Of God and Creatures. An Annotated Translation of the Summa Contra Gentiles of Saint Thomas Aquinas* (London: Burns and Oates, 1905), p. 1.

10 Padraic Colum, *The Road Round Ireland* (New York: Macmillan, 1926), p. 316.

11 *Stephen Hero*, p. 33.

12 *Ulysses* 17.1410.

13 James Joyce, *Finnegans Wake* (London: Penguin, 1992), p. 306.17–18. Cited by page and line number.

14 Frank Budgen, *James Joyce and the Making of Ulysses*, p. 20.

15 *Finnegans Wake* 167.32–3.

16 John Henry Newman, *The Idea of a University* (London: Longmans, Green, and Co., 1889), pp. 109–10.

17 Herbert Gorman, *James Joyce* (New York: Farrar & Rinehart, 1939), p. 94.

18 C.P. Curran, *James Joyce Remembered* (London: Oxford University Press, 1968), p. 3.

19 Eugene Sheehy, *May It Please the Court* (Dublin: C.J. Fallon, 1951), p. 14.

20 James Meenan (ed.), *Centenary History of the Literary and Historical Society of University College Dublin 1855–1955* (Tralee: The Kerryman, 1955), p. 47.

21 *Centenary History*, p. 51.

22 George H. Healey (ed.), *The Complete Dublin Diary of Stanislaus Joyce* (Ithaca: Cornell University Press, 1971), p. 53.

23 James Joyce, *A Portrait of the Artist as a Young Man*, ed. John Paul Riquelme, text ed. by Hans Walter Gabler with Walter Hettche (New York, NY: Norton, 2007), V. 466–7. Cited by chapter and line number.

24 James Joyce, *Letters II*, ed. Richard Ellmann (New York, NY: Viking, 1966), p. 28.

25 *Letters II*, p. 38.

26 *Letters II*, p. 71.

27 James Joyce, *Critical Writings*, eds Ellsworth Mason and Richard Ellmann (London: Faber and Faber, 1959), pp. 109–10.

28 Hugh Kenner, 'Joyce and the 19th century linguistics explosion', in *Atti del Third International James Joyce Symposium*, Trieste, 14–18 giugno 1971 (Trieste: Università degli Studi, Facoltà di Magistero, 1974), p. 48.

29 See p. 226 above.

30   *Critical Writings*, p. 103.

31   Richard M. Kain, *Fabulous Voyager. A Study of James Joyce's Ulysses* (New York: The Viking Press, 1967), p. 4.

32   *Stephen Hero*, p. 205.

33   *Critical Writings*, p. 100. The editors of the volume remark in a footnote: 'Here again Joyce shows his devotion to Aristotle's aesthetic.'

34   See Joyce's letter to Stanislaus, 8 February 1903: 'I am feeling very intellectual these times and up to my eyes in Aristotle's Psychology. If the editor of the "Speaker" puts in my review of "Catalina" you will see some of the fruits thereof.' *Letters II*, p. 28. Richard Ellmann comments: 'Aristotle's *De Anima* is not mentioned in the review of *Catalina,* but some phrases are perhaps indebted to it. Joyce later used this work as the basis of much of the *Proteus* episode of *Ulysses.*' Ibid., p. 28, n 2.

35   Cited *Critical Writings*, p. 135, n 1.

36   *Portrait* V. 1215–19.

37   *Met.* 4, 3, 1005b19–21.

38   *The Complete Dublin Diary of Stanislaus Joyce*, p. 100.

39   Mary and Padraic Colum, *Our Friend James Joyce* (London: Victor Gollancz, 1959), pp. 131-2.

40   *Finnegans Wake* 161. 6–14.

41   *Stephen Hero*, p. 186.

42   Joyce had read the following statement in Burnet's book which he had reviewed: 'What we do find is that Theophrastos, Aristotle's immediate successor, founded scientific Botany, as he himself had founded scientific Zoology, and that it was either in such branches of inquiry or in historical research that Aristotle's followers chiefly distinguished themselves.' John Burnet, *Aristotle on Education* (Cambridge: Cambridge University Press, 1928), p. 135.

43   *Stephen Hero*, p. 186.

44   *EN* 1, 3, 1094b13–15.

45   *Contra Gentiles* 1, 3. Translation, Joseph Rickaby, *Of God and His Creatures*, p. 2.

46   Gogarty, Oliver St John. *Mourning Becomes Mrs. Spendlove* (New York, NY: Creative Age, 1948), p. 50.

47   Richard Ellmann, *Ulysses on the Liffey* (London: Faber and Faber, 1974), p. 16.

48   Henri Bergson, *Creative Evolution* (London: Macmillan, 1922), p. 344.

49   *Stephen Hero*, p. 77.

50   Harry Levin, *James Joyce. A Critical Introduction* (London: Faber, 1960), p. 35.

51   See Arthur Koestler, *The Act of Creation* (New York: Macmillan, 1964), p. 176.

52   Forrest Read (ed.), *Pound/Joyce. The Letters of Ezra Pound to James Joyce* (New York, NY: New Directions, 1970), p. 105.

53   *Pound/Joyce*, p. 206, my translation.

54   *Selected Letters of James Joyce*, ed. Richard Ellmann (London: Faber and Faber, 1992), p. 271. I am using this translation in preference to that of *Letters I*, pp. 146–7.

55 See *Part. An.* 1, 4, 644a12–23.

56 *Met.* 14, 6, 1093b18–19.

57 *Met.* 12, 4, 1070a31–3: τὰ δ᾽ αἴτια καὶ αἱ ἀρχαὶ ἄλλα ἄλλων ἔστιν ὥς, ἔστι δ᾽ ὡς, ἂν καθόλου λέγῃ τις καὶ κατ᾽ ἀναλογίαν, ταὐτὰ πάντων. Trans. Treddenick modified, p. 131.

58 Richard Ellmann, '*Ulysses*: A Short History', in James Joyce, *Ulysses* (Harmondsworth: Penguin, 1972), p. 719.

59 *Met.* 14, 3, 1090b19–20. See Fran O'Rourke, *Allwisest Stagyrite. Joyce's Quotations from Aristotle* (Dublin: The National Library of Ireland, 2005), p. 45.

60 *Ulysses* 9.1046–7

61 *Met.* 12, 10, 1075a16–19.

62 Herbert S. Gorman, *James Joyce. His First Forty Years* (New York: Viking Press, 1924), p. 115.

63 *Poet.* 22, 1459a5–8.

64 *Boswell's Life of Johnson*, George Birkbeck Hill (ed.), rev. L.F. Powell, vol. 3 (Oxford: Clarendon Press, 1934), p. 174.

65 *Ulysses* 16.1579–81.

66 James Joyce, *Letters* I, ed. Stuart Gilbert (New York, NY: Viking, 1966), p. 167.

67 Ernestus Diehl, *Anthologia Lyrica Graeca* (Leipzig: Teubner, 1936), vol. 1, p. 241, frag. 103.

68 Jean-Paul Sartre, 'Time in Faulkner: *The Sound and the Fury*', in Frederick J. Hoffman and Olga W. Vickery (eds), *William Faulkner: Three Decades of Criticism* (New York: Harcourt, Brace & World, 1963), p. 226.

69 *Critical Writings*, p. 145.

70 *Stephen Hero*, p. 171.

71 *Gen. An.* 1, 22, 730b29–32.

72 *Part. An.* 1, 1, 639b19–21. Peck's translation modified.

73 Padraic Colum, *Our Friend James Joyce*, p. 150.

74 Ellmann, *James Joyce*, p. 124 (based on Herbert Gorman's notes).

75 *Poet.* 7, 1450b34–35. See *EN* 4, 3, 1123b6: 'Beauty implies a good-sized body, and little people may be neat and well-proportioned but cannot be beautiful.'

76 *Letters II*, p. 35.

77 See Ellmann, *James Joyce*, p. 124: 'This corner Joyce had for himself, and he proceeded to point out to Synge the play's Aristotelian defects. In particular he objected to its catastrophe, because it was brought about by an animal (a pony) rather than by the sea, and to its brevity. It was, he said, a tragic poem, not a drama. He told Synge to make a lasting argument or make none.'

78 *Critical Writings*, p. 250.

79 *Met.* 7, 1, 1028a10.

80 The Greek word '*entelēs*' means 'complete' or 'full' (it contains the word '*telos*', i.e. goal or end).

81 *De An.* 2, 1, 412b5–6. See also *U* 15.106–7: 'the first entelechy, the structural rhythm'.

82 Edmund Spenser, 'A Hymn in Honour of Beauty'.

83 Isaac Newton, *Mathematical Principles of Natural Philosophy* (Berkeley: University of California Press, 1960), p. xvii.

84 Aristotle defines sensation as the power to receive a sensible form without the matter, as wax takes on the shape of a signet-ring without the gold; it 'takes the figure of the gold or bronze but not as bronze or gold'. See *De An.* 2, 12, 424a17–21, quoted by Joyce in his Paris notebook. Is it possible that Joyce took the celebrated phrase 'bronze by gold', central to 'Sirens', from Aristotle's psychology?

85 *De An.* 3, 5, 430a23.

86 See O'Rourke, *Allwisest Stagyrite*, pp. 19–21. A possible explanation for this misquotation is that Joyce was misled by the line of an Irish song he frequently sang, *An Cruiscín Lán*, a line of which runs: 'Immortal and divine great Bacchus god of wine'. This song is included on the CD *JoyceSong. Irish Songs of James Joyce*, Fran O'Rourke and John Feeley, Live Concert Monaco, St Patrick's Day 2015. See www.joycesong.info.

87 *Ulysses* 2.380–1.

88 *Ulysses* 2.48–51.

89 Aristotle quotes the poet Agathon: 'Of this alone even God is deprived, the power of making things that are past never to have been.' See *EN* 6, 2, 1139b8–11. An echo and variation of Aristotle is found when Stephen later 'ponders things that were not: what Caesar would have lived to do had he believed the soothsayer: what might have been: possibilities of the possible as possible' (*U* 9.348–50). The contrast hinges upon Aristotle's definition of movement as mistakenly understood by Joyce. See also *U* 9.1041–42: 'He found in the world without as actual what was in his world within as possible.'

90 *Ulysses* 2.67–70.

91 *Métaphysique d'Aristote*, traduction J. Barthélemy-Saint-Hilaire (Paris: Librairie Germer-Baillière, 1879), 3 vols.

92 J. Tricot, *Aristote. La Métaphysique*, tome I, Paris: Vrin, 1940, p. x. Tricot correctly translates the relevant passages from the *Metaphysics*: 'Etant donné la distinction, en chaque genre, de ce qui est en puissance et de ce qui est en entéléchie, l'acte de ce qui est en puissance en tant que tel, je l'appelle mouvement' (11, 9, 1065b16); 'c'est l'entéléchie de l'être en puissance, en tant qu'il est en puissance, qui constitue le mouvement' (11, 9, 1065b33). While Barthélemy-Sainte-Hilaire translated many of Aristotle's writings, they are generally ignored in the scholarly literature on Aristotle.

93 See O'Rourke, *Alwisest Stagyrite*, pp. 40–2.

94 *Ulysses* 2.74–6.

95   Sheldon Brivic, *Joyce the Creator* (Madison: University of Wisconsin Press, 1985), p. 46.

96   *Ulysses* 3.1.

97   *Ulysses* 3.13.

98   Robert McAlmon, *Being Geniuses Together* (London: Hogarth Press, 1984), p. 26.

99   *De An.* 3, 3, 428b18.

100 *Ulysses* 3.1–2.

101 *Ulysses* 15. 3629–31.

102 *Ulysses* 9.85–6.

103 Frank Budgen, *James Joyce and the Making of Ulysses*, p. 109.

104 *Ulysses* 9.48–53.

105 *Ulysses* 9.80–1.

106 *Ulysses* 9.89.

107 *Stephen Hero*, p. 33.

108 *Ulysses* 9.84–5.

109 *Ulysses* 9.212.

110 *Ulysses* 9.213.

111 See Joyce's review of *Humanism: Philosophical Essays*, by F.C.S. Schiller, 'the leading European exponent of William James's philosophy', *Critical Writings*, pp. 135–6.

112 William James, *The Principles of Psychology* (London: Macmillan, 1901), vol. 1, p. xi. See p. 342: 'The passing Thought then seems to be the Thinker.'

113 *Ulysses* 15.107. The Aristotelian associations are continued in the ensuing exchange between Lynch and Stephen: 'Pornosophical philotheology. Metaphysics in Mecklenburgh street! [...] Even the allwisest Stagyrite was bitted, bridled and mounted by a light of love' (*U* 15.109–12). The latter reference to Aristotle, native of the Macedonian town of Stagira, is to the medieval conflation of Aristotle with the protagonist in a tale, imported from the East, of a wise man who, attempting to seduce a woman, allows himself to be bridled, mounted, and whipped.

114 *Stephen Hero*, p. 175.

115 *The Notebooks of Samuel Taylor Coleridge* I, Kathleen Coburn (ed.) (New York, NY: Pantheon, 1957), p. 1770.

116 Anthony Burgess, *Joysprick. An Introduction to the Language of James Joyce* (London: Andre Deutsch, 1979), p. 48.

117 Mario Vargas Llosa, *Bloom* (Dublin: Kingstown Press, 1966), p. 17.

118 Letter of Harriet Weaver to James Joyce, 4 February 1927, cited by Ellmann, *James Joyce*, p. 590.

119 Letter of James Joyce to Harriet Weaver, 24 November 1926. *Letters III*, ed. Richard Ellmann (New York, NY: Viking, 1966), p. 146.

120 Sheldon Brivic, *Joyce the Creator*, p. 50.

121 *Finnegans Wake* 49.35–50.1.

122 *Ulysses* 15.3928.
123 Seamus Deane, Introduction, James Joyce. *Finnegans Wake* (London: Penguin, 1992), p. xii.
124 *Finnegans Wake* 306.17–18.
125 *Poet.* 1461b11–12, Butcher's translation, used by Joyce.
126 *Finnegans Wake* 110.9–21.
127 *Finnegans Wake* 417.16.

ARISTOTLE BIBLIOGRAPHY

I have made use of the translations listed below, primarily those of the Loeb Classical Library (LCL), published by Harvard University Press (Cambridge, MA) and Heinemann (London), and the revised Oxford translation of the *Complete Works of Aristotle* (CW), edited by Jonathan Barnes (Princeton University Press, 1984). Since there are numerous reprints of the Loeb volumes I have not given individual dates of publication. The order in the list below follows the standard Bekker edition of the Prussian Academy of Sciences of Berlin (1831–1870). Line references are to Bekker except for the *Rhetoric* and *Poetics*, where they are to Kassel. Aristotle's works are traditionally known under the Latin titles with which they were known during the Middle Ages. An exception is the *Constitution of Athens*, discovered in Egypt in the late nineteenth century.

De Interpretatione (*De Int.*)	*On Interpretation*, trans. J.L. Ackrill, *CW* 1, pp. 25–38.
Analytica Priora (*An. Pr.*)	*Prior Analytics*, trans. A.J. Jenkinson, *CW* 1, pp. 39–113.
Analytica Posteriora (*An. Post.*)	*Posterior Analytics*, trans. Hugh Tredennick (LCL).
Topica (*Top.*)	*Topica*, trans. E.S. Forster (LCL), 1989.
Physica (*Phys.*)	*Physics*, trans. Philip. H. Wicksteed & Francis M. Cornford (LCL).
	Physics, trans. R. Hardie and R. Gaye, *CW* 1, pp. 315–446.
De Caelo	*On the Heavens*, trans. J.L. Stocks, *CW* 1, pp. 447–511.
	On the Heavens, trans. W.K.C. Guthrie (LCL).
De Generatione et Corruptione (*De Gen. et Corr.*)	*On Generation and Corruption*, trans. H.H. Joachim, *CW* 1, pp. 512–54.
Meteorologica (*Met.*)	*Meteorology*, trans. E.W. Webster, *CW* 1, pp. 555–625.

De Anima (*De An.*)	*On the Soul*, trans. W.S. Hett (LCL).
	On the Soul, trans. J.A. Smith, *CW* 1, pp. 641–92.
De Sensu (*Sens.*)	*Sense and Sensibilia*, trans. J.I. Beare, *CW* 1, pp. 693–713.
De Somno (*Somn.*)	*On Sleep*, trans. J.I. Beare, *CW* 1, pp. 721–8.
De Insomniis (*Insomn.*)	*On Dreams*, trans. J.I. Beare, *CW* 1, pp. 729–35.
De Juventute (*Juv.*)	*Of Youth, Old Age, Life and Death, and Respiration*, trans. G.R.T. Ross, *CW* 1, pp. 745–63.
Historia Animalium (*Hist. An.*)	*History of Animals*, trans. D'Arcy W. Thompson, *CW* 1, pp. 774–993.
	History of Animals I–III, trans. A.L. Peck (LCL).
	History of Animals IV–VI, trans. A.L. Peck (LCL).
	History of Animals VII–X, trans. D.M. Balme (LCL).
De Partibus Animalium (*Part. An.*)	*Parts of Animals*, trans. W. Ogle, *CW* 1, pp. 994–1086.
	Parts of Animals, trans. A.L. Peck (LCL).
De Motu Animalium (*Motu An.*)	*Movement of Animals*, trans. E.S. Forster (LCL).
De Incessu Animalium (*Inc. An.*)	*Progression of Animals*, trans. E.S. Forster (LCL).
De Generatione Animalium (*Gen. An.*)	*Generation of Animals*, trans. A. Platt, *CW* 1, pp. 1111–218.
Problemata	*Problems*, trans. E.S. Forster, *CW* 2, pp. 1319–527.
Metaphysica (*Met.*)	*Metaphysics*, trans. W.D. Ross, *CW* 2, pp. 1552–728.
	Metaphysics, trans. Hugh Tredennick (LCL).
	Metaphysics, trans. H.G. Apostle (Grinnell, IA: Peripatetic Press, 1979).
Ethica Nicomachea (*EN*)	*Nicomachean Ethics*, trans. H. Rackham (LCL).
	Nicomachean Ethics, trans. W.D. Ross, revised J.O. Urmson, *CW* 2, pp. 1729–867.
	Nicomachean Ethics, trans. Terence Irwin (Indianapolis: Hackett, 1999).

Ethica Eudemia (EE)	*Eudemian Ethics*, trans. H. Rackham (LCL).
Politica (Pol.)	*Politics*, trans. H. Rackham (LCL).
	Politics, trans. B. Jowett, *CW* 2, pp. 1986–2129.
Rhetorica (Rhet.)	*The 'Art' of Rhetoric*, trans. John Henry Freese (LCL).
	Rhetoric, trans. W. Rhys Roberts, *CW* 2, pp. 2152–269.
	Aristotelis Ars Rhetorica, ed. Rudolf Kassel (Berlin: de Gruyter, 1976).
Poetica (Poet.)	*Aristotle's Theory of Poetry and Fine Art*, S.H. Butcher *Art* (London: Macmillan, 1923).
	Poetics, trans. W. Hamilton Fyfe (LCL).
	Aristotelis de Arte Poetica Liber, ed. Rudolf Kassel (Oxford: Clarendon Press, 1966).
	Poetics, Malcolm Heath (London: Penguin, 1996).
	Poetics, trans. Ingram Bywater, *CW* 2, pp. 2316–40.
	The Poetics of Aristotle, trans. Stephen Halliwell (London: Duckworth, 1987).
	Poetics, trans. Stephen Halliwell (LCL), 1995.
Constitution of Athens (Ath. Const.)	Trans. H. Rackham (LCL).
	Trans. F.G. Kenyon, *CW* 2, pp. 2341–83.
Fragments	Valentin Rose (ed.), *Fragmenta* (Stuttgart: Teubner, 1967).

General Bibliography

Ackrill, J.L. *Essays on Plato and Aristotle* (Oxford: Clarendon Press, 1997).

Alan of Lille. *De planctu naturae. Patrologia Latina*, vol. 210 (Paris: Migne, 1855).

Allan, D.J. *The Philosophy of Aristotle* (Oxford: Oxford University Press, 1952).

Annas, Julia. 'Plato and Aristotle on Friendship and Altruism', *Mind* 86 (1977), pp. 532–54.

Aquinas, Thomas. *De Spiritualibus Creaturis*, in *Quaestiones Disputate*, vol. 2, eds M. Calcaterra and T.S. Centi (Turin: Marietti, 1965).

—— *Commentary on Aristotle's De Anima* (Notre Dame, IN: Dumb Ox, 1994), trans. Kenelm Foster, O.P. and Sylvester Humphries, O.P.

—— *Summa Contra Gentiles*. Trans. Joseph Rickaby S.J., in *Of God and His Creatures* (London: Burns & Oates, 1905).

—— *Summa Contra Gentiles*, eds C. Pera, P. Marc, and P. Caramello (Turin: Marietti, 1961–67).

—— *De Mixtione Elementorum*, in Raymund M. Spiazzi (ed.), *Opuscula Philosophica* (Turin: Marietti, 1954), trans. V. Larkin, 'On the Combining of the Elements', *Isis* 51/1 (1960), pp. 67–72.

—— *In De Anima*, ed. A.M. Pirotta (Turin: Marietti, 1959).

—— *In Metaphysicorum Aristotelis Expositio*, eds M.-R. Cathala OP & R.M. Spiazzi (Turin: Marietti, 1950).

—— *Summa Theologiae* I, ed. P. Caramello (Turin: Marietti, 1952).

Arendt, Hannah. *The Human Condition* (Chicago: University of Chicago Press, 1958).

Atkins, J.W.H., *Literary Criticism in Antiquity. A Sketch of its Development*, vol. 1 (London: Methuen, 1952).

Avicenna. *Liber de philosophia prima sive scientia divina*, ed. Simone Van Riet (Louvain: Peeters / Leiden: Brill, 1977).

Ayala, Francisco J. 'Teleological Explanations in Evolutionary Biology', *Philosophy of Science* 37/1 (March, 1970), pp. 1–15.

Bacon, Francis. *Works* I, eds James Spedding, Robert Leslie Ellis & Douglas Denon Heath (New York: Garrett Press, 1968).

—— *Works* IV, eds James Spedding, Robert Leslie Ellis & Douglas Denon Heath (New York: Garrett Press, 1968).

Baldry, H.C. *The Unity of Mankind in Greek Thought* (Cambridge: Cambridge University Press, 1965).

Balme, David. 'Aristotle's Biology was not Essentialist', *Archiv für Geschichte der*

Philosophie 62 (1980), pp. 1–12. Reprinted with two appendices in Allan Gotthelf and James G. Lennox (eds), *Philosophical Issues in Aristotle's Biology* (Cambridge: Cambridge University Press, 1987), pp. 291–312.

Barnes, Jonathan. *Aristotle. A Very Short Introduction* (Oxford: Oxford University Press, 2000).

Barthélemy-Saint-Hilaire, J. *Métaphysique d'Aristote*, traduction (Paris: Librairie Germer-Baillière, 1879), 3 vols.

Bergson, Henri. *Creative Evolution* (London: Macmillan, 1922).

Berti, Enrico, 'Aristote était-il un penseur dualiste?', *Thêta-Pi* 2 (1973), pp. 73–111;

Bien, Günther. *Die Grundlegung der politischen Philosophie bei Aristoteles* (Freiburg/München: Alber, 1973).

Black, Max. *Models and Metaphors. Studies in Language and Philosophy* (Ithaca: Cornell University Press, 1962).

—— 'More About Metaphor', *Dialectica* 31 (1977), pp. 431–57.

—— 'How Metaphors Work: A Reply to Donald Davidson', *Critical Inquiry* 6/1 (Autumn 1979), pp. 131–43.

Blanshard, Brand. *Reason and Analysis* (London: George Allen & Unwin: 1962).

Bodéüs, Richard. 'L'animal politique et l'animal économique', in A. Motte & C. Rutten (eds), *Aristotelica. Mélanges offerts à M. De Corte* (Bruxelles: Éditions Ousia / Liège: Presses Universitaires, 1985), pp. 65–81.

Bolton, Robert. 'Aristotle on Essence and Necessity in Science', *Proceedings of the Boston Area Colloquium in Ancient Philosophy* 13 (1997), pp. 113–38.

—— 'The Material Cause: Matter and Explanation in Aristotle's Natural Science', in W. Kullmann & S. Föllinger (eds), *Aristotelische Biologie. Intentionen, Methoden, Ergebnisse* (Stuttgart: Steiner, 1997), pp. 97–126.

Bonitz, Hermann. *Index Aristotelicus* (Berlin: De Gruyter, 1975).

Borach, Georges. 'Gespräche mit James Joyce', in James Joyce, *Die Toten* (Zürich: Diogenes, 1948), pp. 329–34.

—— 'Conversations with James Joyce', trans. Joseph Prescott, *College English*, 15/6 (Mar. 1954), pp. 325–7.

Boswell, James. *Life of Johnson*, ed. George Birkbeck Hill, rev. L.F. Powell, vol. 3 (Oxford: Clarendon Press, 1934).

Boylan, Michael. *Method and Practice in Aristotle's Biology* (Washington, DC: University of America Press, 1983).

Bradley, F.H. *The Principles of Logic*, vol. 2 (Oxford: Oxford University Press, 1967).

Brivic, Sheldon. *Joyce the Creator* (Madison: The University of Wisconsin Press, 1985).

Broch, Hermann. *Gesammelte Werke* 10 (Zürich: Rhein-Verlag, 1967).

Budgen, Frank. *James Joyce and the Making of Ulysses* (Oxford: Oxford University Press, 1991).

Burgess, Anthony. *Joysprick. An Introduction to the Language of James Joyce* (London: Andre Deutsch, 1979).

Burnet, John. *Aristotle on Education* (Cambridge: Cambridge University Press, 1928).

Butcher, S.H. *Aristotle's Theory of Poetry and Fine Art* (London: Macmillan, 1902).

Bywater, Ingram (trans.), *Aristotle's Poetics* (Oxford: Clarendon Press, 1909).

Camus, Albert. *L'homme révolté* (Paris: Gallimard, 1951).

Charles, David. *Aristotle on Meaning and Essence* (Oxford: Oxford University Press, 2001).

Chesterton G.K. *Heretics* (London: Bodley Head, 1928).

Chomsky, Noam. *Reflections on Language* (London: Fontana, 1976).

Clark, Ronald William. *Einstein: The Life and Times* (New York: Wings Books, 1995).

Clark, Stephen R.L. *Aristotle's Man. Speculations upon Aristotelian Anthropology* (Oxford: Clarendon Press, 1983).

—— *Biology and Christian Ethics* (Cambridge: Cambridge University Press, 2000).

Clarke, William Norris. *The Universe as Journey. Conversations with W. Norris Clarke, S.J.* (New York: Fordham University Press, 1988).

Code, Alan. 'The Priority of Final Causes over Efficient Causes in Aristotle's PA', in W. Kullmann & S. Föllinger (eds), *Aristotelische Biologie. Intentionen, Methoden, Ergebnisse* (Stuttgart: Franz Steiner, 1997), pp. 127–43.

Coleridge, Samuel Taylor. *The Notebooks of Samuel Taylor Coleridge* I, ed. Kathleen Coburn (New York: Pantheon Books, 1957).

—— *The Friend* I, ed. Barbara E. Rooke, Collected Works 4 (London: Routledge & Kegan Paul, 1993).

—— *Biographia Literaria* I, Collected Works 7 (London: Routledge & Kegan Paul, 1983).

—— *Aids to Reflection*, ed. John Beer, Collected Works 9 (London: Routledge & Kegan Paul, 1993).

Colum, Mary & Colum, Padraic. *Our Friend James Joyce* (London: Victor Gollancz, 1959).

Colum, Padraic. *The Road Round Ireland* (New York: Macmillan, 1926).

Connell, Desmond. *Essays in Metaphysics* (Dublin: Four Courts, 1996).

Connell, Sophia M. 'Toward an Integrated Approach to Aristotle as a Biological Philosopher', *The Review of Metaphysics* 55/2 (December, 2001), pp. 297–322.

Connolly, Thomas E. (ed.), *Scribbledehobble, the Ur-Workbook for* Finnegans Wake (Evanston: Northwestern University Press, 1961).

Cooper, John M. 'Political Animals and Civic Friendship', in G. Patzig (ed.), *Aristoteles' Politik* (Göttingen: Vandenhoeck & Ruprecht, 1990), pp. 221–48.

—— *Reason and Emotion. Essays on Ancient Moral Psychology and Ethical Theory* (Princeton: Princeton University Press, 1999).

Cope, E.M. *The 'Rhetoric' of Aristotle, with a Commentary*, rev. and ed. J.E. Sandys, vol. 3 (Cambridge: Cambridge University Press, 1877).

Croce, B. *The Philosophy of Giambattista Vico*, trans. R.G. Collingwood (New York: Russell & Russell, 1964).

Curran, C.P. *James Joyce Remembered* (London: Oxford University Press, 1968).

D'Arcy, Wentworth Thompson. *On Growth and Form* (Cambridge: Cambridge University Press, 1942).

Darwin, Charles. *The Variation of Animals and Plants under Domestication*, vol. 2 (London: John Murray, 1868).

—— *The Life and Letters of Charles Darwin*, ed. Francis Darwin, vol. 3 (London: John Murray, 1888).

—— *On the Origin of Species* (London: Penguin, 1985).

—— *The Descent of Man, and Selection in Relation to Sex* (London: Penguin, 2004).

Dawkins, Richard. *The Blind Watchmaker* (London: Penguin, 1991).

—— 'God's Utility Function', *Scientific American* 273/5 (November 1995), pp. 62–7.

—— *A River out of Eden* (London: Weidenfeld & Nicholson, 1995).

—— 'You Can't Have It Both Ways: Irreconcilable Differences?', *Skeptical Inquirer* 23/4 (July 1999), pp. 62–4.

—— *The Selfish Gene* (Oxford: Oxford University Press, 2009).

Day-Lewis, Cecil. *The Poetic Image* (London: Jonathan Cape, 1947).

De Chardin, Teilhard. *The Phenomenon of Man* (London: Collins, 1960).

De Lubac, Henri. *Sur les chemins de Dieu* (Paris: Aubier, 1956).

—— *The Discovery of God* (New York: Kennedy, 1960).

De Ste Croix, G.E.M., 'Aristotle on History and Poetry (*Poetics*, 9, 1451a36–b11)', in Amélie Oksenberg Rorty (ed.), *Essays on Aristotle's Poetics* (Princeton: Princeton University Press, 1992), pp. 23–32.

De Vio, T. (Cardinal Cajetan). *Scripta Philosophica (De Nominum Analogia, De Conceptu Entis)*, ed. P. Zammit (Rome: Angelicum, 1952).

—— *The Analogy of Names and the Concept of Being*, trans. E.A. Bushinski (Pittsburgh: Duquesne University Press, 1953).

Deane, Seamus. Introduction, James Joyce, *Finnegans Wake* (London: Penguin, 1992), pp. vii–xlx.

Delbrück, Max. 'Aristotle—totle—totle', in J. Monod and E. Borek (eds), *Of Microbes and Life* (New York: Columbia University Press, 1971), pp. 50–5.

Dennett, Daniel. *Darwin's Dangerous Idea. Evolution and the Meanings of Life* (London: Penguin, 1995).

Depew, David J. & Weber, Bruce H. (eds), *Darwinism Evolving* (Cambridge, MA: MIT Press, 1995).

Depew, David J. 'Humans and Other Political Animals in Aristotle's *History of Animals*', *Phronesis* 40/2 (1995), pp. 156–81.

—— 'Etiological Approaches to Biological Aptness in Aristotle and Darwin', in W. Kullmann & S. Föllinger (eds), *Aristotelische Biologie. Intentionen, Methoden, Ergebnisse* (Stuttgart: Franz Steiner, 1997), pp. 209–27.

Dewey, John. *The Influence of Darwin on Philosophy and Other Essays* (New York: Henry Holt and Company, 1910).

Diehl, Ernestus, ed. *Anthologia Lyrica Graeca*, vol. 1 (Leipzig: Teubner, 1936).

Diels, Hermann & Kranz, Walter. *Die Fragmente der Vorsokratiker* I (Zürich: Weidmann, 1992).

Diogenes Laertius. *Lives of Eminent Philosophers*, vol. 1. trans. R.D. Hicks (Cambridge, MA: Harvard University Press, 1995).

Dudley, John. *The Evolution of Chance in the Physics and Ethics of Aristotle* (Amersfoort: Acco, 1997).

—— *Dio e contemplazione in Aristotele. Il fondamento metafisico dell' Etica Nicomachea* (Milano: Vita e Pensiero, 1999).

Düring, Ingemar. *Aristotle in the Ancient Biographical Tradition* (Göteborg: Elanders Boktryckeri 1957).

—— *Aristotle's Protrepticus. An Attempt at Reconstruction* (Gothenburg: Acta Universitatis, 1961).

—— *Aristoteles. Darstellung und Interpretation seines Denkens* (Heidelberg: Carl Winter, 1966).

Eco, Umberto. *Semiotics and the Philosophy of Language* (London: Macmillan, 1984).

Edmonds, J.M., ed. *Lyra Graeca* II (Cambridge, MA: Harvard University Press, 1958).

Eliot, George. *The Mill on the Floss* (Oxford: Clarendon Press, 1980).

Ellis, Brian. *Scientific Essentialism* (Cambridge: Cambridge University Press, 2001).

—— *The Philosophy of Nature. A Guide to the New Essentialism* (Chesham: Acumen, 2002).

Ellmann, Richard. *The Identity of Yeats* (London: Faber and Faber, 1968).

—— '*Ulysses*: A Short History', in James Joyce, *Ulysses* (Harmondsworth: Penguin, 1972), pp. 705–19.

—— *Ulysses on the Liffey* (London: Faber and Faber, 1974).

—— James Joyce (Oxford: Oxford University Press, 1983).

Else, Gerald F. *Aristotle's Poetics: The Argument* (Leiden: Brill, 1957).

Emerson, Ralph Waldo. *The Selected Writings of Ralph Waldo Emerson*, ed. Brooks Atkinson. (New York: Modern Library, 1950).

Feuillerat, Albert (ed.), *The Prose Works of Sir Philip Sidney* III (Cambridge: Cambridge University Press, 1963).

Ficino, Marsilio. *Theologia Platonica*, XIII, 3 (Hildesheim: Olms, 1975).

Finley, M.I. *Politics in the Ancient World* (Cambridge: Cambridge University Press, 1991).

Frankfurt, Harry G. 'Freedom of the Will and the Concept of a Person', *Journal of Philosophy* 68 (1971), pp. 5–20.

Freeman, Kathleen. *Ancilla to the Pre-Socratic Philosophers* (Oxford: Basil Blackwell, 1962).

Frege, Gottlob. *Begriffsschrift und Andere Aufsätze* (Hildesheim: Olms, 1964).

Friar, Kimon. *Modern Greek Poetry* (New York: Simon Schuster, 1973).

Furley, D. J., & Nehamas, A. (eds). *Aristotle's* Rhetoric. *Philosophical Essays* (Princeton: Princeton University Press, 1994).

Furth, Montgomery. *Substance, Form and Psyche: An Aristotelian Metaphysics* (Cambridge: Cambridge University Press, 1988).

Futuyma, D.J. *Evolution* (Sunderland, MA: Sinauer Associates, 1986).

Ghiselin, Michael. 'Darwin's Language may Seem Teleological, but his Thinking is Another Matter', *Biology and Philosophy* 9 (1994), pp. 489–92.

Gigon, Olof. *Aristoteles, Politik* (München: Deutscher Taschenbuch Verlag, 1973).

Goethe, Johann Wolfgang von. *Maximen und Reflexionen*, Werke 12 (Hamburg: Wegner, 1967).

Gogarty, Oliver St John. *Mourning Becomes Mrs. Spendlove* (New York: Creative Age, 1948).

Gorman, Herbert S. *James Joyce. His First Forty Years* (New York: Viking Press, 1924).

—— *James Joyce* (New York: Farrar & Rinehart, 1939).

Gotthelf, Allan and Lennox, James G. (eds), *Philosophical Issues in Aristotle's Biology* (Cambridge: Cambridge University Press, 1987).

Gotthelf, Allan. 'Aristotle's Conception of Final Causality', *The Review of Metaphysics* 30/2 (1976–7), pp. 226–54. Reprinted with a postscript in A. Gotthelf and J.G. Lennox (eds), *Philosophical Issues in Aristotle's Biology* (Cambridge: Cambridge University Press, 1987), pp. 204–42.

—— 'Understanding Aristotle's Teleology', in R.F. Hassing (ed.), *Final Causality in Nature and Human Affairs* (Washington, DC: Catholic University of America Press, 1997), pp. 71–82.

—— 'Darwin on Aristotle', *Journal of the History of Biology* 32 (1999), pp. 3–31.

Gottschalk, H.B. *Heraclides of Pontus* (Oxford: Clarendon Press, 1980).

Gould, Stephen Jay. 'Self-Help for a Hedgehog Stuck on a Molehill', *Evolution* 51/3 (1997), pp. 1020–3.

—— *The Panda's Thumb. More Reflections in Natural History* (New York: Norton, 1980).

Grene, Marjorie. *The Understanding of Nature* (Dordrecht: Reidel, 1974).

Griswold, Charles L. Jr. *Self-Knowledge in Plato's Phaedrus* (New Haven: Yale University Press, 1986).

Guthrie, W.K.C. *In the Beginning. Some Greek Views on the Origin of Life and the Early State of Man* (London: Methuen, 1957).

Guthrie, W.K.C. *The Greek Philosophers from Thales to Aristotle* (London: Methuen, 1978).

—— *A History of Philosophy VI, Aristotle: an Encounter* (Cambridge: Cambridge University Press, 1981).

Hall, Barry G. 'Evolution of New Metabolic Functions in Laboratory Organisms', in M. Nei and R.K. Koehn (eds), *Evolution of Genes and Proteins* (Sunderland, MA: Sinauer Associates, 1983), pp. 234–57.

—— 'Evolution on a Petri Dish', *Evolutionary Biology* 15 (1982) pp. 85–150.

Halliwell, Stephen. *The Poetics of Aristotle. Translation and Commentary* (Chapel Hill: University of North Carolina Press, 1987).

—— 'Pleasure, Understanding, and Emotion in Aristotle's *Poetics*', in Amélie Oksenberg Rorty (ed.), *Essays on Aristotle's Poetics* (Princeton: Princeton University Press, 1992), pp. 241–60.

—— 'Aristotelian Mimesis Reevaluated', in Lloyd Gerson (ed.), *Aristotle. Critical Assessments*, vol. 4 (London: Routledge, 1999) pp. 316–36.

—— 'Aristotelian Mimesis and Human Understanding', in Ø. Andersen and J. Haarberg (eds), *Making Sense of Aristotle. Essays in Poetics* (London: Duckworth, 2001), pp. 87–107.

—— *The Aesthetics of Mimesis. Ancient Texts and Modern Problems* (Princeton: Princeton University Press, 2002).

Hamlyn, D.W. *Aristotle, De Anima* (Oxford: Clarendon Press, 1993).

Hartmann, Nicolai. *Aesthetics*, trans. Eugene Kelly (Berlin: De Gruyter, 2014).

Heath, Malcolm. 'The Universality of Poetry in Aristotle's *Poetics*', *Classical Quarterly* 41 (1991), pp. 389–402.

—— *Aristotle. Poetics* (London: Penguin, 1996).

Hegel, Georg Wilhelm Friedrich. *Vorlesungen über die Geschichte der Philosophie* II (Frankfurt am Main: Suhrkamp, 1986).

Heidegger, Martin. *Erläuterungen zu Hölderlins Dichtung* (Frankfurt am Main: Klostermann, 1971).

—— *Wegmarken* (Frankfurt am Main: Klostermann, 1976).

Herodotus, *The Persian Wars*, trans. A.D. Godley (Cambridge, MA: Harvard University Press, 1960).

Hesiod. *Theogony*, trans. Glenn W. Most (Cambridge, MA: Harvard University Press, 2006).

Highet, Gilbert. *The Art of Teaching* (New York: Vintage, 1950).

Hill, George Birkbeck (ed.), *Boswell's Life of Johnson*, vol. 3 (Oxford: Clarendon Press, 1934).

Ho, Mae-Won & Saunders, Peter (eds.), *Beyond Neo-Darwinism: An Introduction to the New Evolutionary Paradigm* (London: The Academic Press, 1984).

Hodge, M.J.S. 'Darwin as a Lifelong Generation Theorist', in D. Kohn (ed.), *The Darwinian Heritage* (Princeton: Princeton University Press, 1985), pp. 207–43.

Höffe, Otfried (ed.), *Aristoteles. Politik* (Berlin: Akademie Verlag, 2001).

——'Aristoteles' Politische Anthropologie' in Otfried Höffe (ed.), *Aristoteles. Politik*. Berlin: Akademie Verlag, 2001), pp. 21–35.

Horace. *Satires, Epistles, Ars Poetica*, trans. H.R. Fairclough (Cambridge, MA: Harvard University Press, 1942).

House, Humphry. *Aristotle's Poetics* (London: Rupert Hart-Davis, 1956).

Hübner, Johannes. 'Die Aristotelische Konzeption der Seele als Aktivität in de Anima II 1', *Archiv für Geschichte der Philosophie* 81 (1999), pp. 1–32.

Hume, David. *A Treatise on Human Nature*, ed. L.A. Selby-Bigge (Oxford: Clarendon Press, 1973).

—— *An Enquiry Concerning the Principles of Morals*, ed. Jerome Schneewind (Indianapolis: Hackett, 1983).

—— 'Of Suicide', in S. Copley & A. Edgal (eds), *David Hume: Selected Essays* (Oxford: Oxford University Press, 1993).

Iamblichus. *De Vita Pythagorica*, ed. L. Deubner (Leipzig: Teubner, 1937).

Irwin, T.H. *Aristotle's First Principles* (Oxford: Clarendon Press, 1990).

Jaeger, Werner. *Aristotle. Fundamentals of the History of his Development* (Oxford: Oxford University Press, 1934).

—— *Early Christianity and Greek Paideia* (Oxford: Oxford University Press, 1962).

James, William. Review of Wilhelm Wundt, *Grundzüge der physiologischen Psychologie*, *North American Review* 121 (1875), pp. 195–201.

—— *The Principles of Psychology*, vol. 2 (New York: Dover, 1950).

Johncox, Louise. 'Trip to the Top', *The Times*, 28 Oct. 1995.

Joyce, James. *Die Toten* (Zürich: Diogenes, 1948).

—— *Ulysses*, ed. Hans Walter Gabler with Wolfhard Steppe and Claus Melchior (New York: Vintage, 1986).

—— *Letters II*, ed. Richard Ellmann (New York: Viking, 1966),

—— *Critical Writings*, eds Ellsworth Mason and Richard Ellmann (London: Faber and Faber, 1959).

—— *Scribbledehobble, the Ur-Workbook for 'Finnegans Wake'*, ed. Thomas E. Connolly (Evanston: Northwestern University Press, 1961).

—— *Stephen Hero* (New York: New Directions, 1963).

—— *Selected Letters*, ed. Richard Ellmann (London: Faber and Faber, 1992).

—— *Finnegans Wake* (London: Penguin, 1992).

—— *A Portrait of the Artist as a Young Man*, ed. John Paul Riquelme, text ed. by Hans Walter Gabler with Walter Hettche (New York: Norton, 2007).

Joyce, Stanislaus. *The Complete Dublin Diary of Stanislaus Joyce*, ed. George H. Healey (Ithaca: Cornell University Press, 1971).

Kahn, Charles H. 'Aristotle and Altruism', *Mind* 90 (1981), pp. 20–40.

Kain, Richard M. *Fabulous Voyager. A Study of James Joyce's Ulysses* (New York: Viking Press, 1967).

Kant, Immanuel. *Critique of Pure Reason*, trans. Norman Kemp Smith (London: Macmillan, 1929).

Kaufmann, Stuart. *At Home in the Universe* (New York: Oxford University Press, 1995).

Kenner, Hugh. *Dublin's Joyce* (London: Chatto and Windus, 1955).

—— 'Joyce and the 19th Century Linguistics Explosion', Atti del Third International James Joyce Symposium, Trieste, 14–18 giugno 1971 (Trieste: Università degli Studi, Facoltà di Magistero, 1974), pp. 45–60.

Keyt, David. 'Three Fundamental Theorems in Aristotle's Politics', *Phronesis* 32 (1987), pp. 54–79.

Kierkegaard, Søren. *Philosophical Fragments* (Oxford: Oxford University Press, 1936).

Kirby, J.T. 'Aristotle on Metaphor', *American Journal of Philology* 118 (1997), pp. 517–54.

Kirk, G.S. & Raven, J.E., *The Presocratic Philosophers* (Cambridge: Cambridge University Press, 1977).

Kitcher, Philip *Vaulting Ambition* (Cambridge, MA: MIT Press, 1985).

Koestler, Arthur. *The Act of Creation* (New York: Macmillan, 1964).

—— *The Ghost in the Machine* (London: Picador, 1967).

—— 'Beyond Atomism and Holism – the Concept of the Holon', in A. Koestler (ed.), *Beyond Reductionism. New Perspectives in the Life Sciences* (London: Hutchinson, 1969), pp. 192–232.

Kohl, J.G. *Travels in Ireland* (London: Bruce and Wyld, 1844).

Kraut, Richard. *Aristotle on the Human Good* (Princeton: Princeton University Press, 1989).

—— (ed.), *The Cambridge Companion to Plato* (Cambridge: Cambridge University Press, 1992).

Kullmann, Wolfgang. 'Der Mensch als Politisches Lebewesen bei Aristoteles', *Hermes* 108 (1980), pp. 419–43.

—— 'Man as a Political Animal in Aristotle', in *A Companion to Aristotle's Politics*, eds David Keyt and Fred D. Miller, Jr. (Oxford: Blackwell's, 1991), pp. 94–117.

—— *Il pensiero politico di Aristotele* (Milano: Guerini, 1992).

—— *Aristoteles und die moderne Wissenschaft* (Stuttgart: Steiner, 1998).

—— *Η Πολιτική Σκέψη του Αριστοτέλη* (Αθήνα: Μορφωτικό Ίδρυμα Εθνικής Τραπέζης, 2003).

Kyrkos, Basileios A. *Die Dichtung als Wissensproblem bei Aristoteles* (Athen: Gesellschaft für Thessalische Forschung, 1972).

Labarrière, Jean-Louis. 'Aristote penseur de la différence entre l'homme et l'animal', *Anthropozoologica*, 33–34 (2001), pp. 105–12.

Lear, Jonathan, 'Katharsis', in Amélie Oksenberg Rorty (ed.), *Essays on Aristotle's Poetics* (Princeton: Princeton University Press, 1992), pp. 315–40.

Leibniz, Gottfried Wilhelm. *Selections*, ed. Philip P. Wiener (New York: Scribner, 1951).

—— *Philosophical Papers and Letters*, vol. 2, ed. Leroy E. Loemker (Chicago: University of Chicago Press, 1956).

—— *Philosophical Writings* (London: Dent, 1973).

—— *Sämtliche Schriften und Briefe* II, 1 (Berlin: Akademie Verlag, 1987).

Lennox, James G. 'Are Aristotelian Species Eternal?', in Allan Gotthelf (ed.), *Aristotle on Nature and Living Things* (Pittsburgh: Mathesis Publications, 1985), pp. 67–94. Reprinted in Lennox, *Aristotle's Philosophy of Biology*, pp. 131–59.

—— 'Teleology', in E. Fox Keller & E.A. Lloyd (eds), *Keywords in Evolutionary Biology* (Cambridge, MA: Harvard University Press 1992), pp. 324–33.

—— 'Darwin *was* a Teleologist', *Biology and Philosophy* 8 (1993), pp. 409–21,

—— 'Nature does nothing in vain...', in H.-Chr Günther. & A. Rengakos (eds), *Beiträge zur antiken Philosophie, Festschrift für Wolfgang Kullmann* (Stuttgart: Franz Steiner, 1997), pp. 199–214. Reprinted in Lennox, *Aristotle's Philosophy of Biology*, pp. 205–23.

—— *Aristotle's Philosophy of Biology. Studies in the Origins of Life Science* (Cambridge: Cambridge University Press, 2001).

Lenski, Richard E. and Mittler, John E. (eds), 'The Directed Mutation Controversy and Neo-Darwinism', *Science* 259/5092 (Jan 8, 1993), pp. 188–94.

Levin, Harry *James Joyce. A Critical Introduction* (London: Faber, 1960).

Lewes, George Henry. *Aristotle: A Chapter from the History of Science* (London: Smith, Elder and Co, 1864).

Lewis, C.S. *The Abolition of Man* (London, Macmillan, 1947).

Lewontin, Richard. *How the Leopard Changed its Spots: The Evolution of Complexity* (New York: Charles Scribner's Sons, 1994).

Lloyd, G.E.R. *Polarity and Analogy* (Cambridge: Cambridge University Press, 1966).

—— *Aristotle: The Growth and Structure of his Thought* (Cambridge: Cambridge University Press, 1968).

—— 'Empirical Research in Aristotle's Biology', in Allan Gotthelf & James G. Lennox (eds), *Philosophical Issues in Aristotle's Biology* (Cambridge: Cambridge University Press, 1987), pp. 53–64.

—— *The Revolutions of Wisdom* (Berkeley: University of California Press, 1989).

—— *Methods and Problems in Greek Science* (Cambridge: Cambridge University Press, 1991).

—— *Aristotelian Explorations* (Cambridge: Cambridge University Press, 1996).

Luther, Martin. *Life and Letters of Martin Luther*, ed. Preserved Smith (Boston: Houghton Mifflin, 1911).

—— *Works*, vol. 2 (Philadelphia: A.J. Holman, 1915).

MacIntyre, Alasdair. 'Analogy in Metaphysics', *The Downside Review* 69 (1951), pp. 45–61.

—— 'Egoism and Altruism' *Encyclopedia of Philosophy*, vol. 2 (New York: Macmillan, 1967), pp. 462–6.

—— 'The Logical Status of Religious Belief', in Stephen Toulmin, Ronald W. Hepburn & Alasdair MacIntyre, *Metaphysical Beliefs. Three Essays* (London: SCM, 1970), pp. 157–201.

—— *After Virtue* (London: Duckworth, 1981).

—— *Whose Justice? Which Rationality?* (Notre Dame: University of Notre Dame Press, 1988).

—— *Dependent Rational Animals* (Chicago: Open Court, 2008).

—— *God, Philosophy, Universities. A Selective History of the Catholic Philosophical Tradition* (Lanham, MD: Rowman and Littlefield, 2009).

MacNeice, Louis. *Collected Poems* (London: Faber and Faber, 1979).

McAlmon, Robert. *Being Geniuses Together* (London: Hogarth Press, 1984).

McMullin, Ernan. 'The Motive for Metaphor', *Proceedings of the American Catholic Philosophical Association* 55 (1981), pp. 27–39.

Madigan, Arthur. 'Eth. Nic. 9.8: Beyond Egoism and Altruism?', in J.P. Anton & A. Preus (eds), *Essays in Ancient Greek Philosophy IV, Aristotle's Ethics* (Albany: SUNY Press, 1991), pp. 73–94.

Malebranche, Nicolas. *Oeuvres complètes*, vol. 12 (Vrin: Paris, 1965).

Mansion, Suzanne. *Le jugement d'existence chez Aristote* (Louvain: Éditions de l'Institut Supérieur de Philosophie, 1976).

Marcel, Gabriel. *Being and Having* (Westminster: Dacre Press, 1949).

Marks, Jonathan. *What It Means to Be 98% Chimpanzee: Apes, People, and Their Genes* (Berkeley: University of California Press, 2003).

Maugham, W. Somerset. *The Summing Up* (New York: Mentor, 1957).

Mayr, Ernst. *The Growth of Biological Thought. Diversity, Evolution, and Inheritance* (Cambridge, MA: Harvard University Press, 1982).

—— *Toward a New Philosophy of Biology. Observations of an Evolutionist.* (Cambridge, MA: Harvard University Press, 1988).

Meenan, James (ed.), *Centenary History of the Literary and Historical Society of University College Dublin 1855–1955* (Tralee: The Kerryman, 1955).

Mertens, Jos. 'De Artistieke Mimèsis bij Plato', *Tijdschrift voor Filosofie* 43 (1981), pp. 642–98.

Miller, Fred D., Jr, 'Aristotelian Natural Form and Theology – Reconsidered', *Proceedings of the American Catholic Philosophical Association* 49 (1995), pp. 69–79.

—— *Nature, Justice, and Rights in Aristotle's Politics* (Oxford: Clarendon Press, 1997).

Miller, Kenneth R. *Finding Darwin's God. A Scientist's Search for Common Ground Between God and Evolution* (New York: Harper Collins, 1999).

Miłosz, Czesław. *The Figured Wheel*, trans. Robert Pinsky (New York: Farrar, Straus & Giroux, 1966).

Mosby, Thomas Speed. *Little Journeys to Parnassus* (Jefferson City: Hugh Stephens, 1922).

Mulgan, R.G. 'Aristotle's Doctrine that Man is a Political Animal', *Hermes* 120 (1974), pp. 438-45.

Muller, Herbert J. *Science and Criticism: the Humanistic Tradition in Contemporary Thought* (New Haven: Yale University Press, 1943).

Murry, John Middleton. *Countries of the Mind: Essays in Literary Criticism.* Second Series (London: Oxford University Press, 1937).

Needham, Joseph. *A History of Embryology* (Cambridge: Cambridge University Press, 1959.

Needham, N.J.T.M. *Science and Civilisation in China*, vol. 1 (Cambridge: Cambridge University Press, 1954).

Nelkin, Dorothy. 'Less Selfish Than Sacred? Genes and the Religious Impulse in

Evolutionary Psychology', in H. Rose and S. Rose (eds), *Alas, Poor Darwin, Arguments against Evolutionary Psychology* (London: Vintage, 2000), pp. 14–27.

Newman, John Henry. *The Idea of a University* (London: Longmans, Green, and Co., 1889).

—— 'Poetry with reference to Aristotle's Poetics', in E.D. Jones (ed.), *English Critical Essays (Nineteenth Century)* (Oxford: Oxford University Press, 1959).

Newman, W.L. *The Politics of Aristotle*, vols. 1 & 2 (Oxford: Clarendon press, 1887).

—— *The Politics of Aristotle* , vols. 3 & 4 (Oxford: Clarendon Press, 1902).

Newton, Isaac. *Mathematical Principles of Natural Philosophy* (Berkeley: University of California Press, 1960).

Nichols, Terence. 'Aquinas' Concept of Substantial Form and Modern Science', *International Philosophical Quarterly* 36/3 (September 1996). pp. 303–18.

—— *The Sacred Cosmos* (Grand Rapids, MI: Brazos Press, 2003).

Niemann, Hans-Joachim (ed.), *Karl Popper and the Two New Secrets of Life* (Tübingen: Mohr Siebeck, 2014).

Nietzsche, Friedrich. *On the Genealogy of Morals* (New York: Vintage Books, 1967).

Nightingale, A.W. *Spectacles of Truth in Classical Greek Philosophy* (Cambridge: Cambridge University Press, 2004).

Noon, William T., S.J. *Joyce and Aquinas* (New Haven: Yale University Press, 1957).

Nussbaum, Martha. *The Fragility of Goodness. Luck and Ethics in Greek Tragedy and Philosophy* (Cambridge: Cambridge University Press, 1986).

O'Hear, Anthony. *Beyond Evolution: Human Nature and the Limits of Evolutionary Explanation* (Oxford: Clarendon Press, 1997).

O'Rahilly, Thomas F. *Dánfhocail: Irish Epigrams in Verse* (Dublin: Talbot Press, 1921).

—— *A Miscellany of Irish Proverbs* (Dublin: Talbot Press, 1922).

O'Rourke, Fran. '*Virtus Essendi*: Intensive Being in Pseudo-Dionysius and Aquinas', *Dionysius* 15 (1991), pp. 55–78.

—— *Allwisest Stagyrite. Joyce's Quotations from Aristotle* (Dublin: National Library of Ireland, 2005).

—— *Pseudo-Dionysius and the Metaphysics of Aquinas* (Notre Dame: University of Notre Dame Press, 2005).

Owens, Joseph. 'Aristotelian Ethics, Medicine, and the Changing Nature of Man', in J.R. Catan (ed.), *Aristotle. The Collected Papers of Joseph Owens* (Albany: SUNY Press, 1981, pp. 173–80.

—— 'The Self in Aristotle', *Review of Metaphysics* 41/4 (1988), pp. 707–22.

—— *Cognition. An Epistemological Inquiry* (Houston: Center for Thomistic Studies), 1992.

Pascal, Blaise. *Oeuvres* 13, *Pensées* II, ed. Léon Brunschvicg (Paris: Hachette, 1904. Reprint Liechtenstein: Kraus, 1976).

Patzig, Günther (ed.), *Aristoteles' Politik* (Göttingen: Vandenhoeck & Ruprecht, 1990).

Peck, A.L. Preface, *Generation of Animals* (Cambridge, MA: Harvard University Press, 1942).

—— Introduction to Aristotle, *Parts of Animals* (Cambridge, MA.: Harvard University Press, 1945).

Pellegrin, Pierre. *Aristotle's Classification of Animals. Biology and the Conceptual Unity of the Aristotelian Corpus* (Berkeley: University of California Press, 1986).

Pender, E.E. *Images of Persons Unseen. Plato's Metaphors for the Gods and the Soul* (Sankt Augustin: Akademia, 2002).

Philippe, M-D. '*Analogon* and *Analogia* in the Philosophy of Aristotle', *The Thomist* 33 (1969), pp. 1–74.

Phillips Simpson, Peter L. *A Philosophical Commentary on the Politics of Aristotle* (Chapel Hill: The University of North Carolina Press, 1998).

Pieper, Josef. *Leisure the Basis of Culture* (New York: Mentor, 1963).

Pinsky, Robert. *The Figured Wheel* (New York: Farrar, Straus & Giroux, 1966).

Pittendrigh, C.S. 'Adaptation, Natural Selection, and Behavior', in A. Roe & G.G. Simpson (eds), *Behavior and Evolution* (New Haven: Yale University Press, 1958), pp. 390–416.

—— Letter to Ernst Mayr, in *Toward a New Philosophy of Biology* (Cambridge, MA: Harvard University Press, 1988), pp. 63–4.

Plato. *Complete Works*, ed. John M. Cooper (Indianapolis: Hackett, 1997).

—— *Dialogues*, trans. B. Jowett, 2 vols. (New York: Random House, 1937).

—— *Apology*, trans. G.M.A. Grube, *Complete Works*, ed. John M. Cooper (Indianapolis: Hackett, 1997), pp. 17–36.

—— *Cratylus*, trans. Harold North Fowler (Cambridge, MA: Harvard University Press, 1977).

—— *Ion*, trans. W.R.M. Lamb (Cambridge, MA: Harvard University Press, 2001).

—— *Ion*, trans. Paul Woodruff, *Complete Works*, ed. John M. Cooper (Indianapolis: Hackett, 1997), pp. 937–49.

—— *Phaedo*, trans. Harold North Fowler (Cambridge, MA: Harvard University Press, 1966).

—— *Phaedrus*, trans. Harold North Fowler (Cambridge, MA: Harvard University Press, 1966).

—— *Republic*, trans. Paul Shorey, 2 vols. (Cambridge, MA: Harvard University Press, 1982).

Plotinus. *Enneads* IV, trans. A.H. Armstrong (Cambridge, MA: Harvard University Press, 1984).

Plutarch. *De Audiendis Poetis*, trans. Frank Cole Babbitt, *Moralia*, vol. 1 (Cambridge, MA: Harvard University Press, 1927).

—— *Isis and Osiris*, trans. Frank Cole Babbitt, *Moralia*, vol. 5 (Cambridge, MA: Harvard University Press, 1936).

Pope, Stephen J. *Human Evolution and Christian Ethics* (Cambridge: Cambridge University Press, 2007).

Popper, Karl. 'A New Interpretation of Darwinism' (The first Medawar Lecture to The Royal Society, 1986) in Hans-Joachim Niemann (ed.), *Karl Popper and the Two New Secrets of Life* (Tübingen: Mohr Siebeck, 2014), pp. 115–20.

Porphyry. *Quaestiones Homericae*, ed. H. Schrader (Leipzig: Teubner 1882).

—— *In Aristotelis Categorias Commentarium*, ed. A. Busse (Berlin: Reimer, 1887).

—— *On Aristotle, Categories*, trans. S.K. Strange (Ithaca: Cornell University Press, 1992).

Pound, Ezra. *Pound/Joyce. The Letters of Ezra Pound to James Joyce*, ed. Forrest Read (New York: New Directions, 1970).

Premack, David. 'Language and Intelligence in Ape and Man', *American Scientist* 64 (1976), pp. 681–2.

Preus, Anthony. '*Eidos* as Norm in Aristotle's Biology', in J.P. Anton & A. Preus (eds), *Essays in Ancient Greek Philosophy II* (Albany: SUNY Press, 1983), pp. 340–63.

—— 'Aristotle and Respect for Persons', in J.P. Anton and A. Preus (eds), *Essays in Ancient Greek Philosophy IV, Aristotle's Ethics* (Albany: SUNY Press), 1991), pp. 215–26.

Proclus. *In Platonis Timaeum Commentarii*, ed. E. Diehl (Leipzig: Teubner, 1903).

Quine, W.V. *Ontological Relativity and Other Essays* (New York: Columbia University Press, 1969).

—— 'Three Grades of Modal Involvement', in *The Ways of Paradox* (Cambridge, MA: Harvard University Press, 1976), pp. 158–76.

Randall, John Herman, Jr., *Aristotle* (New York: Columbia University Press, 1960).

—— Introduction to Frederick J.E. Woodbridge, *Aristotle's Vision of Nature* (New York: Columbia University Press, 1965).

Read, Forrest (ed.), *Pound/Joyce. The Letters of Ezra Pound to James Joyce* (New York: New Directions, 1970).

Rees, Martin. *Our Cosmic Habitat* (Princeton: Princeton University Press, 2001).

Richards, I.A. *The Philosophy of Rhetoric* (London: Oxford University Press, 1936).

Rickaby, Joseph. *Of God and Creatures. An Annotated Translation of the Summa Contra Gentiles of Saint Thomas Aquinas* (London: Burns and Oates, 1905).

Ritter, Joachim. *Metaphysik und Politik* (Frankfurt am Main: Suhrkamp, 1969).

Roberts, Jean. 'Political Animals in the *Nicomachean Ethics*', *Phronesis* 34 (1989), pp. 185–204.

Robinson, H.M. 'Aristotelian Dualism', *Oxford Studies in Ancient Philosophy* 1 (1983), pp. 123–44.

Robinson, Howard. 'Form and the Immateriality of the Intellect from Aristotle to Aquinas', *Aristotle and the Later Tradition: Oxford Studies in Ancient Philosophy*, Supp. vol. 2 (1991), pp. 207–26.

Rorty, Amélie Oksenberg (ed.), *Essays on Aristotle's Poetics* (Princeton: Princeton University Press, 1992).

—— (ed.), *Essays on Aristotle's Rhetoric* (Berkeley: University of California Press. 1996).

Rose, Hilary & Rose, Steven (eds), *Alas Poor Darwin, Arguments against Evolutionary Psychology* (London: Vintage, 2000).

Rose, Steven. *Lifelines: Biology, Freedom, Determinism* (London: Penguin, 1998).

Rose, Valentin (ed.), *Aristotelis Fragmenta* (Stuttgart: Teubner, 1967).

Rowe, Christopher J. 'Aristotle for and against Democracy', in D.N. Koutras (ed.), *Political Equality and Justice in Aristotle and the Problems of Contemporary Society* (Athens: Society for Aristotelian Studies 'The Lyceum', 2000), pp. 408–16.

Ruse, Michael. *Taking Darwin Seriously* (Oxford: Basil Blackwell, 1989).

——*The Darwinian Paradigm: Essays on its History, Philosophy, and Religious Implications* (London: Routledge, 1989).

——'Evolutionary Ethics. A Defence', in *Biology, Ethics, and the Origins of Life*, ed. Holmes Rolston, III, pp. 89–112 (Boston: Jones & Bartlett, 1995).

——'Evolutionary Ethics: A Phoenix Arisen', in Paul Thompson (ed.), *Issues in Evolutionary Ethics* (Albany: SUNY Press, 1995), pp. 225–47.

—— 'Evolutionary Ethics. A Defence', in *Biology, Ethics, and the Origins of Life*, ed. Holmes Rolston, III (Boston: Jones & Bartlett, 1995) pp. 89–112.

—— Review of Holmes Rolston's *Genes, Genesis, and God*, 1 September 2011, Metanexus Institute website: http://www.metanexus.net/book-review/review-holmes-rolstons-genes-genesis-and-god. Accessed 1 September 2015.

Ruse, Michael & Wilson, E.O. 'The Evolution of Ethics', *New Scientist* 108/1478 (17 October 1985), pp. 50–2. Also in J.E. Huchingson (ed.), *Religion and the Natural Sciences. The Range of Engagement* (Orlando: Harcourt Brace Jovanovich, 1993), pp. 308–11.

Russell, Robert. 'Special Providence and Genetic Mutation: A New Defense of Theistic Evolution', in R.J. Russell, W.R. Stoeger, F. Ayala (eds), *Evolutionary and Molecular Biology. Scientific Perspectives on Divine Action* (Vatican City: Vatican Observatory, 1998), pp. 191–223.

Sakellariou, M.B. *The Polis-State. Definition and Origin* (Athens/Paris: National Hellenic Research Foundation/De Boccard, 1989).

Santoro, Liberato. *The Tortoise and the Lyre* (Dublin: Irish Academic Press, 1993).

Sartre, Jean-Paul. 'Time in Faulkner: *The Sound and the Fury*', in F.J. Hoffman and O.W. Vickery (eds), *William Faulkner: Three Decades of Criticism* (New York: Harcourt, Brace & World, 1963), pp. 225–32.

Schelling, Friedrich. *Sämtliche Werke* 13 (Stuttgart: Cotta, 1858).

—— *Philosophie der Offenbarung* I (Darmstadt: Wissenschaftliche Buchgesellschaft, 1955).

—— *The Grounding of Positive Philosophy*, trans. Bruce Matthews (Albany: SUNY Press, 2007).

Schrader, H. (ed.), *Quaestiones Homericae* (Leipzig: Teubner, 1882).

Sheehy, Eugene. *May It Please the Court* (Dublin: C.J. Fallon, 1951).

Shields, Christopher. 'Some Recent Approaches to Aristotle's *De Anima*', in Aristotle. *De Anima* Books II and III, trans. D. W. Hamlyn, rev. ed. Christopher Shields (Oxford: Clarendon Press, 1993), pp. 157–81.

Short, T.L. 'Darwin's concept of final cause: neither new nor trivial', *Biology and Philosophy* 17 (2002), pp. 323–40.

Sidney, Philip. *The Prose Works of Sir Philip Sidney* III, ed. Albert Feuillerat (Cambridge: Cambridge University Press, 1963).

Siebeck, H. 'Platon als Kritiker aristotelischer Ansichten', *Zeitschrift für Philosophie und Philosophische Kritik (Neue Folge)* 108 (1896), pp. 5–9.

Siger of Brabant. *Quaestiones in IV Metaph.*, ed. W. Dunphy (Louvain-la-Neuve: Éditions de l'Institut Supérieur de Philosophie, 1981).

Simplicius. *In Aristotelis Categorias Commentarium*, ed. Karl Kalbfleisch (Berlin: Reimer, 1907).

—— *On Aristotle's 'Categories 1–4'*. Trans. Michael Chase (Ithaca: Cornell University Press, 2003).

Simpson, Peter L. Phillips. *A Philosophical Commentary on the Politics of Aristotle* (Chapel Hill: University of North Carolina Press, 1998).

Singer, Peter. 'Ethics and Sociobiology', *Philosophy and Public Affairs* 11/1 (Winter 1982), pp. 40–64.

—— *The Expanding Circle. Ethics and Sociobiology* (Oxford: Oxford University Press, 1983).

Smith, Preserved (ed.), *Life and Letters of Martin Luther* (Boston: Houghton Mifflin, 1911).

Sophocles. *Ajax, Electra, Oedipus Tyrannus*, trans. Hugh Lloyd-Jones (Cambridge, MA: Harvard University Press, 1994).

—— *Antigone, Women of Trachis, Philoctetes, Oedipus at Colonus*, trans. Hugh Lloyd-Jones (Cambridge, MA: Harvard University Press, 1994).

Spenser, Edmund. *Shorter Poems of Edmund Spenser*, ed. William A. Oram et al. (New Haven: Yale University Press, 1989).

Spurgeon, Caroline F.E. *Shakespeare's Imagery and What It Tells Us* (Cambridge: Cambridge University Press, 1936).

Stanford, W.B. *Greek Metaphor. Studies in Theory and Practice* (Oxford: Blackwell, 1936).

Strabo, *Geography*, vol. 1, trans. Horace Leonard Jones (Cambridge, MA: Harvard University Press, 1960).

Swift, Jonathan. *The Works of Jonathan Swift* (Edinburgh: William P. Nimmo, 1869).

Swiggers, Pierre. 'Cognitive Aspects of Aristotle's Theory of Metaphor', *Glotta* 62 (1984), pp. 40–5.

Thomas, O. *Metaphor and Related Subjects* (New York: Random House, 1969).

Thompson, D'Arcy Wentworth. *On Growth and Form* (Cambridge: Cambridge University Press, 1942).

Thoreau, Henry David. *Walden, or Life in the Woods* (Harmondsworth: Penguin, 1938).

Thucydides, trans. Charles Foster Smith (Cambridge, MA: Harvard University Press, 1956).

Tipton, Jason A. 'Aristotle's Study of the Animal World. The Case of the *kobios* and *phucis*', *Perspectives in Biology and Medicine* 49/3 (Summer 2006), pp. 369–83.

—— 'Aristotle's Observations of the Foraging Interactions of the Red Mullet (Mullidae: *Mullus* spp) and the Sea Bream (Sparidae: *Diplodus* spp)', *Archives of Natural History* 35/1 (2008), pp. 164–71.

Tricot, J. *Aristote. La métaphysique* I (Paris: Vrin, 1940).

Trigg, Roger. *The Shaping of Man. Philosophical Aspects of Sociobiology* (Oxford: Basil Blackwell, 1982).

—— *Ideas of Human Nature. An Historical Introduction* (Oxford: Basil Blackwell, 1988).

Trivers, Robert L. 'The Evolution of Reciprocal Altruism', *The Quarterly Review of Biology* 46 (1971), pp. 35–57.

Valéry, Paul. *Oeuvres* II (Paris: Gallimard, 1960).

Vargas Llosa, Mario. *Bloom* (Dublin: Kingstown Press, 1966).

Verbeke, Gérard. 'Comment Aristote conçoit-il l'immatériel?', *Revue philosophique de Louvain* 44 (1946), pp. 205–36.

—— *Moral Education in Aristotle* (Washington, DC: Catholic University of America Press, 1990).

Vico, Giambattista. *New Science*, trans. T.G. Bergin and M.H. Fisch (Ithaca: Cornell University Press, 1968).

Wallace, William A. *Causality and Scientific Explanation*, vol. 2, *Classical and Contemporary Science* (Ann Arbor, MI: University of Michigan Press, 1974).

—— 'Are Elementary Particles Real?', in *From a Realist Point of View. Essays on the Philosophy of Science* (Washington, DC: University Press of America, 1979), pp. 187–99.

—— 'A Place for Form in Science: The Modeling of Nature', *Proceedings of the American Catholic Philosophical Association* 69 (1995), pp. 35–46.

—— *The Modeling of Nature, Philosophy of Science and Philosophy of Nature in Synthesis* (Washington, DC: Catholic University of America Press, 1996).

—— 'Is Finality Included in Aristotle's Definition of Nature?', in R.F. Hassing (ed.), *Final Causality in Nature and Human Affairs* (Washington, DC: Catholic University of America Press, 1997), pp. 52–70.

Ward, Keith. *The Battle for the Soul: The End of Morality in a Secular Society* (London: Hodder and Stoughton, 1985).

Wells, H.G. *A Modern Utopia* (Lincoln: University of Nebraska Press, 1967).

Whitehead, Alfred North. *Science and the Modern World* (New York: Macmillan, 1967).

Wieland, Wolfgang. 'The Problem of Teleology', in J. Barnes, M. Schofield, R. Sorabji (eds), *Articles on Aristotle*, vol. 1, *Science* (Duckworth: London, 1975), pp. 141–60.

Wild, John. *Plato's Theory of Man* (New York: Octagon Books, 1964).

William, Clark Ronald. *Einstein: the Life and Times* (London: Hodder and Stoughton, 1995).

Wilson, Edward O. *Sociobiology: The New Synthesis* (Cambridge, MA: Harvard University Press, 1978).

—— *On Human Nature* (Cambridge, MA: Harvard University Press, 1978).

—— *Naturalist* (New York: Warner 1995).

—— *Consilience: The Unity of Knowledge* (London: Little, Brown, 1998).

Wilson, M. *Aristotle's Theory of the Unity of Science* (Toronto: Toronto University Press, 2000).

Wittgenstein, Ludwig. *Tractatus Logico-Philosophicus* (London: Routledge & Kegan Paul, 1969).

Wörner, Markus. 'Elements of an Aristotelian theory of political discourse', in D. Koutras (ed.), *Aristotle's Political Philosophy and its Influence* (Athens: Society for Aristotelian Studies 'The Lyceum', 1999), pp. 56–73.

Wöhrle, Georg. 'Aristoteles' biologische Schriften heute lesen?', in H.-Chr. Günther & A. Rengakos (eds), *Beiträge zur antiken Philosophie. Festschrift für Wolfgang Kullmann* (Stuttgart: Franz Steiner, 1997), pp. 231–44.

Wolfe, Tom. 'Sorry, But Your Soul Just Died', *Forbes ASAP*, 2 December 1996, p. 212.

Woodger, J.H. *Biological Principles* (London: Kegan Paul, Trench, Trubner & Co., 1929).

Woolcock, Peter G. 'The Case against Evolutionary Ethics Today', in J. Maienschein & M. Ruse (eds), *Biology and the Foundation of Ethics* (Cambridge: Cambridge University Press, 1999), pp. 276–306.

Wordsworth, William. *Poetical Works*, eds E. de Selincourt and Helen Darbishire (Oxford: Clarendon Press, 1968).

Yeats, William Butler. *The Poems*, ed. Daniel Albright (London: Everyman's Library, 1992).

Index Locorum

INDEX NOMINUM

On pages where an author is discussed, but not explicitly named, the associated footnote reference identifies the relevant passage.